Tom Paine and Revolutionary America

National Portrait Gallery, London

Tom Paine and Revolutionary America

Updated with a new preface

ERIC FONER

New York   Oxford
OXFORD UNIVERSITY PRESS
2005

Oxford University Press

Oxford   New York
Auckland   Bangkok   Buenos Aires   Cape Town   Chennai
Dar es Salaam   Delhi   Hong Kong   Istanbul   Karachi   Kolkata
Kuala Lumpur   Madrid   Melbourne   Mexico City   Mumbai   Nairobi
São Paulo   Shanghai   Taipei   Tokyo   Toronto

First published by Oxford University Press, Inc., New York, 1976.
First issued as an Oxford University Press paperback, 1977.

Published by Oxford University Press, Inc.
198 Madison Avenue, New York, New York 10016
www.oup.com

Library of Congress Cataloging-in-Publication Data
Foner, Eric.
    Tom Paine and Revolutionary America / Eric Foner. — Updated ed.
        p. cm.
    Includes bibliographical references and index.
    ISBN 0-19-517486-0 — ISBN 0-19-517485-2 (pbk.)
    1. Paine, Thomas, 1737–1809. 2. United States—Politics and government—1775–1783.
3. Political culture—United States—History—18th century. 4. Radicalism—United
States—History—18th century. 5. Artisans—Pennsylvania—Philadelphia—Political
activity—History—18th century. 6. Working class—Pennsylvania—Philadelphia—Political
activity—History—18th century. 7. Philadelphia (Pa.)—History—Revolution, 1775–1783.
8. Philadelphia (Pa.)—Social conditions—18th century. 9. Philadelphia (Pa.)—Economic
conditions—18th century. I. Title.

JC177.A4F66 2004
320.51'092—dc22   2004054799

Printing number: 9 8 7 6 5 4 3 2 1

Printed in the United States of America
on acid-free paper

To the memory of my father
Jack D. Foner (1910–1999)

My motive and object in all my political works, beginning with Common Sense, *the first work I ever published, have been to rescue man from tyranny and false systems and false principles of government, and enable him to be free.*

Thomas Paine, 1806

Contents

☆ ix ☆

Preface to the
Updated Edition

Like every work of history, *Tom Paine and Revolutionary America*, which first appeared in 1976, is a product of the time in which it was written. This updated edition, a source of personal gratification as well as a disquieting reminder of the passage of time, offers the opportunity to consider briefly how the book reflects the intellectual, political, and historiographical currents of its era, and how writing on Paine and his times has changed in the past three decades.

Tom Paine and Revolutionary America explores the historical conjunctures of a man and the world in which he lived, and between the political ideas and social movements of the Age of Revolution. The way I conceived the project reflects my education at Columbia University, the turbulent political atmosphere of the 1960s, the impact of British neo-Marxian social history on my generation of American historians, and the impact of the "new labor history" at home.

As both an undergraduate and graduate student at Columbia, I was fortunate enough to study with Richard Hofstadter, the finest historian of his generation, whose writings directed me toward subjects that have defined much of my scholarly career—the history of political ideologies and the interconnections between social development and political culture. My doctoral dissertation, *Free Soil, Free Labor, Free Men*, completed in 1969 and published the following year, was an examination of the ideology of the Republican party before the Civil War.[1] In many ways it exemplified what was then known as the "Columbia school" of political and intellectual history, which centered on the careful analysis of political ideas, symbols, and institutions.

Having been swept up as a student in the civil rights and anti-war movements of the 1960s, I decided that my next book would be a history of American radicalism. Loosely modeled on Hofstadter's classic, *The American Political Tradition*, it would devote chapters to abolitionists, feminists, Radical Republicans, Irish-American land reformers, socialists, and leaders of the Old and New Lefts. Tom Paine was to be the subject of the book's first chapter. My aim was to illuminate the various strands that make up the American radical tradition and to provide modern-day social activists with a "usable past."

Thanks to a fellowship from the American Council of Learned Societies, I was able to spend the 1972–73 academic year in England, where I conducted research for the chapters on Paine and the Irish-Americans. It was then that I first encountered the scholarship of British social and labor history, which had not formed part of my graduate education. I also came to know some of its leading practitioners—inspiring individuals like E. P. Thompson, Eric Hobsbawm, and George Rudé, who generously shared with me their ideas about Paine and his times. I vividly recall taking part in Hobsbawm's pathbreaking monthly seminar on labor history at London's Institute for Historical Research and spending a day with Thompson at his home near Worcester, where he periodically interrupted our conversation about Paine to dash into the adjoining room for a televised update on the cricket "test match" between England and New Zealand. When I returned to the United States, I took a job at New York's City College, where Herbert G. Gutman, an indefatigable advocate of recovering the experience of forgotten Americans from coal miners to slaves, had assembled a remarkable group of young social and labor historians.

Today, when we take for granted that history must include the experience of previously neglected groups—racial minorities, women, laborers, and others—it is difficult to recapture the sense of intellectual excitement first produced by "history from below." The experience of studying in England and of working alongside my City College colleagues powerfully influenced my approach when I sat down to write my chapter on Paine. Like my first book, this was in large part a study of political ideas, but this time I tried to ground Paine's writings in the social history and political movements of his diverse environments, especially lower-class London and Philadelphia. When I finished writing the "chapter," it ran well over one hundred pages. How should I cut it down to size? The late Warren Susman, a brilliant historian who generously agreed to read my draft and offer advice, urged me to expand the unwieldy essay into a book on Paine and the Revolution. He observed that the kind of analysis I was attempting could not be condensed into a single chapter and sagely pointed out that the bicentennial of American independence was fast approaching, so a book on Paine might attract a wide readership. Sheldon Meyer, my editor at Oxford University Press, readily agreed to this detour from the book on radicalism. *Tom Paine and Revolutionary America* was published in January 1976, two hundred years to the day, more or less, after Paine's great pamphlet *Common Sense* first appeared in Philadelphia.

Tom Paine, the introduction announces, is "intended to be both less and more than another biography of Paine." Rather than offering a detailed account of Paine's life, whose outlines have long been known, the book examines the roots of Paine's thought in eighteenth-century England, the elaboration of his ideas in America, and his relationship to specific issues that arose during the American Revolution—the decision for independence, the expansion of political democracy, the battle between advocates of price controls and adherents of laissez-faire, and the contest over the Bank of North America. An epilogue traces Paine's career after his return to Europe in 1787, including the writing of his great pamphlets of the 1790s—*The Rights of Man*, *The Age of Reason*, and *Agrarian Justice*. While the book concentrates on the American side of Paine's career, it also reflects research I had conducted in England on Paine's influence on that country's radical movements of the 1790s and the way those movements affected his evolving outlook. The book ends with a brief look at how Paine's legacy was kept alive after his death by freethinkers, labor activists, and radicals more generally.

The book argues that Paine's greatest contribution lay in his role as the pioneer of a new political language and mode of political discourse. Paine played a pivotal role in the expansion of what scholars would soon call the "public sphere"—the arena of political debate outside the direct control of government. In language carefully crafted to appeal to a mass audience of ordinary readers, Paine dismantled the traditional justifications for monarchy and hereditary privilege. He also articulated a vision of the worldwide historical significance of the American Revolution, identifying the new nation as an "asylum for mankind," a beacon of liberty in a world overrun with oppression.

Tom Paine was conceived as a social history of ideas. In some sense, it represents an early effort to overcome what critics were already calling the "fragmentation" of the American past into autonomous subfields of political, social, and intellectual history. The book links Paine's ideas and political language, especially his social egalitarianism and passion for economic improvement, to his experiences during the first half of his life, spent in England, and to the political struggle for independence in America. Finally, the book emphasizes Paine's "modernity." At a time when many of his contemporaries were inspired by nostalgia for an imagined "ancient constitution" or pristine agrarian past, Paine's was a forward-looking vision that united natural rights, political democracy, and compassion for the poor with a belief in economic progress linked to expanding commerce.

My book formed part of a revival of interest in Paine that did not subside when the bicentennial commemoration of 1976 ended. Indeed, by the late twentieth century, Paine had achieved what one scholar calls "near celebrity" status.[2] (The director Richard Attenborough is now even said to be planning a major Hollywood movie on Paine's life.) Because his outlook does not fit neatly with modern political alignments, Paine has been claimed as a forebear by individuals and movements with very different political purposes. His democratic and egalitarian ideas, along with his disdain for established authority, make him a hero of the Left; his identification of government as a source of evil, his growing adherence to laissez-faire economics, and his call for lowered taxes appeal to the modern Right.

During the 1980s and 1990s, indeed, many conservatives laid claim to Paine. Beginning with his speech accepting the Republican nomination in 1980, Ronald Reagan frequently quoted Paine's words about the possibility of radical change in human affairs: "we have it in our power to begin the world over again." Despite the long-standing aversion to Paine among evangelical Protestants because of his attack on revealed religion in *The Age of Reason*, some of the most conservative members of Congress spearheaded a drive to have a statue of Paine erected in the nation's capital. Among the bill's seventy-two Senate sponsors were ultra-conservatives Jesse Helms of North Carolina and Steve Symms of Idaho. (In 1992, Congress authorized the building of a Paine monument. But in keeping with the spirit of the times, it was to be financed entirely by the private sector, at "no cost to the taxpayer." As of this writing, private funds have not been forthcoming, and Washington remains without a monument to Paine.)[3]

On the other hand, Paine continues to be invoked by critics of established authority. Jon Katz, who hailed the World Wide Web as a revolutionary public forum where ideas flow freely without government interference or corporate control, called Paine "the patron saint of the Internet." "He made us possible. We need to resurrect him and hear him again," Katz proclaimed. "Tom Paine should be our hero."[4] When liberals critical of the drift of public policy established an online "public interest journal" to promote their views, they called it TomPaine.com.

Scholars, too, continue to direct their attention to Paine. Although no book on Paine has achieved the best-seller status of works on other founding fathers,[5] the past thirty years have seen a steady flow of new lives of Paine, more specialized studies, and anthologies of his writings.[6] These works offer insights on themes touched on only lightly in my book, especially Paine's career in England and France, but do not, I think, fundamentally alter the portrait of Paine presented here.[7]

Probably the fullest new biography is by the British political scientist John Keane, who examined much new material on Paine's years in revolutionary France. Keane sees Paine as a forerunner of modern democracy and of "the modern fight for the rights of citizens against warring states and arbitrary governments, social injustice, and bigotry."[8] A careful study of Paine's thought by Gregory Claeys also concentrates on his European career. The book says little about the American Revolution but goes much further than my own study in showing how Paine influenced popular radicalism in England by attempting to reconcile commercial society with an uncompromising commitment to natural rights and the pursuit of the public good.[9] A different element of Paine's thought emerges in two books by Jack Fruchtman, Jr., which find the key to Paine in his religious, if non-doctrinal, understanding of nature and faith in human perfectibility.[10] Scholarly articles have elaborated on Paine's role in "modernizing" American political consciousness by severing political thought from belief in hereditary succession, creating a new American reading public, and outlining the principle of "idealistic internationalism," which figured prominently in the diplomatic outlook of the founding fathers.[11]

If historians' portraits of Paine himself seem not to have changed dramatically during the past three decades, the historiography concerning his intellectual and political milieu has expanded enormously. This book attempts to unite the history of political ideas with social history, subfields that since 1976 have undergone remarkable transformation and growth, making possible new understandings of Paine and his era.

Beginning in the 1980s, intellectual history came to be dominated by the "linguistic turn." Fearful of being "conquered and colonized" by social historians, as one scholar put it, intellectual historians increasingly focused on language itself as the prime subject of historical investigation, while rejecting the reduction of language to a transparent mode of expressing ideas that arise from an underlying political or social reality. The most extreme practitioners of the linguistic turn assume that "nothing exists beyond meanings," or that historical categories like class, politics, and ideology can only be apprehended through language and must be approached primarily through linguistic analysis. More generally, scholars of ideas affirmed that political language has its own integrity and at least relative autonomy from social causes. The task of the intellectual historian is less to locate ideas in a specific moment in history than to reconstruct the conceptual framework, the internal logic and references, within which texts are written.[12] Some of the new work on Paine adopts this perspective, seeking to understand his writings in terms of what ideological sources and pre-existing political languages he drew on and how his pamphlets worked as political arguments.[13]

The linguistic turn was more pronounced in European than Amer-

ican intellectual history. In Britain, it inspired a widespread repudi-
ation of many of the assumptions of the new social and labor history, including its "easy derivation of political from social forces" and
its underlying historical trajectory of expanding working-class consciousness.[14] (In part, this reflected a sense that the coming to power
of Margaret Thatcher in 1979 had halted the once seemingly irreversible "forward march" of labor.) In the United States, scholars
did not stop seeking the roots of ideas, but they increasingly tended
to find the meaning of a text either within its own mode of "discourse" (the assumptions and modes of expression of the text itself)
or in its cultural milieu, rather than in social history. Thus, historians came to rely more and more on the methods of art history, lin-
guistics, cultural anthropology, and other disciplines, rather than social and labor history, to interpret political ideas. How social reality
was represented in culture, not how language reflected underlying
class interests, became the dominant mode of intellectual history.[15]

One important insight of the linguistic turn was that numerous
"discourses" can coexist at any historical moment, even within a single text. At the time *Tom Paine* was written, historians of the ideas
of the American Revolution were locked in a debate over whether
the revolutionaries should be described as "republicans" or "liberals." Republicanism celebrated active participation in public life by
virtuous, economically independent citizens as the highest aim of
politics and the essence of political freedom. Tracing its lineage back
to Renaissance Florence and beyond that to the ancient world, republicanism held that as a social being, man reaches his highest ful-
fillment in setting aside self-interest to pursue the public good. Liberalism stressed that liberty requires limits on governmental
authority so that individuals can pursue their myriad private ambitions without outside interference. Republicanism was deeply suspicious of capitalist economic development for undermining public-
spirited virtue; liberalism severed the public good from private
character and did not fear the pursuit of personal gain by self-
interested individuals.

During the late 1940s and 1950s, scholars like Richard Hofstadter
and Louis Hartz described liberalism as the hegemonic American
ideology from the earliest days of colonial settlement. While some

scholars celebrated this putative liberal consensus, Hartz and Hofstadter lamented it as the product of a society that seemed incapable of producing original ideas or of understanding the social realities of the modern world. By the time I began writing *Tom Paine*, however, Bernard Bailyn, Gordon Wood, and J. G. A. Pocock had succeeded in substituting one or another variant of republicanism as the dominant discourse of the revolutionary era. Although my book stresses Paine's embrace of economic progress and laissez-faire economics and his sharp distinction in *Common Sense* between society and government (ideas typical of "liberalism"), it tries to assimilate him into the republican tradition. In this, it formed part of what was then a flourishing literature that linked variants of republicanism to social conflict in American history.

Tom Paine and Revolutionary America connects Paine's brand of republicanism to the social and political history of radical artisans on both sides of the Atlantic. A few years after this book appeared, Sean Wilentz expanded the concept of "artisan republicanism" to describe the ideology of the labor movement in early nineteenth-century New York City. Other scholars of labor and social history found evidence of republicanism in movements like Populism. For a time, republicanism became a shorthand for any political movement or ideology that seemed to reject the market capitalism of nineteenth- and twentieth-century America.[16] Simultaneously, political theorists dissatisfied with what they considered the excessive individualism and lack of civic-mindedness of political liberalism rediscovered republicanism as an ideology committed to what they considered a more laudable pursuit of common public purposes.[17]

Partly because of this overextension and partly because of the increasingly schematic nature of the republicanism-liberalism debate, the tide of republican interpretation eventually receded. Some scholars reemphasized the liberal roots of important elements of revolutionary-era thought, especially the emphasis on individual rights and the power to resist tyrannical authority. Others stressed the common strands within both liberalism and republicanism, or redefined these outlooks so that liberalism came to embrace not simply self-interest but concern for the public good, while republicanism now included a commitment to commercial and material progress. Americans of the revolutionary generation, it became clear, did not see themselves as confronted by two rival or mutually exclusive ideologies, nor did they believe that every political debate could be interpreted as either an extension of republicanism or a reaction against it. Both political ideologies, moreover, could inspire a commitment to constitutional government, freedom of speech and religion, and restraints on arbitrary power.

By the end of the 1980s, previously acrimonious debates among intellectual historians had been superceded by a truce in which participants acknowledged the insights of their former antagonists. Today, the revolutionary generation is widely seen as simultaneously liberal and republican. (One scholar calls the founders "liberal republicans.")[18] Perhaps more importantly, historians have become far more aware of the existence of other political "languages" independent of both. A recent article by the political scientist Isaac Kramnick identifies no fewer than six distinct discourses that shaped the era's intellectual history—along with republicanism and liberalism, he lists Protestantism, utilitarianism, Scottish "moral sense" philosophy, and Enlightenment rationalism.[19] This new awareness of the complexity of political ideology in the age of revolution and its multiplicity of sources helps make greater sense of Paine, who drew on elements of all of the political languages identified by Kramnick.

Valuable as this work on the history of ideas has proven to be, the relationship between rhetorical meaning and social experience seems as elusive as ever. Many books focus so single-mindedly on the writings of the era's leading political figures that they seem oddly divorced from a second major development of the past thirty years, the flourishing social history of the American Revolution. The study of the Revolution "from below," only in its infancy when *Tom Paine* was written, has grown enormously. This scholarship has confirmed the book's picture of the Revolution as a time of social conflict and political democratization, while expanding the cast of historical characters well beyond the colonial cities and the artisan classes, the focus of my investigation.

In the 1960s, writers like Thompson and Hobsbawm had identified artisans as the crucial exponents of political radicalism in preindustrial Europe. *Tom Paine* extends this interpretation to the

United States, tracing the awakening to political consciousness of Philadelphia's artisan class during the Revolution, the mobilization of the "lower orders" through service in the militia, and Paine's relationship to the city's social and political cleavages. Since the book appeared, works on urban politics of the revolutionary era have reconfirmed the picture of the lower classes emerging into full political participation during the struggle for independence, catalyzing the expansion of political democracy.[20]

Far more striking, however, has been the expansion of the era's social history to include rural communities, where the vast majority of the American colonists lived. It is now clear that the mobilization of political participation and the decline of a deferential political culture, which I identified with the cities, also took place in the countryside, and that egalitarian ideas similar to those I identified with the urban artisans flourished in rural America. Throughout the colonies, free-wheeling debates ensued on the fundamentals of government in which annual elections, universal manhood suffrage, religious toleration, even the abolition of slavery were discussed by artisans, small farmers, and laborers.[21]

The fact that local Committees of Safety, established throughout the colonies in 1774 and 1775, had already begun the process of transferring effective political power from established governments to extralegal grassroots bodies helps to explain Americans' receptivity to Paine's argument for independence in *Common Sense* and his demand for an expansion of the right to vote during the struggle for independence. This mass politicization helps us appreciate more fully Paine's role in creating an enlarged public sphere and underscores why in many colonies, not just Pennsylvania, elites feared that the struggle for independence threatened to unleash anarchy and undermine traditional forms of deference and local structures of power.[22]

Recent works on the transformation of American society and social thought from an emphasis on hierarchy and patronage to a more democratic, egalitarian, and competitive culture highlight even more strongly Paine's role in articulating an egalitarian ideology for a mass audience. In rejecting the crown, as well as the principle of hereditary aristocracy, many Americans also rejected the very idea of human inequality and the society of privilege, patronage, and fixed status that these traditions embodied. If, as Gordon Wood has written, "equality was in fact the most radical and most powerful ideological force let loose in the Revolution," Paine, more than any other individual, championed and explained equality to a mass audience.[23] And unlike many of his contemporaries, Paine recognized the liberating implications of market ideology in a society where status traditionally rested not on individual merit but on one's place in a complex web of privilege and patronage.

Equally striking has been the proliferation of scholarship that chronicles the experience of African-Americans, Native Americans, and women, groups that did not share fully in the era's democratizing tendencies. These studies complicate our understanding of the Revolution. They underscore the "contagion of liberty," while pointing to the limits of change. Studies of individual communities scattered across the colonies reveal that by the end of the revolutionary era, many blacks had gained their freedom, bound labor among whites had all but disappeared, women enjoyed higher status, and ordinary men greater political power. On the other hand, slavery remained well entrenched, loyalists and those accused of insufficient patriotism had suffered persecution, and Native Americans were victims of savage fighting on the frontier and continued appropriation of their lands.[24] The Revolution looks far more complex and multifaceted today than a generation ago.

The burgeoning literature on the era's social history has exposed some of the gaps and silences in revolutionary political thought, including some in Paine's own works. Written at a time when women's history was just emerging as a dynamic field of investigation, my book contained virtually no discussion about the role of gender in Paine's thought or the era's history. Since then, historians have made clear that while the Revolution brought some improvement in the status of American women, gender formed an impenetrable boundary, separating those fully entitled to the blessings of American freedom from those who were not. Feminist political theorists have emphasized how the era's political language identified the citizen as the male head of household. Dependence, an increasingly illegitimate status for men, remained the "natural" role of women, and the division of society into public and private realms excluded them from claims to political recognition.[25]

Similarly, it is now quite clear that whatever the private views of some founders, the revolutionary generation failed to confront the challenge of slavery and indeed left the institution more deeply embedded than ever in American economic and political life. Jefferson, once seen as an ancestor of abolitionism, has been severely criticized for his failure to act against the institution, his apparent sexual exploitation of a female slave, and his inability to conceive of America as an interracial society. Paine's own antislavery credentials have been called into question. He did not support slavery and hoped for its eradication, and he certainly did not share the xenophobic and racist views of contemporary English radicals like William Cobbett. But Paine wrote little about slavery and took no significant public action against it.[26] Paine's language and his insistence that mankind possesses natural rights no government can violate opened the door for the disenfranchised, women, and even slaves to challenge limitations on their own freedom. But at the same time, the universal language of Paine and his contemporaries obscured the fact that lines of exclusion were inherent in the revolutionary vision itself.

Social and economic historians have also directed new attention to the "consumer revolution" of the eighteenth century—the proliferation in England and its North American colonies of inexpensive, mass-produced consumer goods and the rise of a flourishing Atlantic commerce in such items. Indeed, some scholars now see the eighteenth century as an era of Anglicization, in which the cultural norms of the American colonies moved closer to British patterns. The tendency was strongest among the colonial elites, who frequently sent their children to London for social seasoning and emulated British styles of dress and architecture. But common consumer tastes flourished among the middle and even lower classes as well. The Atlantic, it seems, was more a bridge than a barrier between Britain and America, a vast arena for the transmission of goods, cultures, and peoples.[27]

These works powerfully underscore the radicalism of Paine's wholesale assault on the British constitution in *Common Sense*, while helping to make sense of his conviction that free commerce was part of the meaning of American independence. Overall, at a time when scholars are increasingly adopting an "Atlantic perspective" on the era's history, Paine, whose career knew no national boundaries and whose influence criss-crossed the Atlantic, seems more relevant than ever to our understanding of the American Revolution.

I never did write the book on American radicalism in which Paine was supposed to appear, although two proposed chapters on Thaddeus Stevens and Irish-American radicalism were eventually published separately.[28] Even as I was finishing *Tom Paine and Revolutionary America*, my scholarly career took an unexpected turn when Richard Morris asked me to write the volume on Reconstruction for the New American Nation series, a project that took over a decade to complete. Subsequently, I became interested in the history of the idea of freedom in the United States, and then composed a survey textbook of the American experience from the earliest days of European conquest and settlement to the early twenty-first century.[29] These and other writings deal with new issues and time periods and reflect the impact of the new approaches to historical analysis of the past thirty years. But in some ways, the central concerns of my scholarship have remained the same as they were three decades ago—the country's evolving political culture, the nature of its democracy, the relationship between political ideas and America's social and economic development, and the role of radical social movements in helping to shape the modern world. As for *Tom Paine and Revolutionary America*, it was a product of the 1960s and 1970s. Readers today will undoubtedly approach Paine with different questions and assumptions than readers of thirty years ago. But Paine's protean intellect and far-reaching vision of political and social change ensure that, like every generation since his death, Americans of the twenty-first century will continue to find him relevant, challenging, and inspiring.

NOTES

1. Eric Foner, *Free Soil, Free Labor, Free Men: The Ideology of the Republican Party Before the Civil War* (New York, 1970).
2. Harvey Kaye's forthcoming book on Paine, which he kindly allowed me to read in manuscript, offers many examples of what he calls Paine's emergence as a "near celebrity."

3. Steve Symms to Eric Foner, March 19 and June 22, 1992, letters in my possession.

4. Jon Katz, "The Age of Paine," *Wired*, 3 (May, 1995).

5. Joseph Ellis, *Founding Brothers: The Revolutionary Generation* (New York, 2000); David G. McCullogh, *John Adams* (New York, 2001); Walter Isaacson, *Benjamin Franklin: An American Life* (New York, 2003).

6. Recent anthologies include my own *Paine* (New York, 1995); Bruce Kuklick, *Political Writings: Thomas Paine* (New York, 2000); Mark Philp, eds., *Rights of Man, Common Sense, and Other Writings* (Oxford, 1995); and Michael Foot and Isaac Kramnick, eds., *Thomas Paine Reader* (New York, 1987).

7. One author recently credited *Tom Paine and Revolutionary America* with advancing "the dominant modern interpretation of Paine." David Wootton, ed., *Republicanism, Liberty, and Commercial Society, 1649–1776* (Stanford, 1994), 32.

8. John Keane, *Tom Paine: A Political Life* (Boston, 1995), ix–xiv.

9. Gregory Claeys, *Thomas Paine: Social and Political Thought* (Boston, 1989). Other studies of Paine's ideas include A. Owen Aldridge, *Thomas Paine's American Ideology* (Newark, Del., 1984), a detailed examination of his writings between 1775 and 1787 without any sense of historical context; A. J. Ayer, *Thomas Paine* (New York, 1988), an odd, brief work by one of the twentieth century's most esteemed philosophers, which offers chapters on the writings of Thomas Hobbes, John Locke, and David Hume, seemingly unrelated to Paine himself; and Mark Philp, *Paine* (Oxford, 1989).

10. Jack Fruchtman, Jr., *Thomas Paine and the Religion of Nature* (Baltimore, 1993) and *Thomas Paine: Apostle of Nature* (New York, 1994).

11. Jack P. Greene, "Paine, America, and the 'Modernization' of Political Consciousness," *Political Science Quarterly*, 93 (Spring, 1978), 73–92; Edward Larkin, "Inventing an American Public: Thomas Paine, the Pennsylvania Magazine, and American Revolutionary Discourse," *Early American Literature*, 33 (1998), 250–76; David M. Fitzsimmons, "Tom Paine's New World Order: Idealistic Internationalism in the Ideology of Early American Foreign Relations," *Diplomatic History*, 19 (Fall, 1995), 569–82. See also Alfred Y. Young, "*Common Sense* and the *Rights of Man* in America," in Kostas Gavoglu *et al.*, eds. *Science, Mind, and Art: Essays on Science and the Humanistic Understanding in Art, Epistemology, Religion and Ethics in Honor of Robert S. Cohen* (Boston, 1995), 411–39, which offers a careful examination of the circulation of *Common Sense* in America and responses to it.

12. John E. Toews, "Intellectual History After the Linguistic Turn: The Autonomy of Meaning and the Irreducibility of Experience," *American Historical Review*, 92 (October 1987), 879–907 (quotes on 881, 882).

13. For example, Claeys, *Thomas Paine: Social and Political Thought*; Philp, *Paine*; and Robert A. Ferguson, "The Commonalities of *Common Sense*," *William and Mary Quarterly*, 3 ser., 57 (July, 2000), 465–504, a careful examination of the rhetoric, tone, and literary style of Paine's great pamphlet.

14. Gareth Stedman Jones, *Languages of Class: Studies in English Working Class History 1832–1982* (Cambridge, 1983), 2. See also the editorial introduction to the Autumn 1980 issue of the British social history journal *History Workshop*,

entitled "Language and History," and the debate on "History and Post-Modernism," *Past and Present*, 133 (November, 1991), 204–13.

15. For example, T. J. Jackson Lears, *No Place of Grace: Antimodernism and the Transformation of American Culture* (New York, 1981); Richard J. Fox and T. J. Jackson Lears, eds., *Power of Culture: Critical Essays in American History* (Chicago, 1993); Kenneth Cmiel, *Democratic Eloquence: The Fight over Popular Speech in Nineteenth-Century America* (New York, 1990). Some American historians continued to try to combine intellectual, social, and economic history, for example Nancy Cohen, *The Reconstruction of American Liberalism, 1865–1914* (Chapel Hill, 2002), and James Livingston, *Pragmatism and the Political Economy of Cultural Revolution, 1850–1940* (New York, 2001).

16. Sean Wilentz, *Chants Democratic: New York City and the Rise of the American Working Class, 1788–1850* (New York, 1984). I discuss some of this literature in "Why Is There No Socialism in America?" written in 1984 and reprinted in *Who Owns History? Rethinking the Past in a Changing World* (New York, 2002), 119–24. Daniel Rodgers, "Republicanism: The Career of a Concept," *Journal of American History*, 79 (June, 1992), 11–38, is an influential summary of and valedictory for the republicanism debate.

17. Michael J. Sandel, *Liberalism and the Limits of Justice* (New York, 1982); Sandel, *Liberalism and Its Critics* (New York, 1984).

18. Lance Banning, "The Republican Interpretation: Retrospect and Prospect," *Proceedings of the American Antiquarian Society*, 102, pt. 1 (1992), 162.

19. Isaac Kramnick, "Ideological Background," in Jack P. Greene and J. R. Pole, eds., *A Companion to the American Revolution* (Oxford, 2000), 88–93.

20. Gary B. Nash, *The Urban Crucible: Social Change, Political Consciousness, and the Origins of the American Revolution* (Cambridge, 1979); Richard A. Ryerson, *The Revolution Is Now Begun: The Radical Committees of Philadelphia, 1765–1776* (Philadelphia, 1978); Steven Rosswurm, *Arms, Country, and Class: The Philadelphia Militia and "Lower Sort" During the American Revolution* (New Brunswick, 1987).

21. Works on rural political mobilization include Alan Taylor, *Liberty Men and Great Proprietors: The Revolutionary Settlement on the Maine Frontier, 1760–1820* (Chapel Hill, 1990); Albert H. Tillson, Jr., *Gentry and Common Folk: Political Culture on a Virginia Frontier 1740–1789* (Lexington, 1991); Alfred F. Young, ed., *Beyond the American Revolution: Explorations in the History of American Radicalism* (DeKalb, 1993); Ray Raphael, *The First American Revolution* (New York, 2002); Alan D. Watson, "The Committees of Safety and the Coming of the American Revolution in North Carolina, 1774–1776," *North Carolina Historical Review*, 73 (April, 1996), 131–55.

22. Joseph S. Tiedermann, *Reluctant Revolutionaries: New York City and the Road to Independence, 1763–1776* (Ithaca, 1997).

23. The transformation from a hierarchical to a democratic social order is the key theme of Gordon S. Wood, *The Radicalism of the American Revolution* (New York, 1992) (quote on 232). Marc W. Kruman, *Between Authority and Liberty: State Constitution Making in Revolutionary America* (Chapel Hill, 1997), discusses the expansion of the right to vote.

24. Woody Holton, *Forced Founders: Indians, Debtors, Slaves, and the Making of the American Revolution in Virginia* (Chapel Hill, 1999); Jean B. Lee, *The Price of Nationhood: The American Revolution in Charles County* (New York, 1994); Francis S. Fox, *Sweet Land of Liberty: The Ordeal of the American Revolution in Northampton County, Pennsylvania* (University Park, 2000); Barbara Clark Smith, "Food Rioters and the American Revolution," *William and Mary Quarterly*, 3 ser., 51 (Jan., 1994), 3–38; Colin G. Calloway, *The American Revolution in Indian Country* (New York, 1995).

25. Linda K. Kerber, " 'I Have Don . . . much to Carrey on the Warr': Women and the Shaping of Republican Ideology," *Journal of Women's History*, 1 (Winter, 1990), 231–43; Carol Pateman, *The Sexual Contract* (Cambridge, 1988); Wendy Brown, "Finding the Man in the State," *Feminist Studies*, 18 (Spring, 1992), 7–34.

26. Ira Berlin and Ronald Hoffman, eds., *Slavery and Freedom in the Age of the American Revolution* (Charlottesville, 1983); Gary Wills, *"Negro President": Jefferson and the Slave Power* (Boston, 2003), is the most recent attack on Jefferson's relationship to slavery. Linda Colley, "I Am the Watchman," *London Review of Books*, November 20, 2003, 16–17, discusses Cobbett. For Paine and slavery, see James V. Lynch, "The Limits of Revolutionary Radicalism: Tom Paine and Slavery," *Pennsylvania Magazine of History and Biography*, 123 (July, 1999), 177–99.

27. On the consumer revolution, see T. H. Breen, *The Marketplace of Revolution: How Consumer Politics Shaped American Independence* (New York, 2004); Margaret E. Newell, *From Dependency to Independence: Economic Revolution in Colonial New England* (Ithaca, 1998); Cary Carson et al., eds., *Of Consuming Interest: The Style of Life in the Eighteenth Century* (Charlottesville, 1994). The trans-Atlantic transmission of ideas is discussed in P. J. Marshall, "Britain and the World in the Eighteenth Century: II, Britons and Americans," *Transactions of the Royal Historical Society*, 6 ser., 9 (1999), 1–16, and Peter Linebaugh and Marcus Rediker, *The Many-Headed Hydra: The Hidden History of the Revolutionary Atlantic* (Boston, 2000).

28. "Thaddeus Stevens, Confiscation, and Reconstruction," and "Class, Ethnicity and Radicalism in the Gilded Age: The Land League and Irish-America," both reprinted in *Politics and Ideology in the Age of the Civil War* (New York, 1980), 128–200.

29. *Reconstruction: America's Unfinished Revolution, 1863–1877* (New York, 1988); *The Story of American Freedom* (New York, 1998); *Give Me Liberty! An American History* (New York, 2004).

INTRODUCTION

The Problem of Thomas Paine

On January 9, 1776, one of the most remarkable political pamphlets in the history of English writing appeared in Philadelphia. *Common Sense*, a forceful and brilliant argument for the independence of the American colonies from Great Britain and the superiority of republican government over hereditary monarchy, had an enormous impact on the subsequent decision for independence. By the end of the year, no fewer than twenty-five editions had been printed, reaching hundreds of thousands of Americans. The exact circulation of *Common Sense* is not known, but every scholar of the American Revolution agrees it was totally unprecedented in eighteenth-century America. In an age of pamphleteering, *Common Sense* was unique in the extent of its readership and its influence on events.

The author of *Common Sense* was Thomas Paine, "a gentleman," as John Adams described him, "about two years ago from England, a man who . . . has genius in his eyes." *Common Sense* marked the emergence of Paine as the greatest pamphleteer of the Age of Revolution, a career he would pursue in his *Crisis* papers in America, in *The Rights of Man*, *The Age of Reason* and *Agrarian Justice* in Europe, and in countless other pamphlets and newspaper articles. "I

know not," Adams observed in 1806, "whether any man in the world
has had more influence on its inhabitants or affairs for the last
thirty years than Thomas Paine."[1]

Yet, while universal agreement exists on the importance of
Paine's writings, considerable mystery still surrounds the man and
his career. One can begin with the paradox of *Common Sense* itself:
a document instinctively identified with the American Revolution,
it was written by a man with only the briefest experience in this
country. Until now, historians have failed to explain either its
unique impact or the roots of the ideas expressed by Paine.

The problem of *Common Sense*, however, is only one facet of the
larger problem of Thomas Paine. Paine's biographers have always
faced an unenviable task, and not only because of the complexity
of Paine's personality and the fact that most of his correspondence
and papers were accidently burned over a century ago. To depict
Paine in his entirety requires a knowledge of the history of America, England and France in the Age of Revolution and familiarity
with eighteenth-century science, theology, political philosophy and
radical movements. Paine's connections must be traced among the
powerful in Europe and America and also in the tavern-centered
world of politically conscious artisans in London and Philadelphia.
The questions central to an understanding of Paine's career, in
fact, do not lend themselves to exploration within the confines of
conventional biography.

It is hardly surprising, then, that while several biographies of
Paine now exist, they have not resolved the many perplexing questions about this remarkable man. Paine's ideas, indeed, have never
been grasped in their full complexity, nor have they been successfully located within the social context of his age. Some writers
have isolated individual strands of Paine's thought—Newtonian science, deism, political egalitarianism, the promotion of business enterprise—and found in one or another the "key" to Paine's ideas,
but no one has shown why, when and how the various strands became integrated into the coherent ideology of which, for Paine at
least, they were components.[2] Uncertainty still shrouds the apparent inconsistency between Paine's advocacy of the most democratic
state constitution of the era and his defense in the 1780s of the

Bank of North America in league with anti-democratic Philadelphia business interests. The tremendous impact of Paine's writings
in Europe and America has never been adequately explained, and
Paine's relationship to the expansion of popular participation in
politics—a major achievement of the Age of Revolution—is still
not clear. Nor have reasons been offered for the exclusion of Paine
from the roster of revolutionary leaders canonized in nineteenth-
century popular culture.

These are some of the issues addressed in this study, a book
which is intended to be both less and more than another biography of Paine. Less, because there is no need to retrace with the
detailed hand of the biographer the chronology of Paine's life or
to explore again his complex personality.[3] More, because the book
is an early attempt to trace a special set of processes: the relationships between a particular individual and his times and between a
particular brand of radical ideology and the social and political
history of revolutionary America.

Rather than traditional biography, what follows is an attempt to
explore crucial moments in Paine's career while investigating as
well specific aspects of Paine's America. Following Paine's career
as it unfolded, the subjects range from an examination of the roots
of Paine's thought in eighteenth-century England and the nature
of his republican ideology in America, to the specific issues which
dominated his career during the American Revolution—the movement for independence and the controversy surrounding the
Pennsylvania Constitution of 1776, the popular movement for
price controls in 1779 and the contest over the Bank of North
America in the 1780s. An extended epilogue traces the remainder
of Paine's life—his experiences in England and France during the
1790s, the impact of his last great pamphlets *The Rights of Man,
The Age of Reason* and *Agrarian Justice,* and his years in America from
1802 to his death in 1809—and considers briefly the history of his
reputation among both radicals and American society in general.
The history of Philadelphia in the revolutionary era—the city to
whose fortunes Paine's destiny was so closely tied during his years
in America—plays a special role in this analysis. The reader may
feel, perhaps, that Paine himself all too often disappears from the

narrative. My rationale is the conviction that a fuller appreciation of Paine as well as the America that both made and unmade him requires a thorough exploration of the contexts within which Paine lived.

This is an "early attempt" because despite the abundance of historical literature about the American Revolution, our knowledge of its social history is still in many ways in its infancy. We do not even possess a common language in which to describe the society of that era. Certainly, to look for a "working class," in the modern sense of the term, during the eighteenth century would hardly be appropriate; historians have tended, rather, to use terms like "the lower classes" in describing the social order of the period.[4] The most influential of recent works on the Revolution—those of Bernard Bailyn and his students—have been confined largely to intellectual history. This is not to disparage these studies, which afford us a far more sophisticated understanding of the republican ideology of the revolutionary generation, an understanding without which Paine himself is incomprehensible.[5] These books, however, have proven more successful in describing perceptions Americans shared in common than in explaining the radical differences which arose among them or in delineating the various strands of republican thought.[6]

Without returning to an older view that ideas are simply "propaganda"—masks for narrow economic interests—it should be possible to develop a more organic understanding of the relationship between ideas and social structure in the American Revolution. A full understanding of Paine, in other words, involves less a study of ideas (although Paine's thought certainly merits careful analysis), than a social history of intellectual endeavor and political communication. Of course, as one perceptive student of this subject, J. G. A. Pocock, writes, "the slogan that ideas ought to be studied in their social and political context is . . . in danger of becoming a shibboleth; too many of those who pronounce it assume, often unconsciously, that they already know what the relations between ideas and social reality are. . . . " As Pocock reminds us, ideas and the language in which they are expressed are more than a simple reflection of "reality": they are as much a part of social reality as

the institutional and class structure of a society. "Language is both
a product of history and possesses a history of its own"; indeed,
one of the keys to social change is a change in the nature of language itself, both in the emergence of new words and in old words
taking on new meanings.[7] (Anyone who has lived through the
1960s should understand the importance of changes in modes of
expression and communication as an index of social change.)

To understand Paine we must begin with his role as a pamphleteer of revolution. "The American and French Revolutions,"
Eric Hobsbawm has written, "are probably the first mass political
movements in the history of the world which expressed their ideology and aspirations in terms of a secular rationalism and not of
traditional religion."[8] Paine was one of the creators of this secular
language of revolution, a language in which timeless discontents,
millennial aspirations and popular traditions were expressed in a
strikingly new vocabulary. The very slogans and rallying cries we
associate with the revolutions of the late eighteenth century come
from Paine's writings: the "rights of man," the "age of reason," the
"age of revolution" and "the times that try men's souls." Paine
helped to transform the meaning of the key words of political discourse. In *Common Sense* he was among the first writers to use "republic" in a positive rather than derogatory sense; in *The Rights of
Man* he abandoned the old classical definition of "democracy," as
a state where each citizen participated directly in government, and
created its far broader, far more favorable modern meaning. Even
the word "revolution" was transformed in his writing, from a term
derived from the motion of the planets and implying a cyclical view
of history to one signifying vast and irreversible social and political change.[9]

Paine's importance was not simply, or even primarily, that of a
political philosopher and it hardly discredits him to acknowledge
this. There were numerous political writers of the eighteenth century far more original and sophisticated in their ideas. What made
Paine unique was that he forged a new political language. He did
not simply change the meanings of words, he created a literary
style designed to bring his message to the widest possible audience.
His rhetoric was clear, simple and straightforward; his arguments

rooted in the common experiences of a mass readership. Paine
helped to extend political discussion beyond the narrow confines
of the eighteenth century's "political nation" (the classes actively
involved in politics, to whom most previous political writing
had been addressed). Through this new language, he communi-
cated a new vision—a utopian image of an egalitarian republican
society.

One of the most astute contemporary assessments of Paine's
virtues and weaknesses was made by Madame Roland during the
French Revolution:[10]

> The boldness of his thoughts, the originality of his style, the incisive
> truths, audaciously flung before the very persons they offend, have
> doubtless produced a great sensation; but I find him more fit, as it
> were, to scatter these kindling sparks than to lay the foundation or
> prepare the formation of a government. Paine is better at lighting
> the way for revolution than drafting a constitution. He grasps, he es-
> tablishes those great principles whose exposition attracts everyone's
> attention, ravishing a club and exciting a tavern gathering; but as for
> the dispassionate committee discussion or the day-to-day work of a
> legislator, I consider [the English reformer] David Williams infinitely
> more suited than he.

Paine, as Madame Roland suggests, was unsuited by tempera-
ment and talents both to the creation of governments and to their
conduct—a judgment underscored by his unhappy experience as
a member of the National Convention in revolutionary France and
his relative indifference and shifting attitude toward the details of
governmental structure in America. He was at his best at the moment of revolutionary crisis, when his utopian vision of the future
stirred men to action. First in America in 1776 and then in England during the years 1791–92, Paine was precisely the right man
at the right time: articulating ideas which were in the air but only
dimly perceived by most of his contemporaries, helping to promote revolution by changing the very terms in which people
thought about politics and society.

But the conjunction of Paine and his times is even more complex than this. Paine's writings helped to shape the history of the

Age of Revolution, but they themselves were shaped by Paine's own experiences and by the rapid social and political changes American society underwent in the revolutionary era. In both England and America, Paine's brand of republican ideology struck its deepest chords among the artisans; for this reason, the history of that class in this period will be a major focus of this book. In the late eighteenth century, artisans on both sides of the Atlantic awakened to political consciousness and became themselves the cradle and transmitters of democratic and egalitarian ideas. Newly emerging into political consciousness, they found their voice in Paine's writings—a new vision of the future and a new means of expressing their political and social grievances.

A full appreciation of Paine's career in America must include the process by which his artisan audience and other groups, previously excluded from meaningful political participation, suddenly entered the "political nation." Such an investigation must draw on the important work of European scholars, most notably Edward Thompson, who have so ably traced the political and social history of the English and French lower classes in this era.[11]

The American Revolution, of course, was, in general, conducted and controlled by an alliance of the colonial ruling classes—merchants, lawyers and large landowners in the northern colonies, slaveholding planters in the South. But like all colonial movements for independence, the resistance to Great Britain involved a wide range of social groups from the very outset, some of whom desired to transform it into a struggle for internal change as well. In a famous letter of April 1776, John Adams explained:

> We have been told that our struggle has loosened the bonds of government everywhere; that children and apprentices were disobedient; that schools and colleges were grown turbulent; that Indians slighted their guardians, and negroes grew more insolent to their masters.

Adams was here responding to his wife Abigail's mild suggestion that the Continental Congress "remember the ladies" when it drafted a "new code of laws." What he described was the radical edge of the American Revolution, demands for far-reaching changes in the nature of American government and society some of which were fulfilled and some—including Abigail Adams' plea—frustrated in the 1770s and 1780s. Adams himself gave Paine a large share of the blame for the social turmoil which accompanied the movement for independence. In 1776 he rushed into print to combat the "democratical" influence of *Common Sense* and in the 1790s he would ridicule the spread of egalitarian ideas on both sides of the Atlantic as "Paine's yellow fever."[12]

Of course, in discussing the radical impulse which so alarmed Adams, it is extremely important to bear in mind "the pastness of the past"[13]—to avoid reading nineteenth- and twentieth-century definitions of radicalism into the eighteenth century. Rather than positing an abstract conception of radicalism and then ransacking the past for predecessors in a radical family tree—a tendency among almost every radical group in American history—radicalism should be defined within each specific historical context. The problem is compounded by the fact that many persons who were "radical" in opposing British measures and supporting independence in the mid-1770s—men like John and Samuel Adams—were frequently "conservative" in their political ideas. Samuel Adams, as one historian has written, was "a revolutionary without being a radical."[14] Certainly, many staunch Whigs and republicans were dismayed by the outpouring of popular politics that accompanied the struggle for independence.

That Paine was a radical is indubitable, if we understand that term to refer to one who thinks forcefully and originally about the possibility of changing existing institutions and attempts to put those ideas into effect. But Paine was an eighteenth-century radical, not a contemporary one. His views were far more democratic than those of most of his contemporaries (including men like Sam Adams and Patrick Henry, usually regarded as the "radicals" of the Revolution), but even Paine did not entirely reject the contemporary notion that some proof of personal independence should be required of voters. Similarly, Paine's republicanism envisioned a society guided by a single harmonious general good, rather than one divided into conflicting, self-conscious classes. His ideas were firmly rooted in a society that had not as yet experienced the process of industrial revolution which gave birth to modern radical ideologies.

Nor was Paine's the most radical voice of the Age of Revolution in either America or Europe. His unhappy experiences during the French Revolution are well known (although not necessarily well understood), and in England and America there were those who took Paine's new political language and, unlike Paine, forged it into a weapon against the existing distribution of property. But it was precisely because he raised the possibility of total change that Paine's ideas could be used in this way. What gave coherence to Paine's social outlook was his complete rejection of the past. A man of the eighteenth century, Paine was nonetheless strikingly modern in ideas, language and social role. He was modern in his commitment to republicanism, democracy and revolution—as redefined in his writings—modern in his secularism, modern in his belief in human perfectibility and the possibility of unceasing progress, modern in his peculiar combination of internationalism (he called himself "a citizen of the world") with his defense of the powers of the national state (he was an early advocate of a strong central government for America). In America, Paine was the first professional pamphleteer,[15] the first writer to have the single-minded goal of stirring public opinion in support of the war effort, the first to become a paid publicist for the federal government.

To be sure, tensions and ambiguities existed in Paine's thought, tensions inevitable in an era of rapid change. But what unified Paine's ideology was that he embraced the dual transformation which overtook America in these years—the emergence of mass political participation and the expansion of market relations in the economy and society. Many who were "radical" in their political outlook were "conservative" or at least nostalgic in seeking to preserve a social order of agrarian self-sufficiency and opposing the development of such capitalist institutions as banks, corporations and the national debt. Much of the popular protest of this period, indeed, was conservative in the literal sense of seeking to preserve traditional customs and values against the onslaught of massive social change. Ironically, Paine's very modernism sometimes cut him off from the popular politics his writing helped to inspire. On the other hand, men like the great merchant Robert Morris, who helped to revolutionize economic life and shared with Paine a commitment to American commercial expansion, were remarkably elitist in their political views.

What makes Paine's radicalism relevant today is not simply the specific tenets of his belief, but the cast of his mind—his impatience with the past, his critical stance toward existing institutions, his belief that men can shape their own destiny. Paine's invention of a new political language and his creation of one of the first designs for an iron bridge went hand in hand: they symbolize the twofold nature of the revolution to which he was committed and the modern world which he helped to usher in.

Tom Paine and Revolutionary America

CHAPTER ONE

The
Making of a Radical

The town of Thetford was one of the innumerable market centers which dotted the English countryside in the eighteenth century. Located in Norfolk, seventy miles northeast of London, Thetford had centuries before known a certain prominence as a center of rural manufacturing, and while most of its inhabitants in the eighteenth century were farmers, many still spun yarn in their homes for the thriving weaving industry of Norwich, only twenty miles away. But while Thetford, according to one contemporary account, "hath a good Market weekly on Saturday, and a Fair on May 1," it was, to say the least, off the beaten path. A local historian listed as the major occurrences of the eighteenth century the erection of a bridge, the removal of a market and "the capture of two very fine sturgeon in the Mill Pond."[1] It would have been foolhardy indeed to predict that a child born in Thetford would become one of the leading figures of the eighteenth-century world.

Thomas Paine was born in Thetford in 1737 into a humble but

by no means impoverished family. His father, a Quaker stay-maker and small farmer, and his mother, an Anglican and the daughter of a local attorney, were able, although not without sacrifice, to send Paine to the local grammar school, where he studied for seven years. At age thirteen, Paine left school to apprentice himself to his father's craft of staymaking, the manu-facture of whalebone stays for corsets.[2]

Paine spent the next twelve years of his life following the traditional path from apprentice to journeyman to master stay-maker, but it seems that he was unhappy in a trade which required great physical strength and "a tolerable share of assur-ance" in dealing with women, rather than education or great native intelligence. At sixteen, he ran away from home to serve aboard a privateer, but he soon returned and in 1756 worked as a journeyman for a Mr. Morris, "a very noted stay-maker" of London. Two years later Paine moved to the seacoast town of Dover, again working as a journeyman, and in 1759 his master loaned him ten pounds to set up his own shop in the nearby town of Sandwich. There Paine met and married Mary Lambert, a maid employed by the wife of a local shopkeeper. Within a few months, the couple moved to neighboring Margate, where Mary Paine died in 1760, less than a year after their wedding.[3]

Mary Lambert's father was an officer in the Customs and Excise Service, and he seems to have inspired Paine to abandon staymak-ing. Paine returned to Thetford to study for the excise officers' examination, which required a grounding in mathematics and an ability to write clear English. In 1762 he was appointed to the low-level position of collecting excise taxes in Alford, Lincolnshire. But three years later, he was dismissed for committing the not uncommon offense of "stamping his whole ride," that is, filing a report without in fact examining the goods involved. After a brief attempt to re-establish himself as a staymaker in Norfolk, Paine moved to London. There, in 1766 and 1767, he taught English in a local academy for the poverty-level salary of twenty-five pounds per year, half his former excise salary. An early biographer claims that he also preached to small groups in his London lodgings.

In 1768, after three years of near indigence, Paine's situation improved. He wrote a humble letter of apology for his previous infraction, which the Excise Board accepted, and he was appointed to a post in Lewes, Sussex, a market town fifty miles south of London. Paine lodged in the home of Samuel Ollive, the owner of a tobacconist shop and one of the leading citizens of Lewes (he had been elected one of the town's two constables earlier in the 1760s). When Ollive died in 1771, Paine married his daughter and ran the shop in addition to performing his excise duties. But Paine was discontented. He spent the winter of 1772–73 in London, leading excise tax collectors in a movement for higher salaries. The movement failed, and during the next year Paine's life virtually disintegrated. He was again dismissed from his government position—this time for abandoning his post to participate in the campaign in London—his Lewes shop failed and he and his wife separated. At the age of thirty-seven, in 1774, Paine decided to seek a new beginning in America.

Such, in brief, is our knowledge of the first half of Paine's life, a period of almost unrelenting failure. Paine was well into middle age before his talents received any recognition, but it is not unreasonable to assume that many of his ideas were fixed by the time he arrived in America. He once attributed the success of his early writings to the fact that he had brought to America "a knowledge of England."[4] What had life in England taught Paine? What were the formative influences on his thought?

We can be certain that Paine's father's Quakerism influenced his son's rejection of hierarchies in church and state and his support for reforms ranging from anti-slavery to the abolition of dueling. It was also natural that the son of a Quaker always criticized the laws excluding Protestant Dissenters from public office, the universities and many professions and favored the separation of church and state. But because so little is known about Paine's early career—most of it deriving from hostile biographies commissioned by the British government during the 1790s—any answers beyond this must be somewhat tentative and speculative.

It seems safe to say that through his acquaintance with various parts of England, his work as a tax collector and his ill-fated attempt to petition the Excise Board and Parliament for a salary increase, Paine had learned a good deal about the workings of English society and government. He had lived in Thetford, Dover, Sandwich, and Lewes, towns in which the inequities of the system of Parliamentary representation and the dominance of the landed aristocracy in political life were all too apparent. Each of these tiny towns sent two representatives to the House of Commons—the Thetford members of Parliament were selected by a closed corporation limited to thirty-two voters who followed the orders of the local magnate, the Duke of Grafton—while the city of Manchester, with 60,000 inhabitants, had no representation at all.[5]

The position of revenue officer, moreover, as Paine later declared, put him in a unique position "to see into the numerous and various distresses which the weight of taxes even at that time of day occasioned."[6] Paine could hardly have escaped the signs of economic distress and decay which abounded in southeastern England during the eighteenth century. Sandwich was "an old, decay'd, poor, miserable town" and Dover an "ill repair'd, dangerous and good for little harbour." The economic history of Sussex in the period has been described as "a record of povery, disaster and lawlessness."[7] Paine lived in or near London in the 1760s and 1770s, when population growth coupled with a series of bad harvests led to rising prices, falling real wages, food riots and industrial disputes. In 1766 the government was forced to forbid the export of wheat, flour and corn to stem discontent over food prices, and in 1773 a group of London weavers petitioned the

"Imagination pales before the horrors of the times in the back streets and alleys of London," writes the historian Margaret George. William Hogarth's well-known print *Gin Lane* (1751) offers a satiric glimpse of the wretchedness of lower-class life in Paine's London. *Library Company of Philadelphia*

King to "have pity upon the poor, and to remove those evil ministers who will not lower the price of provisions and relieve us."[8] Although as a master staymaker, petty government official and teacher, Paine would not have wanted himself to be classed with the unskilled laborers and paupers at the bottom of the city's social scale, Paine had known poverty himself and had lived in the Covent Garden area, one of the "dreadful places" of eighteenth-century London, known for its wretchedness, crime and disorder. Paine's writings would always express a genuine compassion for the plight of the English poor.[9]

During his years in England, Paine once recalled, "The natural bent of my mind was to science." Like so many other figures of the eighteenth century, Paine's thought about the political and social world was influenced by Newtonian science. The Newtonian universe was one of harmony and order, guided by natural laws. It thus seemed to follow that men could create a science of society, that is, that every human institution could and should be brought to the bar of reason for judgment. In reality, however, the basic principle of the English system of government, which Paine described as "that of following precedents," was antithetical to the spirit of inquiry, criticism and improvement which animated eighteenth-century science. This contradiction made popular Newtonianism a breeding ground for radical politics, especially as the English governing elite in the second half of the eighteenth century increasingly viewed the rationalistic frame of mind as a threat to tradition and existing institutions. To many it seemed axiomatic that, as Paine's sometime friend and political associate in Philadelphia Benjamin Rush put it, the sciences were "ever fond of liberty."[10]

It was the study of science, Paine once wrote, perhaps referring to his own experience, which lifted "the soul of an islander" beyond the concerns of everyday life, to questions of universality. During one of his stays in London, Paine purchased some scientific equipment and attended the lectures of Benjamin Martin and

James Ferguson, two of the itinerant lecturers who helped bring scientific knowledge to audiences which otherwise had little opportunity for advanced education. There was no overt political content to these lectures, but the listeners were composed largely of religious Dissenters and self-educated artisans and shopkeepers, many of whom leaned toward deism and political radicalism. "What began as scientific curiosity," one student of the period writes, "often ended in political and moral speculation."[11]

Paine retained scientific interests for the rest of his life—in later years he would investigate the causes of yellow fever, experiment with a kind of internal combustion engine and with smokeless candles and would spend years developing and promoting his design of an iron bridge. Newtonian science strongly influenced Paine's critical cast of mind and brought him into contact with articulate critics of English government. Through his scientific connections in London, Paine became acquainted with the astronomer John Bevis, the celebrated mathematician and Commissioner of the Board of Excise George Lewis Scott, and, as a result of an introduction from Scott, with Benjamin Franklin.[12]

We can only speculate about Paine's contact with the coterie of nonconformist artisans, clergymen and intellectuals who made up Franklin's "Club of Honest Whigs" in London. The group was a center of scientific, religious and political speculation and of support for the American colonies in the developing conflict over British policies. Among the members of this group who seem to have influenced Paine were three writers: James Burgh, a London schoolmaster; Richard Price, a Dissenting minister and teacher; and Joseph Priestley, a Dissenting clergyman and scientific and political experimenter.[13]

These men were part of the third generation in a tradition of criticism of political and social life in eighteenth-century England. They traced their intellectual ancestry to such republican theorists of the seventeenth century as James Harrington, to coffeehouse radicals and opposition politicians of the early eighteenth century and to disaffected landed gentry like the well-known political writer Henry St. John, Viscount Bolingbroke. Such earlier publicists, variously known as "Commonwealthmen," "Country party," or "radical Whigs," had developed a pervasive critique of the "corruption" overtaking English life as a result of the political and financial innovations of the eighteenth century. They condemned the development of cabinet government and the manipulation of Parliament by the Crown and its ministers through patronage, control of elections and the growing number of government appointees and army officers in the House of Commons. They exalted instead the ideal of balanced government and called for the expulsion of "placemen" from Parliament and the election of men of "independence"—landed gentry—who could not be controlled by the ministry. They decried the financial revolution that witnessed the rise of a large national debt and of the Bank of England and other great moneyed companies and lamented the increase of such social types as "stockjobbers," "speculators" and other men whose bureaucratic positions, pensions or speculation in public funds made them dependent on the government for their wealth. The Commonwealthmen looked with nostalgia on an imagined time of individual and governmental virtue, when social position and political influence were not determined by allegiance to one or another Parliamentary "interest" attached to mighty aristocrats or manipulating ministers, when English liberties rested on the sturdy independence of the country gentry. It was the Commonwealthmen who in mid-eighteenth-century England demanded shorter Parliaments, changes in the distribution of seats in the House of Commons, a broader suffrage and other such reforms intended to bolster the independence of the Commons against the aggrandizement of executive power.[14]

Despite the vigor of their lamentations, the Commonwealthmen had little success within England. "The scale of their operations was small, their impact on important politicians slight, and their influence on the public at large neglibible."[15] But their

writings, especially the works of such third generation opposition
writers as Priestley, Price, Burgh and the noted historian Catherine Macaulay, were avidly devoured in the American colonies and
helped shape an image of England as a nation of rapidly deterio-
rating liberty and virtue. In addition to supporting the earlier
Country party ideology, these writers of the 1760s and 1770s
demanded full political and civil rights for the Protestant Dissenters of eighteenth-century England, a demand which they increasingly broadened into a concern for the liberty of individual
conscience on secular as well as religious matters. Dissenting
radicalism, with its stress on individual liberty, freedom of
thought, the right of resistance to tyrants, religious toleration and
Parliamentary reform, flourished among those segments of the
population most independent of the hierarchy of paternalistic
relationships that dominated rural England—men like the craftsmen and traders of London and the growing industrial cities of
the North, men from the middle ranks of society, "having neither
poverty nor riches." Such men were likely to applaud a critique of
a political system which deprived them of the political influence
they felt their talent and wealth had earned.[16] Paine himself
almost certainly read the *Essay on the First Principles of Government*
(1771) by Joseph Priestley and *Political Disquisitions* (1774–75) by
James Burgh, both of which combined a stress on individual
liberty of conscience with demands for Parliamentary reform,
and he was acquainted with the reformer John Horne Tooke,
who shared these writers' critical attitude toward British political
institutions.[17]

Despite a certain nostalgia for the days of the Cromwellian
commonwealth of the 1640s and 1650s, most of the "radical
Whig" spokesmen were firmly committed to the English "balanced" constitution of King, Lords and Commons. Their aim was
to preserve this system from degeneration, not to replace it.
James Burgh did indicate that theoretically, republicanism had
certain advantages over "regal" government, but he hastened to

add that he had not "the least thought" of advocating the establishment of a republic.[18]

In America, this radical Whig ideology would eventually be
transformed into republicanism—although not without dissent
from Tories and moderate patriots, many of whom embraced the
critique of British "corruption," but could not abandon the axiom
of eighteenth-century politics that the British constitution was the
most perfect political structure in the world. In England, republicanism would not become a public political movement until the
1790s—and then largely as the result of the American and
French Revolutions and of Paine's great pamphlet *The Rights of
Man*. In the 1760s and 1770s, English republicanism existed primarily as an underground tradition of anti-monarchical belief
inherited from the days of the Civil War of the 1640s and 1650s.
The tradition of the "Good Old Cause" survived among Dissenting artisans and the politically and economically dispossessed into
the eighteenth century, but the extent to which it influenced
Paine remains unknown.[19] Some writers claim to have found
affinities between Paine's style of thought, his complete rejection of English political institutions, and the radical democracy of the Levellers of the 1640s. Indeed, a contemporary critic
claimed that Paine's attack on monarchy in *Common Sense* was
simply a rewritten version of the arguments of the Cromwellian
writer John Hall, whose anti-monarchical pamphlet of the 1650s
was republished in London in 1771.[20]

If Paine did come into contact with underground radical ideas
stemming from the seventeenth century, this exposure is likely to
have taken place in London and in Lewes, where he spent the six
years before his departure for America. Both were centers of
political disaffection. London had a history of chronic opposition
to the government, an opposition grounded in the resentments of
the middling merchants, shopkeepers and artisans who, because
of the capital's wide franchise, controlled local political life but
exerted little influence on a government dominated by the landed

aristocracy. Most of these critics, of course, were loyal to the Crown, but there were "little knots of republicans and radicals scattered throughout London and its suburbs."[21]

London's citizenry was much more highly politicized than the rural population. There were countless discussion clubs meeting at taverns and alehouses, where apprentices and workingmen participated in public debate along with more substantial Londoners and where the ideas of men like James Burgh circulated. "Deference was not an outstanding quality of London life," writes one historian, a judgment amply confirmed by the popular movement for "Wilkes and Liberty" which dominated the city's politics between 1768 and the mid-1770s and which illustrates the nature of London radicalism at the time of Paine's residence there.

The Wilkes movement played an important role in engaging the political energies and broadening the political education of the artisans, shopkeepers and humbler professional men among whom Paine moved. In 1762 and 1763 John Wilkes published the *North Briton,* a journal whose audacious ridicule of the government led to his arrest on a charge of seditious libel. After several years of exile, Wilkes returned to London in 1768 and was three times elected to a seat in Parliament, each time being barred because of of his previous "crime." Wilkes developed an enormous popularity in London, owing to his adroit appeals to such issues as freedom of the press, ministerial corruption and Parliamentary reform, and to the more general anti-authoritarian tradition of the "free-born Englishman" which lay at the heart of the city's popular political culture. Although the Wilkes movement bore little resemblance to the self-conscious, self-directed radicalism of the 1790s (the crowds which shouted "Wilkes and Liberty" were carefully directed by agents of Wilkes), it did allow underground republican sentiments to surface in such crowd slogans as "Wilkes and no King."[22]

It is not entirely clear at what point in his life Paine's own republican beliefs originated. In 1777, Paine observed that while he had not "troubled others with my notions till very lately," he had a strong "aversion to monarchy, as being too debasing to the dignity of man."[23] Such an outlook may well have been influenced by Paine's experiences in the politically charged atmosphere of London, but it is even more likely that it stemmed from his years in Lewes. Lewes had been a republican center in the 1640s and 1650s, and one of its leading ministers had been a millennial Fifth Monarchist—a believer in the imminent establishment of the Kingdom of God on this earth. Seventeen Protestant martyrs had been executed there in the days of Queen Mary, and the anti-Popery tradition was still strong in the eighteenth century. The Lewes celebration of Guy Fawkes' Day was the most famous in Sussex; it involved elaborate pageantry, anti-Popery speeches, bonfires and a carnival atmosphere. Paine's early writings in America would include appeals, possibly influenced by his stay in Lewes, to anti-Popery sentiments and to the millennial vision of a total change in the human condition which inspired so much of popular radicalism in eighteenth-century England and America.[24]

The people of Lewes seem to have been a rather recalcitrant lot during the time of Paine's residence there and throughout the eighteenth century. Attempts to suppress the Guy Fawkes' Day celebrations in the 1770s led to violent clashes between authorities and large crowds of protestors. When John Wilkes, the symbol of opposition to the government, visited Lewes in the 1770s, "vast crowds of people" assembled to see him.[25] The local newspaper, which Paine almost certainly read (his wife advertised her boarding school for young ladies in it, and its publisher printed Paine's petition for a salary increase for excise officials) gave extensive coverage to the Wilkes affair in London and carried articles denouncing George I and George II as "avowed enemies to freedom" (while prudently remaining silent about the current monarch, George III). It also carried the letters of the mysterious "Junius," an anonymous member of the inner circle of the political world who used an adroit combination of gossip, malice and political criticism to discredit the government. Paine would later refer to the letters of Junius in his own writings.[26]

The spirit of political independence in Lewes was demonstrated in still other ways. In 1734, there was an attempt to establish "the right of the inhabitants generally to vote," which resulted in a Parliamentary warning that only householders could legally cast ballots. The town was a stronghold of the Pelham-Newcastle family, whose agents included local officials, innkeepers and local clergy, but in a heated election campaign just before Paine's arrival at Lewes, the Duke of Newcastle's hand-picked Parliamentary candidate was defeated. The result promped the astonished Duke to order his stewards to evict tenants who had voted the wrong way and to "call in the bills of such tradesmen at Lewes, who have been employed by me, and did not vote as above, and not employ them again on my account."[27]

There was also a continuous "spirit of opposition"[28] in Lewes to the payment of local taxes, and the neighborhood was a center of smuggling, which made Paine's job as an excise official an unenviable one. A virtual "guerrilla war" had prevailed in the 1740s between the authorities and armed gangs of smugglers, and while many of the gangs had been suppressed, smuggling continued into the 1770s. During Paine's tenure a number of excise officials in nearby towns were badly beaten by smugglers, often with the covert sympathy of the inhabitants who dispised the excise, an extremely regressive tax on such articles of common consumption as beer, ale, salt and soap. Most Englishmen probably agreed with Dr. Samuel Johnson that it was "a hateful tax levied upon commodities, and adjudged not by the common judges of property, but by wretches hired by those to whom the excise is paid."[29]

That Lewes, a center of political disaffection, did have an influence on Paine seems clear, but, as with so much of his early life, the precise details of the effect remain problematical. What we know of his activities in Lewes is somewhat inconsistent. Paine, on one occasion, wrote that during his years in Lewes he "had no disposition for what is called politics," while at another time he declared that it was in Lewes in the 1770s that he had begun to think about "systems of government." In the 1790s, in an address to the people of Lewes, Paine wrote, "many of you will recollect, that whilst I resided among you, there was not a man more firm and open in supporting the principles of liberty than myself."[30] Here Paine was probably referring to his participation in a debating club which met regularly at the White Hart Inn in Lewes, one of the numerous debating societies in Hanoverian England which helped men like Paine to crystallize their attitudes on a wide range of political and social issues. Paine gained a reputation both for obstinacy in debate and for Whig views in politics, and on one occasion he earned three guineas by composing an election song for a Whig Parliamentary candidate in a nearby district (an action that probably violated the rule against any form of participation by excise officials in political campaigns). Paine also took some part in public affairs in Lewes; his name appears in the town records of local government meetings and of church vestry activities distributing poor relief.[31]

Aside from these small pieces of evidence, the only other direct indication of Paine's beliefs before his arrival in America is *The Case of the Officers of Excise*, his only experience in England in political pamphleteering. Paine described himself as "the principal promoter" of the officers' movement for higher salaries, and he was one of the eight who put their signatures on the document submitted to the Commissioners of Excise. *The Case*, four thousand copies of which were printed, contains in embryo a number of Paine's later ideas, and reflects that deep disaffection from eighteenth-century English society which would characterize so much of his subsequent writing. Paine complained of "the voice of general want" in England, the "want and misery" resulting from ever-increasing prices, which he blamed on the "increase of money in the kingdom." Moreover, Paine expressed the fear that impoverishment would affect the morals of the petitioners. "Nothing tends to a greater corruption of manners and principles than a too great distress of circumstances," Paine wrote, and he warned that low salaries were an inducement to corruption in the excise service: "poverty and opportunity corrupt many an honest man." A man who had known poverty himself, Paine would never romanticize it. But he also displayed a hostility, seemingly out of place in a "humble" petition, toward "the rich, in ease and affluence," whose wealth was "the misfortune of others."[32]

With *The Case of the Officers of Excise,* Paine assumed the social role which would identify him for the remainder of his career— that of political pamphleteer. The eighteenth century witnessed the steady expansion of literacy among the English middle class and artisans. The emergence of a new "reading public" explained the popularity of novelists like Defoe and Richardson, political pamphleteers such as Swift, Addison and Steele, and newspaper writers like Wilkes and the mysterious Junius who attacked those in authority during the 1760s and 1770s. The growth in numbers and influence of booksellers and printers and the emergence of public opinion as an independent force in politics reflected the opportunities open to men, like Paine, who could wield the power of the printed word. The fact that Paine was asked by his fellow officers to draft the excise petition suggests that his talent as a writer was already known to others before his departure for America.[33]

Paine spent the winter of 1772–73 in London, attempting to gain support for the petition. But, as a contemporary noted, "a rebellion of excisemen, who seldom have the populace on their side, is not much to be feared." In the end, the Excise Commissioners took no action, and Parliament ignored the petition while increasing the appropriation for the King's expenses. Within a year, Paine was dismissed from the excise service for the second time, his marriage dissolved and "all the household furniture, stock in trade, and other effects of Thomas Paine" were sold at auction in Lewes.[34]

By 1774, Paine had lived for thirty-seven years in England. He had matured during a time of widespread economic distress and had spent much of his life in centers of political disaffection. He had moved among critics of English government and society and was possibly familiar with underground currents of republican thought and religious millennialism. A man of skill in a craft, knowledge of science and with enough intellectual ability to work as a teacher and tax collector, his experience had been largely one of disappointment and frustration. A passage in *The Case of the Officers of Excise* very likely referred to his own experience:[35]

Persons first coming into the excise form very different notions of it. to what they have afterwards. The gay hopes of promotion soon expire. The continuance of work, the strictness of duty, and the poverty of the salary, soon beget negligence and indifference . . .

It is hardly surprising that such a man in the eighteenth century would look to America for a new start in life. The image of America in Paine's England, especially among critics of British society, was of a land of abundance and equality, where individual merit, not social rank, set the limits to a man's achievement.[36] It is likely that Paine shared this utopian image of the New World with countless other immigrants of the eighteenth century—certainly his writings would soon do much to promote this very vision of America.

In one respect, however, Paine was far more fortunate than the average immigrant. The majority, even in the 1770s, came as indentured servants (or as slaves). But Paine, because of a separation settlement of thirty-five pounds from his wife, was able to travel first class—on a ship also transporting over one hundred German indentured servants—and arrived in America owing service to no one.[37] Most immigrants arrived with no connections whatsoever in the New World, but Paine brought letters of introduction from Benjamin Franklin. Paine arrived in America with a unique combination of resentments against the English system of government and opportunities for immediate self-advancement and self-expression. Like a seed transplanted from a hostile environment to friendly soil, Paine's latent radicalism, nourished by his experiences in England, would suddenly blossom in the New World.

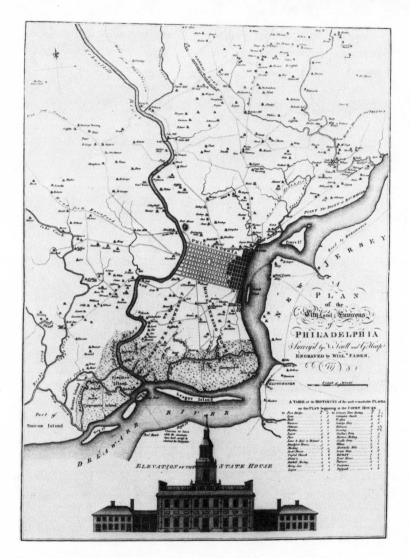

A map of Philadelphia and its environs in 1777 by the engraver William Faden. Note the limited size of the actual city and the large number of country seats of wealthy Philadelphians dotting the surrounding area. *Historical Society of Pennsylvania*

CHAPTER TWO

Paine's Philadelphia

The Philadelphia where Paine arrived in the fall of 1774 was "the capital of the new world."[1] With a population of some 30,000, it was the largest city in English America, and its heterogeneous citizenry included Quakers, Anglicans and Catholics of English descent, German Lutherans and Mennonites and Scotch-Irish Presbyterians. Many of its citizens, like Paine, were recent arrivals; in the decade beginning in 1764, no fewer than 215 ships carrying immigrant indentured servants had reached the city from German and Irish ports alone, and on the eve of the Revolution, these two ethnic groups comprised about half the city's population. As a result of this influx, the population of Philadelphia had more than doubled between 1750 and 1770, and would exceed 42,000 by the time of the first federal census of 1790.[2] Physically, the city was tiny by modern standards—it covered an area of less than one square mile and extended only about seven blocks westward from the shore of the Delaware River. But as the financial and commercial center of the colonies, as well as the home of the arts, the theater and educational and philanthropic institutions, it more closely resembled a major European metropolis than did any other American city. One characteristic which Paine immediately found congenial was the widespread interest in science. "Almost every Philadelphian, it seemed, had some scientific interest or business" and as in London, popular lectures on scientific subjects attracted large audiences.[3]

During the period of his residence there, from 1774 until his return to England in 1787, Paine's Philadelphia would undergo enormous political, social and economic changes. New classes, particularly the city's artisans, would emerge into political consciousness, challenging the dominance of a previously entrenched elite and often finding their voice in Paine's writings. The War for Independence would destroy old economic patterns and social relations and would create new financial institutions and opportunities for economic innovation. Some of these changes were already under way at the time of Paine's arrival, some were the direct consequence of the struggle for independence and of the Revolutionary War, others may simply have coincided with the Revolution. But all would disrupt the lives of the city's population and affect the political issues which framed Paine's own career. Because Paine was so intimately involved in the political and social turmoil which convulsed Philadelphia during his residence there, it is impossible to understand his ideas and role without first examining the structure of the city at the time of his arrival, as well as the nature of the transformations it experienced during the American Revolution.

I

"The size of all towns in America," an astute Irish visitor observed in the 1790s, "has hitherto been proportionate to their trade, and particularly to that carried on with the back settlements." Philadelphia was a prime example of this economic axiom, for its prosperity rested on the city's dominance of a well-settled countryside embracing eastern Pennsylvania, the Delaware Valley, western New Jersey and northern Maryland—one of the most affluent areas of commercial farming in the eighteenth-century world. The key figure in the economy of this region was the Philadelphia merchant, who organized the collection of farm produce, supplied rural storekeepers with imported goods and extended credit to rural customers.[4] A portion of the farm goods were sold in Philadelphia itself; a visitor in 1769 was struck by the "abundance and goodness of the provisions of every kind" in the city's markets. But most of the wheat, flour, bread and meat was exported to other colonies, to southern Europe and especially to the West Indies. Philadelphia merchants engaged in a complex series of triangular trades; they gathered the sugar, rum and molasses produced by the slave plantations of the British Caribbean and used the profits of trade with the islands to pay for the import of ever-increasing quantities of manufactured goods from the mother country.[5]

By 1774, Philadelphia was the busiest port in America, and its shipping tonnage was exceeded only by London and Liverpool in England. Commerce dominated the lives of Philadelphians. Not only were the city's merchants its leading entrepreneurs and economic innovators, but the livelihoods of many artisans and laborers were tied to trade, from the shipwrights, joiners, sailmakers and others who built and outfitted the ships to the carters and laborers who loaded and unloaded them and the bakers, distillers and millers who transformed flour and sugar into the crucial commercial commodities of bread and rum. The entire city, wrote Pennsylvania's Governor Thomas in 1744, "in some way or other depends upon the merchant, and if he cannot trade to advantage, it will soon be very sensibly felt by the whole." This was no less true a generation later. It was the interdependence of the city's economic interests which led Alexander Hamilton to conclude (somewhat inaccurately, as we shall see), that urban artisans could be counted upon to vote for merchants for office: "They know that the merchant is their natural patron and friend."[6]

WILLIAM COATS,

Takes this method of acquainting the PUBLIC in general, and his FRIENDS in particular, that he has for SALE, at his STORE, at the sign of the SUGAR-LOAF, contiguous to the PUBLIC WHARF, in FRONT-STREET, and near POOL's BRIDGE, WHOLESALE and RETAIL;

WEST-INDIA and PHILADELPHIA RUM, Jamaica spirits, brandy, geneva, anniseed, cordials; Madeira, Lisbon, and Teneriff WINES ; lamp oil; loaf, lump and muscovado SUGARS; molasses ; green, souchong, and bohea TEA ; chocolate, rice, oatmeal, starch, indigo, pepper, ginger, allspice, cloves, mace, cinnamon, and nutmegs; cotton ; 3d, 4d, 8d, 10d, 12d and 20d, nails ; powder and shot, soap and candles, brimstone, allum, salt-petre, copperas, raisins, currants, madder, red-wood, fine an d coarse salt, WESTON's SNUFF, mustard, Florence Oil, &c. &c. &c.

Sea stores, shallop-mens bills, &c. put up with care, and all orders from Town or Country thankfully received, and carefully executed.

PHILADELPHIA, Printed by JOHN DUNLAP, at the *Newest Printing-Office*, in *Market-street*.

This 1772 broadside affords a rare view of the interior of a Philadelphia shop and enumerates some of the many European and West Indian wares available in the city. *Library Company of Philadelphia*

Although the wealthy merchants of Philadelphia lacked the titles and hereditary legal privileges of the British upper class, they dominated the city's economic, political and social life and could justifiably be called its "aristocracy." In 1775, the richest 10 per cent of Philadelphia's population owned over half the wealth in the city, more than triple the amount controlled by the 10 per cent immediately below them. (The poorest 40 per cent owned only 4 per cent of the total wealth.)[7] Increasingly, the urban elite aped the fashions and conspicuous consumption of the British aristocracy. In addition to a comfortable but usually unostentatious town house located not far from the Philadelphia waterfront, the typical member of Philadelphia's merchant elite owned a country estate near the city, where sumptuous dinners and entertainments provided the focus of upper-class social life. A map of the city published in 1752 revealed over one hundred fifty such "country seats" within a dozen miles of the city. The lavish appointments of these houses—mahogany furniture, four-wheeled carriages, silver service and the like—set the lifestyle of the wealthy merchants far apart from that of ordinary Philadelphians.

Closely related by ties of business and kinship, the elite dominated the municipal government of Philadelphia, which by the 1770s had become "well divorced from the interests of the citizenry."[8] But to the merchant upper class, such political dominance was only their due. They had no use for what they called "levelling principles," and treated men of lesser rank with "surly pride" and "insulting rudeness." The Revolution only strengthened such attitudes. A visitor in the 1790s would find that "amongst the uppermost circles in Philadelphia, pride, haughtiness, and ostentation are conspicuous; and it seems as if nothing would make them happier than that an order of nobility should be established, by which they might be exalted above their fellow citizens, as much as they are in their own conceit."[9]

It is difficult to know precisely how to characterize the economic life of revolutionary America. In a certain sense, it is true that as one historian has put it, in America, "capitalism came in the first ships." In the northern colonies, a large majority of the citizens were yeoman farmers who owned their own land with titles free from the complex restrictions of feudal land law which still persisted in Europe. Even the most isolated rural areas had some artisans, shopkeepers and local merchants, and few farmers were totally cut off from cash transactions and the commercial marketplace.[10]

On the other hand, business organization and market development in the colonial economy were still embryonic. Transportation and communication were extremely primitive, and neither farming and manufacturing technology nor the economy's dependence on agriculture had changed significantly during the eighteenth century. The pace of economic life was excruciatingly slow by modern standards. Business life ebbed and flowed with the seasons; even in international commerce, little business was done in winter and summer. Urban merchants might have dealt in the international capitalist market, but they did not have to spend much time in the countinghouse. Apprentices and clerks kept the accounts and copied letters; not a few merchants retired from the city altogether, or spent most of their time in their country estates.[11]

A perceptive study of mercantile activity in Boston concludes that business life there bore more resemblance to commerce in the Middle Ages than to that of the modern world. Philadelphia was probably more advanced economically than Boston, but it too had virtually no corporate enterprises—the typical business activity was carried on by an individual entrepreneur or a loose partnership. Most business relations were face-to-face transactions between men who knew one another personally, and a merchant's standing often depended more on his family and religious contacts and his personal reputation than on his business acumen. Even the wealthiest merchants did not specialize in a single economic activity. Not only did they conduct trade in a variety of products and with a number of areas (although it was only the wealthiest who engaged in the import trade from England), but they were forced to act as banker, insurance underwriter, wholesaler, retailer, and shipowner for their own commercial ventures.[12]

Despite the great wealth of some Philadelphia merchants, their business activities were often in a precarious state. Britain's Navigation Acts restricted most of their commerce to the British Empire, and because of the lack of reliable information about market conditions overseas, individual cargoes often sold at a loss. Much of the merchants' capital was supplied on credit from Britain. Indeed, Philadelphia's traders often were little more than agents or factors for London merchants seeking access to Pennsylvania's wheat and flour and a market for British manufactured goods. In the 1760s and 1770s, London houses not only restricted credit, but initiated the practice of dumping large amounts of goods on the American market through auction sales and direct dealings with shopkeepers, bypassing the established merchants altogether. Naturally, this development caused great consternation among Philadelphia's merchant community. They reacted by attempting to suppress auction sales altogether, an action deeply resented by poorer residents of the city who appreciated the bargain prices at these auctions.[13]

Another restraint on business development was the chronic shortage of specie and reliable paper currency which afflicted the colonies in the eighteenth century. There were no banks in colonial America, and while Pennsylvania was more successful than other colonies in issuing and stabilizing the value of paper money, much trade, even in Philadelphia, utilized such substitutes for currency as personal promissory notes, credit and even barter. The lack of a banking system and the high interest rates in colonial Pennsylvania (averaging between 6 and 10 per cent, as opposed to 3 to 4 per cent in England), made it extremely difficult to mobilize the money accumulated by merchants for investment as productive capital. Some merchants did, to be sure, invest in shipbuilding, iron manufacturing, flour and saw mills and other such ventures, but they invested much more of their money either in real estate or in bonds issued by the British government or, if they acquired specie, had it converted into plate by local silversmiths. Such activities were motivated in part by a desire to balance more stable investments against the high risks involved in maritime commerce.[14]

On the eve of the Revolution, then, capitalist development was still at an early stage, and the market did not exert the dominance over economic life which it would come to exercise in the nineteenth and twentieth centuries. Many economic relations were based on subsistence, barter or personal ties rather than cash transactions. Prices of imported goods in Philadelphia seem to have been determined by supply and demand, but there was relatively little inflation except for short periods, and traditional notions of a "just price" lingered.[15] Involuntary labor—slaves, indentured servants and apprentices—as we shall see, still supplied a significant portion of the workforce, and from the little we know about wage rates during the period, they seem to have been based as much on custom as on supply and demand.[16]

The point of this brief excursion into economic history is not simply to outline the nature of Philadelphia's economic life at the time of Paine's arrival there, but also to indicate that the period of the War for Independence and its immediate aftermath would witness a great extension and development of capitalist institutions and market orientation in the city's life. The war experience greatly expanded the horizons of the merchant class, enabling them to trade in areas previously restricted by the British Navigation Acts. The need to supply the army and obtain assistance from France, the issuance of paper currency and the creation of a national debt to finance the struggle stimulated the emergence of large-scale business ventures and the development of a national business class. The great Philadelphia merchant Robert Morris took advantage of the war situation to accumulate a fortune by organizing an extensive group of associates in joint supply, insurance and trading operations.

The investment of money accumulated during the war and of capital loaned from overseas, moreover, was facilitated by the emergence in the 1780s of capitalist institutions almost unknown in the colonial era. Banks were organized in Philadelphia, Boston and New York in the 1780s, and some thirty-three corporate business charters were issued in that decade. The consolidation and funding of the national debt by the federal government in the early 1790s marked the final step from the colonial practice of personally supervised investments to more modern financial institutions. And at the same time the flood of paper money issued during the war and the tremendous inflation for which it was partly responsible, greatly expanded the familiarity of Americans with the marketplace and the circulation of money.[17]

Of course, these developments did not transform the American economy overnight from underdevelopment to modernity. To some extent, they were simply an acceleration of tendencies already apparent in the late colonial period. The windfall profits of the flour trade in the late 1760s and 1770s had already facilitated the emergence of large-scale enterprises like the famous partnership of Willing and Morris, with its agents and correspondents in the major ports of Europe.[18] The war unleashed a whole new set of business conditions to which merchants responded creatively by moving into new ventures, with new forms of organization and new credit mechanisms. And much of the social conflict of the 1770s and 1780s—conflict in which Paine would be deeply involved—would center on the disrupting effects on American life of large accumulations of wealth, the destruction of traditional notions of price by paper money and the marketplace and the new financial institutions like banks and the national debt which had been spawned during the struggle for independence.

II

The merchant aristocracy may have dominated the economic life of Philadelphia, but it goes without saying that they comprised only a small minority of the city's population. Beneath them in the social scale were the city's aritsans, who comprised about half the population of Philadelphia. Historians have been unable to agree about the economic and political status of the artisans, or even about the correct terminology to use in describing them. Some have restricted the term to self-employed craftsmen while others use it, or its synonym "mechanic," to apply to the entire urban working population from skilled master craftsmen and their wage-earning journeymen to laborers, apprentices and indentured servants. This is possibly too broad a definition for, in their own minds and the minds of contemporaries, masters and journeymen—men who possessed a skill, owned their own tools and had usually served an apprenticeship—were clearly distinguished both from merchants and professionals above them and from the pre-industrial, pre-proletariat class of sailors and laborers below.[19]

Even if we restrict our definition of artisans to masters and journeymen, however, one of the crucial characteristics of the group is its economic heterogeneity. Artisans included a few entrepreneurs in such highly capitalized enterprises as shipyards and distilleries, a larger group of highly skilled craftsmen in prestigious trades like clock and instrument making and gold and silversmithing and large numbers of relatively poor "inferior craftsmen" like tailors, shoemakers and weavers, whose work required far less skill and only a few inexpensive tools and whose ranks were continually being augmented by immigrants who knew the craft. There were master carpenters, who combined a knowledge of mechanics and architecture with their carpentry skill, and many journeymen who were no better off in terms of income than unskilled laborers.[20] Half the male residents of Philadelphia in the early 1770s whose occupations are known can be classified as artisans, and this broad spectrum of the population possessed between 30 and 40 per cent of the city's wealth. Although many artisans were poor, most seem to have been able to escape want, to acquire some property and to educate their children.[21]

Colonial Philadelphia was the great center of American craftsmanship. More goods were produced in Philadelphia than in any other American city, and craftsmen in other localities were frequently trained in Philadelphia. But no single industry dominated the city—the largest concentration of artisans, the building trades, comprised only one-fifth of the total craftsmen. Next in importance were the various clothing trades (tailors, weavers, hatters, etc.), then leather crafts, food processing (butchers and bakers), shipbuilding and metal crafts.[22]

On the eve of the Revolution, only a few of Philadelphia's crafts were organized on a large-scale basis. The typical artisan either worked in a small workshop, often his own home, along with one or two journeymen, apprentices and indentured servants, or was an independent craftsman like a bricklayer who owned his own tools but worked for wages. The artisan's occupation required both manual labor and the ability to make administrative and commercial decisions and to handle capital. Some craftsmen produced for the marketplace in anticipation of demand, and a few were even engaged in the export business (1500 pairs of shoes, for example, were exported from Philadelphia to the West Indies in 1771). But large numbers, especially in the clothing trades, worked for custom orders, personally taking customers' measurements and delivering the garments when the work was completed.[23] "When I was a boy," a Philadelphian recalled long after the Revolution,

> there was no such thing as conducting their business in the present wholesale manner, and by efforts at monopoly. No masters were seen exempted from personal labour in any branch of business— living on the profits derived from many hired journeymen. . . .

These early nineteenth-century engravings of artisans at work illustrate as a group the wide disparity which existed within the artisan community. The silversmith and jeweller were among the most prestigious and wealthy craftsmen, while the shoemaker and weaver represented the far more numerous humbler tradesmen. Note the difference in attire and in sophistication of tools among the crafts and the fact that spinning and carding were often assigned to women, usually members of the weaver's family.

Four more crafts of Paine's Philadelphia. Brewing was one of the few trades which employed numerous men at one workplace; the hat-maker exemplified the more typical craftsman working with only his young apprentice. Coopers were among the many artisans whose fortunes were directly tied to the success of Philadelphia's maritime commerce, and the harness-maker represented the city's important leather crafts.

Thus every shoemaker and tailor was a man for himself; thus was
every tinman, blacksmith, hatter, wheelwright, [and] weaver. . . .

At any one time, the majority of the men engaged in these trades
were probably wage-earning journeymen, but most probably had
a reasonable opportunity to set themselves up as independent
masters after a few years of employment.[24]

The nature of artisan production reflected the nascent condition of the capitalist economy. The market for urban manufacturing was extremely limited since large numbers of rural families
produced their own goods and British imports supplied the
demands of many other Americans. Operations requiring an
extensive market, like a large china works built in the Southwark
suburb of Philadelphia in 1770, were speculative ventures indeed;
this one failed, and its organizers went bankrupt. The shortage of
money, high interest rates, the abundance of cheap land drawing
urbanites to rural areas and the high cost of labor in America
compared with Europe, all further hindered the development of
manufacturing. In a situation in which technology was stagnant,
the market limited, prices fairly constant and credit often unavail-
able, the artisan had little opportunity to save money, accumulate
property or launch large-scale enterprises. Only a little capital was
required for a skilled worker to set up in business for himself, and
in prosperous times the number of small-scale enterprises mush-
roomed. But by the same token, the economic fortunes of artisans
were extremely vulnerable to fluctuations in trade. In times of
recession, many were wiped out, and not a few landed in debtor's
prison.[25]

Despite the great disparity in their wealth, an intricate web of
economic and social relationships linked artisan and merchant,
creating an apparent community of interest between them. Artisans were economically independent in the sense that they had
control over the means of production—their own tools and skill—
but they relied heavily on merchants for credit and access to
capital—the keys to business success. Merchants controlled the

An elaborate trade card issued by the kettle-maker Benjamin Harbeson to advertise his wares. Such cards were frequently circulated by artisans in Philadelphia and other colonial cities. *Historical Society of Pennsylvania*

artisans' supply of raw materials from nearby rural areas—wood for carpenters, coopers and shipbuilders, hides for tanners and shoemakers, iron for metalworkers. And since the market for many goods was so limited, wealthy merchants were the main consumers of the products of many craftsmen. This was especially true for such luxury crafts as silver and goldsmithing, coachmaking, clock making and the luxury branches of clothing manufacture. Furniture craftsmen, including the chairmakers who produced the highly regarded Windsor chairs of Philadelphia, also depended on the patronage of men of wealth. And other artisans, especially in the shipbuilding and cooperage trades and, more indirectly, the building trades, recognized that their fortunes were closely tied to the rise and fall of commercial shipping.[26]

On the other hand, during the 1760s and 1770s, increasing numbers of artisans would come to regard the importation of manufactured goods from Great Britain as a principal threat to their economic well-being. They would become ardent economic nationalists, supporters of the various nonimportation agreements of the pre-war years and of state tariffs on imported goods after independence. They would strongly support the federal Constitution of 1787 which they hoped would create a government strong enough to protect American manufacturers. Not all artisans, of course, suffered from British competition. The building trades had a natural monopoly of their craft, and most of the furniture in Philadelphia homes seems to have been of local manufacture. But there were many trades which, as General Thomas Gage noted when he visited the city in 1768, hoped to supply Americans "with many necessary articles which they now import from Great Britain." The great bulk of British imports consisted of textiles, linens and hats, with lesser amounts of shoes, metal goods and luxury products of all kinds. Thus, the large leather, clothing and metal crafts suffered the most from British imports, and the shipbuilding industry often felt the sting of competition as well. A majority of the city's artisans were members of trades which had economic reasons to resent the merchants who imported British goods, and many craftsmen placed advertisements in the Philadelphia press, extolling the quality of their own products at the expense of imports.

Not all merchants, however, imported from Great Britain—those concentrating in the West India trade did not compete with artisans and, in fact, sometimes exported the products of Philadelphia craftsmen to the islands. And other merchants would come to see the encouragement of manufacturing as integral to a general program of American economic independence. Here lay the economic basis of the alliance of artisans, West India merchants and proponents of home manufacturing which would take the lead in the opposition to British measures between 1770 and 1775.[27]

The cultural and political hero of the Philadelphia mechanics was Benjamin Franklin. The personification of the successful

Top: *Library Company of Philadelphia*
Bottom: *American Philosophical Society*

Ship-building and house construction were industries which required the coordination of large numbers of crafts. The beautiful engraving by William Birch concludes his series, "The City of Philadelphia as It Appeared in the Year 1800." The glimpse of a construction site is one of a series of illustrations of the maxims of Franklin's *Poor Richard's Almanac*. Note the well-dressed foreman directing each group of workmen.

artisan who had emerged from their ranks to international celebrity, Franklin was "a sort of tribune of the people," and not only in Philadelphia. As late as the 1790s, mechanics in New York would drink a toast on July 4 to "the memory of our late brother mechanic Benjamin Franklin." The maxims of *Poor Richard's Almanack* (which sold an average of ten thousand copies per year in the 1750s and 1760s), celebrating the virtues of hard work, sobriety, moderation, thrift and self-improvement, powerfully influenced artisan culture, and were reinforced in turn by the Presbyterianism and German Lutheran outlook of a significant portion of the Philadelphia mechanics.[28] "Mr. Printer," an artisan wrote to a Philadelphia newspaper, "the mechanics of Philadelphia are in general a set of sober, prudent, and industrious people." "Corruption, extravagance and luxury," said another, "are seldom found in the habitations of tradesmen. Industry, economy, prudence, and fortitude generally inhabit there."[29] And partly because of the intimate cultural and ideological links between the master craftsman and his journeymen and laborers, it was through the artisans that these values entered the lower-class world.

But there was much more to artisan culture than the stark individualism and emphasis on the accumulation of money in Franklin's maxims. Franklin exhorted workingmen to remember that "time is money," and condemned British laborers' practice of observing the traditional pre-industrial "holiday" of "Saint Monday" and spending the day "at the alehouse." But in Philadelphia, too, shoemakers had "from time immemorial" observed the custom of not working on "blue Monday."[30] Unfortunately, we know far too little about work habits in pre-industrial America, but it is clear that large numbers of artisans worked in their own homes and were not subjected to rigid work discipline or direct supervision. And the nature of many artisan crafts, in which one man performed a variety of tasks until he completed a finished product—picking up and putting down tools, changing from one type of work operation to another—strongly encouraged breaks in the work day. The artisan's control over his own time was one of his most precious possessions; it gave him much more scope than the common laborer to take part in political affairs, and it enabled him to participate more or less at will in the leisure and organizational activities of his community.

Historians have only recently begun the task of reconstructing the social life of the artisan community of revolutionary Philadelphia. It is not yet fully clear to what extent artisans were a group apart from other elements of the city's population. On the one hand, neither mechanics nor the urban elite were sequestered in any one neighborhood of the city. They lived side by side and on occasion belonged to the same organizations. Some volunteer fire companies—as much social clubs as fire protection groups—embraced both artisans and merchants, and the friendly societies of the city's numerous ethnic groups (organizations which provided both camaraderie and an early form of unemployment and funeral insurance) were also composed of citizens of all ranks. On the other hand, the life-style of the merchant aristocracy, with their country estates and social graces and pretensions, was far removed from that of the average artisan. Aristocratic society before the Revolution, according to one account, excluded "the families of mechanics however wealthy." Social divisions were clearly visible in the dress of eighteenth-century Philadelphians: the upper classes modeled their attire on the latest fashions of the English aristocracy, mechanics wore leather aprons, and servants and hired laborers wore linen shirts and striped trousers.[31]

In their daily lives, Philadelphia artisans were much more likely to come into contact with fellow craftsmen than with upper-class merchants. Many artisans worked with and depended upon men of related trades. Crafts like shipbuilding, furniture making and house construction were minutely subdivided, often requiring the cooperation of a dozen or more crafts. Artisans generally apprenticed their sons to relatives or other craftsmen, and successful artisans were often themselves the sons of artisans. In their leisure activities, too, artisans were part of a closely knit community. Living in tiny houses on Philadelphia's crowded streets and back alleys, they often repaired with their friends to local taverns, centers of conviviality and the meeting place for political and social organizations.[32]

The artisan of revolutionary Philadelphia was literate, self-educated and often interested in science. The majority of craftsmen appear to have owned books while most wage-earning laborers did not. The printer and bookseller Robert Aitken extended credit not only to Franklin and Paine, but to shoemakers, calico printers, soap boilers, stonecutters and other artisans. According to a contemporary account, visitors to the library set up under the will of James Logan were "obscure mechanicks who have a turn for mathematics." The very nature of craft work required dexterity with tools, mastery of physical materials and a technical knowledge which often stimulated a further interest in science. As in Paine's London, artisans made up a large portion of the audiences at Philadelphia's popular lectures on scientific subjects. In the days before the professionalization of science and the mechanization of work, interest in science brought the artisan together with the scholar, teacher and physician. The great scientists of colonial Philadelphia, Benjamin Franklin and David Rittenhouse, had begun life as artisans.[33]

"He that hath a Trade, hath an Estate," wrote Franklin in his almanac. The key to the life of an artisan was his skill, the possession of which set him apart from the unskilled laborer, and on which opportunities for advancement depended. Artisans identified themselves as members of a particular craft and only secondarily as artisans (although the period of the Revolution would see the rise of the first inter-craft artisan political organizations and of a "mechanic consciousness" cutting across craft lines). Several guild-like organizations promoting the interests of specific trades had long existed in eighteenth-century

Philadelphia, although the steady influx of immigrants, the ease of transfer from journeyman to master and the high cost of labor made it almost impossible for organizations like the Taylor's Company and the Cordwainer's Company to set prices and wages successfully or to limit entrance to the craft. The closest approximation to a successful guild was the Carpenter's Company, composed of wealthy builder-architects, whose Carpenter's Hall still stands in Philadelphia today. By the 1780s, almost every trade had some kind of craft organization, replete with flags and insignias. Almost all such groups were restricted to master craftsmen, but this limitation in no way contradicted the belief that the interests of journeymen, as the masters of tomorrow, were embraced in the "good of the trade."[34]

The great aspiration of the artisan was "independence"—the status of master craftsman. This was why Franklin set aside in his will funds for loans to assist "young married artificers in setting up their business." By its very nature, this desire for independence implied a fierce respect for private property. But it is important to distinguish between the private property of the artisan and that of the wealthy merchant. The property of the artisan included his skill, his tools, perhaps his shop and his trade or customers, while that of the merchant comprised liquid assets, his warehouse and ships, extensive holdings in real estate and commercial investments, an elegant residence and personal possessions. There was more than a simple difference in wealth here; there was a fundamental difference in attitude. To the artisan, property was legitimate and natural only if it were the product of visible labor. This was the typical attitude of the small producer in the age of the small shop and the family farm. As a committee of mechanics put it in 1773, "our property . . . [as] the clear-earned fruits of our labour" should be "at our own disposal."[35]

The differences between merchant and artisan attitudes toward private property would influence many of the political disputes and alignments of the 1770s and 1780s. The conceptions of both groups were framed by the Lockean theory of property which dominated eighteenth-century thought, holding that private property was a natural right derived from each individual's "property in his own labor" and whatever materials he mixed his labor with. Yet on crucial points, Locke's theory was decidedly ambiguous and open to both conservative and radical interpretation. In general, Locke seemed to sanctify existing inequalities by emphasizing that all private property was inviolate, a position the merchant community embraced with enthusiasm. In his discussion of the state of nature, however, Locke had tied the legitimacy of property directly to individual labor and to the provision that men accumulate only enough to meet their own needs, leaving sufficient property for others. Although Locke himself stated that the creation of civil society superceded these limitations, radical artisans and, in the 1790s, Paine himself, would use this mode of analysis to attack large concentrations of property, especially when such accumulations did not seem to derive from productive labor. The artisan's respect for the principle of private property, in other words, did not necessarily preclude an attack on the existing distribution of wealth.[36]

Philadelphia's artisan culture was pervaded by ambiguities and tensions, beginning with the inherent dualism of the artisan's role, on the one hand, as a small entrepreneur and employer and, on the other, as a laborer and craftsman. Culturally, there was a recurrent tension between the sense of mutuality and community, whether confined to a specific craft or extended to all artisans, and the strong tendency toward individualism and self-improvement. Socially, the artisans insisted on recognition of the distinction between themselves and the common laborers below them, yet they shared with these same men not only a wide variety of leisure activities, but the resentment of ordinary Philadelphians against the pretensions and arrogance of the city's would-be aristocracy.

These and other tensions were inevitably reflected in artisan politics during the revolutionary era. The artisans' impulse toward egalitarianism, their nationalism and their position as urban consumers, would often cast them as the ideological leaders of the lower class in fights for the extension of political rights, independence and, for a time, price controls. In such struggles, the artisans would view themselves not as spokesmen for a particular class interest, but as representatives of the entire "people," or the "producing classes," against a narrow "aristocracy." But their commitment to private property and business enterprise also pulled artisans into alliances with Philadelphia's mercantile community, leaving those below them bereft of the sustained political leadership which, in this period, only politically conscious artisans could provide.

It was during the era of the Revolution that Philadelphia's artisans, like those in other cities, awakened to their common political and economic interests. Yet, ironically, this same period witnessed the emergence of significant conflicts of interest within the artisan community itself, resulting from the commercialization of a sizeable group of artisans. Until the 1770s, few artisans dealt with a large clientele or participated in any significant way in a wide market. Artisans had traditionally attempted to solve their economic problems outside the framework of the competitive market—by imposing guild-like restrictions upon their trades or by asking for governmental regulation of the prices of raw materials.

During the 1770s and 1780s, however, a significant number of artisan entrepreneurs took advantage of the new opportunities offered by war production, urban growth and the development of modern financial institutions. They moved into the merchant's realm of economic activity, attempting to gain control of their own sources of raw materials and becoming involved in importing, exporting and wholesaling. For this commercially oriented segment of the artisan community, such activities marked a fundamental break from the modest business methods of the majority of artisans and led to an increasing identity of interests with large merchants. By 1779 and the 1780s, a substantial number of

Philadelphia artisans would embrace the merchants' doctrine of laissez-faire in opposition to the traditional policy of price controls and would support the establishment of banks to facilitate their access to credit.

The emergence of the entrepreneur who combined the functions of merchant and artisan marked a fundamental step forward in capitalist development. It also had the effect of widening the gap between the master craftsman and his journeyman employees. For the entrepreneurial artisan who produced wholesale for a wide market inevitably sought to reduce wages as a means of cutting costs.[37]

Of course, the idea that today's journeyman was the master of tomorrow did not suddenly disappear; it would persist well into the nineteenth century. A journeyman not only worked at his master's side, but often lodged in his master's home and ate at his family's table. On the other hand, it is unlikely that all journeymen accepted, even in the 1770s, the traditional belief that their interests were identical to their masters'. After all, one of the purposes of organizations of master craftsmen like the Taylor's Company had been to establish maximum wage rates for journeymen.

Nevertheless, before the 1780s, there had been only a handful of journeymen's strikes in America—and none in Philadelphia— and no organized expression of distinct journeymen's interests. Journeymen united with masters in movements for nonimportation and the protection of home industry. When food prices rose, journeymen were more likely to blame farmers, bakers and merchants and to call for governmental regulation of prices, than to demand higher wages. But in the 1780s and 1790s, distinct organizations of journeymen appeared and strikes occurred, based on the assumption that journeymen were as much wage-earners as future independent craftsmen. The first strike in Philadelphia took place among journeymen printers in 1786. By the 1790s journeymen's organizations had been created in at least eleven crafts, and although most were short-lived, the shoe-makers' group conducted a number of strikes in that decade and the following one, culminating in the famous trial and conviction for conspiracy of the group's leaders in 1806.[38]

In addition to artisans being propelled into the market econ-omy and the growing gap between entrepreneurial masters and their wage-earning journeymen, other basic changes affected both the artisan community and the economy of Philadelphia as a whole in these years. These were the precipitous decline of var-ious forms of unfree labor during the revolutionary generation and the rise of the market as the basic means of mobilizing the labor force.

Until the very eve of the War for Independence, various forms of unfree labor—slavery, indentured servitude and apprentice-ship—comprised a high percentage of the city's work force. Although reliable figures are extremely hard to come by, it would appear that in 1775 there were at least as many slaves, appren-tices and servants in the city as free wage-earning laborers and journeymen.[39] The large number of unfree laborers illustrates how, especially within the artisan community, traditional patriar-chal labor relations had not yet been fully supplanted by mone-tary values and the free market. Slave labor had long been utilized by many artisans and as late as 1772, some 10 per cent of the craftsmen owned slaves. A far larger number employed inden-tured servants and apprentices. Over 80 per cent of the young men apprenticed in the city in the early 1770s were bound to craftsmen, who were obligated to teach them the "mystery" of their trade and provide food, lodging, clothing and education in exchange for the apprentice's obedience and labor. Precisely how many masters used the labor of servants and apprentices is not certain, but it seems to have been a large majority. When the Cordwainers' Fire Company asked its members in 1767 for con-tributions to enable it to take action against "the frequent losses sustained by servants and apprentices running away," only one announced that he had "no servant or apprentice" and would therefore refuse to contribute.[40]

If a "market society" is one in which labor as well as the products of labor are commodities valued in terms of cash and subject to the operations of the market, then the persistence of pre-market, patriarchal labor systems in pre-revolutionary Philadelphia is another index of the embryonic state of capitalist development in the city.[41] By the time of Paine's arrival, however, these unfree systems of labor were already in the process of breaking down. Because of a fall-off in slave imports and a high death rate among blacks, the number of slaves in the city declined sharply in the years preceding independence: the 1392 slaves of 1767 had been reduced to less than half that number in 1775. The great influx of immigrants in the early 1770s augmented the number of indentured servants, but at the same time the freeing of those who had served their time—usually four or five years— was constantly increasing the free labor force. As for apprenticeship, despite the fact that large numbers of boys continued to be apprenticed to merchants and artisans, usually for six or seven years, the ethical content of the master-apprentice relationship was increasingly superceded by a more commercial bond, in which the master's obligations were clearly specified, often in monetary terms. To many employers, apprenticeship, slavery and indentured servitude had become no more than business propositions—a relatively inexpensive way of mobilizing a work force, given the high cost of wage labor in America.[42]

As in other areas of Philadelphia's economic life and social relations, the revolutionary generation witnessed the commercialization of labor relations. In 1780, the state legislature provided for the gradual abolition of slavery; by the time of the first census ten years later there were only a little over two hundred slaves in the city. The war cut off the flow of indentured servants, and while the trade resumed in the 1780s and continued, in fact, into the nineteenth century, it never regained the importance of the colonial years when from one-half to two-thirds of the white immigrants had arrived bound to labor. And, for reasons which are not yet entirely clear, the apprenticeship system seems to have waned considerably in the 1780s and 1790s. The Revolution brought the free labor market and a significant class of wage-earners to Philadelphia.[43]

III

The decline of unfree labor, the freeing of servants who had worked for a required period of time and the steady influx of immigration into the city, all augmented Philadelphia's free lower class, of whom sailors, dockworkers, hired servants and unskilled laborers comprised the largest portion. It is difficult to say how many such men lived in Philadelphia at the time of the Revolution, for one of the chief characteristics of this lower class was its impermanence. Many stayed only a short time in the city before moving on in search of work. A local official estimated that there were not fewer than one thousand sailors in Philadelphia in November 1770, but most of these men never showed up on any tax list.[44] What is clear is that a large proportion of such workers were poor, and that during the 1760s and 1770s poverty for the first time became a social problem of significant proportions in Philadelphia. Poverty in Philadelphia was, of course, of a different magnitude than existed in the great cities of eighteenth-century Europe, where between one in four and one in three inhabitants were beggars and paupers and another one-third were "labouring poor" who could easily become destitute in times of crisis. "You see no where in America," one European visitor remarked, "the disgusting and melancholy contrast, so common in Europe, of vice, and filth, and rags and wretchedness in the immediate neighborhood of the most wanton extravagance."[45]

Nonetheless, in the 1760s and 1770s there was a steady

increase in the number and percentage of poor persons and the gap in wealth between the poorest and richest Philadelphians steadily widened. By the early 1770s, some 410 adult males spent part of the year in such institutions as the almshouse, the workhouse or the hospital for the sick poor, and another 469 were designated as insolvent or without sufficient property to pay taxes. Uncounted others were aided by various church charities and ethnic societies, like the Friendly Sons of St. Patrick and the Deutsche Gesellschaft, or various craft organizations. Each winter, the number of persons in need of assistance rose dramatically because navigation of the Delaware River was likely to be blocked by ice for weeks or even months, and many jobs related to trade simply disappeared.[46]

The decade before Paine's arrival were years of chronic economic dislocation in Philadelphia, and there was considerable newspaper comment on the increase in the number of poor, the growing burden of taxes for poor relief and the problems caused by "vagabonds" and "rogues." Poverty had become a problem which affected many more Philadelphians than the aged, infirm, widows and orphans who traditionally had received the bulk of relief. And among the working population, a large number of shoemakers, weavers and bricklayers, in addition to sailors and laborers, received institutional relief.

In order to deal with the new poverty problem and to lower the poor rates, the House of Employment, a new workhouse, was opened in 1767 with the aim, according to its directors, of subjecting the "indolent and supine to the necessity of labouring for their support." Within a few months it housed almost three hundred men and women who were set to work sewing or spinning flax and wool. Supported by private donations from Quaker families, the workhouse was "a source of pride to public-spirited Philadelphians." But a visitor to the city who was given a tour of the institution soon after its opening reported that some of the inmates "begged me to try to get them out."[47]

There were also private efforts to provide employment for the poor. Benjamin Franklin subscribed to a sale of stock in a Linen Manufactory in 1764, whose prospectus commented on the increase of poverty in the city, and eleven years later the United Company of Philadelphia for Promoting American Manufactures announced its hope that its new textile factory would "excite a general and laudable spirit of industry among the poor, and put the means of supporting themselves into the hands of many, who at present are a public expense." By the fall of 1775 the factory employed some five hundred persons, including poor women who spun flax and woolen yarn in their homes, and it turned a handsome profit for the stockholders. "Private interest, charity to the poor, and the public good," were all, the directors exulted, united in the venture.[48]

We have already seen that a great social gulf existed between skilled masters and unskilled laborers. It was the artisan's property—including his skill and his ownership of tools—which set him off from the laborers who lived solely by manual work, were hired often day to day, moved readily from job to job and were excluded from craft organizations. Artisans lived throughout the city, while laborers lived on the fringes in crowded, unsanitary housing where periodic epidemics of yellow fever took a fearful toll. And while the gap in income between artisans and laborers was far less than that between merchants and artisans, there is no evidence that mechanics identified, except on relatively rare occasions, with the urban lower class. While it is not clear that artisans fully accepted the common association of poverty with idleness, dissipation and drunkenness (many craftsmen, after all, lived on the edge of poverty), Franklin's writings certainly lent credence to the belief that it was lack of "industry, frugality, and sobriety" which accounted for economic misfortune. Indeed, the stress on self-discipline, thrift and self-improvement which dominated much of artisan culture reflected an attempt to preserve the artisan's personal pride and self-confidence and to avoid dropping down into the ranks of the dependent and poor.[49]

Before we can understand fully relations between prosperous

artisans and the poor or between skilled craftsmen and laborers and sailors, we need to know more about social life and group consciousness of all social classes in Philadelphia. The city contained such distinct subcultures as German immigrants, many of whom never learned English, attended their own schools and churches and resisted assimilation, and Afro-American slaves who still spoke the languages of Africa and celebrated holidays with African dances. A distinct cultural life may also have existed among sailors and shipbuilding craftsmen, whose homes were concentrated in the southern part of the city and the adjacent district of Southwark.[50]

There were also many cultural activities in which men of all classes participated. Taverns were social centers whose clientele cut across class lines. True, merchants had their elegant coffee houses near the waterfront where imported madeira and port were served and business was conducted with ship captains, many taverns catered particularly to members of one or another artisan craft and unlicensed groggeries seem to have drawn most of their clientele from the lower class. But the typical Philadelphia tavern catered to customers from a wide range of ethnic groups and occupations and were social centers where "dissipated young bloods" rubbed shoulders with the poverty stricken. Horse-racing, cock-fighting and bear- and bull-baiting—the blood sports— were popular among servants, laborers, artisans and gentlemen and afforded opportunities for gambling and drinking in which class lines were, for a short time, erased. Popular sporting events were often sponsored by tavern keepers; one footrace between a Philadelphia champion and a Virginian attracted five thousand spectators to a tavern in the city.[51]

It does seem, however, that a distinct lower-class subculture also existed in eighteenth-century Philadelphia, embracing apprentices, servants, slaves, and perhaps some journeymen, laborers and sailors. It should not be surprising that such a culture cut across racial lines. Many slaves worked side by side with appren-

Hogarth's famous engraving recreates a cockfight in eighteenth-century England. This popular sport, on both sides of the Atlantic, was an occasion at which class lines were momentarily set aside as rich and poor shared in the excitement of the spectacle and the accompanying gambling. *Library Company of Philadelphia*

tices and servants in the workshops of artisans, other slaves were owned by tavern keepers, and still others were employed in the shipyards or on board ships. The legal status and life of slaves were far closer to those of white servants than in the plantation colonies to the south. There were constant complaints in the eighteenth century against retailers who sold liquor to slaves as

well as servants and apprentices. The practice, introduced by
Germans and adopted by servants and slaves, of "shooting out"
the old year with gunpowder, firecrackers and general revelry
continued until the Revolution. The Philadelphia grand jury
more than once complained of the "great disorders" committed
on Sundays by "servants, apprentice boys, and numbers of
Negroes." There was a similar problem on weekday evenings,
when "many disorderly persons" gathered at the courthouse,
"and great numbers of negroes and others sit there with milk
pails, and other things, late at night, and many disorders are there
committed." Complaints and legislation against these and other
practices, including revels, masques, street-fighting and the celebration of May Day—on which parties of young men and women
spent the day feasting and dancing in the woods outside the city
and fishermen danced around maypoles—generally proved to be
ineffectual.[52]

Among the most important occasions for recreation and enjoy-
ment in the lower-class world of Philadelphia were the semi-
annual three-day fairs held every May and November, which
drew to the city dealers in all sorts of goods as well as strolling
entertainers and liquor salesmen. Throughout the eighteenth
century, there were complaints about the "license, riot, races,
gambling, and drunkenness" which accompanied the fairs. As
early as 1731, "diverse inhabitants" of Philadelphia observed that
servants "by custom think they have a right to liberty of going out"
at fair time. Some not only engaged in drinking and disorders but
also conspired to "run away more than at any other time." Fairs,
this petition insisted, tended "to corrupt the morals, and destroy
the innocence of our youth; who are at such times induced to
drinking and gaming, in mix'd companies of vicious servants and
negroes." But in spite of such complaints, the fairs continued to
be held until 1775, when the mayor and Common Council,
speaking for "the respectable inhabitants" of the city, convinced
the Assembly to abolish them.[53]

It should be clear that many aspects of this bawdy lower-class culture violated the ideals and standards of artisans, especially the most intellectually aware and politically conscious. In many ways, popular culture was "decidedly pre-Enlightenment." Scientific interests were spreading among artisans, but in 1770 the home of Dr. William Shippen was attacked by a mob, enraged by rumors that he had removed bodies from cemeteries for medical research (offending the fundamentalist Protestant objection to desecration of the human body). Belief in fortune-telling, conjuring, "cunning men," haunted houses and witches was still widespread; in the same year that Joel Barlow proclaimed America "the empire of reason" (1787), a woman accused of being a witch was killed by a Philadelphia crowd.[54]

Many artisans, of course, participated in popular entertainments like cock-fighting, and were not averse to spending their leisure time in taverns. But they must have felt uncomfortable with the "high-minded contempt of the plodding and industrious" which was present in tavern culture.[55] More important, the most politically conscious artisans recognized how popular entertainments like cock-fighting, fairs and races were sponsored by men of wealth in part as a means of establishing the hegemony of their own style of life. Indeed, to many artisans, the life-styles of the rich and poor had more in common than either had with the life of the craftsman. This hostility to both high and low in society, and the identification of their values and life-styles with each other, is illustrated by an article in a Philadelphia newspaper describing social classes in the city:[56]

> The first class consists of commercial projectors: those who make enormous gains of public confidence; speculators, riotous livers, and a kind of loungers. . . . These people are so complaisant to each other as to call themselves the Better Sort of People. . . . The second class are a set of honest sober men, who mind their business; very little regarded at present, excepting, as they are the prey of the first and third classes.

The third class are thieves, pick-pockets, low-cheats and dirty sots. These are not restrained by principle, but only by want of wealth and public trust, from being of the first class. . . . A fellow who could cheat at cards, or wretch that could betray private confidence, needs only to be entrusted with a few millions of Continental property, to become, instantly, one of the Better Sort of People. A highway-man, in some situations, would have shone like a star of the first magnitude. . . .

Another gap between the "third class" and the artisans who awakened to political consciousness in the early 1770s, was that lower-class political life was still permeated by deferential political attitudes. A writer in 1776 certainly exaggerated when he declared that the political attitudes of the rich and "the common people" were equally "aristocratical." But there was much truth in his observation: "The rich, having been used to govern, seem to think it is their right; and the poorer commonalty, having hitherto had little or no hand in government, seem to think it does not belong to them to have any." And another writer, a year later, commented, "putting the rich and poor on an equal footing is giving the wealthy an amazing advantage. The people in general have a predilection to the great, and are ever fond of bestowing the highest offices upon them." The tremendous gap in wealth and life-style between the wealthiest Philadelphians and the great majority of their fellow-citizens, and the dependence of most urban economic interests on commerce, encouraged this attitude. Political deference did not, to be sure, prevent "the common people" from ignoring laws designed to suppress their disorderly recreations; it did not prevent Philadelphia servants from gaining the reputation of being "insolent and extravagant." But the whole circumstances of life of common laborers and the poor made any kind of independent political identity virtually impossible. To politically conscious artisans like the portrait-painter and one-time leather-worker and silversmith, Charles W. Peale, it seemed self-evident that it required a certain control over one's own time to "improve" oneself and make a man "fit for public stations."[57]

In an age of deference, the characteristic expression of lower-class discontent was not sustained political organization, but sporadic crowd activity. Although there was considerably less crowd violence in Philadelphia than in Boston during the decade preceding independence, Philadelphia, like other eighteenth-century European and American cities, did have something of a tradition of crowd activity. And as elsewhere, there were two kinds of crowds in Philadelphia—spontaneous popular protests against the infringement of customary rights or practices and, far more frequent, crowds called into being and sanctioned by men of wealth for their own political purposes. Examples of the first kind were the crowd which in 1738 assaulted constables enforcing an ordinance barring the erection of fishing weirs in the Schuykill River, the crowd in 1741 which forced bakers to resume the making of bread during a controversy over currency and prices, and the so-called "Dutch riot" of the early 1780s, when a crowd of German women tore down the fences of a man who killed some pigs caught grazing in his wheat field.[58]

In general, however, crowd actions were inspired and directed by members of the ruling elite for their own purposes. Crowd activity was an accepted, almost "constitutional" part of eighteenth-century political life, and as one contemporary wrote, "merchants, assemblymen, magistrates, etc. united directly or indirectly in the riots." Thus, for example, the crowd of fifty to seventy sailors armed with clubs who attacked Quakers who were assembled to vote at the Courthouse in 1742, would appear to have been instigated by the Quakers' political foes. (This is not to say, however, that the sailors did not have their own reasons for acting. Some exclaimed, "You are damned Quakers, you are enemies to King George, and we will knock you all in the head.") In 1769 and 1770 there were a series of violent attacks by sailors and other persons of "the lower sort" on customs officials and men who had informed against smugglers. Several of the crowd's targets were first subjected to the traditional sailor's punishment of tarring and feathering and then were brutally beaten and paraded through the streets of Philadelphia. The local customs collector assumed that the sailors had been "set on by the merchants" to discourage action against smugglers, but he also noted that large numbers of Philadelphians "in their hearts approve of it," because the customs official "is looked upon as an enemy to the community." But again, the sailors had their own grievances as well: they traditionally had had the right to bring small amounts of goods on shipboard and sell them in port, but customs collectors had recently begun seizing such goods.[59]

Unfortunately, the aims and composition of these crowds remain uncertain. Sailors seem to have been a particularly volatile element of the urban population, and typical contemporary accounts described crowds as composed of a "rabble of boys, sailors, and negroes." This may have been more an attempt to discredit the crowd than describe its composition accurately; but perhaps it correctly rooted crowd activity in the lower-class subculture.

Some crowds, however, seem to have been drawn from a wide variety of social groups. The men who attacked a customs official in 1771 were said to be dressed in sailor's jackets, "but some of them had white stockings" (the attire of the merchant elite). In 1773, when an attempt was made to extend a public market on a street where "men of wealth" resided, the residents pulled apart the construction each night until the city abandoned the plan. It seems likely that, as in London, there were more poor men and wage-earners in Philadelphia crowds than merchants and master mechanics, but at the same time the lead was often taken by what one contemporary called "these Mobbing Gentry."[60]

The relationship between the tradition of crowd activity and colonial and revolutionary political life is extremely complex. On the one hand, sporadic crowd activity was most emphatically a "pre-political" form of expression. Crowds either were instigated from above or were reactions to immediate popular grievances; they aimed at the correction of specific injustices, rather than at

A rare contemporary illustration of a Philadelphia crowd scene, this engraving from a Pennsylvania German almanac depicts the procession prior to the burning of an effigy of Benedict Arnold in 1780. The figure of Arnold holds a letter from Beelzebub and sits before a representation of the devil, illustrating how popular rituals often combined religious and political symbolism. Like many eighteenth-century crowds, this one was led by "several gentlemen mounted on horseback." *Historical Society of Pennsylvania*

fundamental political or social change. Law enforcement could be so lax by modern standards, and crowd activity so "acceptable," precisely because crowds so often looked to the upper classes for a warrant for their behavior. On the other hand, colonial Whig leaders found during the 1760s and 1770s that crowds, once raised, sometimes got out of hand. In Boston, for example, a Stamp Act crowd, against the wishes of its leaders, ransacked the homes of royal officials and then destroyed the house of Lieutenant Governor Thomas Hutchinson. As in England, colonial crowds sometimes expressed a raw hostility to men of wealth. And they embodied the popular tradition which accorded legitimacy to direct action against unjust or authoritarian official actions.[61]

Nonetheless, the most politically conscious mechanics, while certainly willing to embrace crowd activity on occasion, did not view the crowd as an effective means of sustained political activity. Poor Richard had long since declared "a Mob's a monster," with

many heads but no brain, and Franklin himself cited the preval-
ence of crowds in London as evidence of the general debauchery
of British life. The leadership of the resistance to British measures from the 1760s to the time of independence usually sought
to restrain crowd violence and set resistance on an orderly path,
even while they used the threat of violence as a political weapon.
The First Continental Congress strongly condemned "routs, riots,
or licentious attacks upon the properties of any person whatever,
as being subversive of all order and government."[62] But behind
such resolutions lay a variety of attitudes—fear among some
colonial leaders that mobs, once unleashed, would be difficult to
control, and the desire of others to transform the nature of
popular politics. A radical artisan like David Rittenhouse had "a
singular antipathy to all mobs and riots," not because of social
conservatism, but because he wanted to move men from the
streets into committee rooms, to create permanent forms of
popular political expression. Such an attitude illuminates one
of the fundamental transformations in political life of the revolutionary period. The 1770s and 1780s would, to be sure, be
decades of great political and social turbulence, and crowd activity
would continue to play a major role in political life. But at the
same time men of all classes would increasingly be drawn into
more "modern" forms of political expression and participation.
This politicization was what struck, and alarmed, the perceptive
conservative Gouverneur Morris at a mass meeting in New York
in 1774: "the mob begin to think and reason."[63]

IV

The politicization of the mass of Philadelphians—from the master craftsmen to a significant segment of the laborers and poor—
was the most important development in Philadelphia's political
life in the decade before independence. First to emerge as a

self-conscious element in politics, with their own organization and demands, were the master mechanics, in their accustomed role as spokesmen for the entire artisan community. Most artisans were probably able to take part in politics because, while a majority could not meet the legal voting requirement of ownership of fifty acres of land or fifty pounds of property, these requirements were rarely enforced with any strictness. But until the 1770s, Philadelphia's artisans played little independent role in politics and to all outward appearances accorded the merchant aristocracy the deference it demanded.

The reasons for the politicization of the artisan community lay as much in the realm of provincial politics as in the affairs of the city. Provincial Pennsylvania "was ruled by a narrow, privileged minority, whose power and policies were maintained in a political structure that had changed but little since 1701." The Penn family, proprietors of Pennsylvania, combined the roles of chief executive and chief landowners in the province. Governor Thomas Penn, resident in Britain, appointed a lieutenant-governor and council to represent him, while he lived off the income of his vast Pennsylvania estates, one of the most valuable landholdings in the western world. His followers created the Proprietary party, utilizing the governor's power to appoint judges, sheriffs and other officials and to regulate investment and speculation in western lands. The Assembly, in which an inequitable distribution of seats gave control to the commercial farming counties surrounding Philadelphia while vastly under-representing the swiftly growing back country to the west, was dominated by the Quaker party. Originally a closely knit group dominated by wealthy Quaker merchants of Philadelphia, the party had, under the leadership of Benjamin Franklin, been broadened in the 1750s to include able professional men from a variety of religious backgrounds. It won strong support from Quaker and German voters of the eastern counties and from Philadelphia artisans, who generally followed Franklin's political lead.[64]

Pennsylvania politics was transformed in 1764 by the movement, engineered by Franklin and his political associate Joseph Galloway, to replace the Penn family's proprietorship with direct royal government. The Proprietary party, faced with this threat to its very existence, for the first time attempted to achieve a wide popular following. It won support among back country Scotch-Irish Presbyterians, who resented their under-representation in the Assembly and that body's seeming indifference to their continual pleas for protection against Indians, and from the Presbyterian clergy in Philadelphia, who feared that the institution of royal government would be a threat to the religious toleration the Penn family had guaranteed.

In the election of 1764, both the Quaker and Proprietary parties made exceptional efforts to gain popular support, distributing vitriolic leaflets and political pamphlets throughout the city, entertaining voters in taverns and organizing street demonstrations. In the end, almost four thousand Philadelphians, an unprecedented number, cast ballots. Both Franklin and Galloway lost their Assembly seats. The artisan community probably split along religious lines, with Presbyterians voting with the Proprietary group, but many others remaining loyal to Franklin and the Quaker party.

The political situation was further complicated by the Stamp Act controversy of 1765–66. The Proprietary party took the lead in opposing the measure, to further discredit the idea of royal government, while Franklin, from his position as Pennsylvania representative in London, supported the act and even arranged for his friend John Hughes to be appointed stamp commissioner in Philadelphia. The governor's party helped to stir up opposition to the Stamp Act, while those in control of the Assembly supported it or remained silent—an ironic reversal of the political situation in other colonies. The Sons of Liberty never caught on in Philadelphia because the artisans, who were prominent in its rank and file in other cities, remained loyal to Franklin, even defending his house against a threatened crowd assault. The "unfortunate dissentions in Provincial Politics keeps us rather a divided people," one Philadelphian lamented in 1766.[65]

The movement for royal government died in the late 1760s, but the constant appeals for popular support by the contending parties altered the style of Pennsylvania politics. Although both Proprietary and Quaker parties were firmly under the control of men of great wealth—the Proprietor's dependents and Anglican and Presbyterian merchants, on the one hand, and the Quaker elite and its allies, on the other—increasing numbers of artisans and even laborers had been drawn into political participation as the leadership sought their votes through pamphlets, speech-making and personal campaigning. In addition, these political appeals had increasingly included virulent attacks on British policies and officials. "It is no uncommon thing," Franklin's ally Joseph Galloway lamented in 1765, to hear high proprietary officials, "in the presence of the attending Populace . . . treat the whole Parliament with the most irreverent abuse. Scarcely anything is too bad to be said of the Ministry, and that worthy Nobleman Lord Bute [the Prime Minister] is openly cursed whenever his name is mentioned."[66]

Until 1770, the results of this new "politics of participation" and the increasing currency of anti-British rhetoric did not threaten merchant control of Philadelphia politics. But in that year, the city's politics was transformed by the controversy over the Townshend duties and the tactic of non-importation. Philadelphia merchants had joined with those of other cities in agreeing to the non-importation of British goods as a means of pressuring the mother country to repeal the new taxes enacted by the British Parliament in 1767. In the spring of 1770, Parliament virtually capitulated and repealed all the new taxes, except the one on tea. Philadelphia merchants who traded with Britain now pressed for an end to non-importation; their trade had been curtailed, while the "wet goods" merchants dealing with the West Indies—generally the lesser merchants—had continued their commercial enterprises as usual. But Philadelphia's mechanics, many of whom were for obvious reasons pleased with the non-importation agreement's elimination of their British competition, now began to desert the Quaker-merchant party. Following the leadership of Franklin's long-time political associate Charles Thomson, a merchant who was a strong advocate of home manufactures, and John Dickinson, a Presbyterian lawyer whose famous *Farmer's Letters* of 1768, rejecting Parliament's right to tax the colonies, also touched on manufacturing interests, the mechanics in 1770 strenuously opposed a resumption of trade with Britain. But in July Philadelphia merchants, following the lead of New York, resumed the commerce.

The controversy of 1770 over non-importation transformed the political alignments in Philadelphia. A new political grouping emerged, led by young Presbyterian merchants, artisans and lawyers like Thomson, Dickinson, Joseph Reed, and the printer William Bradford, and drawing strong support from West India merchants and the artisan community. With the death of the movement for royal government, "the two aristocracies" of the Quaker and Proprietary elites increasingly drew closer together to oppose this rising "Whig" or "Presbyterian" party. The artisans' new political allegiance was strengthened by the support Benjamin Franklin gave to the new alliance and by the unprecedented flood of British imports between 1771 and 1774, which widened the breach between the artisans and their former merchant allies in the Quaker party.[67]

"The opposition to the claims of Britain," a Philadelphian recalled after the Revolution, "originated with the better sort." But "the spirit of liberty and resistance drew into its vortex the mechanical interest, as well as that numerous portion of the community in republics, styled The People; in monarchies The Populace, or still more irreverently, The Rabble, or Canaille." Moreover, "as whiggism declined among the higher classes, it increased in the inferior; because they who composed them, thereby, obtained power and consequence." In 1770 the first political meeting specifically restricted to mechanics was held, and two years later master craftsmen formed a permanent political organization, the Patriotic Society, to promote artisan candidates and policies, especially protection against British imports. By 1774, when the Tea and Intolerable Acts sparked a new round of popular protests and non-importation agreements, the artisans had emerged as a self-conscious, aggressively anti-British element in Philadelphia politics. Virtually no mechanics had served on the various extra-legal committees of the 1760s which had been established to police the non-importation agreements. But in November 1774, just as Paine was arriving in America, a city committee was elected dominated by young merchants, shopkeepers and artisans who were followers of the Thomson-Dickinson party and were determined that non-importation and resistance to British measures would not be dropped as they had been in 1770.[68]

The politicization of the artisan community was one of the fundamental political changes of the revolutionary generation. It would, of course, be wrong to attribute complete political unity to artisans, either in Philadelphia or elsewhere, on any political issue. Like other classes, artisans sometimes divided along religious or ethnic lines. By 1776, most were avid nationalists and friends of independence, but blacksmiths, tailors, coopers, shipwrights and hatters were among those attainted of treason by the Pennsylvania Assembly for their conduct during the British occupation of Philadelphia in 1778.[69]

On one question, almost all artisans saw eye to eye: the need for protection against the competition of British manufactured goods, the issue which breached the traditional artisan-merchant alliance in the Quaker party in 1770. The demand for protection and for the encouragement of home manufactures would be a recurrent strain in artisan politics in the 1770s and 1708s. But why did those artisans who did not compete directly with British imports, who, indeed, often had a personal stake in the fortunes of Philadelphia's commerce, join in self-conscious artisan politics? The answer lies not only in the vitality of the city's artisan community, but in the mechanics' deep social and political grievances.

In the late eighteenth century Philadelphia's artisans, like their counterparts in contemporary England and France, awakened to political consciousness and articulated a fiercely egalitarian ideology. Increasingly, artisans came to resent the wealthy merchants' control of the economic and political life of Philadelphia. By the early 1770s, they were denouncing the pretensions of men of wealth who "have the impudence to assert that Mechanics are men of no consequence," who "make no scruples to say that the mechanics . . . have no right to be consulted; that is, in fact, have no right to speak or think for themselves." They now publicly expressed resentment against the previous political arrangements whereby "a certain company of leading men" chose a slate of candidates before each election, "without ever permitting the affirmative or negative voice of a mechanic to interfere." They took great pride in "the growing interest and importance of the worthy mechanics and manufacturers of this city," and insisted that mechanics be given a share in Philadelphia's elected offices. And they identified themselves with the "noble struggle the citizens of London (chiefly mechanics)" were engaged in during the Wilkes affair.[70]

The "mechanical interest" which emerged as a leading force in Philadelphia politics in the early 1770s was composed of master craftsmen, the upper segment of the artisan community. Like their various craft companies, inter-craft artisan political committees seem to have been restricted to masters. This was only to be expected. As we have seen, the assumption that the masters in a specific craft spoke for the interests of their jouneymen and apprentices was rarely questioned before the 1770s. Protection from British imports would benefit these groups as well as the masters, and the journeymen, as the independent craftsmen of tomorrow, naturally supported the demand for a greater role for artisans in political decision-making.

Between 1772 and 1776, through their participation in meetings of the Patriotic Society and on the numerous committees established to conduct public affairs and police non-importation agreements, several hundred mechanics were for the first time involved in governmental operations and sustained political activity. This in itself was a new thing in Pennsylvania politics.[71] But even more revolutionary was the politicization of the poorer artisans, journeymen, apprentices and laborers, as a result of mobilization into the militia in 1775–76. Representing a very different constituency from the "mechanical interest" of the early 1770s, the militia by 1776 had become an active radical force in Pennsylvania politics.

The military system of Pennsylvania had not changed since 1747, when Benjamin Franklin helped organize a voluntary military Association to circumvent the Quaker party's pacifist objections to the state establishing any form of compulsory military service. It was only in the aftermath of the battles of Lexington and Concord in April 1775 that steps were taken to create a more stable military force and the provincial Assembly began raising money to fight a war. And even then, men were permitted to escape military service by paying a modest fine or by providing a substitute.[72]

Contemporary evidence indicates that the Philadelphia militia was drawn most heavily from the ranks of poorer artisans and laborers and included "a great many apprentices" and servants as well. Although blacks were excluded by law, some may have served illegally in 1775; late that year, "David Owen, a person suspected of enlisting negroes" was "committed to the workhouse" by the city's Council of Safety. Aristocratic Whigs described the militia privates as "in general damn'd riff raff—dirty, mutinous, and disaffected." The militia described themselves as "composed of tradesmen and others, who earn their living by their industry" and who had left behind families "destitute of every means of acquiring an honest living," who deserved public assistance, preference in employment, or even "public works."[73] One militia petition mentioned that some Associators, "through Poverty, are not in the public tax books," and a check of one militia company roster against the published tax lists for Philadelphia reveals that of sixty-seven names, almost half (twenty-nine) appeared on no tax list between 1769 and 1781. Those on the tax lists whose occupations were mentioned included two carpenters, two tailors and one shoemaker, bookbinder, laborer, plasterer, breechmaker and locksmith, almost all listed with very modest amounts of property. That many of these artisans were journeymen rather than masters is indicated by a resolution of another militia company, describing itself as including "persons who by a short neglect of the business of their employer would deprive themselves of their daily bread." It is not surprising that a constant refrain in militia petitions in 1776 was that many militiamen were "not entitled to the privileges of freeman electors" because they could not meet the property qualifications.[74]

For such men, participation in the militia was the first step in the transition from crowd activity to organized politics. Like the New Model Army of the English Civil War, the militia was a "school of political democracy." It quickly developed a collective identity and consciousness, a sense of its own rights and grievances, which included the junior officers, who were all elected by the privates, and even many superior officers as well. Like the New Model Army, it became a center of intense political debate and discussion, in which privates were drawn into contact with radical artisans and intellectuals. And for one group in particular, the Germans, militia service was the first movement out of an apolitical, self-contained ethnic subculture into the mainstream of Pennsylvania politics.[75]

The demands of the militia privates in late 1775 and early 1776 were fairly simple. First, they insisted upon the right to elect all their officers, not simply the junior officers, as provided by the Assembly. Sometimes they even suggested that all officers be selected annually by secret ballot, in the same manner as Assemblymen and local officials, "for annual Election is so essentially necessary to the Liberty of Freemen." Second, they demanded the right of every Associator to vote, regardless of whether or not he met age and property qualifications. This was a far more radical demand than appears at first glance, for it challenged the traditional rationale for excluding apprentices and servants from political life—that being economically dependent on their masters, they could have no political will of their own. Third, they insisted that militia service be made truly universal, or at least that significant financial sacrifices be asked of the men of wealth who avoided service. The Assembly's fine of fifty shillings for nonservice was insultingly low; it offered "the lazy, the timid, and disaffected" an easy way to avoid service and to "ridicule those whose patriotism" led them to enlist.

The petitions drafted by the militia's Committee of Privates, two members of which were elected by each company, were the first articulate expression of resentments from the ranks of lesser artisans and the poor against the widening gap between the top and bottom of Philadelphia society and the growing incidence of poverty. Non-associators, the Committee declared, included "some of the most considerable estates in the Province." Fines should be levied on them "proportioned to each man's property," and the proceeds used to support the families of Associators, "whose maintenance depends on their labour." As for the traditional means of assisting the poor in Philadelphia, one militia petition pointedly observed that public assistance to the families of poor Associators was essential, since "no man, who is able, by his industry, to support his wife and children, could ever consent to have them treated, by the Overseers of the Poor, as the law directs."[76]

Many of the militia's petitions were endorsed by their officers, men of substance who included such leaders of the Presbyterian-Whig party as John Dickinson, Thomas McKean, Joseph Reed and William Bradford. The privates' complaints about the large number of men who escaped military service were echoed by a group of officers, who informed the Assembly that it was "unreasonable" to expect the privates "to remain in the field, while a great number of men equally able to bear arms are suffered to remain at home . . . [and] cowards, disaffected men, and open enemies to the liberties of America are suffered to go abroad sowing sedition."

But there was an underlying tension as well in private-officer relations. In May 1775, "a considerable number of the Associators" complained that the uniforms recommended by their officers were "too expensive" and urged that the privates be allowed to wear "the cheapest uniform . . . a hunting shirt." Not only would the cost be "within the compass of almost every person's ability," but such a uniform would "level all distinctions" within the militia. Many officers believed the rank and file's raw egalitarianism and resistance to discipline were detrimental to proper military organization. Militia meetings were notorious for being attended by "intemperance . . . quarreling, profane swearing, and acts of violence." The officers insisted that those enlisting troops "have great regard to sobriety and moral character in general," and they drew up articles in the summer of 1775 calling for disciplinary action against any soldier using profane language, involved in disturbances or guilty of drunkenness. And, probably in response to complaints from employers, they provided in 1776 that no indentured servant or apprentice be enlisted without the permission of the master. Such rules, of course, may have had much to recommend them in terms of the need for military discipline and respect for the rights of property, but they may also have reflected a middle-class uncomfortableness with the very different life-style of the city's lower classes.[77]

TO THE

ASSOCIATORS

OF THE

CITY OF PHILADELPHIA.

A Confiderable number of the Affociators of this city, on confidering the plan of an uniform recommended by a Committee of the Officers, at a late meeting, are of opinion that it will be found too expenfive for the generality, as well as inconvenient to them; that the aforefaid Officers could not, with propriety, take upon them to adopt of themfelves an uniform for the whole city, without the approbation of the people, who are entitled to an equal confultation. That by adopting the cheapeft uniform, fuch as that of a HUNTING SHIRT, as it will level all diftinctions, anfwers the end of coat and jacket, and is within the compafs of almoft *every* perfon's ability, not cofting at the utmoft above ten fhillings. The officers fay that they did not mean to impofe any particular uniform upon the people, but then they fhould have given the privates an opportunity of making known *their* fentiments. An uniform is granted by *all* to be abfolutely neceffary, but let it be fomething cheap, which the generality can afford. A very material advantage which the HUNTING SHIRTS have above the prefent uniform recommended, is that they will anfwer all feafons of the year, as a perfon may wear neither coat nor jacket in warm weather, and in winter he may cloath under them as warm as he pleafes. Had the hunting fhirts been recommended by the Officers, it would have met the approbation of ninty-nine out of an hundred. It is very far from being the intention of the author of this, to make any diffention among the people; and he is forry to be under the neceffity of propofing any alteration in what is feemingly fixed upon. A meeting of the Affociators ought to be called immediately, that each man may have a voice in what fo nearly concerns himfelf. The author is informed that fome of the Captains of the different companies have propofed, that any of the men, who think they are not able to buy uniforms, may be fupplied by *them*; now there are *hundreds* who could not afford it, yet would never fubmit to *afk any* man for a coat, neither would they appear in the ranks to be pointed at by thofe who *had* uniforms. The author begs leave to affure his fellow citizens, that no interefted motives are the occafion of thefe ftrictures, actuated only by a wifh for the general welfare, the economy of the uniform, and its being peculiarly adapted to the climate, he hopes will induce thofe gentlemen, who have partly fixed upon an expenfive uniform, to concur in fentiment with him.

may 18th 1775

This broadside testifies to the "leveling" spirit that pervaded the Philadelphia militia and to the humble economic circumstances of most Associators. *Library Company of Philadelphia*

☆ ☆ ☆ ☆ ☆

This then was the Philadelphia of the American Revolution and, from 1774 to 1787, of Thomas Paine. It was a city of contrasts, in which impoverished immigrants and the four-wheeled coaches of wealthy merchants driven by liveried slaves, passed each other daily on the streets. It was small enough both physically and in population that men of all classes rubbed shoulders in daily life, but it was a city in which a small number of merchants controlled the bulk of the wealth, and the gap between rich and poor was widening. The premier commercial center of British America, it traded in the international markets of the Atlantic world, but internally the market did not yet fully dominate either investment, business relations, prices or the mobilization of labor. Its political structure was dominated by a system of party competition far more organized and advanced than that of other colonies, but it was only in the 1770s that the tight control of wealthy merchants over the city's affairs was challenged. With the arrival of the Continental Congress in 1774, Philadelphia became the political capital of British America, but it was only in the 1770s that its important artisan community entered political life as an independent force, and a large segment of the lower-class world was still characterized by the politics of the crowd, rather than by sustained political activity. Social stratification was becoming more rigid, but in many ways the great social divide was between "gentlemen" and ordinary men rather than between classes, and class consciousness was probably much more pronounced at the top of society than at the bottom.[78]

The American Revolution would fundamentally alter the life of this city. It would hasten some trends which had been visible for years, and would shatter other traditions and institutions with great suddenness. In a sense, Philadelphia at the time of Paine's arrival stood poised between tradition and modernity; and the Revolution would greatly accelerate the transition between older and more modern forms of economic and political life. The emergence of banks, corporations and other modern financial institutions, the commercialization of an important segment of the artisan community and the extension of the market in free labor, would all propel the city along the path of capitalist development. And Philadelphia's political life would be transformed by the politicization of the mass of its citizens and the overthrow of the provincial system of government. The conflicts and tensions which were an essential part of these fundamental transformations—from the battle over independence and a new system of suffrage, representation and government for Pennsylvania, to debates about inflation, price controls and the legitimacy of institutions like banks and corporations in American society—would frame the career of Thomas Paine in America.

COMMON SENSE,

ADDRESSED TO THE

INHABITANTS

OF

AMERICA,

On the following interesting

SUBJECTS.

I. Of the Origin and Design of Government in general, with concise Remarks on the English Constitution.

II. Of Monarchy and Hereditary Succession.

III. Thoughts on the present State of American Affairs.

IV. Of the present Ability of America, with some miscellaneous Reflections.

Man knows no Master save creating HEAVEN,
Or those whom choice and common good ordain.

THOMSON.

PHILADELPHIA;

Printed, and Sold, by R. BELL, in Third-Street.

MDCCLXXVI.

☆ ☆

CHAPTER THREE

☆ ☆

Common Sense
and Paine's Republicanism

I

Thomas Paine arrived in Philadelphia on November 30, 1774. Political change was in the air; it dominated discussion in the city's taverns and coffee houses, homes and workshops. Already, the port of Boston had been closed as punishment for the Boston Tea Party of December 1773 and the First Continental Congress had assembled in Philadelphia in the fall of 1774, composed of "the ablest and wealthiest men in America." From New England came the "brace of Adamses"—John and his cousin Samuel—advocates of a policy of resistance to British policies and, many feared, secret friends of American independence. In Congress, Pennsylvania's Joseph Galloway urged a policy of reconciliation, but he was narrowly defeated, and instead Congress in October adopted the Continental Association, an agreement banning all commerce with Britain and the West Indies, and called for the establishment of popularly elected local committees to enforce the prohibition. The Whig leaders of Philadelphia—Dickinson, Thomson and

Reed—with their popular base in the artisan community dating from the political conflict of 1770, quickly gained control of the Philadelphia committee, which rapidly replaced the official city government as the real power in local affairs.

Paine arrived in America with the not very revolutionary aim of setting up an academy for the education of young women. But Franklin's letters of introduction soon obtained for him a position as editor of the *Pennsylvania Magazine,* a periodical launched by the publisher and bookseller Robert Aitken. From February to September 1775, Paine worked as day-to-day editor of the publication and contributed poems and essays of his own.[1]

Like *The Case of the Officers of Excise* of 1772, Paine's early American writings provided an inkling—but only that—of the fully developed political outlook and deep resentment against the inegalitarian structure of English society which Paine would soon express in *Common Sense.* In the very first issue of the *Pennsylvania Magazine* (January 24, 1775), Paine spoke of the "profligacy" and "dissipation of manners" of England and the "virtue" of America, language which had long been familiar to Americans in the writings of the British Commonwealthmen and their American disciples. In another early essay, "Reflections on Titles," Paine wrote, "When I reflect on the pompous titles bestowed on unworthy men, I feel an indignity that instructs me to despise the absurdity." "High sounding names" like *"My Lord"* served only to "overawe the superstitious vulgar," and make them "admire in the great, the vices they would honestly condemn in themselves." Paine also gave voice to the anti-Popery which had permeated the culture of Lewes in England and which was widespread among American Protestants. Criticizing the Quebec Act of 1774, which afforded official recognition to the Catholic faith of the inhabitants of Quebec, he observed, "Popery and French laws in Canada are but a part of that system of despotism which has been prepared for the colonies."

Paine thus seems to have identified himself from the beginning

with the fears of many colonials about the intentions of the British
government. But on one issue, as the true son of a Quaker, he was
critical of Americans as well. "With what consistency, or decency,"
he asked in a newspaper piece published in March 1775, could
the colonists "complain so loudly of attempts to enslave them,
while they hold so many hundred thousand in slavery."[2]

Through his connection with the magazine Paine, in 1775,
made the acquaintance of the young physician Benjamin Rush,
who had himself attacked slavery in print a few years before
Paine's arrival in America. Rush, a friend of John Adams and
other members of Congress and of the renowned artisan-scientist
David Rittenhouse, was already advocating in private the establishment of an independent American republic. Friendships like
this and his position as editor of the *Pennsylvania Magazine*
allowed Paine to elaborate and refine his ideas in the charged
political atmosphere of Philadelphia. By the end of his first year
in America he was familiar with the issues and arguments of the
colonists' conflict with Britain and was ready to enlist his literary
talent in the cause of independence and republicanism.

The political situation at the close of 1775 was confused and
ironic. War between British troops and Americans had broken
out in Massachusetts in April, and in May the Second Continental
Congress gathered in Philadelphia, bringing to the city not only
the Adams cousins but such illustrious Virginians as George
Washington, Thomas Jefferson, Richard Henry Lee and Patrick
Henry. Throughout the summer Pennsylvania, like the other
provinces, actively enlisted troops, and military engagements
against the British were fought in New England and the South. At
the same time debate raged in Congress between advocates of
vigorous opposition to the mother country and friends of reconciliation, led by Pennsylvania's Galloway and John Dickinson, no
longer in the forefront of Whig ranks. In November, Congress
learned that the British government had refused to receive the
conciliatory Olive Branch Petition it had approved the previous

July, and in December, the delegates authorized the importation of gunpowder and munitions and the construction of an American navy.

These developments undermined the possibility of reconcilation, and strengthened the hand of the Adamses, Rush and other advocates of separation from Britain. But there were also powerful forces militating against independence. To begin with, the seeming impossibility of defeating the most powerful military authority in the world strengthened the natural reluctance of men to embrace treason. And there were the tradition of obedience to British rule and the protection Americans enjoyed as part of the British Empire. Many of the wealthy merchants, planters and lawyers who dominated Congress, moreover, were alarmed at the upsurge of popular participation in politics which had accompanied the creation of extra-legal non-importation committees in 1774 and 1775. They feared that war and independence would unleash a movement for political change within the colonies themselves. Despite the fact that war was in progress and British authority was in fact suspended, most political leaders still vindicated their actions by invoking the "rights of Englishmen" rather than the goal of independence and the hope persisted that a peaceful accomodation could be reached. As Paine observed, the situation was "strangely astonishing, perfect independence contending for dependence."[3]

It was Paine's *Common Sense,* published in January 1776, which transformed the terms of political debate. Benjamin Rush suggested to Paine that he write a pamphlet broaching the subject of independence, although he specifically warned Paine to avoid both that word and republicanism—advice Paine chose to ignore. At first, no typographer would agree to set the pamphlet in print, but finally the "republican printer" Robert Bell (a notorious Scot who openly kept a mistress and was one of Philadelphia's most enterprising businessmen) agreed. While Rush gave the pamphlet its name and he, Franklin, Rittenhouse, Sam Adams and possibly one or two others read the manuscript and made a few minor changes, the arguments and the means of presenting them were Paine's. He was fully responsible for "the most brilliant pamphlet written during the American Revolution, and one of the most brilliant pamphlets ever written in the English language."[4]

"My motive and object in all my political works, beginning with *Common Sense*," Paine recalled in 1806, " . . . have been to rescue man from tyranny and false systems and false principles of government, and enable him to be free." Paine began *Common Sense* not with a discussion of America's relations with Britain, but with an analysis of the principles of government and an attack on hereditary rule and the validity of monarchy itself. Paine always considered the republican argument of *Common Sense* more important than the pamphlet's call for independence. "The mere independence of America," he later wrote, "were it to have been followed by a system of government modelled after the corrupt system of English Government, would not have interested me with the unabated ardor it did. It was to bring forward and establish the representative system of government, as the work itself will show, that was the leading principle with me in writing."

There had been a few attacks on hereditary authority and calls for republican government in the colonial press before Paine wrote. But, by and large, republicanism had existed as an unarticulated strain of political radicalism and as a component of the evangelical relgious mind. The Country party ideologists whose outlook dominated the writings of previous colonial pamphleteers had not challenged the view that the British constitution, with its balance between monarch, Lords and Commons, was the most perfect system of government in the world, even while they warned that "corruption" was undermining the stability of this finely tuned structure. In *Common Sense*, Paine literally transformed the political language. "Republic" had previously been used as a term of abuse in political writing; Paine made it a living political issue and a utopian ideal of government.[5]

Paine's savage attack on "the so much boasted Constitution of England" contains the most striking passages in *Common Sense*. He not only raised the by now traditional cry that corruption was destroying English liberty, but he denounced the whole notion of the historical legitimacy of the monarchy itself. His description of the accession of William the Conqueror seven centuries earlier would become one of his most frequently quoted passages: "A French bastard landing with an armed banditti and establishing himself king of England against the consent of the natives, is in plain terms a very paltry rascally original. . . . The plain truth is that the antiquity of the English monarchy will not bear looking into." Paine minced no words in his assaults on the principle of hereditary rule: "Of more worth is one honest man to society, and in the sight of God, than all the crowned ruffians that ever lived." And: "One of the strongest natural proofs of the folly of hereditary right in kings is that nature disproves it, otherwise she would not so frequently turn it into ridicule, by giving mankind *an ass for a lion.*" Far from being the most perfect system of government in the world, the king was "the royal brute of England" and the English constitution simply "the base remains of two ancient tyrannies, compounded with some new Republican materials . . . the remains of monarchial tyranny in the person of the king . . . the remains of aristocratical tyranny in the persons of the peers."[6]

Paine was the first writer in America to denounce the English constitution so completely, and with it the idea that balanced government was essential to liberty. To be sure, he could use the familiar language of the Commonwealthmen in denouncing the British government: "in its present state . . . the corrupt influence of the Crown, by having all the places in its disposal, hath . . . effectively swallowed up the power, and eaten up the virtue of the House of Commons." But he differed from contemporary radicals, both in England and America, in idealizing neither the uncorrupted, balanced constitution, nor some mythical Anglo-Saxon past (although his attack on William the Conqueror by implication invoked the popular tradition of the "Norman

Yoke"). Instead, Paine simply urged the establishment of republican government in America, while only hinting at its structure. Paine was always more interested in principles than forms of government, but he did call for the creation of a continental legislature and new unicameral state assemblies based on a broad suffrage, popular representation through frequent elections, and a written constitution guaranteeing the rights of persons and property and establishing freedom of religion.[7]

Common Sense then turned to a discussion of independence, an issue that had been mentioned sporadically in the press in 1775, but one which most colonists still refused to confront. One by one, Paine considered and then demolished the arguments for reconciliation. Was it ungrateful to rebel since Britain was "the parent country"? "The more shame upon her conduct," answered Paine. "Even brutes do not devour their young, nor savages make war upon their own families." Moreover, Paine insisted, it was wrong to consider England "the parent country of America" since "this new world hath been the asylum for the persecuted lovers of civil and religious liberty from *every part of Europe.*" Was America weak in comparison to Britain? Quite the reverse, Paine declared. "There is something absurd in supposing a continent to be perpetually governed by an island." Would independence involve America in wars with European powers while depriving it of British protection? "France and Spain," Paine replied, "never were, nor perhaps ever will be, our enemies as *Americans,* but as our being the subjects of Great Britain." America should "steer clear of European connections, which she can never do" while imprisoned in the British empire. It was monarchial government which caused the wars which perennially afflicted Europe, while "the republics of Europe are all . . . in peace."[8]

Paine also addressed himself to conservatives who, he said, "dreaded an independence, fearing that it would produce civil wars." Independence, he replied, was inevitable. Since the outbreak of war, all plans for reconciliation "are like the almanacks of the last years; which though proper then, are superceded and useless now." The only question was how independence would come—by the legal voice of the people in Congress; by a military power; or by a mob." In effect, Paine was warning conservatives that the very "popular disquietudes" they feared would produce internal upheaval might, if unfulfilled, be harnessed by demagogues in an uprising which would "finally sweep away the liberties of the continent like a deluge.... Ye that oppose independence now, ye know not what ye do: ye are opening a door to eternal tyranny."[9]

"I challenge the warmest advocate for conciliation," Paine declared, "to show a single advantage that this continent can reap by being connected with Great Britain." Not only was America a plaything of British politicians and constantly involved in European disputes, but British mercantilist regulations were inimical to the economic growth of the colonies and responsible for "many material injuries." "No nation in a state of foreign dependence" and "limited in its commerce" could ever achieve "material eminence" or political greatness. Paine outlined a vision of an independent American empire, pursuing a policy of friendship and free trade with all nations, promoted by a strong continental government, complete with a national debt ("a national debt is a national bond") and a powerful navy.[10]

Toward the close of *Common Sense,* Paine moved beyond these material considerations to outline in lyrical rhetoric a breathtaking vision of the meaning of American independence. "We have it in our power to begin the world over again ... the birthday of a new world is at hand." Paine transformed the struggle over the rights of Englishmen into a contest with meaning for all mankind:[11]

> O! ye that love mankind! Ye that dare oppose not only tyranny but the tyrant, stand forth! Every spot of the old world is overrun with oppression. Freedom hath been hunted round the globe. Asia and Africa have long expelled her. Europe regards her as a stranger, and England hath given her warning to depart. O! receive the fugitive, and prepare in time an asylum for mankind.

The immediate success and impact of *Common Sense* was nothing short of astonishing. At a time when the most widely circulated colonial newspapers were fortunate if they averaged two thousand sales per week, when the average pamphlet was printed in one or two editions of perhaps a few thousand copies, *Common Sense* went through twenty-five editions and reached literally hundreds of thousands of readers in the single year 1776. It also reached non-readers; one report from Philadelphia in February said the pamphlet "is read to all ranks." Paine later claimed *Common Sense* had sold at least 150,000 copies, and most historians have accepted this figure as roughly accurate. As Paine exulted, it was "the greatest sale that any performance ever had since the use of letters."[12]

From up and down the thirteen colonies in the spring of 1776 came reports that the pamphlet was read by "all sorts of people" and that it had made "innumerable converts" to independence. A Connecticut man announced, "You have declared the sentiments of millions. Your production may justly be compared to a land-flood that sweeps all before it. We were blind, but on reading these enlightening words the scales have fallen from our eyes." And from Philadelphia itself a writer in February 1776 commented on "the progress of the idea of Colonial independence in three weeks or a month," adding, "surely thousands and tens of thousands of common farmers and tradesmen must be better reasoners than some of our untrammelled *juris consultores,* who to this hour feel a reluctance to part with the abominable chain."[13]

John Adams always resented the fact that *Common Sense* was credited with having contributed so much to the movement for independence. Its discussion of that subject, he insisted, was simply "a tolerable summary of the arguments which I had been repeating again and again in Congress for nine months."[14] To some extent, Adams was right, but he failed to understand the genius of Paine's pamphlet. *Common Sense* did express ideas which had long circulated in the colonies—the separateness of America from Europe, the corruption of the Old World and innocence of the New, the absurdity of hereditary privilege and the possibility of a future American empire. None of these ideas was original with Paine. What was brilliantly innovative was the way Paine combined them into a single comprehensive argument and related them to the common experiences of Americans.

Paine's reference to the colonists' diverse European origins and denial of England as the sole "parent country" was self-evident in a province like Pennsylvania, with its thoroughly heterogeneous population. His discussion of the benefits of isolation from the power struggles of the Old World was all but obvious to Americans who could remember that between 1689 and 1763 the colonies had been involved in four military conflicts between Britain and her European foes. His description of the virtues of republican government confirmed the experiences of colonists, especially in New England, who had long known a kind of republicanism in town meetings and annual elections, and of others who in 1774 and 1775 had witnessed the ability of popularly elected committees to exercise the functions of government. Paine's reference to the material benefits of free trade with Europe was especially persuasive in light of the high profits merchants and farmers had reaped by exporting grain to Portugal in the 1760s and 1770s. And his vision of a powerful American empire was attractive to Americans who had matured in an age of empires and felt an abiding interest in westward expansion. The most far-sighted colonists, like Benjamin Franklin, had long envisioned the New World as the site of a continental state exceeding in population and power any of the nations of Europe. (It is worth noting that Paine, Franklin and others used the word "empire" in its eighteenth-century sense of expanding territorial and commercial sovereignty, with none of the negative emotive implications of more modern usage. Paine, for example, helped to popularize the idea of a benevolent American empire while in 1778 condemning British rule in India as "not so properly a conquest as an extermination of mankind."[15])

Equally striking was the way Paine enlisted the Bible-based

Protestantism of the majority of colonists in the cause of republicanism and independence. Near the beginning of *Common Sense* are several paragraphs with lengthy Biblical quotations designed to show that monarchy was incompatible with true Christianity and the word of God. "The will of the Almighty," he concluded, ". . . expressly disapproves of government by kings." Monarchy was "the most prosperous invention the devil ever set on foot for the promotion of idolatry. . . . [It is] in every instance . . . the popery of government." It may seem ironic that Paine, who twenty years hence condemned the authority of the Bible in *The Age of Reason*, would use such arguments. When John Adams told Paine he thought the Biblical reasoning in *Common Sense* was ridiculous, Paine laughed, "expressed a contempt of the Old Testament and indeed the Bible at large" and announced his intention of one day publishing a work on religion.[16]

However tedious the Biblical arguments of *Common Sense* may seem to the modern reader, however disingenuous Paine may have been in these passages, he understood only too well the necessity of stripping monarchy of its Biblical authority and appealing to the anti-Popery sentiments which suffused the culture of eighteenth-century American and English Protestants, who viewed the Catholic Church as the essence of despotic hierarchy and the denial of individual liberty and self-direction. He utilized Biblical imagery and language throughout the pamphlet, as in his appeal to conservatives, "ye know not what ye do," and his description of the King of England as a "Pharoah." And he invoked, in a secularized form, the millennial hope for the coming of a new world, the vision of a perfect society, which had been "predominant among English-speaking Protestants since the later seventeenth century." Paine transformed the language of an impending millennium into the secular vision of a utopia in the New World. To the millennial view of the American past as a stage in the process whereby God's kingdom would be established on this earth, Paine added the future destiny of America as a society defined by its commitment to liberty and its isolation from the Old World. Paine's image of a New World "could only be created by a man who knew Europe well enough to hate its society and who longed desperately enough for salvation to envision in a flash of illumination the destiny of the New World as libertion from the Old."[17]

John Adams, as we have seen, considered Paine's arguments in *Common Sense* to have been singularly unoriginal. Nothing in the pamphlet was new, he believed, except "the phrases, suitable for an emigrant from New Gate, or one who had chiefly associated with such company, such as 'the royal brute of England,' 'the blood upon his soul,' and not a few others of equal delicacy." Adams was certainly correct in believing that that uniqueness of Paine's pamphlet lay not simply in broaching the hitherto forbidden subjects of independence and republicanism, but in doing so in a new literary tone and style. But he once again failed to recognize the significance of Paine's achievement. If the era of the Revolution witnessed "the massive politicization of American society," *Common Sense,* written in a style designed to reach a mass audience, was central to the explosion of political argument and involvement beyond the confines of a narrow elite to "all ranks" of Americans.[18]

The first thing which contemporaries noticed about *Common Sense* was its tone of outrage. Consider Paine's description of his reaction to the outbreak of hostilities at Lexington and Concord:

> No man was a warmer wisher for a reconciliation than myself, before the fatal nineteenth of April, 1775, but the moment the event of that day was made known, I rejected the hardened, sullen-tempered Pharoah of England for ever; and disdain the wretch, that with the pretended title of Father of his People can unfeelingly hear of their slaughter, and composedly sleep with their blood upon his soul.

What contemporaries described as Paine's "daring impudence" and "uncommon frenzy" was far removed from the legalistic, logical arguments, the "decorous and reasonable" language, of previous American political pamphlets.[19]

But there was more to Paine's appeal than the enraged assaults on hereditary monarchy that so offended Adams and the "indecent expressions" to which Henry Laurens of South Carolina objected. Paine was the conscious pioneer of a new style of political writing, a rhetoric aimed at extending political discussion beyond the narrow bounds of the eighteenth-century's "political nation." "As it is my design to make those that can scarcely read understand," he once wrote, "I shall therefore avoid every literary ornament and put it in language as plain as the alphabet." He assumed knowledge of no authority but the Bible, provided immediate translations for the few Latin phrases he employed and avoided florid language designed to impress more cultivated readers.

Paine was capable, to be sure, of creating brilliant metaphors, such as his famous reply in *The Rights of Man* to Edmund Burke's sympathy for the fate of Marie Antionette: "He pities the plumage, but forgets the dying bird." He could employ humor as a weapon, as when he observed in *Common Sense* that American grain would "always have a market while eating is the custom of Europe." But the hallmarks of his writing were clarity, directness and forcefulness. His vocabulary and grammar were straightforward, and he carried his readers along with great care from one argument to the next. A good example of how he constructed his argument is the beginning of the discussion of monarchy in *Common Sense*. Paine had alluded to the social distinction between rich and poor, and then went on:[20]

But there is another and greater distinction for which no truly natural or religious reason can be assigned, and that is the distinction of men into Kings and Subjects. Male and Female are the distinctions of nature, good and bad the distinctions of heaven; but how a race of men came into the world so exalted above the rest, and distinguished like some new species, is worth inquiring into, and whether they are the means of happiness or misery to the world.

Paine was not the first writer of the eighteenth century consciously to address himself to a wide readership. There are similarities between his literary style and the "plain English," the "clear and easy prose" of English novelists such as Defoe and Richardson and political essayists like Addison, Swift and Junius. Each of these writers developed modes of literary expression addressed to "the plain understanding of the people," elucidated the "plain truth," and drew on the everyday experiences of their readers. (Paine, in fact, originally planned to title his pamphlet *Plain Truth,* but was convinced by Banjamin Rush to call it *Common Sense.*) Nor was Paine the first pamphleteer in England or America to use outrageous and even insulting language. In several colonial electoral contests, including the Philadelphia campaign of 1764, political opponents hurled invective at one another. Paine himself was acquainted with the biting personal satire of Junius in England. But unlike Junius, whose writing was at its best when it attacked prominent individuals, Paine announced at the outset of *Common Sense* his intention of avoiding "everything which is personal" and all "compliments as well as censure to individuals."[21] Paine's concern was not with personalities, but with the principles of government. And his rage was tempered by a conscious effort to engage the reason as well as the passions of his readers. His savage attacks on kingship and his careful exposition of the essential principles of republicanism were two sides of the same coin: both were meant to undermine the entire system of deferential politics.

Paine's message, stated explicitly and conveyed by his tone and rhythm as well as his appeals to common experience, was that anyone could grasp the nature of politics and government. He flaunted his contempt for precedent and authority. "In this part of the debate," Paine wrote in the spring of 1776 of a newspaper antagonist, "Cato shelters himself chiefly in quotations from other authors, without reasoning much on the matter himself; in answer to which, I present him with a string of maxims and recollections, drawn from the nature of things, without borrowing from any one." Rather than invoking authorities and legal precedents, Paine offered "nothing more than simple facts, plain arguments, and common sense." Politics, Paine insisted, could. and must be reduced to easily comprehensible first principles: "Notwithstanding the mystery with which the science of government has been enveloped, for the purpose of enslaving, plundering and imposing upon mankind, it is of all things the least mysterious and the most easy to be understood." And the first axiom of Paine's politics was simply the possibility of change. Men could, by the exercise of reason, throw off the dead weight of tradition and see "government begin, as if we lived in the beginning of time."[22]

To his critics, Paine was as guilty of debasing the language as of attacking the government. Gouverneur Morris scoffed at him as "a mere adventurer . . . without fortune, without family or connexions, ignorant even of grammar" (a remark seemingly more appropriate to a patronage society like Britain than to colonial America). Even Franklin, sending a publication of Paine's to a friend in Paris, felt obliged to remark, "This rude way of writing in America will seem strong on your side." But Paine was indeed a conscious artist, who agonized over his choice of words and wrote and rewrote with great care. He was aware that he was creating a style of writing, "hitherto unknown on this side of the Atlantic," as Virginia's Edmund Randolph put it. Most writers of the eighteenth century believed that to write for a mass audience meant to sacrifice refinement for coarseness and triviality, to reject a "high" or "literary" style in favor of a "low" or "vulgar" one. The American pamphleteers before Paine, with rare exceptions, came from the upper social strata of lawyers, merchants, planters and ministers. Only Paine had sprung from that same mass audience which devoured his works on both sides of the Atlantic. His literary style, his rejection of deference and his political republicanism were all interdependent: for Paine, the medium was of one piece with the message.[23]

In February 1776, the Massachusetts Whig Joseph Hawley read *Common Sense* and remarked: "Every sentiment has sunk into my well prepared heart." The hearts of Hawley and thousands of other Americans had been readied for Paine's arguments by the extended conflict over Britain's right to tax the colonies, the outbreak of war and the pervasive influence of the Country party vision of a corrupt British government and society. The intensification of fighting in the winter of 1775–76—the American invasion of Canada, the burning of Falmouth, Maine by the British, the bombardment of Norfolk coupled with Lord Dunmore's attempt to arm Virginia slaves to fight against the colonists and the arrival of news of the British decision to send German mercenaries to serve beside her own soldiers—all gave added weight to Paine's call for independence. As George Washington observed, "A few more of such flaming arguments as were exhibited at Falmouth and Norfolk, added to the sound doctrine and unanswerable reasoning contained in the pamphlet *Common Sense*, will not leave members [of Congress] at a loss to decide upon the propriety of separation."

Common Sense did not, of course, "cause" either the movement or the decision for independence. Six months would elapse after its publication until Congress approved the Declaration of Independence. But the pamphlet's astonishing impact stemmed from the fact that it appeared at precisely the moment when Americans were ready to accept Paine's destruction of arguments favoring conciliation and his appeal to latent republicanism, to the material interests of the colonists and to the widespread idealistic hopes for the future of the New World. Paine articulated the deepest meaning of the struggle with Britain for an audience still preoccupied with attaining the full rights of Englishmen, and drew new secular, republican conclusions from such deep traditions of popular thought as anti-Popery and the "Norman Yoke." By doing all this in a new style of writing and a new political language, Paine "broke the ice that was slowly congealing the revolutionary movement."[24] The success of *Common Sense* reflected the perfect conjunction of a man and his time, a writer and his audience, and it announced the emergence of Paine as the outstanding political pamphleteer of the Age of Revolution.

II

From 1776 to the end of his life, the hallmarks of Paine's political and social outlook remained remarkably constant. Paine himself asserted that his great pamphlet of the 1790s, *The Rights of Man*, was based on the "same principles" as *Common Sense*: "The only difference between the two works was that one was adapted to the local circumstances of England, and the other to those of America."[25] On certain specific questions Paine's ideas would change after 1776, yet he would always retain the commitment to political and social egalitarianism, the hostility to monarchy and hereditary privilege, the American nationalism (coupled with a cosmopolitan interest in the spread of liberty overseas) and the belief in the virtues of commerce and economic growth, which he articulated in *Common Sense*. All were elements of Paine's comprehensive and distinctive ideology of republicanism.

For Paine, what distinguished republican government was not the "*particular form*" of government but its object: "the public good." Sprinkled through Paine's writings are references to "the cloven foot" of faction," and the need to prevent "governing by party." Both class and party conflict were, in a sense, incompatible with the essence of republicanism, which, Paine believed, "does not admit of an interest distinct from that of the nation."

Legislation, for Paine, should simply reflect the united interest of a homogenous people, rather than private or narrow needs. "Whatever is of consequence to any, is so to all," Paine wrote in 1779, "for wealth like water soon spreads over the surface. . . ."[26]

That the people, especially when set against their rulers, were a homogenous body with a definable common interest, was a view to which most American republican thinkers subscribed. This was why American political leaders viewed organized parties as divisive and dangerous, the instruments of small special interest groups opposed to the common good. Nonetheless, there was an inherent conflict or at least an ambiguity within republican thought between a Lockean emphasis on natural rights, which seemed to posit a society composed of competitive individuals, each engaged in the pursuit of his own happiness, and the notion of the general good, which seemed to hark back to an earlier corporate notion of society.

By the 1780s, American political thought was developing toward the idea that social conflict was inevitable in a society in which the private liberties of individuals were guaranteed. The most explicit statement of this belief was made by James Madison in his writings on the federal Constitution. Madison rejected as "entirely fictitious" the idea that society consisted of individuals who possessed "precisely the same interests." No society "ever did or ever can consist of such a homogenous mass of citizens." As a result, it was necessary to take great care in constructing governments, so as to balance competing group interests and prevent any one faction from attacking the liberty of others. For Madison, representative government was less a utopian experiment than an organizational device to prevent self-interested factionalism from destroying the state. (But Madison's view also represented a stage in the development of a distinctive American philosophy of individualism, in which that concept lost its older connotations of narrow self-interest and took on an identification with moral freedom and the rule of liberty.[27])

Paine himself was hardly free from the tension between the individualist and corporate implications of republicanism. He accepted the cardinal precept of what has been termed "possessive individualism"—that individual freedom was inviolable because it was a form of property. In his early anti-slavery essay of 1775, he criticized slaveowners as thieves, and argued that "the slave, who is the proper owner of his freedom, has a right to reclaim it." And in 1778 he would explicitly assert, "I consider freedom as personal property." But Paine never believed that conflict existed between individual interests and the general good. "Public good," he insisted, "is not a term opposed to the good of individuals. On the contrary, it is the good of every individual collected. It is the good of all, because it is the good of every one."

In a sense, it was Madison, not Paine, who had a more realistic view of the possibilities of class conflict in republican society. Such conflict was inevitable, Madison believed, because the unequal distribution of property created distinct interests among "those who hold, and those who are without property." The irony here is indeed remarkable. Madison's view reflects the recognition by Virginia's planter class, stemming from the time of Bacon's Rebellion in the seventeenth century, of the dangers of discontent among propertyless whites. In the eighteenth century, the massive importation of black slaves had reduced this danger by placing the bulk of the laboring class totally outside political society. By eliminating altogether the question of political rights for the laboring population, slavery enabled the wealthy planters for whom Madison spoke to embrace republicanism and representative government.[28]

Paine was less attuned than Madison to the dangers of class conflict in a republic partially because—like so many other Europeans—what impressed Paine about the New World was its egalitarian distribution of property and high standard of living compared to Europe. "There are not three millions of people in any part of the universe, who live so well, or have such a fund of ability, as in America," Paine wrote in 1782. "The income of a common laborer, who is industrious, is equal to that of the generality of tradesmen in England. . . . In America, almost every farmer lives on his own lands, and in England not one in a hundred does."[29]

This vision of an egalitarian America helps to explain Paine's comparative indifference to governmental structures. Madison and the other founding fathers, spokesmen for an inter-colonial alliance of forward-looking merchants, planters and lawyers, took great care to construct a government in which the various branches and powers (and class interests) were carefully balanced against one another. Paine, a pamphleteer with little direct responsibility in practical political affairs, believed that the simpler government was, the better. Indeed, unlike virtually all the political writers of his time, he did not distinguish sharply between a republic and "democracy." In the political language of the eighteenth century, "democracy" had not yet acquired its modern meanings—it applied only to those states in which the entire people participated directly in the conduct of government, and it implied anarchy and perpetual turbulence. In a large country, direct democracy was clearly impossible, and representation of the people via elections became inevitable. But to most American Whigs there was far more to representation than simply a matter of convenience. Inherent in the Commonwealthman ideology which shaped the American Whig mind was a view of human nature as susceptible to corruption, basically self-interested and dominated by passion rather than reason. It was because of this natural "depravity" of human nature that democracy was inexpedient: a good constitution required a "mixed" government to check the passions of the people, as well as representing their interests.[30]

At times, Paine too seemed to embrace this pessimistic view of human nature. Government, he wrote in *Common Sense,* was "a mode rendered necessary by the inability of moral virtue to govern the world," and in another celebrated passage, which invoked the religious imagery of the fall of man, he explained:

> Government, like dress, is the badge of lost innocence; the palaces of kings are built upon the ruins of the bowers of paradise. For were the impulses of conscience clear, uniform and irresistably obeyed, man would need no other law-giver. . . .

In general, however, Paine took an extremely optimistic view of human nature, or at least of the possibility of human perfectibility. He had faith in the ability of men to act according to the dictates of reason instead of passion and narrow self-interest. As he transformed the millennial Protestant vision of the rule of Christ on earth into a secular image of utopia, Paine helped to create and publicize the new secular ideas of continual progress and human perfectibility which emerged in the eighteenth century. Previous theorists had viewed human history either in terms of the unfolding of a divine plan of redemption or as a cyclical pattern of the rise and fall of empires. The new, modern idea of progress looked not to the goal of a static, perfect state achieved through divine intervention, but to an open-ended process of future improvement, created by the deliberate actions of mankind.[31]

Because of his commitment to the idea of the perfectibility of man and his roseate view of human nature, Paine could reject the need for governmental checks and balances, and even the common contempt for "democracy" as a form of government. Rather than distinguishing sharply between "republic" and "democracy," Paine rejected direct democracy solely because it was "inconvenient," and defined a republic as "representation ingrafted upon democracy." Such a definition was possible only because of Paine's belief that "man, were he not corrupted by governments, is naturally the friend of man, and that human nature is not of itself vicious."[32]

Paine's belief in a simple governmental structure rested not only on his view of human nature, but on a central axiom of his political philosophy, the distinction between society and government. Nowhere did he expound this more clearly than in the opening section of *Common Sense:*

> Some writers have so confounded society with government, as to leave little or no distinction between them; whereas they are not only different, but have different origins. Society is produced by our wants and government by our wickedness; the former promotes our happiness *positively* by uniting our affections, the latter *negatively* by restraining our vices. The one encourages intercourse, the other creates distinctions. The first is a patron, the last a punisher. Society is in every state a blessing, but government, even in its best state, is but a necessary evil.

On the basis of passages such as this, which are repeated throughout his political writings, some writers accord Paine a place in "the pantheon of anarchist ancestors."

Paine's distinction between society and government had as its corollary that society is natural and worthwhile while government is coercive and oppressive. One of the things which struck him most deeply about the situation in America in 1775 and 1776, he wrote in *The Rights of Man,* was that despite "the suspension of the old governments . . . everything was conducted" with "order and decorum." Most of the "order which reigns among mankind is not the effect of government," he concluded. "It had its origin in the principles of society and the natural constitution of man. It existed prior to government, and would exist if the formality of government was abolished."[33]

This idea, like so many of Paine's, was not original with him. For Paine, the concept was intimately related to his Newtonian frame of mind and to his vision of economic progress. Like the Newtonian universe, the natural state of society was harmony and order. It was government—that is, outside interference—which deranged this natural order, corrupted human nature and replaced harmony with competition and oppression.

The cement of the natural order of society, the force holding it together as truly as gravity united the Newtonian universe, was commerce. Paine explicitly used the terminology of science in describing social relations: "No one man is capable, without the aid of society, of supplying his own wants; and those wants acting upon every individual, impel the whole of them into society, as naturally as gravitation acts to a center." Since commercial interchange between individuals and nations was natural, Paine was always, as he described it, "an advocate for commerce." "All the great laws of society," he believed, "are laws of nature. Those of trade and commerce, whether with respect to the intercourse of individuals, or of nations, are laws of mutual and reciprocal interest." Such an outlook would, as we shall see, make Paine extremely receptive to laissez-faire economics since it would be folly to allow governmental interference with the "natural laws" of trade and commerce. But it also underlay his conviction that far less government was necessary than men were used to. Republican government, according to Paine, should be "nothing more than a national association acting on the principles of society."[34]

This distinction between society and government helps to explain Paine's vision of a republic without class conflict or economic oppression. Paine was, to be sure, an eloquent and scathing critic of the social order of Europe. He could comment in moving terms on "the mass of wretchedness" lying "hidden from the eye of common observation" which had "scarcely any other chance than to expire in poverty or infamy." But the cause of this wretchedness was political, not economic: the existence of poverty implied that "something must be wrong in the system of government." Paine singled out oppressive taxation as the primary cause of poverty in Europe—another example of the destructive effects of excessive and unjust government. While he outlined a pioneering and far-reaching program of social welfare measures in *The*

Rights of Man (measures which he never suggested needed to be applied in America), his primary remedy for economic injustices was the establishment of republican government. "When we survey the wretched condition of man under the monarchial and hereditary systems of government . . . it becomes evident that those systems are bad and that a general revolution in the principle and construction of government is necessary."[35]

Paine thus did not attribute inequalities of wealth to economic oppression, although his views on this subject did change during his lifetime. In *Common Sense*, Paine took a typical Lockean view of private property, attributing economic inequalities to differences in talent, industry and frugality among individuals. "The distinctions between rich and poor," he declared, "may in a great measure be accounted for, and that without recourse to the harsh ill-sounding names of oppression and avarice. Oppression is often the *consequence*, but seldom or never the *means* of riches." Almost twenty years later, in his *Dissertation on the First Principles of Government*, Paine repeated the same argument, in virtually the same language.

Only in *Agrarian Justice*, written in 1796 in France, did Paine for the first time blame poverty on the oppression of the poor by the rich. In this pamphlet he called for a government program of direct payments to each citizen reaching adulthood, as compensation for the loss of the natural right to land which private property in land caused. But even in *Agrarian Justice*, Paine rejected an "agrarian law" dividing existing property.[36]

"I see in America," Paine wrote in *The Rights of Man* in 1791, "the generality of the people living in a style of plenty unknown in the monarchial countries; and I see that the principle of its government, which is that of the *equal rights of Man*, is making rapid progress in the world." This association between America's economic abundance and its republican form of government was a crucial element in Paine's social analysis and helps explain why he did not attribute inequalities of wealth to economic oppression. In a republic, there was no reason for antagonism between rich

and poor or employer and employee. In America, "the poor are not oppressed, and the rich are not privileged. Industry is not mortified by the splendid extravagance of a court rioting at its expense. Their taxes are few, because their government is just."
As this passage implies, there was one important exception to Paine's view of a republic without class conflict—the privileged aristocracy and hereditary monarchs of Europe stood outside the harmonious general good. Wealth and property, in other words, were legitimate and contributed to the welfare of society, only if they were obtained by individual effort, not artificial privilege. Nowhere would Paine explain this distinction better than in *The Rights of Man*, in countering Edmund Burke's defense of the House of Lords:[37]

> Why then does Mr. Burke talk of this House of Peers, as the pillar of the landed interest? Were that pillar to sink into the earth, the same landed property would continue, and the same plowing, sowing and reaping would go on. The aristocracy are not the farmers who work the land, and raise the produce, but are the mere consumers of the rent; and when compared with the active world, are the drones, a seraglio of males, who neither collect the honey nor form the hive, but exist only for lazy enjoyment.

Such an indictment, of course, had more radical implications in England, where it challenged the very structure of legal privilege and aristocratic government, than in America, which lacked a titled and legally privileged nobility. Paine never denounced the "aristocracy" of America with the fury he lavished upon their English counterparts. The most he did was appeal to the widespread distrust, shared by all elements in Philadelphia below the elite, toward the men of great wealth and pretensions. As he wrote in 1778:

> There is an extent of riches, as well as an extreme of poverty, which, by narrowing the circles of a man's acquaintance, lessens his opportunities of general knowledge. But the man who by situation is most

likely to steer right, is looked for in the practical world. The knowledge necessary for raising and applying a revenue with the greatest
ease, is drawn from business. It is self business.

The last sentence is of crucial importance. For it grounds
Paine's republicanism firmly in a society of small producers—
artisans and farmers—as opposed to other elements of society
who, Paine wrote "produce nothing themselves." For men in
what came to be called the "producing classes," wealth was the
result of hard work and good fortune, not privilege or family
connections, and there was little possibility of accumulating great
fortunes. But it was the manner of obtaining one's wealth, not the
amount of it, which was of greatest importance.[38] Paine could
speak of a republic as socially harmonious because republican
government would cut the aristocracy off from their sources of
income—hereditary privilege, court sinecures and governmental
favors—and would allow full reign to the natural laws of civil
society, ensuring that all classes would share in economic abundance, and that inequalities of wealth would reflect differences in
individual ability and effort.

And what of the poor? As the above paragraph suggests, Paine
distinguished men of "self business" from those of "an extreme of
poverty" as well as "an extent of riches." Like so many other men
who had known poverty and pulled themselves out of it, Paine did
not romanticize want. As early as 1772, in *The Case of the Officers of
Excise*, he had written, "poverty, in defiance of principles, begets a
degree of meanness that will stoop to almost anything." Despite
his own penchant for drinking and tavern society, Paine clearly
dissociated himself from many aspects of lower-class culture. Like
his friend Charles W. Peale, he believed "rational amusement"
superior to bull-baiting and cockfighting, and in 1775 he published a poem against cruelty to animals in the *Pennsylvania
Magazine*. In 1777, he declared that "the whole race of prostitutes
in New York were Tories," and that "schemes for supporting the

Tory cause" in Philadelphia "were concerted and carried on in common bawdy-houses."[39]

Paine also disapproved of the traditional lower-class means of political expression, crowd activity. "It is time to have done with tarring and feathering," he wrote in 1777, and a year later declared, "I never did, and never would encourage what may be properly called a mob, when any legal mode of redress can be had." Ten years later he was even more insistent that "the republican form and principle leaves no room for insurrection, because it provides and establishes a rightful means in its stead."[40] Paine, moreover, knew that in England, mobs as often rallied to the cause of Church and King as to Wilkes and Liberty. The crowd was often fundamentalist—in Philadelphia and Boston crowds attacked doctors who dissected corpses, and the Boston crowd refused to take action on Saturday and Sunday nights, which were considered holy by New Englanders—while Paine was a deist. Crowd activity, he wrote of England, was too often motivated by "prejudices, which the government itself has encouraged." It was only after the crowd abandoned its "cry and apprehension of arbitrary power, wooden shoe, popery and such stuff," that it would turn its attention "toward the aristocrats of their own nation."[41]

The cause of mobs, for Paine, was poverty, and the cause of poverty, bad government; both would disappear with the advent of republicanism. As Paine explained in *The Rights of Man:*[42]

There is in all European countries, a large class of people of that description which in England is called the "mob." Of this class were those who committed the burnings and devastations in London in 1780, and of this class were those who carried the heads upon the spikes in Paris. . . . Why then does Mr. Burke charge outrages of this kind on a whole people? As well as may he charge the riots and outrages of 1780 on all the people of London. [But] even the beings who commit them have some claim to our consideration. How then is it that such vast classes of mankind distinguished by the appellation of the vulgar, or the ignorant, mob, are so numerous in all old countries. . . . They arise as an unavoidable consequence, out of the ill construction of all old governments in Europe, England included with the rest. A vast mass of mankind are degradedly thrown into the background of the human picture, to bring forward, with greater glare, the puppet-show of state and aristocracy.

What is striking about this passage is not only Paine's distaste for mob actions, but his compassion for the poor. Like so many of the Commonwealthman writers, Paine believed that "freedom is destroyed by dependence." But unlike them, Paine was not content simply to condemn the poor for idleness or to argue, as Rev. Joseph Priestly did, that as the cause of poverty was excessive expenditures on drink, an increase in taxation would be beneficial to the poor, since it would reduce the amount available to spend on liquor.[43] Paine, to be sure, could describe the poor as "bred up without morals," and exposed to "vice and legal barbarity." But if the poor were corrupt, they were made so by government. The establishment of republican government coupled, in Europe, with his social welfare proposals for the abolition of poor rates and regressive taxation, aid to the unemployed, free public education (with direct grants to parents to enable them to decide for themselves where to send their children to school) and public unemployment, would not only eliminate poverty, but end "riots and tumults."[44] Paine despised not the poor, but poverty. Like the other radical leaders of Philadelphia, his aim was to wean the lower classes both from economic poverty and from an entire pattern of deferential relationships into self-respect and full participation in the mainstream of the life of society.

III

The writings of Thomas Paine, one historian has written, contain the voice of "the intelligent artisan come into his own at last."[45] There is an important insight here, but it must be accepted with some caution. Not only did Paine's republicanism have little room for distinct and divergent class interests, but his personal and political associations were limited to no single group; in both England and America they spanned the worlds of the upper-class salon and tavern political debates. His American friends included Washington and Jefferson as well as radical artisans of Philadelphia; his English associations in the early 1790s included Charles James Fox, the Duke of Portland and, until their breach over the French Revolution, Edmund Burke, in addition to middle-class and artisan radicals.

Rather than the consistent spokesman for any single class within American society, Paine should perhaps be considered one of the first intellectuals, a social group which emerged into prominence in the second half of the eighteenth century. Then as now, intellectuals hailed from diverse social origins and as a "relatively classless stratum," often thought of themselves as being above narrow personal, party or class loyalties. "Independence is my happiness," Paine wrote in *The Rights of Man,* and I view things as they are, without regard to place or person; my country is the world, and my religion is to do good."[46]

Paine always tried to live as the exemplary republican; a man guided only by his own conscience and a commitment to the public good. As he wrote in 1787, "I defend the cause of the poor, of the manufacturers, of the tradesmen, of the farmers . . . but above all, I defend the cause of humanity." Paine scrupulously attempted to preserve the appearance of disinterestedness in his writings, insisting his concern was simply "the general good, the happiness of the whole," and donating the profits of *Common Sense* and the *Crisis* essays to the war effort.

Paine's writings, moreover, were read in "all ranks," precisely as he intended. Like all writers he sought the largest possible impact and audience. In *Common Sense* he appealed to conservatives as well as radicals; in the *Crisis* papers he strove to weld an alliance of "property and persons" in support of the war. He may have believed that "only . . . the rich and the moderate are for the connexion" with Britain, but this only emphasized the importance of convincing "men of property" that independence was in their best interest. Not until the 1790s and in an English context, in the second part of *The Rights of Man*, would Paine aim his writings exclusively at the artisans, tradesmen and laboring poor.[47]

Nonetheless, even in America there was a special bond between Paine and the artisan community. Paine had begun life as an artisan, and throughout his life he retained a manual agility with tools and an interest in applied science.[48] In the turbulent world of revolutionary Philadelphia, Paine would often express the outlook of the city's mechanics on political and economic questions. By virtue of its conditions of life, its leading role in the struggle for independence and its demand for a greater voice in the affairs of Pennsylvania, the artisan community was ideally suited to produce and to welcome Paine's particular brand of political thought. Egalitarianism, nationalism, a respect for private property, an insistence on the primacy of the "producing classes" and a hostility to the "aristocracy" and to deferential political and social relationships coupled with a sense of separateness from the poor, were the hallmarks of artisan politics in the revolutionary era. Paine, the artisan of words, helped to create the new language of politics and vision of society which the artisan class required as it emerged into political consciousness in the Age of Revolution.

"As early as the 1780s," the historian Staughton Lynd writes, "there were two alternative sources for an American radical tradition"—the agrarian republicanism associated with Thomas Jefferson and an urban variant of republicanism, which may be identified with Paine and the radical urban artisans.[49] Lynd's argument is somewhat over-simplified, but it is worth exploring. The ideology of republicanism became the common language of politics for Americans during the revolutionary era. Jeffersonian and Paineite republicanism shared many perceptions and values, yet their differing conceptions of the nation's future illuminate the diversity of Americans' reactions to the profound changes which overtook their society in the late eighteenth century.

The Jeffersonian vision of politics stemmed directly from the Country party tradition in England, especially the variant of that ideology associated with Viscount Bolingbroke. On both sides of the Atlantic, Country party spokesmen lamented the political and economic developments of the eighteenth century—the growth of cabinet government and the financial revolution—and rooted governmental "virtue" and the defense of liberty firmly in independent men of landed property. But the social context in which the ideology took root was very different on the two sides of the Atlantic. In England, Bolingbroke spoke for the resentments of the provincial landed gentry. Country party thought there was much concerned with preserving the independence of Parliament but was "little occupied by considerations of inequality of property," and it had strong affinities with a hierarchial vision of state and society.

In America, by contrast, the Jeffersonian constituency was the great mass of yeoman farmers and southern planters and agrarian thought emphasized an approximate equality of property as an essential safeguard of liberty, virtue and republican government. Jefferson even proposed that the government provide fifty acres of land to each citizen. "Those who labor in the earth," Jefferson wrote in a well-known passage in his *Notes on the State of Virginia,* "are the chosen people of God." "Corruption of morals in the mass of cultivators, is a phenomenon of which no age nor nation has furnished an example." It was the independence of the farmer—not simply his means of earning a livelihood—which made him the repository of social virtue since "dependence begets subservience and venality, suffocates the germ of virtue, and prepares fit tools for the designs of ambition."[50]

There was, of course, a strong anti-urban bias in agrarian republican thought. Cities were the home of luxury, dependence and dissipation, of bankers, speculators and rentiers and the new

capitalist institutions which nourished them. Jefferson himself in
the 1780s voiced so extreme a distrust of cities that he even
condemned the artisans as "the panderers of vice, the instruments
by which the liberty of a country are generally overturned," and
said he hoped "never to see our citizens occupied at a work-
bench." Unlike the advocates of home manufacturing, Jefferson
was quite prepared to "let our workshops remain in Europe." But
few of his contemporaries took agrarian republicanism to this
extreme. More typical were the views of James Madison, who
recognized that to avoid dependence on Britain, America would
have to encourage some home industry, although he made it clear
that he had in mind household production, not large-scale manufacture. And even Jefferson himself changed. By the 1790s,
reacting to the urban artisans' enthusiasm for the French Revolution, he accorded them his highest accolade, describing them as
"the *yeomanry* of the city." Jefferson's most extreme anti-urban
pronouncements were abstract declarations in private letters.
During his presidency he, like Madison, would come to embrace
the idea of a balanced economy of agriculture, commerce and
home manufacturing. To be sure, Jefferson never abandoned
his distrust of mercantile and manufacturing interests, with their
penchant for speculation and their dependence on the world
market. But by the same token no one in the revolutionary period
envisioned a manufacturing nation, and even proponents of
American manufactures like Philadelphia's Tench Coxe were prepared to accord agriculture primacy in the nation's economy.[51]

It would be wrong, therefore, to place too much emphasis on
the differences between agrarian and urban republicanism: they
were overlapping strands of the same ideology, rather than
mutually exclusive outlooks. Socially, artisans and yeoman farmers both qualified as independent small producers who could
share an ideology which exalted the "productive classes" and
distrusted the "non-productive" speculators, rentiers and government pensioners. Politically, a majority of small farmers and
artisans embraced the struggle for independence, and while

they divided over the federal Constitution in 1788—the artisans in the major cities were strongly in favor, while large numbers of small farmers were anti-Federalists—the majority of each group would unite again in the 1790s in support of the French Revolution and the Jeffersonian Republican party. And as individuals, Paine and Jefferson shared not only a close friendship, but an optimistic view of human nature, an egalitarian vision of republicanism as a rejection of the class-stratified society of the old world, and scientific interests (although Jefferson's agrarian followers tended to be far less interested in applied science, far more susceptible to anti-intellectualism, than urban artisans).[52]

But Jefferson and Paine did differ in one important respect—their reaction to the changes in economic life and social relations which American society experienced in the era of the Revolution. The difference is much deeper than the fact that Paine was "a city man at heart." As Lynd points out, Jefferson was extremely optimistic about human nature, but pessimistic about the direction of historical change. The golden age of society lay in the past, in a mythical Anglo-Saxon polity of free and equal farmers; economic growth, the expansion of commerce and urbanization were elements of national decay and the corruption of virtue. Jefferson even proposed a design for the seal of the United States with one side depicting Henigst and Horsa, the Saxon chiefs "whose political principles and form of government we have assumed." To Jefferson and Madison, the vast virgin lands of the West held out the prospect of an almost limitless future of a yeoman's republic, guaranteeing the endless reproduction of an egalitarian and unchanging social structure. But, eventually, the West would be filled up, and America would come to resemble Europe, with its crowded cities, landless lower classes, social conflict and governmental corruption. The sturdy yeoman would be transformed into a landless laborer, and the liberty which rested on a wide distribution of property would degenerate into tyranny.[53]

Paine, by contrast, was a man with little interest in the past and

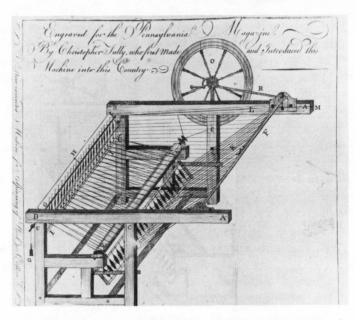

An engraving of America's first spinning jenny. Published in the *Pennsylvania Magazine* during Paine's editorship, it underscores Paine's fascination with applied science and technological progress, interests he shared with Franklin, David Rittenhouse and many artisans on both sides of the Atlantic. *Library Company of Philadelphia*

unbounded optimism about the future. He could not have cared less about the Anglo-Saxon past. Jefferson may have hoped America could insulate itself against the industrial revolution, but Paine was enchanted by the cotton mills, potteries and steel furnaces he saw in England in the late 1780s, and he hoped such enterprises could be "carried on in America as well." As early as 1775, as editor of the *Pennsylvania Magazine,* Paine published a woodcut of the new spinning jenny of the United Company for Promoting American Manufactures and commented on its "usefulness." Jefferson—like Bolingbroke before him—abhorred the national debt as an endless source of manipulation, speculation and corruption; Paine in *Common Sense* saw the debt as an institution binding society together, although, sharing the Country party revulsion against speculators and placemen, he said the debt should bear no interest. Jefferson had a singular distaste for commercial transactions, credit and market relations of all kinds. His objective for the yeoman farmer was a commercial agriculture tempered by self-sufficiency—the truly independent man must also be free from the tyranny of the marketplace. Paine valued the independence which the ownership of property entailed, but he viewed commerce as a natural and progressive force, fostering interdependence among men and nations, stimulating all forms of economic enterprise, benefitting agriculture and manufactures and lifting the concerns of mankind from the parochial to the cosmopolitan.

Agrarian republicanism, then, was essentially nostalgic. It placed primary value on independence and equality, but believed that the only way these virtues could be preserved was by resisting economic growth and capitalist development. To Paine, the past was a burden, not a guide, and the present only a stopping point from which to propel society into the future. Paine's cast of mind was what has been called the "projecting spirit"; it gloried in newness and invention, was impatient with tradition and precedent and embraced economic growth as part of the general progress of mankind. In *The Rights of Man* he exulted in "the rapid progress which America makes in every species of improvement," and held out the prospect of continuing technological and social advance to a future republican Europe as well.

If, as has been argued, there were strong tensions between republicanism and the emerging capitalist order of the era of the Revolution, Paine shows that republicanism and early capitalism could also go hand in hand. In the world of late eighteenth-century America, before Malthus "demonstrated" that society's natural order could produce misery as well as plenty and before the industrial revolution overturned the world of the small producer, Paine envisioned a society in which republican government together with economic progress would produce social harmony, equality and economic abundance.[54]

Paine, then, was an urbanite, a cosmopolitan, a nationalist and a proponent of commerce and economic innovation and growth, as well as a republican and a democrat. In *Common Sense,* these intellectual commitments seemed fully compatible. But at various times in his American career, one or another would take precedence. In the struggle between 1776 and 1779 to create and defend a new ultra-democratic state government for Pennsylvania and, for a time, in the price control movement of 1779, the implications of Paine's egalitarianism would overshadow his commitment to commercial freedom and his high regard for men of business. During the 1780s, his economic values and his support of the Bank of North America would, for a time, push his political commitments into the background. In a sense, having made so signal a contribution to the coming of independence, Paine would be engaged for the rest of the American Revolution in working out the full meaning of his republicanism.

CHAPTER FOUR

Paine,
the Philadelphia Radicals
and the Political
Revolution
of 1776

Common Sense was an attempt to unite all Americans in a struggle
for independence and republican government. Yet the very success of the pamphlet plunged Paine into an intense involvement
in the tangled and divisive politics of Philadelphia and Pennsylvania. For several months in the spring and summer of 1776, he
played a leading role in the struggle which began as a movement
to commit Pennsylvania to independence and soon broadened
into an assault upon the state's government. Paine's vision of
republican government strongly influenced a group of radical
intellectuals, professionals and artisans who emerged into sudden
political prominence in 1776, and played a leading role in over-
turning the established government and drafting a new state
constitution. And the bitter debate over the merits of the constitution which convulsed Pennsylvania politics after 1776 led Paine
to define for the first time his conception of the limits of political
participation under republican government.

I

The heated nature of political debate in revolutionary Philadelphia stemmed from a unique combination of circumstances. In almost every other colony, the established political leadership either stepped wholesale onto the Whig side by the spring of 1776, or split into Tory and Whig factions. But in Pennsylvania, the old elite obstinately opposed any talk of independence, and the Assembly united with the Proprietary interest to fight a prolonged delaying action against separation from Britain. In addition, the leaders of the Whig movement of the early 1770s either were drawn into national affairs, serving with the army or Congress like Charles Thomson and Joseph Reed, or, like John Dickinson, lapsed into political silence as the movement for independence accelerated.

It was this vacuum of political leadership which created the opportunity for the emergence of a new radical party in Philadelphia politics. Basing their political power on the artisan and lower-class communities, now organized in extra-legal committees and the militia, the radicals were also able to form a temporary alliance with supporters of independence in the Continental Congress, who strongly disapproved of their ultra-egalitarian views of government but were willing to join in their attack on the established authorities of Pennsylvania in the hope of removing an entrenched obstacle to independence. With Paine playing a conspicuous role, the radicals provided the ideological leadership and much of the day-to-day political direction for the popular upsurge which committed Pennsylvania to independence, overthrew the provincial government and established in its place the most democratic state constitution of the revolutionary period. Pennsylvania was the only state in which there was virtually no continuity between pre-independence and post-independence political leadership.[1] And because of the intense political struggle of the spring of 1776, it was the state in which republican ideas were pushed to their most radical limits and were made an explicit weapon not only against political privilege, but against a wide range of social and economic inequalities.

Along with Paine, the Philadelphia radicals included Benjamin Rush, Timothy Matlack, Christopher Marshall, James Cannon, David Rittenhouse, Owen Biddle, Thomas Young and Charles Willson Peale. As a group, these were men of modest wealth, who stood outside the merchant elite and had exerted little political influence in Philadelphia prior to 1776. Many were outsiders of one kind or another: Young and Peale, like Paine, were recent arrivals in the city, and Marshall and Matlack had been disowned by their Quaker meetings.[2] Paine had known some of these men in 1775—Rush had suggested that Paine write *Common Sense,* and Rittenhouse had been one of the few to read the manuscript before publication. But it was not until January 1776 that the radicals entered Philadelphia politics as a self-conscious group. Together, they reflected the various ideological strands and political styles which made up the radical wing of the revolutionary movement in Philadelphia.

The Philadelphia radicals, to be sure, shared many of the assumptions about colonial virtue and English coruption which were common among all American Whigs. But there were other political strands as well which made this group more akin to the radical artisans and professionals of London than to the cultured Whig merchants and planters who populated the Continental Congress. Matlack brought to the Philadelphia radicals an immense following in the popular culture of lower-class Philadelphia, Rush and Marshall reflected the evangelical roots of popular republican thought, and Cannon, Young, Rittenhouse, Biddle and Peale, like Paine, were men whose roots lay among the rationalist, politically-conscious artisans.

Timothy Matlack was the son of a Quaker brewer who had fallen into debt and been "torn to pieces" by his creditors. He was himself disowned by the Philadelphia Friends in 1765 for neglecting his business—a hardware store—failing to pay his debts and frequenting the wrong kind of company. His greatest claim to fame before the Revolution was his penchant for gambling, horse-racing, bull-baiting, and especially the immensely popular sport of cock-fighting. Matlack's popularity among Philadelphia's lower classes was assured in 1770 when his prize bantam cocks engaged in a famous match with those of the New York aristocrat James Delancey, who had traveled from New York for the inter-colonial contest. Matlack was, if anything, a pugnacious personality. In 1781 he engaged in a fistfight on Market Street with Whitehead Humphreys, a prominent opponent of the Philadelphia radicals. At the age of seventy-two he offered himself for military service in the War of 1812.

Matlack's associations spanned the upper- and lower-class worlds drawn together in popular recreations like cock-fighting. He was notorious as a tavern habitue and for his friendships with poor men, white and black. It was perhaps not surprising that he was elected one of the five colonels of Philadelphia's militia companies in 1775. But he was also a frequent dinner guest in the 1760s of the wealthy merchant and political leader Joseph Galloway, and a perceptive contemporary noted that Matlack "hath a great notion of being a courtier." He also read scientific papers before the American Philosophical Society.

To the Philadelphia upper class, however, Matlack's rise to prominence and high office during the Revolution was absurd; to them, he always remained "an upstart." Something of their contempt for Matlack comes through in a poetic broadside distributed by Humphreys soon after the fistfight:[3]

> Altho', dear Tim, you've rose so great,
> From trimming cocks to trim the State;
> Yet to a brother lend an ear
> A moment—tho' in humble sphere . . .
> Did you forget, in days of yore,
> When you, like Price, was wretched poor?

> But all at once, you're raised so high,
> Quakers can't safely pass you by!
> And yet, you know, with truth 'twas said,
> Your hapless babes oft' wanted bread;
> While you, unfeeling, idled time
> With Negroes—Cuff and Warner's Prime . . .
> That great day Independence came,
> At such a time you judged it best,
> To have yourself superbly drest;
> You were so greas'd and puff'd with powder,
> No coxcomb sure could e'er look prouder . . .

Far different from Matlack's lifestyle was the austere Presbyterianism of Benjamin Rush and the equally devout Quakerism of Christopher Marshall, a wealthy retired druggist. The lives of both men illustrated how the evangelical religious fundamentalism which flowed from the Great Awakening of the 1740s had become a potent source of egalitarian social and political ideology. "It is perhaps impossible," one historian observes, "for the modern secular mind to grasp the revolutionary implications of an imminent millennium." But the Awakening inspired countless Americans with this very vision. Religious enthusiasm, contemporaries declared, had a special appeal among the poorest colonists, and the evangelical ministry often combined an attack upon the dissipation, luxury and corruption of English life with a critique of increasing selfishness, extravagance and lack of social concern among colonial men of wealth. They pointedly contrasted men who hungered only after "temporary wealth and riches" with the truly virtuous, who enjoyed the "riches of Christ." They implied that separation from England would be only the prelude to a social transformation within America itself, and eventually came to identify the millennium with the establishment of governments which derived their powers from the people and were free from the great disparities of wealth which characterized the old world.[4]

Evangelicism had been a major, continuing element in Philadelphia life ever since the English revivalist George Whitefield attracted "vast multitudes" of listeners, mostly of the "lower orders," to his sermons in the city in 1739. Whitefield returned every few years; just before his death in 1770 he was still preaching "like a dragon, cursing and blessing us all in a breath." His work was also carried on by the well-known American revivalist Gilbert Tennent, pastor of Philadelphia's Second Presbyterian Church from 1744 to 1764.[5] It was among the Scotch-Irish Presbyterians, a majority of whom were artisans, laborers and servants, that the revivalism of the Great Awakening took deepest root in Philadelphia. It is well known that the Presbyterian party took the lead in the independence movement in the state and that the Revolution ousted Quakers and Anglicans from their dominant position in Pennsylvania office-holding. By 1780, General Charles Lee declared, the government of Pennsylvania had become a "Macocracy . . . a banditti of low Scotch-Irish whose names generally begin with Mac and who are either the sons of Imported Servants, or themselves Imported Servants, are the Lords Paramount." Lee's hostility led him to exaggerate: in reality, the Presbyterians in office, like Joseph Reed and George Bryan, came from well-to-do families and were men of substance, although they had not been members of the pre-war economic elite. Yet Lee was right in identifying the Scotch-Irish, both of the back country and of Philadelphia, as major supporters of the new government established in 1776.[6]

Contemporaries believed that the Scotch-Irish of Pennsylvania were "the most God-provoking Democrats on this side of Hell." Many were said to look back fondly to the days of Cromwell, to be of "republican principles" and to desire the creation of "a Republican Empire, in America." Franklin's friend John Hughes, the unfortunate stamp commissioner during the Stamp Act crisis of 1765–66, reported to the British government that "the presbyterians . . . are very numerous in America, and are . . . as averse to Kings, as they were in the days of Cromwell."[7] Certainly, their hatred of Popery was intense. Their entrance into Philadelphia politics in the 1760s was inspired not only by British taxation policies, but by the movement to create an Anglican episcopacy in the colonies, viewed by many Presbyterians as a stalking horse for religious persecution and Catholicism, with which they more or less equated the Church of England. The Quebec Act of 1774 was viewed as the culmination of a series of British attempts to abolish religious liberty in America. As one Philadelphian explained to a London friend in 1776, "The Scotch, in the Province of Pennsylvania, act and speak like their ancestors. They covenanted against the tyranny of a Stewart, their own countryman; and they are determined with us never to become the slaves of any Parliament or Potentate on earth. . . . They are here the very warmest advocates for liberty."[8]

When Benjamin Rush equated "a pope in religion and a king in power," he was speaking for many Philadelphia Presbyterians. Rush, though born an Anglican, was converted to evangelical Presbyterianism as a youth, and attended the College of New Jersey, the bulwark of colonial Presbyterianism. Religion and politics were always closely intertwined for him; he considered republicanism the natural consequence of true Christianity and believed the American Revolution heralded the millennial reign of Christ on earth (in which the conquest of disease would be part of the perfect society—physicians like himself were thus also the servants of Christ).[9]

Rush moved easily among the artisans and poor of Philadelphia. His medical practice, until well into the 1770s, was confined to the lower classes, whom he often treated free of charge. He was a leader in the drive for home manufacturing, arguing that this was a way to provide employment for the poor of Philadelphia, to lessen Americans' dependence on Great Britain with its "luxuries and vices" and to encourage English and Irish artisans to emigrate to America, the "only asylum for liberty in the whole world."[10] And like so many other Presbyterians, Rush equated the

movement for independence with the spirit of the English Civil
War, often invoking the memory of his "great ancestor," John
Rush, who had served in Cromwell's army against the "minions of
arbitrary power." In Rush's opinion, "the republics of America
are the fruits of the precious truths that were disseminated in the
British Parliament" during the 1640s.[11]

That evangelical radicalism was not confined to Presbyterians is
illustrated by Christopher Marshall, who, though a Quaker, was
as influenced by millennial ideas as Rush. Though he was disowned by the Quakers for his political views in the 1770s, Marshall
was a profoundly religious man. His letterbooks are filled with long
dissertations on religious subjects, and his political discourses are
punctuated with Biblical quotations. The wealthy Quakers of
Philadelphia, he believed, were guilty of "covetousness, grasping
and worldliness . . . extreme pride, loftiness, luxury, wantonness,"
and indeed every sin "that Sodom was condemned for." Marshall
was certain that the British government and its supporters in
America were inspired by "the prince of the power of darkness,"
and that England intended "to destroy the liberties and freedom
of this new world" and subject it "to papal power." But he was
equally convinced that the time was near when "the kingdoms of
this world are become the kingdoms of our Lord, and of his
Christ."[12]

All evangelical republicans, of course, did not share the same
political or social beliefs. Evangelicism was marked by an inherent
tension between an individualist strain that held Divine truth to be
revealed directly to believers without the mediation of institutions, and the corporate ideal of a harmonious Christian republic
in which selfishness and competition would be subordinated to
the good of the whole. During the Revolutionary War, in fact,
Rush and Marshall would take opposite sides on the question of
whether the government had the right to regulate prices for the
good of the entire community, with Rush speaking the language
of individual rights and Marshall appealing to the idea that the
needs of society overrode individual self-interest. But in the

period immediately preceding independence, they both represented a strand of radicalism far different from the measured
arguments of the "radical Whig" publicists in England and
America. The "lower-class" Philadelphia Presbyterians who as
early as 1765 exclaimed "No King But King Jesus" also contributed something to the ideological origins of the American
Revolution.[13]

Despite his friendship with Rush and Marshall, Paine's political
outlook had more in common with the rationalism and deism of
professionals like James Cannon and Thomas Young and such
skilled artisans as David Rittenhouse, Owen Biddle and Charles
W. Peale. Cannon, the radical group's leading political thinker
aside from Paine, was a mathematician, teacher and student of
science who had emigrated from his native Edinburgh in 1765. His
first involvement in public affairs came in March 1775 when,
along with Marshall and Matlack, he became a manager of the
United Company for Promoting American Manufactures. In the
fall, he emerged as one of the guiding lights of the militia's
Committee of Privates. As the committee's secretary, Cannon
worked closely with its chairman, Stephen Simpson, a man known
to the elite as "a drunken shoemaker," but who had some standing in the artisan community by virtue of having been treasurer of
the Cordwainer's Fire Company during the 1760s. Under their
guidance, the committee flooded the Assembly and newspapers
with petitions outlining the Militia Associators' grievances, and
early in 1776 they coordinated the radical campaign against the
provincial government.[14]

Thomas Young, a self-educated physician whom John Adams
called "an eternal fisher in troubled waters," was a peripatetic
revolutionary who had already lived in Albany, Boston and New-
port before moving to Philadelphia in 1775. The son of immigrants from Ireland, Young had been hauled into court in the
1750s for abusing the name of Jesus Christ and remained a
lifelong deist. In Albany he was involved in the Sons of Liberty
and in Boston was a close political associate of Samuel Adams.

(Adams, a devout Calvinist, was somewhat embarrassed by Young's religious views, though he defended his ally in public, insisting he should be judged by his politics, not his religion.) Young considered artisans "the most worthy members of society" and counted on them to inspire "the other ranks of citizens" to resist Britain. And like Matlack and Cannon, he was intimately involved in militia affairs, serving as surgeon of Philadelphia's rifle battalion.[15]

David Rittenhouse, Owen Biddle and Charles W. Peale were artisans of great skill who achieved intellectual distinction in other fields of endeavor as well. They participated in the world of eighteenth-century science, where interaction between artisans, intellectuals and professional men was an everyday occurrence. Biddle and Rittenhouse were watchmakers, one of the most difficult and prestigious of colonial crafts, and both had followed the common route from watchmaking into science. Rittenhouse, "Jefferson's idol," was widely regarded as America's leading scientist after Franklin; his orrery, a mechanical representation of the movements of the heavens, was among the most sensational scientific achievements of colonial America. Like Franklin, Rittenhouse had a wide following among Philadelphia mechanics, who chose him in 1774 as a member of an eleven man committee to represent their political interests. Peale, who had risen from poverty to artisan status as a leather craftsman and silversmith and then a clockmaker, also became one of America's leading portrait painters. Since the Stamp Act crisis, Peale had been a republican, who "would never pull off his hat as the King passed by" and he was an early advocate of independence and home manufacturing. Biddle was a Quaker, disowned for his participation in the war, while Peale and Rittenhouse were inclined toward deism.[16]

In some ways, the cooperation between the evangelical and rationalist republicans may seem surprising. There was a seemingly impassable gulf between the universe of the deists, in which God had been relegated to the status of prime mover, and that of the evangelicals, who believed in continuing divine intervention in worldly affairs. Deists like Paine believed that man was perfectible, with an inborn moral sense, and they substituted for the fall of man his corruption by tyrannical governments. Most evangelicals could never abandon the idea that sin was inherent in all men, although certain radical Protestant sects did believe that men could become sinless in this life. Ironically, it was the "liberal," anti-revivalist Christianity of the late eighteenth century, not evangelical Protestantism, which bore a closer resemblance to deism. Like deists, "liberals" believed that men were born with the capacity to choose between sin and righteousness and that human reason could establish the main points of religious and moral obligation (although they did not reject revelation and the divine inspiration of the Bible as deists like Paine did).[17]

Nonetheless, evangelical and rationalist radicals had more in common in the era of the American Revolution than they would a generation later, after the French Revolution weakened the link between them. Both groups were early converts to republicanism and independence, and both believed that, as Rittenhouse put it in 1775, "luxury and her constant follower tyranny" had conquered Europe and were threatening the New World. Both exalted the virtues of industry, frugality and self-discipline, although, as one historian has written, "there was a profound difference between disciplines recommended for the salvation of one's own soul, and the same disciplines recommended as a means to the salvation of a class."[18]

In Philadelphia, all the radicals had strong links to the artisan community, and supported the key artisan demand of encouragement for home manufactures. Both evangelicals and rationalists spoke the language of millennialism and of the primacy of the individual conscience, and both came to envision an internal transformation in American society as a desirable, even necessary counterpart of separation from Britain.

Deists, it must be remembered, were far less militant in the 1770s than they would become two decades later. True, Philadelphia ministers had long been dismayed by the extent of infidelity in the city. Whitefield went out of his way to address a gathering of "reasoning unbelievers," and a leading Presbyterian clergyman denounced the "conversation at taverns or coffee-houses" in which piety, the gospel and the idea of a future life were ridiculed. One artisan organization, the Taylor's Company, specifically provided in its by-laws that "no dispute respecting Divinity shall be introduced into this society." But before the 1780s there were no organizations of deists in America, and most deists contented themselves with a simple belief in God as a first cause and a commitment to virtuous living. It was not until the 1790s, when the French Revolution raised the spectre of anti-clericalism and Paine's *The Age of Reason* ridiculed for a mass audience the divine inspiration of the Bible, a cardinal precept of Protestant Americans, that deists were damned as infidels and cooperation between them and devout Christians seemed impossible.

When Paine returned to America in 1802 after spending fifteen years in Europe, Samuel Adams—who had wanted to transform Boston into a "Christian Sparta"—refused to see him because of *The Age of Reason*.[19] But in the 1770s, the same Calvinist Adams defended the deist Thomas Young, and in 1776 Benjamin Rush argued strongly against a religious oath aimed at preventing deists from holding seats in the Pennsylvania Constitutional Convention. Perhaps Rush himself summed up the diverse sources of radical ideology in revolutionary Philadelphia and the fact that he saw no contradiction between them, in the symbols he chose in designing a seal for a new college in 1784: a Bible, a Telescope and a Cap of Liberty.[20]

II

These, then, were the men with whom Paine associated by the end of 1775 and early 1776. "For two years, he roamed the streets and passed the hours in local taverns talking to the 'common people,' drank coffee with Christopher Marshall, visited with Benjamin Rush, talked away the night with Matlack, Young, and Cannon." And the opportunity for these men to emerge as a major force in Philadelphia politics was created by the immense success of *Common Sense* in transforming the nature of colonial political debate. Paine's pamphlet unleashed a torrent of letters, pamphlets, and broadsides on independence and the meaning of republican government. Between January and July of 1776, scarcely a week went by without a lengthy article in the Philadelphia press attacking or defending, or extending and refining Paine's ideas, and the same was true in other cities as well. Nothing reveals the revolutionary aspects of the struggle for independence better than the vast outpouring of popular politics in 1776 and the swiftness with which established institutions were attacked and overturned and with which established authorities were called into question. In this atmosphere, old ideas were transformed, and new ones entered the political arena with great suddenness. "It seems as if everything was to be altered," came a report from Massachusetts. "Scarcely a newspaper but teems with new projects."[21]

In the Philadelphia press, the leading radical propagandists were Paine himself, writing under the pseudonym "The Forester," and Cannon, Rush, Young, Marshall, and Rittenhouse. The newspaper debate dealt not only with the pros and cons of independence, but with the meaning of republican government. On this question, the old leaders of the movement for resistance to a Britain had little to say in common. As John Adams observed, a republic might mean "anything, everything, or nothing." Everyone agreed that republican government must involve the representation of the people through frequent elections, but there was little consensus on how to translate this ideal into functioning government. *Common Sense* may have introduced "a new system of politics as widely different from the old system of politics as the Copernican system is from the Ptolomaic" (a compliment Paine must certainly have cherished), but the precise meaning of republicanism in America remained to be worked out.[22]

Common Sense catalyzed conservatives as well as radicals: defenders of the connection with England and of balanced government rushed into print to dispute Paine's ideas. Loyalist writers defended the British constitution—"the admiration of mankind"—and denounced Paine as "a crack-brained zealot for democracy" and a "violent republican." (The newspaper debate of 1776 was the last time in American history that the words "republic" and "republican" would be used as terms of political abuse.) They described Paine and the other radicals as "unknown leaders," "adventurers who have nothing to lose," in contrast to "the most amiable and venerable personages . . . who abominate such nefarious practices." They ridiculed Paine's idea that "every silly clown and illiterate mechanic" could take it upon himself to judge the content and nature of government, and declared that independence and republicanism must inevitably degenerate into disorder, violence or Cromwellian dictatorship. One Loyalist voiced a fear of the growing radicalism within the militia, warning that "the soldiers" would find "an Agrarian law" dividing property "very agreeable." This fear that separation from Britain would lead to internal social upheaval helps account for the reluctance of Pennsylvania's old ruling elite to embrace the cause of independence. In a state like Virginia, by contrast, where the resistance movement of the 1760s and 1770s had not seriously eroded the deferential structure of society and politics, the bulk of the planter elite could expound ideas of independence and republicanism without fearing they would have to face a political challenge from their social inferiors.[23]

It was not only Loyalists, however, who attacked Paine's ideas. There were also many Whigs who were convinced of the necessity or inevitability of independence, but felt it necessary to combat Paine's vision of republican government. Foremost among these was John Adams, who applauded Paine's arguments for a separa-

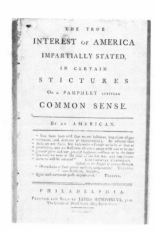

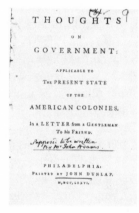

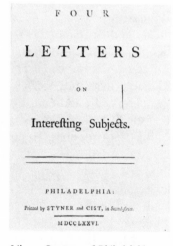

Four of the most important responses to *Common Sense.* The first two, by Loyalist writers, rejected both independence and Paine's democratic republicanism. *Thoughts on Government,* by John Adams, favored independence but was intended to combat Paine's "democratical" ideas, while the anonymous author of *Four Letters* demanded a new constitution for Pennsylvania along the lines outlined by Paine.

tion from England, but considered the ideas of government in *Common Sense* too "democratical." "Indeed," Adams informed his wife Abigail, "this writer has a better hand in pulling down than building up." In order to counteract Paine's pamphlet and give the American people a lesson in "the science of government," Adams composed *Thoughts on Government,* which was widely circulated in the spring and summer of 1776. As Adams later explained, he believed Paine's ideas of government flowed "from simple ignorance, and a mere desire to please the democratic party in Philadelphia, at whose head were Mr. Matlock [sic], Mr. Cannon and Dr. Young. . . . I dreaded the effect so popular a pamphlet might have, among the people, and determined to do all in my power, to counteract the effect of it."

Paine had inclined in *Common Sense* to unicameral legislatures, but Adams insisted on the virtues of balanced government. Behind this structural question lay differing perceptions of the ability of the common people to rule themselves, and whether the people, as well as their rulers, could pose a threat to liberty in America. Adams, who believed self-interest lay at the heart of all human activity, felt it was necessary to check as well as represent the people. In addition, like James Madison, Adams was more realistic than Paine in his assessment of the possibilities of class conflict in a republic. Paine's egalitarian republic was a utopian illusion, Adams believed. In Adams' version of bicameralism, modeled closely on the British Constitution, the structure of government would mirror social reality by giving the wealthy control of an upper house and ordinary men control of the lower. Then neither class would have the power to plunder or oppress the other. Adams' arguments were more appealing than Paine's to the Whig elite in the various states, for it was only in Pennsylvania, Georgia and Vermont that single-house legislatures were established.[24]

Adams was no less of a republican than Paine, but his republicanism had an unmistakable elitist bias. He was alarmed by and sought to counteract the leveling spirit which *Common Sense* had both articulated and intensified. The "one thing" absolutely essential in the new republican governments, he informed one correspondent, was "a decency, and respect, and veneration introduced for persons in authority." Nor was Adams pleased by the growing demand in Philadelphia and elsewhere for a relaxation of property qualifications for voting. Paine had called rather vaguely for a broad franchise in *Common Sense,* and the Philadelphia militia was demanding the vote for all Associators. But Adams reiterated the standard Whig argument, which dated back to James Harrington, that only the ownership of property made men truly independent of the will of others, and therefore suitable to cast ballots. "Men in general, in every society," Adams wrote in May 1776, "who are wholly destitute of property, are also too little acquainted with public affairs to form a right judgment, and too dependent on other men to have a will of their own." "It is dangerous," he went on, "to alter the qualifications of voters. . . . It tends to confound and destroy all distinctions and prostrate all ranks to one common level."[25]

Yet it was precisely this demand that Americans be reduced to "one common level" which seemed to animate much of the egalitarian outpouring. In the spring of 1776 the press teemed with articles challenging the notion that social authority was a necessary prerequisite for wielding political power. What was new in this debate was the sudden emergence of "equality" as the great rallying cry in Philadelphia. To be sure, as with so many slogans of the revolutionary era, the meaning of "equality" lay in the eye of the beholder. Then, as now, when most Americans spoke of equality, they meant equality of opportunity and equality before the law, rather than equality of property or income. But there was a respectable tradition of thought which viewed an approximate equality of property as a necessary precondition of republican government. Since "power follows property," it was only where property was widely distributed that political power could be as well. It was a common idea in the revolutionary generation that large concentrations of property threatened republican government, that, as Noah Webster wrote in the 1780s, "an equality of property . . . is the very *soul of a republic*."[26]

For republican thinkers like Jefferson and Madison, this political axiom led to deep historical pessimism. They believed it inevitable that as commerce and industry developed and the virgin lands of the West were filled with settlers, economic inequality would increase and the stability of republican government would be threatened. Others interpreted the notion of equality more optimisticly, arguing that America was indeed uniquely suited to republicanism. "America," declared a writer in the *Pennsylvania Journal*, "is the only country in the world wholly free from all political impediments at the very time it is laid under the necessity of framing a civil government. Having no rank above that of freeman it has but one interest to consult."[27]

There was, however, another side to the idea of equality, rooted in resentment against the pretensions of Pennsylvania's aristocracy and the growing incidence of poverty and the increasingly rigid social stratification in Philadelphia. In eighteenth-century European usage, "equality" was primarily a "protest-ideal." While those who used it did not envision a literal state of total leveling, the idea of "equality" was a powerful weapon of attack against vast and abusive privileges and inequalities, a call for a government and social structure which minimized the consequences of existing inequalities and advantages. The most radical writers in the Philadelphia press used "equality" in precisely this way.[28] Paine, however, was not one of these writers. While his impudent attacks on established institutions and authorities had certainly helped others to break out of traditional habits of deference, his conviction that America was marked by economic abundance and an approximate equality of condition prevented him from carrying republican egalitarianism to its radical anti-aristocratic extreme.

Paine compared the Philadelphia of 1776 with London, not with the Philadelphia of a generation before. It was left to other writers in the spring of 1776 to take the lead in warning of the movement toward a "feudal revival" in eighteenth-century America. "Candidus" denounced the men of wealth of Pennsylvania for being "petty tyrants" who opposed independence because they dreamed of creating "millions of acres of tenanted soil." James Cannon as "Cassandra" and the anonymous author of a broadside entitled "The Alarm" issued similar warnings that "an aristocratical junto" was "straining every nerve to frustrate our virtuous endeavours and to make the common and middle class of people their beasts of burden." "Eudoxus" admitted that "the Barons of America" did not hold hereditary prerogatives like their English counterparts, but warned that they had "a prodigious itch for such patents." And Dr. Thomas Young, who had long believed in the importance of keeping "the whole people as much on a level as may be," wrote that "men of some rank" desired to establish in America "the system of Lord and Vassal, or *Principal and dependent*," common in Europe.[29]

In one sense, what Cannon and Young were describing was only a tendency toward inequality—they seemed to be expressing concern more about the future than the present, about the intentions rather than the actual social power of "aristocrats." But their argument had radical implications because it located the threat to equality not in impersonal forces of commerce and economic growth, but in the pernicious ambitions of men of wealth. For them, the notion of equality became an argument for "a radical reformation" in the principles of government in Pennsylvania. Young rejected the traditional idea that the right to vote should be dependent on property ownership and that "riches" gave a man any right to office. Both the English and Pennsylvania constitutions, he wrote, destroyed "the right of election" and gave a monopoly of power to "the profligate and *corrupt*."[30] Young and Cannon represented the most radical edge of republican thought in the spring of 1776; their voice was that of the newly politicized militia privates, many of whom had hitherto been excluded from all political participation.

Even Young and Cannon did not in the spring of 1776 advocate a direct attack on the property of the "aristocracy." In good Paineite fashion, they proposed a political solution: that all men "on the tax book" and all those serving in the militia should have the right to vote and that men of wealth should not be entrusted with political power. But it is again worth noting that such a demand had a far more radical meaning in Pennsylvania than it did in the South. Those demanding equality and a broad suffrage in Virginia did not include the bulk of the working population, who were slaves. The Pennsylvania radicals, by contrast, called for the enfranchisement of the vast majority of the lower class, including even apprentices and indentured servants who had enlisted in the militia.[31]

The newspaper debate of 1776 concerned not only principles of government, but the very practical question of committing Pennsylvania to independence. As early as January, the radical group had drafted a ticket of supporters of independence— including forty artisans—which swept the February election for a new hundred-member Philadelphia Committee of Observation and Inspection. During the spring, as the Pennsylvania Assembly continued to favor reconciliation with Britain, the radicals, including Paine, launched an attack on that body as not truly representative of the people of Pennsylvania because its distribution of seats discriminated against the western counties and its suffrage qualifications excluded lesser artisans and the poor. By April, the press was filled with calls for the Assembly to be replaced with a new legislative body, more receptive to demands for independence and more fully representative of the entire people of Pennsylvania.[32]

Paine's articles in April and May 1776, signed "The Forester," were devoted to vindicating independence and republican government and attacking the critics of *Common Sense*. But he did add his voice to the campaign against the Pennsylvania Assembly. He denounced the legislature as "a branch from that power against whom we are contending," and affirmed the right of "the people" to "make such alterations in their mode of government as the change of times and things allows." America, Paine insisted, "hath a blank sheet to write upon" as far as government was concerned, and he added in a footnote, "forget not the hapless African."[33] Other writers reiterated the republican principles of *Common Sense* and extended the pamphlet's attack on the principle of hereditary rule to apply to the Penn family's proprietary control of Pennsylvania. "What right," asked one pamphlet, "could Charles the Second, a deceased tyrant of the last century, have to appoint a governor for the present generation, or declare that the heirs of William Penn should be the Lords and Masters of persons to be born a thousand years hence?" Some radical publicists, including Thomas Young, brought forward an idealized image of the ancient Anglo-Saxon polity, with its direct democracy in local affairs, frequent elections by secret ballot and wide suffrage, as a model for a new Pennsylvania constitution.[34]

In order to counteract this mounting criticism, the Assembly decided to add additional seats for the western counties and Philadelphia, in order to make its composition better reflect the distribution of population within the state. Paine and the other Philadelphia radicals agreed on a ticket of four men for the special election of May 1 and conducted a heated campaign. But three moderates and only one radical were elected. The city was almost evenly divided on the question of independence, and Paine and Young were probably right in attributing the result to the fact that patriots were serving with the military and that certain German voters were barred from the polls on the grounds that they had not been naturalized. Because the result of May 1 was a defeat for the advocates of independence, John Adams soon introduced a motion in Congress calling for the creation of new state governments, with authority deriving from the people rather than the crown. Adams' aim was to replace the Assembly with a body more amenable to independence; he worked in alliance with the Philadelphia radicals despite his distaste for their political opinions. The resolution was adopted by Congress by a narrow margin and seizing on the opportunity, the Philadelphia radicals called for a mass meeting on May 20, which in turn approved a resolution for a Provincial Convention of representatives from local committees throughout the state to meet on June 18. Paine was actively involved in the maneuvering during April, May and June—the diary of Christopher Marshall reveals frequent meetings among Paine and the other radicals—and Cannon, Young and Matlack were sent by the Philadelphia committee to drum up support in the countryside for the coming Convention.[35]

The Provincial Convention which assembled in Philadelphia on June 18 symbolized the political revolution which was overtaking the state. Its delegates represented the radical coalition of backwoods farmers and urban artisans and militiamen which had, in effect, usurped the power of the state's Assembly and committed Pennsylvania to the causes of independence and internal change. Of the 108 delegates chosen by the county and city committees (not by direct popular vote), only Benjamin Franklin—who did not attend—and Thomas McKean were men of any political prominence. But the delegates were not complete political novices: they were veterans of committee politics on the local level, and a majority were officers of the militia.[36]

The main business of the gathering was to issue a call for the election of a Convention to draft a new frame of government for Pennsylvania. On this question there was little debate. At the request of a group of German Associators, the Convention agreed to allow every militia Associator twenty-one years of age or older who had resided in the state for one year and who had been assessed for provincial or county taxes to vote for delegates—a significant expansion of the franchise but one which stopped short of another proposal, that all Associators be enfranchised.[37]

The liveliest moment in the Convention was a heated dispute between Christopher Marshall and Benjamin Rush over a proposed religious oath for delegates to the Constitutional Convention. Rush, despite his own religious enthusiasm, opposed the oath adopted by the Convention requiring delegates to affirm belief in the divinity of Jesus Christ and the divine inspiration of the Bible, pointing out that there were "good men who did not believe in the Divinity of the Son of God"—men, presumably, like Paine and Young. Marshall, who believed deists were "cunning artful sophisters", began to drift away from his former allies, while Cannon and Young berated him as "ignorant in the truths of religion, bigoted" and willing to keep "some of the most best and valuable men out of government." (But when Young died in 1777, Marshall sheathed his sword and raised funds for his widow.)[38]

On June 26, 1776, the day after the adjournment of the Provincial Convention, a broadside appeared written by Cannon and addressed by the Committee of Privates to all military Associators. In discussing the election of delegates to the coming Constitutional Convention, it summarized the egalitarian impulse which had emerged in the previous spring:[39]

It is the Happiness of America that there is no Rank above that of Freeman existing in it; and much of our future Welfare and Tranquility will depend on its remaining so forever; for this Reason, great and over-grown rich men will be improper to be trusted, they will be too apt to be framing Distinctions in Society, because they will reap the Benefits of all such Distinctions. . . . Honesty, common Sense, and a plain understanding, when unbiassed by sinister Motives, are fully equal to the Task. . . . Let no Men represent you . . . who would be disposed to form any Rank above that of Freemen.

Many Pennsylvanians did not vote for delegates to the Constitutional Convention—resenting the required oath renouncing alle-

GENTLEMEN,

THE COMMITTEE of PRIVATES of the City and Liberties of Philadelphia would esteem itself culpable, if it neglected to address you on the most important Subject that can come before Freemen---You are about to hold an Election on the Eighth of next Month ; and on the Judiciousness of the Choice which you then make, depends the Happiness of Millions unborn---The Excellence or Defectiveness of a Constitution which must last for Ages, hangs on the Choice of that Day---and, remember, the Complexion of your Government, and the State of your future Laws, will spring from that Constitution : You ought, therefore, to chuse such Men as are most equal to the Task---Permit us then to point out to you the Qualifications which we think most essential to constitute a Member of the approaching Convention---A Government made for the common Good should be framed by Men who can have no Interest besides the common Interest of Mankind. It is the Happiness of America that there is no Rank above that of Freemen existing in it ; and much of our future Welfare and Tranquillity will depend on its remaining so for-ever; for this Reason, great and over-grown rich Men will be improper to be trusted, they will be too apt to be framing Distinctions in Society, because they will reap the Benefits of all such Distinctions---Gentlemen of the learned Professions are generally filled with the Quirks and Quibbles of the Schools ; and, though we have several worthy Men of great Learning among us, yet, as they are very apt to indulge their Disposition to Refinement to a culpable Degree, we would think it prudent not to have too great a Proportion of such in the Convention---Honesty, common Sense, and a plain Understanding, when unbiassed by sinister Motives, are fully equal to the Task---Men of like Passions and Interests with ourselves are the most likely to frame us a good Constitution---You will, upon this Occasion, no doubt, find Men of otherwise suspicious Characters strive, by every Art in their Power, to recommend themselves to your Favour--- But, remember, the Man who is at any Time solicitous to be employed by you as your Representative, is rarely the most worthy of your Confidence, and at this Time it is sufficient to reprobate him in the Judgments of wise Men--For, be assured, that though Honesty and plain Understanding may be equal to the Task, few Men will ardently long after it who have nothing but your Interest in View--We have now to guard against Proprietary Interest, as the most dangerous Enemy to a good and free Government; be entreated therefore to chuse no Man who was ever suspected of being under Proprietary Influence, and with equal Assiduity avoid the Choice of such as can feel its Influence, and you not know it.---Some who have been very backward in declaring you a free People, will be very forward in offering themselves to frame your Constitution; but trust them not, however well recommended.---Let no Man be made Choice of who has ever discovered the least Desire to retain Power when in his Possession, or to derive it from any Source, but the free and annual Delegation of the People.---Let them be Men fearing GOD and hating Covetousness, and without the Ambition of Self-Aggrandizement.---If Corruption, and the Arts of it, were ever practised in this Country, they will be on this Occasion ; for a Constitution, which effectually guards against it, being once formed, it will shut it out ever after.---We are contending for the Liberty which GOD has made our Birthright: All Men are entitled to it, and no Set of Men have a Right to any Thing higher. Let no Man represent you therefore, who would be disposed to form any Rank above that of Freemen---or who would wish to see any Set of public Officers exist by any other Authority than the free Choice of those over whom they are to exercise that Authority.---You may certainly send from your respective Districts as many Men as fall to your Lot, of unquestionable Principles, Men who were never suspected; and if you are not careful in this Respect, you will deserve to suffer by it.---By this Means your Magistrates, and other Civil Officers, will have their Interest inseparably connected with yours---It is not so now, as too many can witness ; they generally wish to serve him who has granted their Commission.---Magistrates, though chosen annually by Ballot, should, like our Sheriffs, go out at a certain Time, at the End of five or six Years for Instance, to make Room for others.---Remember few Men have

ever

The first page of James Cannon's broadside addressed to the militia, setting forth the qualities to be sought in delegates to the Pennsylvania Constitutional Convention of 1776. This is one of the finest examples of the egalitarian impulse unleashed by the struggle for independence. *Library Company of Philadelphia* giance to George III or the unauthorized way in which the legally elected Assembly was being overturned. Those who did vote seemed to take Cannon's advice. The delegates elected were a collection of "plain countrymen" or, as one critic characterized them, "numsculs." Thomas Smith, a delegate from Bedford County, complained that "not a sixth part of us ever read a word" on the subject of government. He contemptuously reported a motion that every resolution under consideration be printed "for the use of the members, as several of them could read *print* better than writing. Our principle seems to be this: that any man, even the most illiterate, is as capable of any office as a person who has had the benefit of education . . ."[40]

Smith believed that "a few enthusiastic members" who embraced leveling principles dominated the proceedings. Although our knowledge of Convention debates is sketchy, it appears that James Cannon, present as a delegate from Philadelphia, took the leading part in drafting the new constitution. Certainly it later became a commonplace in Pennsylvania politics that "the constitution was framed by a fanatical schoolmaster." Matlack, Rittenhouse and Biddle were also delegates. As for Paine, he was out of the city, having volunteered soon after the signing of the Declaration of Independence to serve as secretary to Daniel Roberdeau, brigadier-general of the state's militia. He later insisted that he "had no hand in forming any part of it, nor knew any thing of its contents." Yet Cannon's political ideas by now were essentially the same as Paine's and the constitution was in line with the governmental structure outlined briefly in *Common Sense*.[41]

Widely regarded as the most radical frame of government created during the American Revolution, the Pennsylvania constitution brought to culmination both the ideological and political developments of 1776. Drafted less than three months after Congress had declared American independence, it symbolized the utopian aspects of the Revolution—a radical break with the

British past, an erasure of historical continuity, the construction of government from first principles. Contemporary European reformers viewed it as the most important of the American state constitutions—it was "the model of an excellent government" according to the French reformer and future friend of Paine's, Brissot de Warville.[42]

In line with Paine's political principles, the constitution rejected the notion of balanced government, providing instead for an all-powerful single-house legislature and replacing the governor with a veto-less plural executive elected by the people. It attempted to prevent the rise of any differences of interest between legislators and the people and to insure the accountability of representatives to their constituents by providing for annual elections, the rotation of office-holders, legislative debates always open to the public and the election every seven years of a Council of Censors, which was to determine if the constitution had been violated. And it dispensed with property qualifications for office-holding altogether, while awarding the suffrage to all men over twenty-one who paid taxes. The constitution thus did not break completely with the traditional idea that voters should have "a sufficient common interest with and attachment to the community," but it extended that notion much of the way toward universal manhood suffrage.

Several clauses of the new constitution looked to the reform of Pennsylvania society. The provisions that debtors not guilty of fraud should not be imprisoned after their property had been given up to creditors, and that schools with low fees be established in every county in the state, spoke directly to the needs and grievances of artisans and others among the middling and poorer elements of the population. The legislature was enjoined to "regulate entails in such a manner as to prevent perpetuities," and the right of Pennsylvanians to "fowl and hunt" on their own land and "on all other lands . . . not enclosed" was guaranteed, provisions which reflected the fear of "feudal revival" shared by rural and urban radicals. There were other hints scattered through the constitution of the hostility to men of wealth which had surfaced the previous spring, but they were coupled with a sense of danger that government could be corrupted from below as well as above. One section admonished citizens to be certain that candidates for office were characterized by "a firm adherence to justice, moderation, temperance, industry and frugality," and another remarked that "every freeman, to preserve his independence, (if without a sufficient estate), ought to have some profession, calling, trade or farm, whereby he may honestly subsist." And finally, the constitution provided that "laws for the prevention of vice and immorality, shall be made and constantly kept in force."[43]

On one question, the Pennsylvania constitution did not fully reflect the views of the Philadelphia radicals. James Cannon had been the leading voice on the committee which drew up the Declaration of Rights. The first fifteen clauses, ranging from guarantees of natural rights to religious freedom, trial by jury and freedom of speech, were taken virtually verbatim from the widely disseminated Declaration of Rights of Virginia, drafted in June 1776 by George Mason. They were adopted by the Convention with only minor changes. But the final clause, strikingly reminiscent of Cannon and Young's earlier warnings about the need for decisive steps against aristocracy, was rejected. It read:

> That an enormous Proportion of Property vested in a few Individuals is dangerous to the Rights, and destructive of the Common Happiness of Mankind; and therefore every free State hath a Right by its Laws to discourage the Possession of such Property.

Here was the closest Pennsylvania radicals would come to the "agrarian law" which Loyalists had warned would follow independence, and it proved too radical for the Convention.[44]

Nevertheless, the Philadelphia radicals could be quite pleased with the new document, for it reflected many of the underlying assumptions of their republicanism. Politically, it was by far the most democratic of the new state constitutions; with its extremely broad franchise and opportunity for office-holding it set the seal of legality on the extension of political participation which the previous years had witnessed. Its unicameral Assembly reflected Paine's principle that in a republic, the entire people had a unitary interest which could best be represented by a one-house legislature. The guiding principle of the constitution, as Thomas Young explained, was that "people at large [are] the true proprietors of governmental power."[45]

Socially, the constitution was based squarely on the idea that the "producing classes" were the backbone of republican government. Despite the rejection of Cannon's "agrarian law" clause, the constitution contained several provisions reflecting the anti-aristocratic resentments which permeated all classes of Pennsylvanians beneath the "gentlemen." But within that vast majority of the population, it still required some proof of independence for political participation. The constitution extended the political nation, but it carefully excluded the unfree—slaves, indentured servants and apprentices—as well as those free citizens so poor they were excused from the payment of all taxes. After all, the same farmers and mechanics who made up the producing classes and were throwing off the legacy of deference to Pennsylvania's elite, still demanded that same deference from their own servants and apprentices. Even as the Convention was sitting, the Council of Safety it appointed, with David Rittenhouse as Chairman and James Cannon, Timothy Matlack and Owen Biddle as members, resolved that all apprentices and indentured servents in the militia be discharged on application of their masters and that none be enlisted in the future without their master's consent. The constitution, in other words, reflected the new political power of the urban master artisans and western farmers, but it did not accede fully to the even more democratic and egalitarian demands of the Philadelphia militia. Its vision of the political nation still had a lower as well as an upper boundary.[46]

III

The Constitution of 1776, wrote one contemporary, "split the Whigs to pieces." Soon after the Convention adjourned, having announced the promulgation of the new frame of government without a popular referendum, moderate Whigs called a mass meeting in Philadelphia which adopted resolutions denouncing the "strange innovations" and calling for amendments to create balanced government, a two-house legislature and a single governor.[47] The debate of 1776 ushered in a period of intense party conflict in Pennsylvania between opponents of the constitution, who styled themselves the Republican party, and the document's supporters, the Constitutionalists. In some ways the division was a continuation of previous political alignments—most Presbyterians supported the constitution while the Quaker and Anglican elite opposed it. Contemporaries described the party division as one between the wealthy and the poor, and the Republican leaders were certainly more closely associated with the state's economic elite than were the Constitutionalists. But the politicians who assumed leadership of the Constitutionalist party—men like George Bryan and Joseph Reed—were hardly impoverished. And in Philadelphia, the artisan community divided over the constitution.[48]

The debate over the constitution which began in the fall of 1776 was conducted in the same rhetoric of class antagonism that had emerged the previous spring. Opponents of the constitution condemned their foes as "coffee-house demagogues" and "political upstarts" and attributed the document's flaws to Cannon's broadside, which had circulated among "the unthinking many, that men of property . . . men of experience and knowledge" were not to be trusted as delegates to the convention.[49] The Constitutionalists characterized their opponents as "all the rich great men and the wise men, the lawyers and doctors," who did not consider that they had "a common interest with the body of the people." They insisted that the Republicans' demand for an upper legislative house was simply an attempt to institute a House of Lords "consisting of a small number of grandees" anxious to increase their own wealth and power. "If the whole body of the people acting agreeable to their own will be tyranny," wrote one defender of the constitution, "I know not what is liberty; for I have no idea of any *being* in society *besides* the people."[50]

Among the defectors from the cause of the constitution was Benjamin Rush, whose position reflected a change in his social position and personal associations. By mid-1776, Rush was no longer an outsider in Philadelphia society. A leader in his profession, a delegate to Congress, a physician with the Army, he was far more prominent than the doctor of a few years before most of whose patients had been lower class. In Congress he had become a close friend of John Adams, and it was Adams who inspired Rush's fiery opposition to the new frame of government. In 1777, Rush published a series of newspaper articles, including long excerpts from Adams' writings on the virtues of balanced government. The new constitution, Rush believed, was "a tyranny. The moment we submit to it we become slaves."

Behind this exaggerated rhetoric lay a sharp departure from the social assumptions which underlay the republicanism of Rush's former allies among the Philadelphia radicals. They viewed equality as an essential prerequisite of republican government; Rush, following Adams, condemned the constitution precisely because it "presupposes perfect equality, and an equal distribution of property, wisdom, and virtues among the inhabitants of the state." In fact, Rush argued, "superior degrees of industry and capacity, and above all, commerce, have introduced inequality of property among us." Rather than attempting to counteract this inequality, the constitution should, in effect, institutionalize it, by isolating the rich in the upper house of a bicameral legislature. (Rush, like Adams, never explained why the rich would not be able to control two houses as easily as one.) It is not surprising, in view of his rejection of the radicals' corporate view of a society governed in accordance with the general good, that Rush opposed government price controls and defended the right of individuals to an unmolested use of their property. Throughout the 1780s, Rush would denounce the government of his state as "a mobocracy," and would urge men of "wisdom, virtue, and property" like his former antagonist John Dickinson, to return to public life to rescue Pennsylvanians from themselves.

Rush's movement away from the radical version of republicanism perhaps reflected a division within the evangelical Protestant tradition which had originally shaped his political outlook. Many evangelical leaders did continue to embrace the millennial vision of republicanism which they had brought with them into the Revolutionary War, but others became increasingly fearful that the American people were not sufficiently regenerate or virtuous to be trusted with unchecked power in a republican government. In the 1780s, as Rush's early utopianism faded, he launched an aggressive assault upon the various forms of pleasure in lower-class culture. Drinking, Rush insisted, was a cause of quarrels, violence and profane language; fairs should be eliminated, for "they tempt to extravagance, gaming, drunkenness, and uncleanness." Horse-racing and cock-fighting "occasion idleness, fraud, gaming, and profane swearing," and Sunday recreations "beget habits of idleness and a love of pleasure which extend their influence to every day of the week," making working people lazy and disorderly. He especially criticized the widespread practice of giving hard spirits to harvest workers and suggested that buttermilk and water be substituted.[51]

Rush, of course, was hardly alone in his distaste for these aspects of lower-class life. The evangelical ministry had long attacked popular recreations as wordly and dissipated; artisan culture had always contained a tendency towards dissociation from the coarser aspects of lower-class life; and the small but growing group of manufacturers in revolutionary Pennsylvania saw this popular culture as inimical to the regular habits of work essential to modern industrial labor. As an intellectual child of evangelical Presbyterianism, a man with ties to the artisan community, an advocate of home manufactures and a stockholder in the society which built one of Philadelphia's first textile factories, Rush combined these various strands of opposition to pre-industrial popular recreations and life styles.

But while Rush's former radical associates, including Paine, may have shared a distaste for aspects of lower-class culture, their aim was to rescue the poor from a life marked by deference and imbue them with the self-respect and self-discipline which sustained involvement in politics required. Rush's reformism, by contrast, went hand in hand with a growing political elitism. He especially condemned militia laws which allowed privates to elect their own officers as productive of lack of discipline and having "an unfriendly influence upon morals." Alarmed by the "excess of the passion for liberty" which the Revolution engendered among the American people, Rush even diagnosed this condition as a new "species of insanity" and gave it a clinical name—"anarchia." It was this lack of self-control among the people, in matters both political and cultural, which made balanced government and checks on the powers of the people's elected representatives necessary. Rush remained a republican, but the only true republic, he came to believe, was "a government consisting of *three* branches, and each derived at different times and for different periods from the people. . . . A simple democracy, or an unbalanced republic, is one of the greatest of evils."[52]

IV

How did Paine react to the fracturing of the Whigs over the constitution of 1776? As we have seen, he was not in Philadelphia when the Convention met, having volunteered to serve without pay as secretary to General Daniel Roberdeau of the Pennsylvania militia. In the fall, he was appointed aide-de-camp to General Nathanael Greene at Fort Lee in New Jersey, sending back dispatches for the Philadelphia press on Washington's campaign at New York City. In November and December, he retreated with the beleaguered Continental troops across New Jersey, and as they settled at Trenton, he returned to Philadelphia. In what he later called "a passion of patriotism," Paine composed *The American Crisis,* which Washington ordered to be read to the troops on Christmas eve shortly before the crossing of the Delaware. It began with words which have since become immortal:[53]

> These are the times that try men's souls. The summer soldier and the sunshine patriot will, in this crisis, shrink from the service of their country; but he that stands it *now,* deserves the love and thanks of man and woman.

Paine produced six more *Crisis* essays in 1777 and 1778, and in April 1777 he was appointed Secretary to the Committee on Foreign Affairs of Congress, a sinecure which enabled him to devote full time to his patriotic writings. Ironically, it was John Adams who nominated Paine for the post, in the hope that his "ready pen" could be put to use for the government. Once again, Paine had assumed a strikingly modern role—the publicist using the mass media to bolster civilian morale in wartime. Published in pamphlet form and reprinted in newspapers throughout the colonies, the *Crisis* papers were superb pieces of propaganda. As in *Common Sense,* Paine appealed both to the passions and the cool deliberation of his readers, to love of country and rage against Great Britain. He ridiculed British commanders, denounced Tories, repeated his critique of the corruption of British life and, in the face of a dismal military situation, insisted on the possibility of American victory.

Paine's rage against his country of birth was enhanced by the armed conflict. "Britain," he wrote in January 1777 in the second

Crisis paper, "as a nation, is . . . the greatest and the most ungrateful offender against God on the face of the whole earth. . . . Whatever a foolish tyrant, a debauched court, a trafficking legislature, or a blinded people may think, the national account with heaven must some day or other be settled." In his seventh essay, of November 1778, Paine even called on the "mercantile and manufacturing" population of England to "risk a revolution" against "your present king and ministry" rather than allowing them to drag the nation "from madness to despair, and from despair to ruin. America has set you the example, and you may follow it and be free."

Paine also turned his pen against internal enemies of the Revolution. "Every Tory," he declared in the first *Crisis* paper, "is a coward; for servile, slavish, self-interested fear is the foundation of Toryism; and a man under such influence, though he may be cruel, never can be brave." He urged that Pennsylvania enact laws requiring a loyalty oath of all voters and office-holders, a policy the new state government soon adopted, further intensifying the political turmoil in the state.

But Paine could also submerge his passion in reasoned analysis of the military situation. He revealed an uncanny grasp of the military advantages of the colonial army, despite its continuing setbacks, and publicized the strategy adopted by Washington which would eventually result in American victory. As early as January 1777, Paine predicted that the British army would find it impossible to conquer the colonies. "Like a game of drafts, we can move out of *one* square to let you come in, in order that we may afterwards take two or three for one. . . . In all the wars which you have formerly been concerned in you had only armies to contend with; in this case you have both an army and a country to combat." The British, he insisted, could capture American cities (General Howe, indeed, would occupy Philadelphia during the winter of 1777–78), but they could never truly subdue the countryside. "I, who know England and the disposition of the people well," Paine declared, "am confident, that it is easier for us to effect a revolution there, than you a conquest here."

Paine spent most of 1777 in Philadelphia and retreated with Congress to the village of York the winter of that year, while the British enjoyed the comforts of Philadelphia and Washington's army suffered at Valley Forge. When the British evactuated the city in the spring of 1778, Congress and Paine returned, and in the fall he issued his sixth *Crisis* essay, supporting the congressional decision not to deal with recently arrived British commissioners on any basis other than a recognition of American independence. America had recently concluded its treaty of alliance with France, and with the promise of military aid from overseas, the prospects for victory seemed brighter. "In France," Paine wrote, "we have found an affectionate friend and faithful ally; in Britain, we have found nothing but tyranny, cruelty, and infidelity."[54]

Paine was thus preoccupied with national affairs and the war effort in 1777 and 1778. But it is not surprising that when he did enter the debate on Pennsylvania's new frame of government, he did so on the side of the Constitutionalists. With the notable exception of Rush, virtually all of Paine's Philadelphia associates were fully committed to the new constitution and state government. Cannon, Matlack and Young had attempted to defend the new frame of government at the October 1776 public meeting in Philadelphia which called for revisions, and the state government organized in 1777 included Matlack as Secretary to the Supreme Executive Council, Rittenhouse as Treasurer, Cannon and Rittenhouse on the Council of Safety and Young as secretary to the Board of War. Young, who considered the constitution "a model, which, with a very little alteration, will, in my opinion, come as near perfection as any thing yet concerted by mankind," created a minor tempest in 1777 when he dispatched a copy of the constitution to Vermont, where his friend Ethan Allen was a leader in what Young called the "struggle with the New York monopolizers." The New York delegates to Congress insisted that a resolution be enacted in June 1777 condemning Young's interference, but Vermont soon declared statehood, and adopted a constitution modeled on the Pennsylvania frame of government.[55]

When his Philadelphia friends created the Whig Society in April 1777 to defend the constitution, with Charles W. Peale as chairman, Paine accepted membership on its Committee of Correspondence. And in a series of letters to the Pennsylvania press in March and June 1777 and again in December 1778, Paine turned his pen to the defense of the constitution. Attempting to maintain his accustomed status as a man above party, he explicitly rejected the rhetoric of class antagonism and attacks upon men of property utilized by other Constitutionalists in the newspapers. After all, in his role as a publicist for the war effort, Paine had been attempting to promote an atmosphere of national unity, not internal conflict. Rather than assaulting the rich, he attempted to convince them that the constitution was in their own best interest:

> I have heard it advanced, by those who have objected against the present constitution, that it was a good one for a poor man. I reply, that for that very reason it is the best government for a rich one, by producing purchasers, tenants, and laborers, to the landed interest, and consumers to the merchants. . . . I am not pleading the cause of the one against the other in either case; for I am clearly convinced that the true interest of one is the real interest of both.

As always, Paine's aim was to cast the widest net in gathering support for republican government.[56]

Paine's letters on the Pennsylvania constitution provided the occasion for the fullest elaboration of his views on equality of political rights. In *Common Sense* he had rather vaguely referred to the utility of a broad suffrage; now he broke explicitly and decisively with the tradition that the right of voting should be linked to the ownership of property. Yet he still remained tied to the idea, which characterized radical thought from the Levellers of the English Civil War to Young and Cannon in 1776, that some sort of guarantee of personal independence was necessary in voters. Indeed, Paine's arguments here are singularly reminiscent of the Leveller idea of freedom, characterized by C. B. Macpherson as "possessive individualism." "I consider freedom as personal property" Paine declared, insisting "wherever I use the words *freedom* or *rights,* I desire to be understood to mean a perfect equality of them." But like the Levellers, Paine allowed that under certain circumstances, freedom could be temporarily forfeited:[57]

> I consider freedom to be inseparable from the man as man; but it may be finally forfeited in the criminal, or the exercise of the right may cease in the servant for the time he continues so. By servitude I mean all offices or employments in or under the state, voluntarily accepted, and to which there are profits annexed. Likewise all servants in families; because their interest is in their master, and depending upon him in sickness and in health, and voluntarily withdrawing from taxation and public service of all kinds, they stand detached by choice from the common floor; but the instant they reassume their original character of a man and encounter the world in their own persons, they repossess the full share of freedom appertaining to that character. The conclusion I mean to draw is, that no *involuntary* circumstance or situation in life can deprive a man of freedom.

Paine was here arguing for what he viewed as the broadest possible suffrage. He insisted that property qualifications were inherently unfair, since property "makes scarce any, or no difference, in the value of the man to the community." It seems clear that in line with his general anti-deferential attitudes, it was *personal* rather than economic independence which he perceived as a necessary qualification for voting. The key to Paine's argument is that servants had "voluntarily" relinquished their independence—an assumption logical enough when applied to indentured servants who in most cases freely entered their contracts, but one which also seemed to take for granted a degree of abundance and economic opportunity that forced no one to give up his personal independence against his wishes.

From 1778 onward, Paine would always condemn property qualifications for voting. But he continued to believe that, as he wrote in 1786, "freedom is destroyed by dependence," and even in *The Rights of Man* he would declare that the right of voting should be "as universal as taxation"—a radical proposal in the English context where virtually every adult male paid some kind of indirect tax, but not quite the same thing as universal manhood suffrage. Not until 1795, in his comments on the French Constitution drafted in that year, would Paine unequivocally state that it was wrong to "disfranchise any class of men," since the right to vote was "the primary right by which other rights are protected."[58]

Even in 1778 Paine's definition of suffrage, which presumably allowed men too poor to pay taxes but not employed as servants to cast ballots, was significantly broader than the provisions in the constitution he was defending, not to mention the much narrower qualifications in other states. But in general, the constitution of 1776 put into practice the basic assumptions of Paine's republicanism. In his defense of the constitution, Paine embraced the expansion of political participation in revolutionary Pennsylvania which his own writings and activities in 1776 had done so much to bring about.

CHAPTER FIVE

Price Controls and Laissez-Faire: Paine and the Moral Economy of the American Crowd

Paine's participation in the debate over Pennsylvania's Constitution in 1777 and 1778 was a prelude to an even more intense involvement in local affairs. The immediate issues agitating Pennsylvania and the rest of the colonies in the turbulent year 1779 arose from the tremendous rise in prices caused by massive congressional printing of paper money and from the efforts of certain merchants to realize windfall profits in army supplies and farm produce destined for the cities. The economic crisis led thoughout the colonies to the formation of extra-legal local committees which attempted to set prices and regulate commercial activities. It generated an explosive debate over the meaning of the republican concepts of "virtue" and "luxury" at a time of immense profits for some colonists and terrible hardships for others and divided colonists over the question of whether property rights were absolute and inviolable or should be regulated for the benefit of the entire community.

Like many Americans in this period of transition, Paine was

caught between older ideas of economic regulation and new notions of laissez-faire. He shared assumptions with both the free trade advocates and the proponents of price control and in the economic crisis of 1779 he found it difficult to maintain a consistent position in relation to an increasingly militant popular movement for extra-legal price regulation. But in the end he found he had more in common with the "modern" idea of laissez-faire than the traditional notion of regulation of economic activity in the interests of the general public.

I

In recent years, historians of England and France have drawn attention to food riots and popular price control as a major form of eighteenth-century crowd activity and to the legitimizing ideas of "moral economy" which animated such actions. The urban and rural poor, and many artisans as well, believed that the operations of the free market worked against their economic interests. They rejected the emerging doctrine of free trade, in so far as it applied to grain, meat and bread, and denied that the farmer, baker, merchant and shopkeeper had an absolute right of property in the necessities of life. Instead, they reaffirmed the traditional idea of a "just price" for bread, which viewed millers and bakers as servants of the entire community, rather than normal entrepreneurs. On occasion, in times of dearth, they resorted to "taxation populaire"—the seizure of food supplies and their sale at a traditional price level. In the popular mind of the eighteenth century, increases in food prices were caused not by the inexorable operation of impersonal market forces, but by the greedy activities of forestallers (merchants who withheld goods from the market), engrossers (those who monopolized vital commodities), and profiteers. The tradition of "moral economy," as E. P. Thompson has described it, rejected the demand for freedom of trade in food as "the liberty of a savage" and upheld an older ideal of an economy regulated by the state in the interests of the consumer.[1]

It would be wrong, of course, to assume that the tradition of "moral economy" existed in exactly the same form in colonial America as it did in Europe. In England, for example, popular price control movements drew support from a legal tradition dating back to medieval days and from a whole set of paternalist relations which still dominated the society. Pennsylvania's rural areas, by contrast, were populated not by peasants and great landowners, but by independent yeoman farmers, many of whom were attuned to the demands of the marketplace and the legitimacy of prices determined by supply and demand. And in Philadelphia, as we have seen, an important segment of the artisan community was becoming disposed toward the free market in the 1770s and 1780s.

On the other hand, the colonial population was constantly augmented by immigrants from England and Ireland for whom "taxation populaire" and the idea that local magistrates should establish maximum prices for food, were part of their cultural inheritance. The large number of English immigrants who arrived in Philadelphia in the late 1760s and early 1770s came from a society which had recently been wracked by food riots. Popular discontent over high prices had led the ministry in 1766 to proclaim the old Edwardian statutes against forestalling and engrossing the market, and in 1768 a London crowd "called on the Butchers in Whitechapel and told them, that unless they would sell their meat reasonable, they would take upon themselves to settle the price."[2] As the events of the 1770s would demonstrate, Philadelphians were well aware of the European traditions of food rioting and "taxation populaire." These traditions, long dormant in the city, could prove extremely resilient under the pressure of economic crisis, especially among poor urban dwellers.

Colonial Americans, like their European contemporaries, were

accustomed to a wide range of governmental economic regulations. The colonial statute books were filled with laws regulating
prices and wages, prohibiting engrossing and forestalling, and
establishing maximum prices for bread, beer, meat and other
foodstuffs. In the eighteenth century, it is true, laissez-faire ideas
made great headway among merchants and the educated classes
generally, and many of the old economic regulations fell into
disuse. But throughout the century, local authorities attempted to
alleviate the sufferings of the poor in times of food shortages by
selling grain at fixed prices, and it seems clear that among wide
segments of the urban population, suspicion of merchants as
nonproductive members of society was widespread. "Everyone
granted the appropriateness of the regulation of social and economic life," concludes a recent study of colonial economic ideas,
and the idea of a "just price" persisted both in popular thought
and in the eighteenth-century legal doctrine that contractual
obligations must be based on fairness or justice, not simply mutual
consent. The idea that economic freedom should be subordinate
to the general good of society also underlay many of the measures
adopted by the colonists in opposing British taxation policies in
the 1760s and 1770s. Nonimportation agreements clearly in-
fringed upon the freedom of trade and usually included provisions
that merchants should not profit from the scarcity of British
goods by raising prices.[3]

Unlike Boston, where a number of eighteenth-century crowds
forcibly prevented the export of food during times of dearth,
Philadelphia was not the scene of food rioting in the colonial
years. Pennsylvania, after all, was an abundant producer and
exporter of foodstuffs, and lush farmlands were cultivated within
a few miles of Philadelphia. For most of the eighteenth century,
the price of food remained low, and the diet of Philadelphians
was more varied and abundant than that of contemporary
Englishmen. But a sudden increase in European demand, the
result of a series of bad harvests in the late 1760s, sent the price of

food in America into a sharp inflation. By the early 1770s, urban consumers were raising their voices against the farmers and merchants they blamed for high prices.[4]

Closely related to the emerging issue of price controls was the immense problem of financing the Revolutionary War. During the colonial period, every American province had reacted to the perennial shortage of specie by issuing paper money, supporting its value not by the promise to redeem the paper in gold and silver, but by a willingness to accept it for taxes and other purposes. Pennsylvania was particularly successful in maintaining the value of its paper currency, with the result that the price level in the province was remarkably stable for the fifty years preceding the Revolution. Since there was little alternative to the colonial system of "currency finance," the practice of issuing paper money was not a major issue before the 1770s; it was the Revolution itself which destroyed confidence in paper money among men of property and led them to embrace the "sound money" policy of tying the currency closely to gold and silver.

At the outset of the war with England, however, the habit of issuing paper to cover government expenses was so deeply ingrained that no other means of finance was seriously considered. (The only alternative, heavy taxation supplemented by borrowing—that is, future taxes—was less than appealing to the men of wealth who dominated Congress.) By the end of 1775, Congress had issued some six million dollars worth of paper notes, and by the time of the Declaration of Independence even that unprecedented amount had been doubled. Paine, who in *The Case of the Officers of Excise* had blamed rising prices in England on the issuance of paper money, included in *Common Sense* a plea that Americans "replace our paper currency with gold and silver." As prices rose precipitously in 1776 and 1777, Paine reiterated his earlier diagnosis. "The prices of goods can only be effectually reduced by reducing the quantity of paper money," he announced in April 1777 in the third *Crisis* paper. Instead of paper money, Paine called for the levying of an annual tax of between 10 and 20 per cent of the value of all property, to finance the war.[5]

Congress, which lacked both the power to levy direct taxes and the sense of self-sacrifice to which Paine was appealing, wrestled with the problems of inflation and paper money during much of 1777 and 1778. An extended debate on the subject took place in February 1777 and revealed that sentiment on price controls followed the division between two emerging "parties"—one an alliance between New Englanders and Virginians, the other concentrated in the commercial centers of the middle states and joined by such conservatives from other areas as John Adams. Among the leading critics of price regulation were two of Pennsylvania's Congressmen, Benjamin Rush and James Wilson. Rush, in medical terminology, assailed the policy as "an opiate" which would not deal with the primary cause of inflation, paper money. Wilson, a prominent attorney, observed, "there are certain things, sir, which absolute power cannot do"—supply and demand alone could establish the price of goods.[6]

Despite his own opposition to the policy, John Adams had to admit that price regulation was "extremely popular in Congress." Even many southerners, skeptical of the effectiveness of such laws, were still anxious to "damp the practice of speculative monopoly" which prevailed "in all the northern states." Richard Henry Lee, for example, blamed "the insatiable avarice of Pennsylvania" for the failure of price control measures and felt such regulations might help to "check the enormity of the evil." During 1777 and the first half of 1778, Congress attempted, with no success, to limit its own issuance of currency and to have the states levy taxes to redeem the paper already issued. At the same time, it admitted that previous measures had been ineffectual and recommended that the states repeal all legislation regulating prices.[7]

The lack of effective national action to control inflation in the first years of the war opened the door for local efforts to regulate prices and prohibit "monopolizing." Not surprisingly, such measures were most popular in New England, with its tradition of a corporate Puritan commonwealth. Massachusetts was the scene not only of "well-nigh universal" demands by urbanites for control of food prices, but of direct actions against merchants suspected of profiteering and engrossing. In 1777 women in Beverly raided merchants' storehouses, and a crowd of women in Boston tossed a leading "engrosser" into a cart, dragged him out of the city and seized his goods while "a large concourse of men stood amazed." In New Windsor, New York, a crowd in 1777 seized a shipment of tea bound for Albany and sold it at the traditional "just price." The southern states, however, were much less enthusiastic about price regulations. George Washington often bemoaned the activities of engrossers and forestallers, the "pests of society," whose activities interfered with the process of supplying the army, but, like most of his fellow planters, he believed that price regulation was "inconsistent with the very nature of things, and impracticable in itself."[8]

In Philadelphia, the local Committee of Observation and Inspection, established in 1775 to oversee nonimportation, fixed the prices of such scarce goods as salt and tea and publicly condemned those merchants who violated the price schedule. Among the artisans, professionals and Whig merchants who comprised the Committee, only Benjamin Rush opposed the price control policy, reading to his colleagues an extract from Hume on the impracticability of price controls in the reign of Edward II. By contrast, Christopher Marshall wanted the Committee to seize and sell at a "just price" the supplies of merchants who withheld goods from the market, but Marshall too was overruled.[9]

Despite the near unanimity of the Philadelphia Committee, many of the city's merchants were never happy with the policy of price controls. In April 1776 a group of ninety merchants petitioned the Committee of Observation and Inspection, denying its power to regulate prices and announcing their intention to refuse further cooperation. The Philadelphia press had already carried complaints blaming rising prices on "monopolizers," and one correspondent pointed out that in England "on a like occasion, the regrated commodities were forcibly taken from the monopolizers, and put into the hands of gentlemen of character, who sold them at a reasonable price to all men alike, and returned the money to the owner." The merchants' petition of April inspired another outburst against the "great merchants" who sought to engross trade and obtain "enormous estates," language which dovetailed neatly with the anti-aristocratic appeals the advocates of independence were utilizing at the very same time.[10]

Despite the merchants' opposition, the state Constitutional Convention of 1776 explicitly authorized local committees to control prices. The type of regulation that continued on the local level can be illustrated by a resolution adopted by the Committee of Bald-eagle township, in the western Pennsylvania county of Northumberland, prohibiting the export of grain from town "until the necessity of the poor is supplied," and warning that the Committee would seize the grain of any person refusing to take his supply to market. The county committee seems to have found this decision a bit extreme, for it reminded Bald-eagle of the prudence of finding a "sort of medium between seizing of property and supplying the wants of the poor."[11]

In response to local price control movements, adherents of the new doctrine of laissez-faire in 1777 and 1778 launched a serious challenge to the traditional idea that government had a responsibility to regulate commerce for the common good. Leading figures of the Revolution had long since assimilated the new doctrine of freedom of trade. "It is contrary to the nature of commerce," Franklin believed, "for government to interfere in the prices of commodities." Jefferson blamed inflation solely on paper money—any other explanation was "nonsensical quackery." Respectable merchant opinion had no use for price-fixing legislation; the maxim that "trade can best regulate itself" had won virtually universal approval in the mercantile community. General Nathanael Greene, himself a leading merchant, expressed the views of his class in mid-1777 when he condemned price-fixing not only as ineffectual, but as wholly inconsistent with "the principles of commerce," and founded "in public covetousness, a desire to have the property of a few at a less value, than the demand will warrant to the owners." And a New York merchant observed that price legislation was "a check to industry which is the principal part of the wealth of every country."[12]

The philosophical underpinnings for such laissez-faire beliefs were articulated most systematically in the writings of Adam Smith. Smith's *The Wealth of Nations* was published in Britain in 1776, but as "a grand central terminus to which many important lines of discussion in the middle of the eighteenth century . . . all run," it expressed ideas which had been widely circulated on both sides of the Atlantic in previous years. The world of Smith was not the corporate and paternalistic commonwealth of a previous age, but a collection of competitive, self-interested individuals whose very competing ambitions, through the operations of the marketplace, produced the greatest public benefit. Smith transferred the age-old function of distributing goods according to some standard of justice from the government to the impersonal mechanism of the market. For the notion of "just price" he substituted "the price of free competition," and in place of all "the absurd laws against engrossers, regraters, and forestallers," he relied on the natural operations of supply and demand to keep the price of food low. "It is not from the benevolence of the butcher, the brewer, or the baker that we expect our dinner," he wrote, "but from their regard to their own interest." The self-interested pursuit of gain, unregulated by legislation or popular prejudices, ensured the greatest benefit to society.[13]

Smith's view of economic life shared great affinities with the Madisonian political outlook that emerged in the 1780s and located government stability in the competition of diverse interests and ambitions, rather than in the virtues of men or the conscious pursuit of an undifferentiated public good. And for this reason, a certain tension existed between laissez-faire economics and Paineite republicanism. Paine still embraced the older view of a society founded upon a uniform general interest consciously perceived and pursued by all members of society, rather than one which was no more than a collection of competing individuals and in which progress was not the result of conscious planning.[14] Smith seemed to leave little room for any human quality save narrow self-interest, at least in economic affairs, while Paine always believed that reason could play a leading role in shaping human behavior.[15]

Despite this, Paine could hardly have escaped the influence of Smithian ideas. He lived in and near London during the prolonged Parliamentary debate on free trade in grain that culminated in the repeal of statutes against forstalling in 1772. Laissez-faire ideas circulated widely among intellectual and reforming circles in Paine's England; "any thinking man" would find in *The Wealth of Nations* "the ideas which he himself was already beginning to form, under the pressure of historical events, and with the tacit and permanent collaboration of all enlightened people." The modes of thought of Paine and Smith were essentially alike. Smith's economic world was a "consistently scientific system"—his admirers called him the Newton of economics and *The Wealth of Nations,* the *Principia* of human affairs. Like the physical universe of Newton and the political world of Paine, the economic system of Smith reflected the fundamental harmony and order of a creation one of whose principles was the natural identity of human interests. Like Paine, Smith distinguished radically between society and government. Economic interchange between men was as natural and inevitable as political intercourse; both stemmed from inherent human desires and the fact that no man could satisfy by himself more than a small portion of his wants. Left to itself, the development of "commercial society" would inevitably create an affluence in which all members of society would share. As in Paine's critique of monarchy, it was only the interference of government which disrupted the natural workings of economic society and created poverty and decay rather than abundance and harmony. As Smith explained:[16]

> The natural effort of every individual to better his own condition, when suffered to exert itself with freedom and security, is so powerful a principle, that it is alone, and without any assistance, not only capable of carrying on the society to wealth and prosperity, but of surmounting a hundred obstructions with which the folly of human laws too often incumbers its operations.

Laissez-faire economics, and its child the self-regulating market, would become "the fount and matrix" of nineteenth-century civilization. Smith's seeming annunciation of the self-interested pursuit of gain would make his ideas particularly appealing to the middle and upper classes on both sides of the Atlantic, until eventually laissez-faire would become synonymous with narrow self-interest, insensitivity to the plight of the poor and opposition to all kinds of social legislation. But in the late eighteenth century it was a doctrine with profoundly liberating implications. Smith, like Paine, suggested that all the old systems of authority and coercion were illegitimate interferences with the natural workings of society. Although he had little interest in politics, Smith seemed to lean toward republicanism and "rational religion." He opposed not only governmental interference with commerce, but all those social institutions impeding competition and individual effort— the established church, privileged corporations, primogeniture and laws limiting the mobility and occupational choice of laborers.[17]

Adam Smith never called his economic system "laissez-faire"— it was "the natural system of perfect liberty and justice" and the watchwords of the natural order were freedom, equality and the liberation of human energies. He did not deny that the market exerted its own coercion on individuals, but insisted that such coercion was more legitimate and just than political authority. The economic decisions of the market were not only just, but in a sense "democratic," since they represented the collective judgment of all consumers and producers. This same assumption that economic society, if left to its own laws, inevitably tended toward justice and equality also informed Paine's social outlook—it makes explicable his preoccupation with government as the cause of poverty and inequality.[18]

Both Paine and Smith envisioned an egalitarian society of small producers animated by a desire for self-improvement and economic gain, in which competition prevented the accumulation of excessive wealth. Smith's model, later used as a justification for monopoly and large corporations, by its very nature excluded the idea that in a truly free market any producer could influence supply, demand or market decisions by his own individual activities. Both men distinguished between productive and unproductive labor—for Smith, "some of the more respectable orders in the society," including the King, army, Church, lawyers, and landlords, were "idle people who produce nothing." Nineteenth-century capitalists would find much of Smith extremely congenial, but they would conveniently ignore his strictures on the cupidity of employers. In the famous Philadelphia shoemakers' trial of 1806, the counsel for the union, not the employers, quoted Adam Smith: "Masters are always and everywhere in a sort of tacit and uniform combination, not to raise the wages of labour above their actual rate."[19]

Understandably, then, the social outlook of Adam Smith was highly congenial to Paine. It would not be long before Thomas Malthus and other writers would come to see the laws of nature not as inherently progressive and beneficial, but as relentless decrees of the inevitable poverty under which the mass of the population labored. For Malthus, nature worked its will through war, disease and starvation. By contrast, the world of Smith and Paine was one of quiet progress and optimism, in which the increase of the wealth of nations spelled "universal opulence" even among "the lowest ranks of the People."[20]

Yet there is a revealing irony here. For, as one historian has explained:[21]

> Custom was one of the people's basic defenses; it was one of the normative weapons of the weak against the strong, one of the ways in which power was disciplined and concessions enjoyed. Custom was a constraint on the behavior of the propertied classes; it restricted their freedom of action (especially their freedom to dispose of property), imposed on them certain obligations, and in many cases limited their profits.

The tradition of "moral economy" looked to the past—to an organic community in which all classes were linked by ties of personal dependence and subordination. An assertion of the superiority of custom over innovation, of popular tradition over new economic theories, it proved extremely effective during the American Revolution in mobilizing mass political activity.

And yet Paine's entire frame of mind was forward looking rather than traditional. "The reasonableness and propriety of things," he insisted, "must be examined abstractly from custom and usage; and, in this point of view, the right which grows into practise today is as much a right, as if it had the customary sanction of a thousand ages." Paine did still cling to an older view of self-sacrificing virtue and an undifferentiated public good as the animating spirit of a republic. But he also looked to a society in which freedom of choice, the right to self-betterment and opportunities for mass political participation were guaranteed. He came to view the self-regulating market—a fundamental break with historical development and custom—as serving these ends better than the traditional "moral economy." And so it should not be surprising that in the economic crisis of 1779, although not without considerable mixed feelings, Paine would abandon the old economics for what one Philadelphian called "the clear and bright light of [Adam] Smith."[22]

II

In the turbulent year 1779, it was the specific national situation that initially determined Paine's reaction to the issue of price controls. In December 1778 and January 1779 he suddenly found himself in the midst of an acrimonious controversy over the conduct of Silas Deane, a Connecticut merchant who had been sent to France three years earlier to purchase supplies for the army. The immediate issue centered on whether a shipment of supplies was a gift from the French government or a commercial transaction on which Deane could claim a commission. But behind the Deane affair lay far larger issues. One was a growing disgust with war profiteering and the questionable ethical standards of merchants like Robert Morris who simultaneously served both the government and their own private gain, often purchasing supplies from their own companies or business partners at inflated prices and using their inside knowledge of governmental needs as a guide to speculation. Deane himself acted at the same time as an agent of Congress, of various private commercial firms, and in his own behalf, and "consistently confused private and public account." Then there was the perennial issue of inflation and the renewed tendency of many in Congress to blame it on the operations of profiteers, engrossers and monopolizers. And uniting these and other issues were widely held traditional ideas: the notions that "luxury" and "corruption" were incompatible with republicanism and that "virtue" should take precedence over private interest and profit.[23]

As with so many other aspects of political language during the Revolution, the precise meaning of terms like "luxury" and its opposite, "virtue," depended on the user. In general, "virtue" denoted a willingness to sacrifice individual self-interest to the greater good of society. This quality was widely believed to be "the essence of republicanism," although growing numbers of adherents of laissez-faire believed that "private vices"—the selfish pursuit of individual advancement—were the mainspring of economic growth. To exponents of the traditional Country party ideology, "luxury" and "corruption" implied a distaste for commercialization and the growth of mercantile and financial capitalism during the eighteenth century. But their assault upon commercial motives often went hand in hand with an emphasis on spartan self-denial and adversity that was compatible with a high degree of hierarchy and social control. Many who denounced "luxury" in the eighteenth century viewed the idleness and dissipation of the poor as a more pernicious example of the fault than the machinations of men of commerce. By contrast, in the hands of the evangelical ministry and urban advocates of popular price controls, condemnations of luxury and lamentations about the decline of "virtue" were directed against the life-style of the rich, with its conspicuous consumption, and against the entire commercial ethos and profit motive.[24]

The most radical implications of the idea of "virtue" were to be found not in Congress, but in the streets of Philadelphia. But the congressional group that attacked Deane railed against "commercial plunder" and denounced the evil operations of "engrossers" that were the "bane of patriotism." Taking the lead in denouncing Deane was the Adams-Lee faction in Congress, a coalition of New Englanders like Samuel Adams, whose social outlook envisaged a "Christian corporate Commonwealth" in which luxury, extravagance and avarice had no place, and southerners like Richard Henry Lee, an admirer of the "frugal, diligent" New England character, and Henry Laurens, the president of Congress and a self-disciplined importer and entrepreneur. In the winter of 1778–79, Adams' letters included more than his usual moralizing about luxury, dissipation, "vice of every kind," and the lack of "sobriety of manners, . . . temperance, frugality, fortitude and other manly virtues" among Americans. Lee joined in the assault on "the demon of avarice, extortion and fortune-making" which had seized "all ranks" of society and which seemed to be eroding the moral distance between a "corrupt" England and a "virtuous" America. To Deane's defense rallied wealthy merchants like Robert Morris and a majority of the southern delegations, men whose life-style partook more of luxury and extravagance than Lee's, whose sober demeanor led the French Ambassador to mistake him for a Presbyterian.[25]

Paine did not share the distaste for commerce which for many Americans lay behind the concept of "virtue." "In all my publications," he later observed, " . . . I have been an advocate for commerce," and in *Common Sense* he had specifically tied the economic hopes of the new nation to commercial freedom while associating restraints on trade with British rule. And in the *Crisis* papers of 1777 and 1778, Paine had reiterated his belief that "trade flourishes best, when it is free, and it is weak policy to attempt to fetter it," and had attributed rising prices to an excess of paper money—the same diagnosis put forward by opponents of price controls.[26]

It was Paine's involvement in the Deane affair which led him to abandon temporarily his high regard for men of commerce and launch an attack on "monopolizers." (The two were not, of course, mutually exclusive—the Smithian free market, as we have seen, was based on the assumption that the marketplace was free from monopoly.) A close associate of Lee and Laurens, Paine rushed into print to defend their side of the Deane controversy, only to find himself under attack for referring in his writings to secret diplomatic correspondence regarding French aid to America. This indiscretion antagonized both Congress and the French Ambassador, and in January 1779 Paine was forced to resign from his position as Secretary to the Committee on Foreign

Affairs. He found himself denounced in the press as a "stranger, without either connections or apparent property in this country," undeserving of a position of public trust. The newspaper debate continued well into spring. As late as May, Paine was still calling Deane an embezzler and denouncing his business partner Robert Morris as corrupt, while Deane and Morris were equally outspoken in presenting their side of the story.[27]

This prolonged controversy temporarily suspended Paine's association with the national war effort and brought him back into Pennsylvania politics as an outspoken critic of merchants who appeared to be putting their personal self-interest ahead of the public good. Paine quickly took a job as clerk to his radical associate from 1776 Owen Biddle, now head of the Pennsylvania Board of War. For eighteen months, Paine did not produce a *Crisis* paper. His popularity in Congress waned, but out of doors it remained high while, according to contemporaries, Deane and his supporters "lapsed into general contempt" in Philadelphia.[28] The Deane controversy propelled Paine into a leading role in the popular movement for price controls which shook the social fabric of Philadelphia in 1779.

As in the other states, prices in Pennsylvania had begun to rise in 1776, and by mid-1778 were increasing at a truly alarming rate. By the beginning of 1779, inflation was totally out of control—in one month, prices rose 45 per cent. And the inflation did not halt there. By the end of 1779, the overall price level was seven times that of 1777. Not all items, however, rose with equal speed. Early in the war, the price of domestic foodstuffs had remained relatively stable while imported goods like rum, tea and molasses led the advance. But in 1778 and 1779, the situation was reversed. The increase for such staples as corn, wheat and flour far outpaced that for West Indian goods. In the single year 1779, for example, the price of corn rose at the astonishing rate of 1255 per cent, while the price of rum did not even double.[29]

Most historians have agreed with Paine and with such contemporary advocates of laissez-faire as John Adams and Benjamin Rush that the primary cause of inflation was the continuing emission of paper money by the federal and state governments. But if this were the only reason, why did the prices of some items rise so much more sharply than others? The special circumstances of the war economy completely disrupted the familiar patterns of trade and marketing of food. One reason for the increase in food prices was the sudden demand for foodstuffs by army supply agents, operating on a cost-plus profit basis, and by the recently arrived French fleet, which often paid for its purchases in gold. Commercial farmers, who profited greatly from the inflation, refused to accept paper money for their produce, and millers refused to sell flour in the Philadelphia market when they could obtain higher prices in Maryland or from the French. By May 1779, Philadelphia's pre-war position as the chief outlet for the grain and flour of Pennsylvania, Delaware and western New Jersey had been thoroughly disrupted; indeed during the summer, these products sometimes had to be shipped to the city from Baltimore. Finally, there is little question that some merchants took advantage of the chaotic economic situation by withholding goods from the market in anticipation of rising prices, and others, like Robert Morris, used their connections with the French and resulting access to large orders and gold to corner the market in goods which could be sold later at a large profit.[30]

In a sense, the actual cause of rising prices is less important than the popular reaction to inflation, which was framed by the traditional values of "moral economy." The outcry over inflation which swept Philadelphia went hand in hand with a growing identification in the popular mind of Tories, speculating and engrossing merchants, and men of wealth in general. It was widely believed that anyone whose wealth increased "in such times as the present," was "an enemy to his country." The "*mistaken* principle of leaving trade to regulate itself" was identified with both Tories and "the Better Sort of People" who gloried "in . . . debaucheries" and "harrangued upon the doctrine, of private vices being public benefits."[31]

The evacuation of Philadelphia in June 1778, after several months of British occupation, unleashed demands for vengeance against Tories and collaborators. Under the British, large segments of Philadelphia's upper class had participated in the balls and theatrical performances sponsored by the occupying forces and in the great *Meschianza* of May 1778, an extravaganza which included a regatta, a procession of medieval knights and a jousting tournament. Entertainments only slightly less ostentatious continued into the fall under the auspices of Benedict Arnold, the American commander in the city. Arnold himself lived in grand style, traveling about the city in a gaudy coach, while Washington's army lived not far away on short rations and real wages plummeted in the city because of inflation. Bitter comments appeared in the Philadelphia press on the expediture of huge sums on "public dinners and other extravagancies" while many in the city were "destitute of the necessaries of life."[32]

This hostility to men of wealth was reinforced by a strain of puritanism which had been associated with the American Revolution for several years. The Continental Association of 1774 had included a condemnation of "every species of extravagance and dissipation, especially all horse-racing, and all kinds of gaming, cock-fighting." In Philadelphia, an unusual alliance of Quakers, evangelical Presbyterians and German Lutherans had long attacked the theater as an encouragement to "vanity, licentiousness . . . dissoluteness and debauchery," and by the time of the Revolution, there was in the recurrent attacks on the theater as much secular hostility to the rich as religious objections to worldliness. The city's playhouses were closed in 1774, but they reopened during the British occupation and continued to operate under Arnold. In March 1779 the state Assembly, dominated by rural Presbyterians of the Constitutionalist party, enacted a law to suppress "Vice and Immorality," outlawing not only the theater, but cock-fighting, all Sunday recreations, "profane swearing, cursing, drunkenness," gambling, horse-racing and "such evil practices which tend to debauch the minds and corrupt the morals of the subjects of the Commonwealth." Obviously, the measure was directed at no single social class, but it won the approval of many Philadelphians resentful of the elite's extravagant behavior. It was said, however, that "gentlemen" continued to believe "they had a right to game, and drink and swear: the law meant to forbid these amusements only to the vulgar."[33]

The vote on the law against "immorality" cut across Pennsylvania's party lines, but in general the social turmoil of 1779 was reinforced by the state's intense party conflict. Opponents of the state constitution included such leading critics of price control as Benjamin Rush and merchants like Robert Morris and Thomas Willing, members of the small but highly visible group of government contractors who profited immensely from their privileged position in the war economy. Their creation of the Republican Society in March 1779, dedicated to constitutional revision, led defenders of the state's frame of government, including some of Paine's friends and associates from 1776, to form the Constitutional Society and to link up with the anti-Deane faction in Congress. Given the character of the Republican leadership and the general outrage over rising prices, it is not surprising that the Constitutional Society was soon denouncing the "decline of decency and public virtue," the "inundation of vice, fraud, and extortion" and the machinations of "forestallers and monopolizers." At the same time the Assembly outlawed the sale of food except at established markets, forbade merchants and farmers to buy or sell "the necessaries of life" for hard money instead of paper, and provided that anyone violating these provisions "shall be deemed a forestaller" and dealt with accordingly.[34]

But as this measure, like its predecessors, failed to halt rising prices, increasing numbers of Philadelphians concluded that only extra-legal action could resolve the economic crisis. As early as December 1778, a writer styling himself "Mobility" had issued "A

Hint" in the Philadelphia press, which graphically illustrated the
vitality of the European tradition of "moral economy:"[35]

> This country has been reduced to the brink of ruin by the infamous
> practices of Monopolizers and Forestallers. Not satisfied with
> monopolizing European and West-Indian goods, they have lately
> monopolized the Staff of Life. Hence, the universal cry of the
> scarcity and high price of Flour. It has been found in Britain and
> France, that the People have always done themselves justice when
> the scarcity of bread has arisen from the avarice of forestallers. They
> have broken open magazines—appropriated stores to their own use
> without paying for them—and in some instances have hung up the
> culprits who have created their distress, without judge or jury. Hear
> this and tremble, ye enemies to the freedom and happiness of your
> country. We can live without sugar, molasses and rum—but we
> cannot live without bread.—Hunger will break through stone walls
> and the resentment excited by it may end in your destruction.

In January 1779, over one hundred sailors armed with clubs
paraded the streets demanding higher wages. In the spring, as in
1776, the militia took the lead. The privates had long resented the
fact that while they had "bravely stepped forward" to defend their
country, "the monied men of the community" were "sculking
about" depreciating the currency and "basking in the sunshine of
monopoly, forestalling and extortion and withal pampering their
vile natures in ease, superfluities and luxury." On May 12, the
First Company of Philadelphia Militia Artillery presented a
lengthy memorial to the Assembly, reviewing the rise in prices
since 1776 and the distress it caused their families. "We had arms
in our hands, and knew the use of them," said the memorial in a
scarcely veiled threat of direct action, but "instead of avenging
ourselves . . . we patiently waited the interference of the Legislative Authority." Signed by thirteen officers and thirty-eight men,
three of whom gave only the mark of X, the petition revealed the
desperation of "the midling and poor" at the enormous and
continuing increase in prices.[36]

As the threat of violence mounted, the Constitutional Society—

in which Peale, Rittenhouse, Marshall and other radicals of 1776 played leading roles—called for a mass meeting on May 25 to deal with the price question. Already, "threatening handbills" had appeared demanding a lowering of prices and on the day of the meeting a group of men armed with clubs compelled a number of shopkeepers to lower prices. The mass meeting was the most important extra-legal gathering in Philadelphia since pre-independence days. Daniel Roberdeau, brigadier-general of the militia, a West India merchant and long-time political ally of Franklin, and reputedly one of the most popular men in the city, was chosen as chairman. His address illuminated the popular justification for extra-legal action:

> I have no doubt but combinations have been formed for raising the prices of goods and provisions, and therefore the community, in their own defense, have a natural right to counteract such combinations, and to set limits to evils which affect themselves.

Roberdeau then presented a plan drawn up by "some worthy citizens"—probably the leaders of the Constitutional Society—by which prices would immediately be lowered to the level of May 1, and would be further reduced on the first day of each succeeding month. Two committees were appointed, one to investigate the affairs of Robert Morris, who was accused of holding food from the market, and another to carry out the price reductions. To both committees were appointed Matlack, Rittenhouse, Peale— and Thomas Paine.[37]

The meeting of May 25 did little to heal the smoldering social tensions caused by the economic crisis. The attitude of the city's elite toward the gathering was expressed by one Quaker-Loyalist poet who ridiculed the "grand town meeting" as a collection of "printer's devils, barber's boys, apprentice lads" and militiamen who believed that, like alchemists, they could change "old rags and lampblack [Continental money] into gold." But there was

Committee-Room.

May 28. 1779.

RESOLVED,

THAT the Retail Prices of the underwritten Articles on the firſt Day of May were as follows----

Coffee.	per pound,	£ 0 : 17 : 6	
Bohea Tea,	ditto,	4 : 15 : 0	
Loaf Sugar,	ditto,	2 : 15 : 0	
Muſcovado Sugar,	ditto,	from 0 : 18 : 9 to £1 : 5 : 0	
		according to Quality.	
Weſt India Rum,	by gallon or quart,	7 : 0 : 0	
Country Rum,	by do. or do.	5 : 5 : 0	
Whiſkey,	by do.	2 : 0 : 0	
Rice,	per pound,	0 : 3 : 0	

And as it is abſolutely neceſſary, that Dry Goods, and all other Commodities, whether imported or the Produce of the Country, ſhould fall in Price as well as thoſe Articles which are already Publiſhed; therefore,

Reſolved, That this Committee do earneſtly requeſt and expect, that no Perſon do ſell any Commodity whatever, at a Higher Price than the ſame was ſold for on the firſt Day of this Month.

By Order of the Committee,

WILLIAM HENRY, CHAIRMAN.

§*§ *The Committee meets at Nine o'Clock preciſely, on Monday Morning next, at the Court-Houſe.*

PHILADELPHIA: Printed by FRANCIS BAILEY, in *Market-Street.*

A broadside printed by the extra-legal Philadelphia price control committee, setting the retail prices of various commodities. *Library Company of Philadelphia* perhaps a grain of truth in his observation that the meeting's organizers, fearing it would lead to turbulence and violence,

> Were fill'd with grief and pity;
> And soon dismiss'd the rabble rout—
> Concluding what they met about
> With choosing a Committee.

For in one sense, the purpose of the mass meeting was to divert popular discontent into structured channels and to reduce the danger of violence.

In this the new Committee was, for the time being, successful. True, after the town meeting, "thousands of the common people" assembled along the riverside, "clamoring for bread," and a merchant, a butcher and a "speculator" accused of raising prices were marched to the city jail. But during the summer there was little overt violence as the Committee went about its business by setting price levels, questioning merchants accused of charging exorbitant prices, prohibiting the export of goods from the city and distributing bread and flour among the poor. The Committee, to be sure, was not averse to using the threat of violence. In June it urged merchants to cooperate, reminding them that "the want of flour has in all Countries produced the most fatal resentments," and it called on local committees outside the city to search for hoarded grain and if necessary "break open and enter the same by force," seize the flour and pay an appraised, regulated price to the owner.[38]

By July 1779, the example of Philadelphia had inspired the creation of extra-legal price-control committees throughout Pennsylvania, and in other states as well. Christopher Marshall, long a critic of the "specious pretense . . . that trade ungoverned will always regulate itself," helped to organize a mass meeting in Lancaster, which adopted a plan similar to Philadelphia's and attempted to mollify urban-rural hostility by appealing to farmers and town-dwellers alike to concur "in measures for the mutual benefit of both."[39] In Boston, following warnings in the press that vengeance would "burst on the heads of monopolizers, as it did on the odious stamp-masters" a decade earlier, merchants themselves adopted a schedule of regulated prices. A report from Albany carried in the Philadelphia press praised the residents of the Quaker City "who lately had the name of the greatest extortioners on the continent," and announced that Albany and surrounding areas had "followed [Philadelphia's] example." Two merchants who sold rum at exorbitant prices were "publicly cried through the city by order of the committee" and were forced to acknowledge their guilt at the Albany marketplace—a traditional crowd "punishment" of colonial days.[40]

As the committee movement expanded, so did resistance both among opponents of the concept of price control, and critics of action by extra-legal committees. To some, the committee movement seemed little more than "a Mob assembled to regulate prices." In July, the Philadelphia press carried articles by "A Farmer of Virginia" charging that price regulation threatened the very basis of society, "which is established for the security of property," and denying that the present movement could be equated with pre-independence extra-legal committees which, he claimed, had been "systematically conducted, and proceeded with as much moderation as could have been expected." In response to such criticism, the Philadelphia Committee issued lengthy justifications of its activities, explicitly repudiating the idea "that trade will regulate itself" and reiterating the concept, central to the traditional notion of "moral economy," of the supremacy of the common good over individual ambitions:[41]

> The social compact or state of civil society, by which men are united and incorporated, requires that every right or power claimed or exercised by any man or set of men should be in subordination to the common good, and that whatever is incompatible therewith,

must, by some rule or regulation, be brought into subjection thereto. . . . If the freedom of trade is to be [absolute] then must all and every species of forestalling, monopolizing and engrossing be sanctioned thereby, because [merchants'] idea of a free trade is, for every man to do what he pleases; a right, which . . . is repugnant to the very principles on which society and civil government are founded.

Not surprisingly, the loudest opposition to such beliefs came from the merchants of Philadelphia, who generally agreed with their political and economic leader, Robert Morris, that trade should be "free as air" and that the private interest of the merchant and the good of the public went "hand in hand." The economic and social crisis of 1779 forced the merchants to elaborate these views more fully and coherently than ever before. Their position was best expressed by Pelatiah Webster, a Connecticut-born trader who published a series of essays in the summer of 1779. "Freedom of trade, or unrestrained liberty of the subject to hold or dispose of his property as he pleases," Webster insisted, "is absolutely necessary to the prosperity of every community." "Gain" was "the soul of industry," the motive force of economic growth. Webster condemned the "torrent of censure and abuse" which he claimed was being directed against farmers, merchants and tradesmen and attributed rising prices solely to "our having too much money." His solution to rising prices was pure Adam Smith:

Take off every restraint and limitation from our commerce. Let trade be as free as air. Let every man make the most of his goods and in his own way and then he will be most satisfied. . . . It is a sad omen to find among the first effects of independence, greater restraints and abridgements of natural liberty, than ever we felt under the government we have lately renounced and shaken off.

In September 1779, Webster and Morris were among eighty Philadelphia merchants who petitioned the city Committee to rescind its price regulations as an invasion of "the laws of property." The merchants went so far as to argue that despite the "popular odium" against engrossers, such men actually promoted the public good by pursuing their own private interests, by creating artificial scarcities which lessened consumption and made real dearths less severe. They admitted, however, that this might be considered a "novel" idea.[42]

Opposition from the merchants was predictable. Much more worrisome for the Committee was a memorial presented in July by a group of tanners, shoemakers and curriers. An attack on the price schedule established for these leather trades, it revealed that the artisan community was itself divided over the wisdom of price controls. As urban consumers, all artisans shared an identity of interest with other groups in opposing high food prices, but as producers and retailers the masters felt obligated to pass on the increase in the cost of their raw materials to their consumers. The price of leather had increased more than sevenfold between May 1778 and July 1779, but the leather trades had been singled out as the first craft to be regulated by the Committee. Yet the petition was based on more than resentment against the Committee's "partial proceedings" which left other trades free to pursue their own interests without regulation. It pointed out that many craftsmen sold their products on credit and therefore suffered from the continuing depreciation of the currency. The only way to make up this loss was by raising prices. Indeed, the leather artisans adopted precisely the same language as the merchants: "Trade should be free as air, uninterrupted as the tide" and would always find its own natural level.[43]

It is difficult to say how typical the petition was of the sentiments of the entire artisan community. The leather trades were one of the largest collection of crafts in the city, representing about one-seventh of all artisans. The shoemakers, generally lesser artisans in income and scale of operations, had traditionally sought guild and legislative regulation of their trade and had complained periodically during the colonial years about the activities of merchants who raised leather prices by engrossing the available supply and exporting leather from the colony. In 1772 the Assembly, responding to a shoemakers' petition, had enacted a statute regulating the quality of leather and prohibiting engrossing, but it was repealed a year later at the behest of the tanners, men of large capital and one of the few pre-war artisan groups to condemn "restraints on trade generally."

How many of the 1779 petitioners were tanners and how many shoemakers is impossible to say. But "A Whig Shoemaker" claimed that the petition had been drawn up by "master workmen . . . disaffected to the common cause" who had willingly served the British during the occupation. Whatever the truth of the charge of Loyalism, it does seem that the petitioners were master craftsmen—for their protest referred to the danger that the regulation of prices would force them to dismiss their journeymen. Not all shoemakers, however, resisted the work of the Committee. Ten announced their intention to work at the regulated rates—an action which, the protesting petitioners replied, would reduce the ten to "the most wretched circumstances in life."[44]

Although artisans participated in every phase of the price control movement of 1779—there were at least nine of them, including two shoemakers and a tanner, on the twenty-six man Committee established in May—there can be little question that many master craftsmen were becoming disillusioned with price controls as the summer wore on. The militia who had inspired the movement in the first place, after all, was primarily composed of laborers, journeymen and poorer artisans, men who were primarily urban consumers and had little real involvement with the marketplace. But groups like the tanners spoke for the increasing number of master artisans who during the Revolution "completed the transition from the guild mentality to the commercial mentality." The price control controversy was symptomatic of a growing gap within the artisan community, as the commercially-oriented artisans came to sense a community of interests with merchants in rejecting the older "moral economy" and, like the merchants, increasingly looked to the self-regulating market as the only legitimate arbiter of their economic activity.[45]

The developing opposition to price controls posed a serious dilemma for the Committee, and for Paine. In May, June and July, Paine was closely identified with the price control movement. He served not only on the Committee establishing price schedules, but on the smaller group investigating the conduct of Robert Morris. Paine drafted a report which, while admitting that there was no specific evidence of engrossing, declared "we are at a loss to find any other name" for Morris' conduct.[46]

Throughout the summer, public controversy swirled about Paine. He was denounced in the press as "a disturber of the public peace, a spreader of falsehoods, and sower of dissension among the people."[47] At the end of July, a crowd composed of several hundred of "the lower orders" descended on the house of Whitehead Humphreys, a proprietor of a Philadelphia steel furnace who had attacked Paine in the newspapers. At a mass meeting a few days later General John Cadwalader, who rose to denounce this "riot," was prevented from speaking by a group of armed men, and the meeting unanimously adopted a resolution "that Mr. Thomas Paine is considered by this meeting as a friend to the American cause."[48]

Nonetheless Paine, and probably others among his radical friends, were not happy with the turbulent atmosphere which pervaded Philadelphia in the summer of 1779. Charles Willson Peale, a radical of 1776, had attempted to disperse the crowd at Humphreys' house. Paine, as always, sought a means of uniting the entire community for the common good. In July, Paine and Owen Biddle devised a "Citizen's Plan" for reducing prices and uniting "public and private interest" in support of the government and the war effort. Paine had always believed—as did the merchants and laissez-faire advocates—that paper money was the primary cause of inflation. Now his plan called for a commitment on the part of Congress to stop emitting paper money and to establish a subscription list to which men could voluntarily contribute funds to support the war effort, their donations to be credited against their next three years' state taxes. Presumably, stopping the printing presses would restore confidence in the currency and reduce prices, while the public subscription would both finance the government and enable men of wealth to prove their loyalty to the cause.[49]

The Citizens' Plan, in effect, was an alternative to price control, but Paine continued to be involved in the Committee movement. At the beginning of August, he was one of 120 members elected to an expanded city Committee, along with Matlack, Biddle, Peale and Rittenhouse, all associates from 1776. The successful ticket, which overwhelmingly defeated a slate headed by Robert Morris, included nine merchants, five shopkeepers, a pilot, captain and mariner and at least forty-seven artisans, including seven shoemakers. It was a cross-section of Philadelphia society, except for the very top and very bottom. But the enlarged Committee proved unwieldy and ineffectual and by the end of September suspended operations, attributing its failure to its inability to regulate the prices of country produce and goods in neighboring states. Farmers were continuing to refuse to sell goods at regulated markets, and merchants were suspending operations in goods like salt, which cost them more than twice the price established by the Committee for sale in the city. Paine was convinced by events of the inability of price control measures to regulate the marketplace adequately. By September, he was arguing for a lifting of the embargo on the export of food from the state, in order to allow exported flour and bread to pay for needed salt and rum.[50]

The demise of the city Committee and the reluctance of the state government—headed by Joseph Reed, the son of a wealthy merchant and believer that "the commerce of mankind must be free, or almost all kinds of intercourse will cease"[51]—to take effec-

Philadelphia august 10.ᵗʰ 1779

WHEREAS the rapid and alarming depreciation of the Currency in the Months of January, February, March, April, and May laſt, occaſioned a Town Meeting to be held, in the State-Houſe Yard in this City on the 25th Day of the laſt mentioned Month ; at which it was reſolved (as the only expedient immediately practicable) to reduce the Prices of ſeveral Articles then mentioned and others, to what they were on the firſt Day of the Month preceding : But as in ſo doing, the Prices of ſeveral of thoſe Articles, as well of Merchandize as Manufacture, became, by the unavoidable fluctuation of Trade, diſproportionate to each other.

And Whereas the General Committee have appointed us the undermentioned Perſons, viz. Blair McClenaghan, J. B. Smith, Timothy Matlack, Thomas Paine, Matthew Irvine, Jacob Shriner, Thomas Fitzſimmons, Robert Smith, George Orde, James Budden, Charles W. Peale, Emanuel Eyre, and John McCulloch to be a Committee for enquiring into the State of Trade. Therefore,

RESOLVED, That in order to enable this Committee to do Juſtice to all Perſons concerned, it be requeſted of the Importers, and Retailers of Wet and Dry Goods, and of the ſeveral Traders and Manufacturers in this City and Liberties, to ſend to this Committee an atteſted Account of the Prices they ſeverally ſold for, or charged at, in the Year 1774, with an Account of their Prices and Charges for the ſame Articles, &c. at this Time, together with ſuch information reſpecting their preſent ſituation in Trade, as they may find it proper to give.

BLAIR McCLENAGHAN,
Chairman of the Committee for
enquiring into the State of Trade.

N. B. The above Committee will meet at Four o'Clock preciſely each Day at the Court-Houſe, and requeſt the information of all perſons concerned, as ſoon as poſſible.

PHILADELPHIA: Printed by F. BAILEY, in *Market-Street.*

One of the few contemporary broadsides mentioning Paine's name, this printed resolution records Paine's involvement in the popular movement for price controls. *Library Company of Philadelphia*

tive action, set the stage for the "Fort Wilson riot" of early October 1779. With the failure of structured channels for the expression of popular grievances, resentments against the wealthy merchants deemed responsible for inflation exploded into the traditional form, crowd activity. On October 4, a militia group began to march into the center of the city, eventually making its way to the house of James Wilson. Wilson had long since "become obnoxious to a large portion of the community," because of his opposition to price controls, his legal defense of two Tories executed in 1778 and his strenuous opposition to the constitution of 1776. With him in the house were some twenty political allies, including Robert Morris. Someone fired a shot, the militia attacked the house and within a few minutes Reed and Timothy Matlack arrived with drawn swords in hand, leading a troop of the City Light Horse, the aristocratic "silk stocking brigade" of Philadelphia. The militia were driven off and many were arrested, although they were released the next day when a group of militia officers threatened to force the jail door to free them.[52]

Benjamin Rush, who believed the militia "were enraged chiefly by liquor" said their objects were "unknown," but it seems clear that while the battle at the house was not premeditated, the purpose of the militia march had been to demonstrate support for "The Constitution, the laws and the Committee of Trade," to round up "Tories" and to oppose "internal enemies" who were held responsible for inflation. Rush was perceptive, however, when he wrote of the crowd: "their leaders abandoned them." Charles W. Peale refused to lead the march and Timothy Matlack headed the brigade that helped to break it up. As for Paine, he published a gloomy letter which seemed to place primary blame for the incident on the men gathered within Wilson's house, but he insisted it would be wrong to condemn Wilson and his friends as Tories: "The difference is exceedingly great, between not being in favor and being considered as an enemy." Paine attributed the incident to misguided patriotism, but he revealed some-

By His Excellency JOSEPH REED, *Esq*; President, *and the* Supreme Executive Council *of the Commonwealth of* Pennsylvania,

A PROCLAMATION.

THE late melancholy Events in this City muft fill the Mind of every good Man and virtuous Citizen with the deepeft Regret and Concern. They muft imprefs every one with the Neceffity of Obedience and Refpect to public Authority, as the only fure Foundation of Tranquility and Peace. The undue Countenance and Encouragement which has been fhewn to Perfons difaffected to the Liberty and Independance of *America*, by fome whofe Rank and Character in other Refpects gave Weight to their Conduct, has been the principal Caufe of the prefent Commotion---the unwearied Oppofition, and the Contempt manifefted in many Inftances to the Laws and public Authority of the State, have alfo contributed---and Juftice alfo requires us to declare, that fome licentious and unworthy Characters, taking Advantage of the unhappy Tumult artfully kindled by themfelves, have led many innocent and otherwife well-difpofed Perfons into Outrages and Infults, which, it is hoped, on cool Reflection they will condemn. But as it is become highly neceffary that all farther Tumult fhould ceafe, and the Laws and good Order prevail, We think proper to declare, that all thofe who were immediately concerned in the unhappy Tranfaction of the fourth Inftant in *Walnut-ftreet*, without Diftinction, fhall as far as poffible be amenable to Juftice; and for that Purpofe do require all thofe who marched down from the Commons, in hoftile Array, to the Houfe of *James Wilfon*, Efq; and alfo all thofe who had previoufly affembled in the faid Houfe, with Arms or otherwife, immediately to furrender themfelves to the Sheriff of the City and County of *Philadelphia*, or to fome Juftice of the Peace, who is directed to commit them to Prifon, there to remain until Examination can be had, and they be delivered in due Courfe of Law. And we do alfo enjoin and require all Officers, both civil and military, and all other the faithful Inhabitants, to fupport and maintain the Peace, Tranquility and good Order of the City, as they would approve themfelves Friends to Government and to *American* Liberty, and as they will anfwer the contrary at their Peril.

GIVEN, by Order of the Council, under the Hand of His Excellency JOSEPH REED, *Efquire, Prefident, and the Seal of the State, at Philadelphia, this Sixth Day of* October, *in the Year of Our Lord One Thoufand Seven Hundred and Seventynine.*

JOSEPH REED, Prefident.

Att. T. MATLACK, Secretary.

GOD Save the PEOPLE.

Printed by HALL and SELLERS. 1779.

While there are no pictorial accounts of the Fort Wilson riot, this proclamation issued two days later reflects in its strongly worded call to order the horror with which government officials and many others viewed that crucial event. *Library Company of Philadelphia* thing of his distaste for crowd activity in chastizing the militia: "Those whose talent it is to act, are seldom much devoted to deliberate thinking."[53]

III

The "Fort Wilson riot" was a major turning point in the history of popular radicalism in revolutionary Philadelphia. The incident irrevocably split the artisan-intelligentsia radical leadership from mass crowd activities, just as the debate over price controls widened the gap between the commercially oriented upper segment of the artisan world and lesser artisans, journeymen, laborers and the poor. It came as the culmination of a year of popular action against inflation and "Tories," animated by an intense egalitarianism and hostility to the economic activities and style of life of the city's merchant elite. But its outcome marked the beginning of a decade in which such activity would be sporadic and ineffectual.

Certainly the defeat of the policy of price controls seemed complete. There was one last flurry of governmental activity in 1779 in the aftermath of the Wilson incident, aimed at preventing a repetition of the violence. The Assembly distributed flour among the Philadelphia poor, with preference shown to families of militia privates, and enacted yet another law against "the evil practice of monopolizing and forestalling." And Joseph Reed pointedly warned merchants that they could hardly expect to "live in ease, plenty, and safety, while such a body of your fellow citizens were destitute of all the necessaries of life."[54]

The final chapter of the price control story was written early in 1780, when delegates assembled at Philadelphia for a convention of the states from New England south to Virginia to establish a general schedule of regulated prices. Apparently, the advocates of price control in Philadelphia had high hopes for this meeting— Benjamin Rush observed sarcastically that "our political quacks (both *within* and without doors) expect to see all the mysteries of alchemy performed in an instant upon our currency." In the end, however, like so many other such efforts of the period, the Philadelphia convention proved abortive. Delegations from New York and Virginia did not appear, and the meeting adjourned to April to await action by those states. It never reconvened.[55]

"We hope," the Connecticut delegates to this Philadelphia gathering reported to their governor in February, "that some measures will soon be adopted for introducing a stable medium of trade, that will render a limitation of prices unnecessary." Stabilization of the currency was thus seen as the alternative to price controls and in March 1780, Congress devalued the continental currency at the rate of forty to one and authorized the issuance of new bills redeemable in six years and bearing 5 per cent interest. The measure did not result in an end to inflation, but it signaled a basic shift in attitudes toward the currency and price questions and was the first evidence of the emergence of Robert Morris to ascendency in financial policy. By 1781, Morris, a firm opponent of the whole "detestable tribe of restrictions on commerce," an advocate of hard money and "fiscal responsibility" and a spokesman for those who wished to forge a strong alliance between urban business interests and the continental government, was the virtual dictator of congressional financial policies.[56]

Pennsylvania quickly capitulated to the new fiscal order. In 1780 and 1781 the laws establishing continental and state currency as legal tender, prohibiting "monopolizing" and barring the export of flour were swept away by the state Assembly, although it was still dominated by Morris' erstwhile political foes of the Constitutionalist party. Philadelphia's merchants rallied to the new policy, agreeing to receive the new congressional money as the equivalent of gold and silver, a policy which involved monetary loss but perhaps was a response to Morris' promise that the "people will grow less turbulent" once "our finances turn for the better." And the majority of the city's artisans, by now thoroughly disillusioned with the experiment in price controls, supported the Morris policies in the hope they would finally stabilize the currency, reduce prices and restore economic confidence. In the fall election of 1780, Morris' Republican party swept the Philadelphia elections.[57]

After the congressional devaluation of March 1780, state and local efforts at price regulation ceased. Both major parties in Philadelphia quickly adopted the position of the merchants of 1779, that price controls flew in the face of the rights of property. When the Council of Censors met in 1783 to consider violations of the state constitution, the Constitutionalist party leadership endorsed a report which condemned the earlier price controls not only as "absurd and impossible" but as "unconstitutional invasions of the rights of property." In the early 1790s, Pennsylvania suspended the traditional practice of having local officials establish the price, weight and content of a loaf of bread, following the judgment of a legislative committee that "the practice of most nations and ages to limit the prices of bread" was a violation of the equality of rights established by the state constitution.[58]

The demise of the notion that government had a responsibility to regulate prices in the interest of the consumer did not, of course, mean that all forms of governmental intervention in the economy suddenly ceased. Various kinds of economic regulations persisted well into the nineteenth century, especially when state action seemed necessary to stimulate economic enterprise. The doctrine of a free market within the republic often went hand in hand with belief in a rising American empire whose commercial and territorial expansion was promoted by a strong central government. Even in the 1780s, the same merchants and artisans who opposed the regulation of prices strongly supported the establishment of a federal government with the power to promote American commerce, offer protection to home manufactures and encourage the nation's economic development.

Nor does it seem likely that traditional "moral economy" ideas suddenly disappeared among the urban lower classes, although the occurrence of Philadelphia's first strikes in the 1780s and 1790s reflected the emergence of a more "modern" response to the problem of inflation among wage-earners. Customary ideas doubtless survived, but they no longer found expression in the realm of politics or in the legal system, where the separation of moral and economic questions and the replacement of traditional notions of a "just price" and an equitable contract by the more modern doctrine of *caveat emptor*—let the buyer beware—were well underway by the early nineteenth century. And even before this, it no longer seemed unusual for political leaders to assert forthrightly that competition alone established "the just value of every commodity," and that it was an advantage of "a perfectly free trade" that it ensured "the farmer the highest price for his produce."[59]

For Paine too, 1779 marked a fundamental shift in thinking on economic matters. Or, perhaps, it forced him to a full realization of his affinities with the "modern" school of laissez-faire economics. Paine enthusiastically endorsed the Morris economic program of 1780. Never again would he support the regulation of prices. In 1793, during the French Revolution, he would warn Danton that the price controls demanded by the Parisian sans-culottes would be both ineffective and counter-productive since farmers would simply refuse to bring their goods to market.[60]

Paine had seen at first hand the failure of the old moral economy to regulate successfully prices whose ultimate determinants depended on national and even international economic conditions. But there was more here than a question of impracticality. Paine came to accept the self-regulating market—in labor as well as in goods—as an instrument of progress. In *The Rights of Man*, he would condemn laws limiting the wages of workingmen: "Why not leave them as free to make their own bargains, as the law-makers are to let their farms and houses? Personal labor is all the property they have."[61] Paine's experiences in 1779 not only propelled him into the economic world of Adam Smith, but led him to embrace the swift expansion of market relations which occured during the American Revolution. And they set the stage for his unusual alliance during the 1780s with his erstwhile antagonist, Robert Morris, and his defense of one of the most controversial institutions of Philadelphia's post-war economy, the Bank of Pennsylvania.

CHAPTER SIX

Paine and
the New Nation

The demise of the popular movement for price controls in 1780 inaugurated one of the most controversial and puzzling periods of Paine's career. During the 1770s, he had been associated with the "democratic party in Philadelphia" in the struggle for independence and the Pennsylvania Constitution. Now he found himself increasingly at odds with some of his erstwhile allies, while appearing to find his former political enemies congenial. Courted by men of wealth and political standing, he seemed closer in outlook to the merchant elite of Philadelphia. He entered into a close alliance with his former foe Robert Morris and employed his pen to defend Morris' plan for strengthening the continental government and his fiscal creation, the Bank of North America.

Many writers have pictured Paine as drifting toward conservatism in the 1780s. Yet Paine's activities did not represent a complete break with his previous political and economic outlook. He had long been a proponent of strong central government, had been a strong critic of state-issued paper money and had defended such new capitalist institutions as the Bank as essential props of American economic development. Paine had seen in 1779 that the tradition of "moral economy" was unable to regulate economic life effectively, an experience which only strengthened his faith—shared by his new allies—in unregulated market relations. Moreover, Paine's alliance with Morris did not represent a full break with his artisan constituency, a majority of whom joined with Philadelphia merchants in opposing a repetition of price controls and in supporting Morris' financial program of the 1780s. A large portion of the artisan community sided with Paine and Morris and against the agrarians who led the attack on the Bank of Pennsylvania. At the same time, the Bank War led Paine to rethink some of his assumptions about the nature of republican government and to develop in rudimentary form an interpretation of American politics which encompassed conflicts based on divergent economic interests.

I

At the beginning of 1780, despite his disillusionment with the price control movement, Paine was still firmly allied with Pennsylvania's Constitutionalist party. In October 1779, a week after the Fort Wilson "riot," Philadelphians had flocked to the polls to give an overwhelming victory to Constitutionalist candidates, ousting Robert Morris from the Assembly and electing Charles W. Peale and George Bryan to two of the city's seats. Despite the Constitutionalist leaders' condemnation of the Wilson affair, that incident had only reinforced the hostility of the bulk of the Philadelphia electorate toward wealthy merchants and Republicans like Morris. The new Assembly appointed Paine to the post of clerk and embarked on an ambitious reform program which included the gradual abolition of slavery, the confiscation of the estates of the Penn family and the reorganization of the College of Pennsylvania, a stronghold of conservative Whigs and Loyalists. A new Board of Trustees was appointed, including David Rittenhouse and such Constitutionalist party leaders as George Bryan and Joseph Reed. James Cannon was called back from Charleston, where he had moved in 1778, to assume a professorship, and in July 1780, at the first graduation ceremony of the reformed institution, Paine was awarded an honorary master's degree.[1]

In fact, however, men like Paine, Cannon and the other surviving Philadelphia radicals of 1776 exerted little influence among the Constitutionalists. By 1780, leadership of that party was firmly in the hands of a group of backcountry farmers, merchants, land speculators and up and coming small town capitalists. The Philadelphians George Bryan and Joseph Reed still exerted considerable influence in party circles, but the emerging leaders were rural Presbyterians like William Findley, John Smilie and Robert Whitehill. Constitutionalists still employed the egalitarian rhetoric which had permeated Pennsylvania politics in the 1770s, while the Republicans continued to argue for a bicameral legislature, a single governor and an increase in the property qualification for voting. One Constitutionalist broadside identified the Republicans with "wealth, influence, pride and grandeur," and many contemporaries believed that Pennsylvania parties were indeed divided between "the few and the many . . . aristocraticks and democraticks."[2]

Yet, as a party dominated by rural leaders, the Constitutionalists had little in common on many issues either with Paine or the bulk of Philadelphia's artisans. For one thing, they sometimes exhibited the traditional agrarian distrust of cities, proposing that Congress and the state Assembly be removed from Philadelphia. The rural Constitutionalists, moreover, were enthusiastic advocates of the issuance of large amounts of state paper money, which Paine and many urban artisans opposed. But the key issue, as far as the artisans were concerned, was protection against the influx of British manufactured goods. Philadelphia's mechanics had enjoyed a period of welcome prosperity between 1781 and 1783—for which many thanked the fiscal policies of Robert Morris. But following the Peace of Paris of 1783 the city was flooded with British manufactured goods, and the mid-eighties were punctuated by artisan appeals for protection. "Shall these industrious citizens," one mechanic asked, "who have so capitally contributed to the independence of this country, now be forgotten, and with their families become objects of the greatest distress, for want of employment in their respective trades?" (The artisans' conversion to the supremacy of the market in 1779 was thus not complete; what they demanded was the free market in one country.) But whether rural Constitutionalists or merchant-dominated Republicans were in control, the state legislature did virtually nothing to protect the artisans from the ruinous competition of British imports.

In fact, a distinct note of hostility underlay the artisan-Constitutionalist discourse, a hostility already apparent in the price control conflict of 1779, when many urbanites denounced farmers who refused to bring their goods to regulated markets. In 1785 one "Constitutionalist" reminded mechanics that farmers were the "pride and support of our land," and urged unemployed artisans to leave the city "for a more independent support in the country" as husbandmen. A "Tradesman" replied that the farmers coveted the "hard-earned estates" of the mechanics, and pledged that whatever the adversity, mechanics "will stay in defiance of thee and thy whole race . . . will stay to watch thy ugly cloven foot, thou Judas!"[3]

On certain issues, then, no love was lost between the rural Constitutionalists and urban artisans. Increasingly in the 1780s voices within the artisan community called on mechanics to abandon both parties and concentrate instead on electing men like themselves to office. "A Brother Mechanic" declared: "the contention between the two parties which divide the state is for power only." One artisan warned that the Constitutionalist party had "a different aim from the mechanics in general," and another

charged that party decisions, as in the 1760s, were made by a
secret junto to which "no mechanics or Germans" were admitted.
Artisans even charged that an election law enacted by the Consti-
tutionalist-controlled legislature in 1785 was "insidiously"
designed to exclude from voting "every man ... who is a
mechanic or manufacturer and happens to have no taxable property." In reply to what they considered the haughtiness of aristocrats and the indifference of farmers, mechanics reasserted the
dignity of the craftsman:[4]

> Pray was not St. Paul a tent maker? ...
> Pray who began the present opposition to Great
> Britain in Philadelphia? was it not the tradesmen?
> ... And pray was not Dr. Franklin, our Ambassador
> at the Court of France, a printer? aye, that he was
> and a journeyman printer too.

At the same time that the drive for protection reinforced a
consciousness of their own interests as a distinct segment of
society, and that they found they could not identify with either of
the two parties which dominated the state's politics, the artisans,
in the aftermath of 1779, pulled back from leadership of lower-
class direct action. As a result, lower-class politics in Philadelphia
reverted to its pre-revolutionary forms. In 1781, for example,
news of Cornwallis' surrender inspired "a set of people who have
no name" to break the windows of houses which were not illuminated in celebration—a throwback to long familiar crowd behavior.

This is not to suggest that popular political consciousness had
not been altered by the Revolution. A foreign visitor in Philadelphia in 1783 was struck by the absence of deferential attitudes in
the city: "People think, act, and speak here as it prompts them;
the poorest day-laborer on the bank of the Delaware holds it his
right to advance his opinion, in religious as well as political
matters, with as much freedom as the gentleman." But what
remained of the popular radicalism of the 1770s was a set of

stubbornly democratic and egalitarian attitudes and a hostility to Tories and the rich, which lacked both articulate leadership and organized political expression.[5]

This political situation is essential for understanding Paine's own career in the 1780s. In the previous decade, along with the other Philadelphia radicals, he had helped provide ideological leadership to a mass movement for independence and republicanism which united the entire lower-class world of Philadelphia and which found political expression in the constitution of 1776 and the party which grew up to defend it. But in the 1780s the old radical group was no longer an active force in politics, the artisans were alienated from both political parties, and those below them in the social scale reverted to "pre-political" crowd action to express their resentments and grievances. It should not be surprising that in the early 1780s, Paine withdrew altogether from Pennsylvania politics. But he was still firmly committed to the support of the war effort. As his attention returned from state to national affairs, it was perhaps inevitable that he drew closer to men like Robert Morris, who possessed the continental breadth of vision, the capital and the organizational ability which the army and Congress so sorely needed.

Paine's first direct involvement with Morris and his merchant associates came in May of 1780. As clerk of the Assembly, it was Paine's unhappy task to read to a closed-door legislative session a letter from General Washington describing the distress of the army and the bleak military situation in the wake of the fall of Charleston to the British. The letter led one legislator to cry out that the American cause was lost, but Paine immediately helped to organize a voluntary subscription campaign among Philadelphia merchants to raise funds for the badly depleted congressional treasury, adding his own salary to the collection. His aim was to create a fund for the supply of the army, and to arouse the broadest possible support for the war effort—an alliance of "property and popularity."[6]

Paine's shift from state to national concerns was further illustrated toward the end of 1780, when he published the pamphlet
Public Good, an argument against the western land claims of
Virginia which insisted that such lands belonged collectively to all
the states, through the continental government. His friends the
Lees of Virginia bitterly attacked Paine's work, but Virginia soon
ceded her claims to the Northwest Territory to Congress. Paine
also shifted his efforts to the nation's needs abroad. Early in 1781,
he accompanied Colonel John Laurens on a trip to France to
obtain further aid from the French government. He spent most
of 1781 on this mission, assisting Laurens in drafting numerous
progress reports to be sent back to Congress, but apparently
playing no part in the delicate negotiations conducted by Laurens
and Franklin, now American ambassador at Paris, which succeeded in obtaining a large shipment of arms, clothing and
money from the French.[7]

Paine returned to America toward the end of 1781, without any
immediate means of support or direct connection with Pennsylvania or national politics, except, of course, for his continuing commitment to the war effort. In February 1782, he entered
into a secret agreement with Superintendent of Finance Robert
Morris, Secretary of State Robert R. Livingston and Commander
in Chief George Washington to compose public letters and pamphlets "in support of the measures of Congress and their ministers," and "to prepare the minds of the people for such restraints
and such taxes and imposts" as were "absolutely necessary for
their own welfare." Four years earlier, in his letters on the Pennsylvania Constitution, Paine had denounced "the wretch" who
wrote "on any subject for bread, or in any service for pay," but
he now accepted the salary of eight hundred dollars per year
paid from a secret fund under Morris' control as Superintendent of Finance. During 1782 Paine often checked his writings
with Morris.[8]

The liaison of Paine and Morris was perhaps less unlikely than it appeared, although the wealthy merchant and Paine were in some ways strange bedfellows. Morris was an elitist in politics—his private correspondence reveals only contempt for the common people. The movement to strengthen the continental government which he spearheaded between 1781 and 1783 was motivated in part by the belief that stronger central government was needed to "restrain the democratic spirit" in the states. Paine would never share such attitudes, but on certain basic questions he had more in common with Morris than with the agrarian opponents of strong central government in Pennsylvania and other states. The politics of the agrarians were locally oriented; their leaders were gener- ally state politicians who had seen little or no service in Congress or the continental army during the war. Paine was a recent emigrant from England without deep local roots and he had devoted much of his time to promoting the national war effort during the years since 1776. As secretary to General Roberdeau and confidant of General Washington, as propagandist for the war effort in the *Crisis* papers, and as aide to a diplomat abroad in 1781, Paine's career had more in common with that of cosmopoli- tans like Morris than with agrarian localists.

Morris, moreover, looked forward to an American empire of "power, consequence and grandeur"—and such a vision of the future had been implicit in *Common Sense.*[9] Paine had never seen any contradiction between capitalist business enterprise and "vir- tue"; indeed, ever since *Common Sense* he had viewed commerce and a national debt as sources of national strength (again reveal- ing his differences with the agrarian Country party mentality, which viewed the debt as a potential source of corruption and loss of virtue). And Paine agreed with Morris on the necessity of a stable currency and on the evils of paper money, especially after witnessing the failure of price controls in 1779. In 1780 and 1781, before his financial arrangement with Morris, Paine had endorsed the new policies of "fiscal responsibility." Thus, when Paine joined in supporting the economic and nationalist policies of the Morris group in the 1780s he was neither being false to his principles in exchange for pay, nor abandoning his belief in egalitarianism and wide popular participation in government in favor of Morris' elitism. Paine, like so many of the Philadelphia artisans, combined a political outlook of intense egalitarianism with a devotion to free enterprise, commercial expansion and national economic development.

Paine's first major effort for the Morris group in 1782 and 1783 was a series of public letters on the 5 per cent tariff on imported goods which Congress had adopted as a means of providing a permanent revenue for the continental government. Cornwallis' surrender at Yorktown in October 1781 had for all practical purposes ended the War for Independence, but both Paine and Morris were determined that national government not expire with the war effort. Paine believed, as did Morris, that the nation's economic difficulties were "ascribable to the loose and almost disjointed condition of the Union," and he hoped the tariff would be the first step toward strengthening the federal government. When the state of Rhode Island rejected the measure, Paine issued a series of letters forcefully arguing the need for stronger central government. The union of the states, he declared, was "our Magna Carta—our anchor in the world of empires. . . . It is on our undivided sovereignty, that our greatness and safety, and the security of our foreign commerce, rest." He even warned opponents of the congressional measure that their opposition "serves only to unhinge the public mind, even in their own State, from every obligation of civil and moral society, and from all the necessary duties of good government; and to promote a profligacy, that may in time think all property common." This exaggerated language was the closest Paine would come to the Morris group's belief in a stronger central government as a barrier to dangerous radical tendencies in the states; it was an appeal specifically directed to the Rhode Island merchants who led that state's opposition to the congressional tariff.[10]

With Rhode Island's veto of the tariff and the end of the Revolutionary War, much of the steam went out of the nationalist movement of the early 1780s. Paine continued to pen appeals for a stronger central government in his final *Crisis* papers, published in April and December 1783, but his secret salary had been discontinued when Morris fell from his post as director of congressional finances early in 1783. Paine more or less withdrew from political concerns. He spent several months each year in the mid-1780s with his friends Colonel and Mrs. Kirkbridge who owned a farm in Bordentown, New Jersey. He wrote little in 1784 and 1785, spending much of his time in a campaign to receive financial remuneration from Congress and the state legislatures for his services during the Revolution (he had devoted the profits of his pamphlets, from *Common Sense* onward, to the war effort). Washington and Jefferson urged his case in Virginia, but the legislature refused to act, probably because of Paine's argument against the state's land claims in *Public Good*. But New York granted him the confiscated estate of a New Rochelle loyalist and in 1785 Congress voted him the sum of three thousand dollars, enough to enable him to avoid want for the next twenty years of his life.[11]

II

Paine did not re-enter the political arena until the end of 1785. The issue was the Bank of North America, the nation's first bank, established late in 1781 by Robert Morris and his associates as part of a policy of cementing relations between the business community and the federal government. A private, profit-making enterprise, it was chartered by both Congress and the Pennsylvania legislature. At a time when the financial resources of Congress and the states were all but exhausted and paper money was still almost without value, Morris hoped the Bank would become a "pillar of American credit" and would create a stable, widely accepted, noninflationary currency. By the fall of 1782, the Bank appeared to be eminently successful in both its public and private aims: its notes circulated at par with gold and silver in Philadelphia, and its stockholders realized sizeable profits.

Controlled by a close-knit group of Morris' business associates and Republican party politicians—the first president, Thomas Willing, had been Morris' partner in the 1770s—the Bank speeded up the economic transformation already underway in revolutionary Philadelphia. Its insistence on punctuality in the payment of debts profoundly affected the business practices of the city's merchants and its issuance of short-term loans facilitated the expansion of commerce. But the Bank quickly aroused charges of favoritism in making loans and of seeking to monopolize the business of banking in Philadelphia. One of its purposes was to supply loans to Philadelphia merchants, whose credit had previously emanated from England, but its loan policy tended to be highly conservative, favoring friends and relatives of the directors and merchants with long-established reputations for stability and business sense, rather than up and coming entrepreneurs.

In 1784 a group of Quaker merchants and Philadelphia businessmen attempted to form a new, competitive bank, a venture strongly opposed by Morris. The new group represented no particular political interest; it was a coalition whose members had in common the desire for easier credit, hostility to Morris and the fact that they were excluded from stockholding in the Bank of North America. In the end, Morris' Bank simply expanded its stock and took the new group under its umbrella. The printer William Bradford remarked, "You might have seen the violent Whig, the bitter tory and the moderate man laying their heads together. . . . The Constitutionalist and Republican were arm in arm; and the Quaker and Presbyterian forgot their religious antipathies in this coalition of interests."[12]

The Bank weathered this first challenge, but it soon faced a

more serious one when the rural Constitutionalists who dominated the state Assembly moved to undermine Morris' financial
program. The legislature authorized a new issue of state paper
money and assumed the federal debts owed to citizens of Pennsylvania—a direct challenge to the nationalists' plan of using the
federal debt as a means of strengthening the central government.
And when the Bank refused to accept the new state paper money
at par, the legislature in September 1785 repealed the Bank's
charter.[13]

The Bank was a major subject of debate in Pennsylvania for
most of 1785 and 1786. To its foes it was a citadel of the Republican
party, an instrument of special privilege and a closed corporation
established under authority of the state, which by its very nature
threatened the republican ideal of equality. In the legislature, the
attack on the Bank was led by the triumvirate of western Constitutionalist leaders, William Findley, John Smilie and Robert Whitehill. The Bank, Findley declared, was "inconsistent with our
laws—our habits—our manners." The essence of republicanism
was equality "of wealth and power," while "enormous wealth,
possessed by individuals," always posed a "danger in free states."
The sole purpose of the Bank charter, Findley added, was to "give
a special law to enable monied men to increase their gain," since
"none but men of wealth," possessed "money to spare to be
bankers." Whitehill echoed the charge that the Bank and the state
as a whole had "opposite interests," and the report of the legislative committee which recommended repeal of the charter insisted
that "the accumulation of enormous wealth in the hands of a
society who claim perpetual duration" was totally inconsistent
with "the public safety."[14]

The arguments of the anti-Bank legislators anticipated strikingly the rhetoric employed against the Bank of the United States
during the Bank War of Jackson's presidency fifty years later.
And in both cases, there was perhaps less social radicalism present
than met the eye. Robert Morris, back in the Assembly as a

representative from Philadelphia, ingenuously observed that if the anti-Bank forces were so concerned with equality, they ought to bring forward "an agrarian law for making an equal division of property." This was unlikely, Morris went on: "each of them, I imagine, possess more now than would fall to his share on such a division." Findley and Smilie, indeed, explicitly rejected the notion that their ideal of equality justified the division of existing property. As Smilie put it, he had no desire to "foment a spirit of hatred against the rich, to cramp the operations of industry by prescribing limits to the property of the citizens of the state . . . [or] to raise a visionary fabric of republican equality on foundations laid in rapine and injustice."[15]

As during the Bank War of Jackson's time, the enemies of the Bank of North America comprised a coalition of rather diverse economic and social groups. They ranged from those who opposed all banks and corporate charters on principle—men in the Country party tradition who viewed such institutions as agents of "corruption" and moral decay—to business competitors of Morris, usurers who resented the low interest rates established by the Bank, speculators in public securities who supported the state's assumption of continental debts and artisans who believed themselves excluded from credit by Morris' Bank and hoped its destruction would lead to the creation of several new banks which could make credit more readily available. As in the 1830s, this coalition found it much easier to agree on the negative policy of eliminating the Bank, than on a positive fiscal program to replace it.[16]

For the agrarian Constitutionalists the alternative to the Bank was a reversion to the colonial practice of creating a state agency to issue paper money and make loans at low interest rates to farmers, with land as security. Such a "land bank" would certainly fit better with republican ideas of equality than a private corporation, but it was hard to see how such an institution would aid artisans who charged that "a few wealthy merchants and those of good credit" were the only ones able to obtain loans from the Bank. Artisans, who generally owned no land, would not qualify for loans from a state land bank.

The Philadelphia artisan community, in fact, was divided on the Bank issue. Many mechanics responded to the Constitutionalists' anti-aristocratic appeal and hoped the destruction of the Bank would result in easier credit, but many others feared it would unleash a flood of paper money and a new round of inflation. Access to capital was a critical issue for artisans in the 1780s, especially the entrepreneurs or aspiring entrepreneurs among them. The former artisan Benjamin Franklin, as we have seen, provided in his will for a loan fund to enable "young married artificers" who had served an apprenticeship to set up shop on their own. What most artisans wanted was access to capital; they opposed not banking itself, but the Bank of North America's monopoly on credit. When the legislature which repealed the Bank charter made no provision for the artisans' economic needs—easier credit and protection from British competition—the Philadelphia artisans swung to electoral support of the Republicans. And their hostility to the Constitutionalists was enhanced by the slowdown in Philadelphia's trade which followed the repeal of the Bank charter.[17]

If artisans were divided, the mercantile and financial community of Philadelphia rallied to the Bank's defense. Some supporters of the Bank forthrightly asserted that inequalities of property were inevitable and proper, even in a republic, and that property deserved special protection from the legislature. "Different degrees of industry and economy (those great republican virtues)," according to one writer—calling himself, appropriately, "Candid"—would "ever create inequality of property, especially in a commercial country." Others, taking perhaps a less impolitic approach, pictured the Bank as an agent of economic equality. "The Bank, instead of creating monopolies, is the greatest leveller that can be devised," one writer argued. "It places the rich and the poor upon equal ground. All that is wanting is industry and a fair character." The agrarians' pet measure, paper money, by contrast, was pictured as the agent of usury, speculation, inflation and moral decline, a preparation "for aristocracy and slavery." Moreover, according to James Wilson, who wrote one of the leading pamphlet defenses of the Bank, repeal of the charter would set a precedent for the repeal of "every other legislative charter in Pennsylvania."[18]

Paine was not particularly anxious to enter the Bank controversy. For one thing, the same legislature which repealed the Bank's charter appropriated five hundred pounds in remuneration for his services during the Revolution. (It is not clear whether Paine ever received the money. In 1786 he complained that nothing had been done to put the appropriation into effect.) Nor was Paine anxious to differ publicly with his friends in the Constitutionalist party, with whom he had often sided in past political conflicts.[19] But in December 1785 he began a series of newspaper letters, added a widely circulated pamphlet, *Dissertation on Government; the Affair of the Bank; and Paper Money,* in February 1786, and continued to press the issue in the Philadelphia newspapers toward the end of that year.

In some respects, Paine in his writings on the Bank simply restated long-established beliefs. His hostility to government-issued paper money had never been expressed more strongly, but it was hardly new. "Paper money, Paper money, and Paper money is now, in several of the states, both the bubble and the iniquity of the day," he declared. ("The bubble" was a phrase with strong historical resonances among his readers, reminding them of the famous South Sea Bubble of 1720: the British government had actively promoted shares in the South Sea trading company, leading to a precipitous rise and then collapse in the value of the stocks, and eventually to the imprisonment of the Chancellor of the Exchequer for fraud.) Paine sent to the press an article by a Rhode Island merchant protesting that state's legislation making it illegal to refuse to accept paper money on the same basis as gold. This, Paine said, was "one of the most vile and arbitrary acts" in any of the states, and a threat to both "liberty and property."

Paine did not believe that the economy could function without paper; but he distinguished sharply between paper money issued by private individuals and corporations like the Bank, which could be accepted or rejected by individuals as they saw fit, and state paper money which, Paine seemed to assume, was automatically legal tender. As he explained:

> The only proper use for paper, in the room of money, is to write promissory notes and obligations of payment in specie. . . . Paper, circulating in this manner, and for this purpose, continually points to the place and person where, and of whom, the money is to be had, and at last finds its home; and, as it were, unlocks its master's chest and pays the bearer. But when an assembly undertakes to issue paper *as* money, the whole system of safety and certainty is overturned, and property set afloat.

Paper, in other words, was legitimate as a convenient representation of gold and silver, but not as a substitute for them. Here again we encounter Paine's distinction between society and government, natural law and human contrivance. "Gold and silver are the emissions of nature; paper is the emission of art," he declared—one was therefore legitimate, the other artificial and coercive. Paine even said that any legislator who proposed a law for legal tender paper money should be sentenced to death. (This, the historian Bray Hammond observes, was "going pretty far."[20])

The Bank, to Paine, was a bulwark against state-issued paper money and, therefore, a boon to the prosperity of the entire community, "one of the best institutions that could be devised to promote the commerce and agriculture of the country." Paine's argument closely paralleled the views of Adam Smith, whose observations on banking from *The Wealth of Nations* were now widely circulated in Philadelphia, having been quoted by James Wilson in his pamphlet defending the Bank of North America. Private banks, Smith argued, invigorated industry and commerce by mobilizing capital for productive enterprises. Like Paine, Smith also approved of paper bank notes as a convenience, but insisted they must be based "upon the solid ground of gold and silver," and he condemned legal tender paper money as a "violent injustice."[21]

The Bank was to play an essential role in Paine's vision of an American republican empire. But the "great improvements and undertakings" which national development required and which the Bank could promote—internal improvements, roads and bridges (Paine himself was in the process of designing an iron bridge)—could not be undertaken in the kind of atmosphere produced by the repeal of the Bank charter. "The faith of government," he complained, "cannot be relied on" if "an act . . . may be made by one assembly and broken by another."

In a new departure in his thinking, Paine distinguished between laws and legislative contracts—the first could be repealed at any time, the latter had to be respected by succeeding legislatures. In a sense, Paine anticipated the later contract theory expounded by John Marshall, which held that the state stood as a "private citizen" in a contract like the Bank charter. But Paine also declared that no act of a legislature could exist "forever." In this respect, the Bank charter was faulty. Since no generation could rightfully bind a future one, all acts of legislation and contract should automatically expire every thirty years. This argument anticipated Paine's later insistence against Edmund Burke that past generations had no legitimate voice in government, that the "rights of the living" should be paramount. Thus, Louis Hartz is right in observing that "Paine on popular sovereignty did not get along easily with Paine on charter contracts." For, as a contemporary opponent of the Bank asked, "where is the benefit of annual election if the wisdom of one assembly may not be extended to correct the errors of a former?" And twenty years later, in one of his last published works, Paine would retreat from his postion regarding the Bank and would argue that all contracts and charters should be proposed in one legislature but voted on in another, to prevent the "very intention, essence and principle of annual election" from being destroyed.[22]

Paine also objected to the idea that the Bank of North America constituted some kind of aristocracy. If the Bank were destroyed, "a few monied men"—the only ones with personal wealth sufficient to finance commercial enterprises—would monopolize the commerce of the state. Credit fueled the economy; by providing credit at nonusurous rates, the Bank enabled aspiring entrepreneurs to challenge the wealthy merchants at the top of Philadelphia's economy. Far from being an engine of privilege, the Bank, for Paine, was an egalitarian institution. It served the needs of the entire economy, and especially small producers and traders, better than the informal pre-war arrangements in which access to capital depended solely on individual wealth and personal connections.

Doubtless Paine's writings on the Bank revealed a certain naiveté concerning the economic interests involved in the Bank War. But, of course, Paine still viewed commerce and economic enterprise as serving the public good, as did the Bank, which stimulated economic activity and established the "credit and confidence among individuals, which for many years was lost, and without which agriculture, commerce, and every species of business, must decline and languish." Significantly, however, Paine added that those who had the most to lose from repeal of the Bank charter were the "manufacturers and mechanics," because these were the groups "against whose immediate interest paper money operates the strongest." Not only did it reduce their real income and render the value of their property insecure, but paper money banished "all the hard money which the exports of the country brought in," sending it abroad "to purchase foreign manufactures and trinkets." Banning paper money would therefore be "the most effectual encouragement" to American manufactures.[23]

In one important respect the ideas expressed in the Bank controversy differed markedly from Paine's previous writings. Paine was shocked by the intensity of party competition in Pennsylvania in the 1780s. As early as 1784 he had condemned "the disagreeable party condition" of the state, blaming "the hotheaded whigs" who, he said, were attempting to "monopolize the government." In his Bank writings he repeated his displeasure at the political situation: a state "rent into factions," legislation enacted under the influence of "party spirit and rancorous prejudice." Laws "founded in party"—like the repeal of the Bank charter—were quite different from republican legislation motivated only by the common good.[24]

This disillusionment led Paine to reconsider his advocacy of a unicameral legislature. "My idea of a single legislature," he explained, "was always founded on a hope, that whatever personal parties there might be in a state, they would all unite and agree in the general principles of good government . . . and that the general good, or the good of the whole, would be the governing principle of the legislature." But experience had shown that this classic vision of a republican utopia had been overwhelmed by party feeling. Paine was forced to conclude that a single house, when under the control of a single party, "is capable of being made a compleat aristocracy for the time it exists." For a unicameral legislature to function properly, "it was absolutely necessary that the prejudices of party should have no operation within the walls of government." But the repeal of the Bank charter showed that Pennsylvanians were motivated by party prejudice, and therefore subject to "passion of arbitrary principles and unconstitutional conduct."

Without quite saying so, Paine seemed to be moving toward the conservative view that a two-house legislature was the only check on the passions and rash proceedings of the people, an argument which circulated widely in the mid-1780s among the merchants and businessmen with whom Paine allied to support the Bank. This was the closet Paine would come in his entire career to the political, as opposed to the economic, outlook of a John Adams or Robert Morris. And in the 1790s he would revert back to the more familiar position of optimistic unicameralism, although coupling it in *The Rights of Man* with a proposal that the single house be divided into two parts, with each debating legislation in turn but eventually voting together, to prevent over-hasty action.[25]

The party conflict of the 1780s also led Paine to rethink his vision of a republican America free from the conflict of class interests. For the first time, Paine moved toward an analysis of political behavior in economic terms, announcing the principle that "a man's ideas are generally produced in him by his present situation and condition." He attributed opposition to the Bank to agrarians whose circumstances limited their views and who had no material interest in the welfare of Pennsylvania. The backwoods farmers who formed the heart of the Constitutionalist party were men isolated from the marketplace. "From their remote situation [they] feel themselves very little, if at all, interested in the prosperity of the more settled and improved areas of the state." They were vastly different from the commercial farmer:

> Their ideas of government, agriculture, and commerce are drawn from and limited to their own frontier habitations. . . . A settler is not yet a farmer . . . In the stage of a settler, his thoughts are engrossed and taken up on making a settlement. If he can raise produce enough for the support of his family, it is the utmost of his present hopes. He has none to bring to market, or to sell, and therefore commerce appears nothing to him; and he cries out, that a Bank is of no use.

Moreover, Paine observed, what exports did emanate from the back-country areas were carried down the Susquehanna River to Baltimore, rather than to Philadelphia and its surrounding counties.[26]

Whatever the virtues of Paine's view as historical analysis, it marked a departure in Paine's thinking. Paine never did accept the political science of Madison—that politics should strive for a balance of selfish interests rather than searching consciously for a unitary public good. He was too repelled by social conflict to favor its institutionalization in government. But in their own way, the Bank writings provided a preview of the greater consciousness of social class which Paine would reveal in his great pamphlets in England and France in the 1790s.

Paine's defense of the Bank, and the attitude he expressed toward the rural Constitutionalists, cost him whatever popularity he still retained in that party. "I cannot conceive in the wide context of creation," declared John Smilie, "a being more deserving of our abhorrence and contempt, than a writer who, having formerly vindicated the principles of freedom, abandons them to abet the cause of a faction, and . . . prostitutes his pen to the ruin of his country." (Smilie appears to have been wrong in suggesting that Paine was in the pay of the Bank, although Paine did keep his cash on deposit there.) But whatever his lack of popularity with the farmers, Paine still retained his following among the artisans of Philadelphia who by and large were abandoning the Constitutionalists. At the height of the Bank controversy, in January 1786, "a numerous company of printers" assembled at the Bunch of Grapes tavern to celebrate the eighty-first birthday of Benjamin Franklin. Their toasts included praise of the printers' craft, freedom of the press, the encouragement of literature, George Washington—and Thomas Paine.[27]

III

The pro-Bank Republican party swept the 1786 elections, including Philadelphia, and the Bank was rechartered the following spring. Paine spent most of 1786 back in Bordentown working on a series of inventions, from a smokeless candle to his design for an iron bridge. With the aid of Franklin, he exhibited his bridge model in the State House yard in Philadelphia in January 1787. In March and April 1787, Paine attended meetings of the newly created Society for Political Inquiries. Dedicated to freeing America from European manners and modes of thought, and to "the advancement of the science of Government and the promotion of human happiness," the Society met weekly in Franklin's library. Its members were a collection of business and political leaders of Philadelphia, including Robert Morris, William Bradford, Jr., and Benjamin Rush. Paine's last "political" act in America was the presentation of a paper to the Society in April, "On the Incorporating of Towns." A few days later, he sailed from New York for Europe, hoping to promote his iron bridge, and planning to return within a year. He believed his "political career" had "closed" and planned to devote himself henceforth to "the quiet field of science."[28] No one, least of all Paine himself, could foresee the turbulent career which lay ahead of him in the 1790s.

Paine had arrived in America an all but penniless unknown; he left with an international reputation and as a member of a transatlantic group of cosmopolitan intellectuals, reformers and scientists. It was typical of his new associations that in 1788 in Paris he followed the debates on the federal Constitution with Jefferson and Lafayette in Paris. It was not surprising that Paine favored the new document. Paine had long been an advocate of stronger continental government. As early as 1776, in *Common Sense,* he had observed, "the continental belt is too loosely buckled," and in 1780, in *Public Good,* he had called for the election of "a Continental convention for the purpose of forming a Continental constitution, defining and describing the powers and authority of Congress." Paine later claimed that he disapproved of several features of the Constitution drafted in 1787: he still preferred a plural executive and he objected to the long duration of the Senate. Quite possibly he also shared Jefferson's concern over the failure of the Constitutional Convention to include a bill of rights in the new frame of government. But Paine, like Jefferson, was a Federalist in 1787, because he was convinced of "the absolute necessity of establishing some Federal authority."[29]

The Constitution of 1787 has sometimes been viewed as a counter-revolution, a betrayal of the ideals of 1776. But Paine did not see it that way. It is true that the leading proponents of the movement for strengthening the federal government were elitists who feared democracy in the states and looked to a strong central government dominated by the "natural aristocrats" of America, to secure republican government from popular excesses.[30] But this was not the only group which supported the Constitution. "To the artisans," one student of the period concludes, "the campaign for the Constitution seemed a direct continuation of the independence struggle." In Boston, New York, Philadelphia, Baltimore and Charleston, the mid-1780s was a period of economic hardship, as British goods flooded the market, wages plummeted and the important shipbuilding industry stagnated. In Philadelphia, only thirteen ships were built in 1786, compared with three times that many in 1784, and "the carpenters, blacksmiths, joiners, and the numerous train of artificers dependent on the various branches of ship-building" suffered grievously. As George Bryan, one of Pennsylvania's leading anti-Federalists, observed, "the situation of our commerce" accounted for the almost unanimous support in Philadelphia for the Constitution.[31]

After the experience of the 1780s, the city's artisans were convinced that Pennsylvania by itself could not "encourage our infant manufactures" or "give sustenance to our starving mechanics." "As times are bad, and I am out of work," a "Bricklayer" declared, "I have more leisure than I used to have to read newspapers;" he concluded, using the language of his craft, that the Constitution was "a noble mansion for the residence of American liberty." Another writer observed that, far from being an aristocratic document, the Constitution truly reflected the conditions of life of the mass of Philadelphians: "We common people

are more properly citizens of *America* than of any *particular state.*
Very many of our sort die in different parts from where they
were born. . . . Taxes on imported goods, which the Congress will
lay, can distress none but the rich." It was what Bryan called the
"golden phantom" of prosperity which swung the artisans, laborers and sailors of Philadelphia behind the movement for a government which:[32]

> . . . will have energy and power to regulate your trade and com-
> merce, to enforce the execution of your imposts, duties, and cus-
> toms. Instead of the trade of this country being carried on in foreign
> bottoms, our ports will be crowded with our own ships, and we shall
> become the carriers of Europe. Heavy duties will be laid on all
> foreign manufactures which can be manufactured in this country.
> . . . The manufactories of our country will flourish—our mechanics
> will lift up their heads and rise to opulence and wealth.

The great Philadelphia procession of July 4, 1788, celebrating the ratification of the Constitution, depicted graphically
the attitudes of the artisan and lower class communities of Philadelphia. Every trade in the city, from ship carpenters to shoemakers, from coachmakers to weavers, from instrument makers
to Paine's old craft of staymaking, took part in this extraordinary
procession, each trade marching in its respective craft association,
with elaborate floats, flags and mottoes. From one point of view,
the procession was "a curious anomaly"—a republican Constitution celebrated by men assembled according to the guild-like divisions of medieval society. The various mottoes and floats expressed the artisans' hopes for the new government. "May
commerce flourish and industry be rewarded," declared the banner of the mariners and shipbuilders; "May the federal government revive our trade," announced the bakers; "May industry ever
be encouraged," said the porters; and, more directly, "Home-
brewed is best" was the motto of the brewers. As the procession
passed through the city, a press was drawn along the street and a

song, reputedly composed by Franklin, was distributed, offering an insight into artisans' pride in craft and skill and optimism for the future at the close of the Revolutionary era:[33]

> Ye merry Mechanics, come join in my song,
> And let the brisk chorus go bounding along;
> Though some may be poor, and some rich there may be,
> Yet all are contented, and happy, and free.
>
> Ye Tailors! of ancient and noble renown,
> Who clothe all the people in country or town,
> Remember that Adam, your father and head,
> The lord of the world, was a tailor by trade . . .
>
> And Carders, and Spinners, and Weavers attend,
> And take the advice of Poor Richard, your friend;
> Stick close to your looms, your wheels, and your card,
> And you never need fear of the times being hard . . .
>
> Ye Shipbuilders! Riggers! and Makers of Sails!
> Already the new constitution prevails!
> And soon you shall see o'er the proud swelling tide,
> The Ships of Columbia triumphantly ride.

For one day, according to Benjamin Rush, "rank . . . forgot all its claims," as 17,000 merchants and apprentices, lawyers and sailors, celebrated the Constitution. (Rush exaggerated slightly, since some trades marched with master craftsmen visibly separated from journeymen and apprentices.) Rush and other observers were particularly impressed by the great float with carding and spinning machines for the manufacture of cotton, and the banner, "May the Union Government Protect the Manufactures of America," sponsored by the Society for the Promotion of Manufactures. This display, Rush believed, was an emblem of "the future wealth and independence of our country." Only four months earlier, the manufacturing society had obtained these carding and spinning machines, exulting that henceforth, "the work of *fifty persons* can be done by a man, a boy and a machine."

Order of Procession,

In honor of the establishment of the CONSTITUTION of the United States.

To parade precisely at Eight o'Clock in the Morning, of FRIDAY, the 4th of JULY, 1788, proceeding along *Third-street* to *Callowhill-street*; thence to *Fourth-street*; down *Fourth-street* to *Market-street*; thence to the Grounds in Front of *Bush-hill*.

Philadelphia: Printed by HALL and SELLERS.

By Order of the Committee of Arrangement,

Francis Hopkinson, Chairman.

Virtually every craft in the city of Philadelphia participated in the procession celebrating the ratification of the federal Constitution. *Historical Society of Pennsylvania*

Yet like Paine and Rush, the parading artisans saw no conflict between the new technology and their own interests. In the July 4 procession, independent hand-loom weavers marched side-by-side with spinners and weavers employed at the new machinery. The time still lay in the future when technological progress would seem a menace, rather than the harbinger of a better life.[34]

Had Paine been present he, like these artisans, would have seen no contradiction between support for the Constitution and a continuing belief in egalitarian politics. In 1788 the hallmarks of his political outlook were basically the same as when he had outlined them in *Common Sense*: republicanism, political egalitarianism, support for a strong central government, the encouragement of commerce and economic expansion. In 1776, these strands of thought had seemed fully compatible; at other times, one had appeared to dominate at the expense of others. But always, Paine had endeavored to unite the entire nation in the struggle to achieve independence and to lay the foundation of a republican empire in America. He had done more than his share to see these goals achieved; in the 1790s, he would help bring the ideals of the American Revolution to Europe.

CHAPTER SEVEN

Epilogue:
England, France, and
America

Paine was fifty years old when he returned to Europe in 1787. Ahead lay two decades that began with exhilarating success as a pamphleteer of revolution, followed by disappointment and ultimately despair. In literary merit and political impact, Paine's greatest pamphlets of the 1790s—*The Rights of Man* and *The Age of Reason*—equaled *Common Sense.* Paine's writings helped to inspire an upsurge of popular radicalism in England and led to his being chosen to sit in the National Convention of revolutionary France. But instead of crowning his career as an international revolutionary, Paine's sojourn in France deteriorated into confusion, isolation and, finally, a year in prison during the Reign of Terror. After being released at the end of 1794, he spent eight more unhappy years in France and finally returned to America in 1802 only to find himself first vilified and then ignored.

It seems likely that a certain mystery will always surround these final two decades of Paine's life. But, as in the case of his participation in the American Revolution, Paine's experiences can best be understood through the relationship of his ideas to his role as a radical intellectual and to his popular constituency. As a revolutionary pamphleteer, Paine was at his best at the very moment of overthrow, when principles of government were called into question and new classes emerged into political life. But Paine was temperamentally and intellectually unsuited for the day-to-day affairs of government, either in time of peace or when the exigencies of a revolutionary situation seemed to require a temporary departure from the abstract principles Paine had enunciated so well. In England, the newly politicized artisan and lower classes made *The Rights of Man* the most popular political pamphlet in English history. In France, however, Paine was out of place as a member of the Convention and, limited by his ignorance of French and his close personal and ideological ties to a circle of Girondin admirers of America, he could not develop the mass constituency he enjoyed in America and Britain. When he returned to America, Paine had relatively little to say about the issues of a political system which seemingly had settled its fundamental principles. In addition, his religious writings of the 1790s had narrowed his personal following to a small band of deists. When Paine died in 1809, Americans almost totally ignored the passing of one of the most celebrated figures of the Age of Revolution.

I

When Paine arrived in England in 1787, reform politics had been moribund for half a decade. The early 1780s had witnessed an alliance of middle-class London radicals demanding an extension of the suffrage, with Rev. Christopher Wyvill's Yorkshire Association agitating for an increase in the Parliamentary representation of the rural "independent gentry." The most extreme of these reformers was Major John Cartwright who, as early as 1776, had advocated universal manhood suffrage, annual elections, equal electoral districts and the payment of members of Parliament. Cartwright was a leading spirit in the Society for Constitutional Information, created in 1780 to distribute reform pamphlets. At their annual dinners, the members of the SCI toasted "The Majesty of the People," but far more members had an "esquire" after their names than a "Mr." before, and the annual fee of one guinea was hardly meant to encourage mass participation.

From 1787 to 1790, Paine devoted far more energy to promoting his design for an iron bridge than to political issues. He shuttled back and forth between London and Paris in 1787 and 1788, seeking endorsements from scientific societies and asking financial support from public officials, and he spent a good deal of time in Yorkshire personally supervising the construction of a model of the bridge. But Paine was not the sort of man to abandon completely his political interests. He had been made an honorary member of the Society for Constitutional Information in 1787 and by 1790 was associating with reformers like John Cartwright, John Horne Tooke and Thomas Hollis of the SCI, the Whig party leader Charles James Fox and the early advocate of women's rights Mary Wollstonecraft. Such persons had supported the Americans in their struggle for independence and viewed Paine as something of a celebrity because of his participation in the American Revolution. And they welcomed with enthusiasm the developing revolution in France.[1]

It was the outbreak of the French Revolution in 1789 which transformed the political situation in England, reinvigorating the SCI and kindred groups and very quickly creating a schism in English life. In 1790 Edmund Burke published *Reflections on the Revolution in France,* a brilliant pamphlet not only attacking the developments in France and extolling the English political system, but dissecting the entire political philosophy on which the rallying cries of equality, revolution and the rights of man were founded. Burke viewed society as a complex amalgam of institutions and

traditions, which could be neither quickly created nor easily transformed. The accumulated wisdom of the past, he maintained, was
a far better guide to political behavior than abstract "prattling
about the rights of men," which had the dangerous tendency to
overthrow long-established institutions and to upset the "principles of natural subordination" which stable government required
of "the body of the people."[2]

Prior to 1790, Burke had been known as a reformer—an
advocate of the American cause in the 1770s and of relieving the
political disabilities of Catholics and Dissenters. He and Paine
became acquaintances of "some intimacy" in 1788 and 1789. But
Paine and his reforming associates were as enthusiastic about the
French Revolution as Burke was alarmed by it. It is not surprising
that Paine decided to take up his pen once again to oppose Burke
and defend revolution and republicanism. The Burke-Paine
debate was the classic confrontation between tradition and innovation, hierarchy and equality, order and revolution.[3]

The Rights of Man was published in 1791. Already, several
reformers had issued replies to Burke, but it was Paine who
captured the public imagination. As in America, Paine's style and
content were of one piece. Burke cited numerous classical and
English authorities in addressing the "political nation" of voters
and office-holders. Paine's audience was the entire adult population. As in his American writings, Paine's very tone, idiom and
rhetoric demonstrated that the issues of politics could be
addressed in the language of common speech. He openly ridiculed Burke's literary style: "As the wondering audience, whom
Mr. Burke supposes himself talking to, may not understand all
this learned jargon, I will undertake to be its interpreter." Never
had Paine's writing been more forceful and direct, never had he
more consciously employed phrases from common life. ("To use a
sailor's phrase," he wrote of Burke, "he has swabbed the deck.")
And never had Paine more explicitly appealed to the cultural
frame of reference of his audience. *The Rights of Man* abounded

in images like "the puppet-show of state and aristocracy," evoking the farces, ballad-operas, pantomimes and other forms of popular theater so common in eighteenth-century England.[4]

Dedicated to George Washington, *The Rights of Man* was in part a vindication of the French Revolution, in part an enunciation of the general principles of republican government. Long sections narrated the overthrow of the ancien régime, the storming of the Bastille, the march on Versailles, and defended these events against Burke's repeated attacks. Paine was particularly outraged by the contrast between Burke's sympathy for the royal family and his seeming indifference toward the victims of the old regime:

> Not one glance of compassion, not one commiserating reflection, that I can find throughout his book, has he bestowed on those who lingered out the most wretched of lives, a life without hope, in the most miserable of prisons. . . . He is not affected by the reality of distress touching the heart, but by the showy resemblage of it striking his imagination. He pities the plumage, but forgets the dying bird.

Paine pointedly contrasted the new French system of government with that of England—the broad French suffrage with the narrow and "capricious" British franchise, the frequent Assemblies based on equal electoral districts with the seven-year Parliaments and system of rotten boroughs, the French guarantee of freedom of conscience with the disabilities faced by religious Dissenters in England. He reaffirmed the American definition of a constitution as "a thing *antecedent* to government . . . not the act of . . . government, but of the people constituting a government." Breaking decisively with the traditional reformers' concern with the corruptions of the constitution, Paine denied that England had a constitution at all. "Can Mr. Burke produce the English Constitution? If he cannot, we may fairly conclude that though it has been so much talked about, no such thing as a constitution exists."

In outlook as in style, *The Rights of Man* resembled Paine's American writings. As in *Common Sense,* he reserved his sharpest barbs for monarchy and hereditary privilege: "The idea of hereditary legislators is as inconsistent as that of hereditary judges, or hereditary juries, and as absurd as an hereditary mathematician, or an hereditary wise man." Once again he defended the necessity of a radical break with tradition, rejecting Burke's invocation of precedent and experience to justify the English system of government:

> Every age and generation must be as free to act for itself, *in all cases,* as the ages and generations which preceded it. The vanity and presumption of governing beyond the grave, is the most ridiculous and insolent of all tyrannies. Man has no property in man; neither has any generation property in the generations which are to follow. . . . I am contending for the rights of the *living,* and against their being willed away by the manuscript assumed authority of the dead.

Paine's conclusion was a classic statement of his secular millennialism: "From what we now see, nothing of reform in the political world ought to be held improbable. It is an age of revolutions, in which everything may be looked for." [5]

As soon as *The Rights of Man* was published, Paine set to work on a companion volume which would, as he later remarked, combine "principle and practice." And in February 1792, what is probably Paine's boldest and greatest work appeared, *The Rights of Man, Part Second.* He began by outlining the general principles of government, almost exactly as he had done in *Common Sense.* Once again, he distinguished between society and government—society, resting on the mutual needs and inherent "social affections" of humanity, was natural and benevolent; government, at least in the Old World, was nothing more than "a disgustful picture of human wretchedness." Once again, Paine assailed the political institutions of his native land. Monarchy had its origins in nothing more than "a band of ruffians" that had overrun the country and then allowed "the chief of the band" to "lose the name of robber in that of monarch." As for the House of Lords, "No reason can be given, why a house of legislation should be composed entirely of men whose occupation consists in letting landed property, than why it should be composed of those who hire, or of brewers, or bakers, or any other separate class of men."

As in his American writings, Paine created a new political language. Not only did he redefine "republican government" as simply "government established and constituted for the interest of the public," but he abandoned the traditional pejorative implications of "democracy"—usually thought of as the anarchic rule of the entire people—and repeatedly used the word in a favorable sense, insisting that representative government was preferable to direct democracy only because it was more convenient. In effect, Paine called upon his audience to recast governments in the Old World on the model of the New. He cited the Pennsylvania experience of 1776 as an example of how the people could create a new constitution, and he painted a utopian picture of the benefits Americans derived from republican government:

> There the poor are not oppressed, the rich are not privileged. Industry is not mortified by the splendid extravagance of a court rioting at its expense. Their taxes are few, because their government is just; and as there is nothing to render them wretched, there is nothing to engender riots and tumults.

So far, little that Paine said was new, although he had never said it better. But suddenly, in chapter five, Paine unveiled a new vision, that of the republican state as an agent of social welfare. Paine first went out of his way to identify himself with his audience. He made it clear that his own origins lay among the lower classes: "My parents were not able to give me a shilling, beyond what they gave me in education; and to do this they distressed themselves." He contrasted the aristocracy (idle "drones") with the productive classes, and included an extended account of the fourteenth-century rebellion led by the mechanic Wat Tyler, concluding: "If the barons merited a monument to be erected in Runneymede [in commemoration of Magna Carta], Tyler merits one in Smithfield."

Having made it clear that he was addressing himself to the laboring population, Paine asserted for the first time that to do away with poverty in Europe, more was required than a simple transition to republican government. Paine outlined an economic program as close to a welfare state as could be imagined in the eighteenth century. The basis of taxation would be changed from poor rates and regressive levies on articles of consumption to direct, progressive taxes on property, especially land. From the proceeds, every poor family would recieve a direct allocation of money to allow it to educate its children; a system of social security would enable all workers to retire at age sixty ("not as a matter of grace and favor, but of right"); public jobs and unemployment relief would be awarded to "the casual poor"; and money would be provided for decent burials for "persons who, travelling for work, may die at a distance from their friends,"—a problem common among "tramping" artisans. Recalling his earliest political cause, Paine even included a salary increase for excise officers. And all of this could be accompanied by a reduction in the taxes of most Englishmen, if the government ceased conducting wars and paying pensions to members of the aristocracy. As Paine observed of the annual stipend of one aristocrat:[6]

> It is inhuman to talk of a million sterling a year, paid out of the public taxes of any country, for the support of any individual, while thousands, who are forced to contribute thereto, are pining from want, and struggling with misery. Government does not consist in contrast between prisons and palaces, between poverty and pomp, it is not instituted to rob the needy of his mite, and increase the wretchedness of the wretched.

The appearance of the second part of *The Rights of Man* marked a turning point in the history of English radicalism. Paine was the first to provide a social program for the English reform movement, to make the traditional demands for Parliamentary reform meaningful to the daily lives of the middle class and workingmen. Paine did not abandon his essential economic outlook—he reaffirmed his respect for rights of property and his belief that commerce was a natural and benevolent system of intercourse among men. He still placed the greatest blame for poverty on the inequities of the political system and their result, unfair and regressive taxation. But he now insisted that a republican government would take decisive steps to ameliorate the pressing problem of poverty in England. In effect, Paine asked that the democratic state assume the social responsibilities of the old paternalist order while jettisoning the deferential and hierarchical social relations that still dominated English society.[7]

The response to *The Rights of Man* can only be described as overwhelming. Some 200,000 copies were sold or distributed free by the end of 1793. The pamphlet reached into every corner of the British Isles. "The avidity with which this work . . . was read by the middle and lower classes of the people, . . . particularly those in the great manufacturing towns both in England and Scotland, is incredible," declared the normally sedate *Annual Register*. Paine's writings became the dividing line of English politics, and numerous reformers retreated from the social vision he offered. The Reverend Christopher Wyvill reiterated his belief in the desirability of Parliamentary reform but insisted it was "unfortunate for the public cause, that Mr. Paine took such unconstitutional ground, and has formed a party for a Republic among the lower classes of the people, by holding out to them the prospect of plundering the rich. . . ."[8]

As in America in 1776, Paine during these years was the right man at precisely the right time. An unprecedented upsurge of radical politics followed publication of *The Rights of Man*. Paine's writings, of course, did not in themselves create the radical movement. The groundwork had been laid by the growth of popular politics in the Wilkes movement of the 1760s, the tracts distributed by the Society for Constitutional Information in the 1780s and the resilient traditions of the "free-born Englishman" which pervaded popular political culture. Most important, the existence of an American republic coupled with the outbreak of revolution in France, by creating living alternatives to the English system of government, had greatly stimulated demands for reform in Britain. As in America, Paine articulated and intensified existing popular discontents and longings, particularly resentments among artisans and laborers against their political powerlessness and often desperate economic conditions. *The Rights of Man* helped to inspire the creation of new radical organizations with a social base far broader than the groups previously involved in the movement for Parliamentary reform. With admission fees as low as one penny per week and the avowed policy of attracting "members unlimited," the societies of the 1790s marked the emergence of "the lower and middling class of society" into organized radical politics.[9]

II

The new radical societies of the 1790s were composed largely of artisans, the great majority of whom were excluded from voting, all of whom were barred from forming unions, and many of whom lived in poverty. They were strongest in London and provincial centers of urban craftsmanship—the "large and respectable manufacturing towns" which, the reformer John Horne Tooke declared, were "the great balance to the aristocratic interests of the country." The first such group was the Constitutional Information Society, organized in late 1791 in Sheffield, a center of skilled and literate artisans and journeymen. "The seditious doctrines of Paine," reported a shocked government official in mid-1792, circulated in Sheffield "to a great degree very much beyond my conception." His explanation illustrated how the nature of small-scale artisan work provided the basis for political activity:

> The manufactures of this town are of a nature to require so little capital to carry them on, that a man with a very small sum of money can employ two, three, or four men, and this being generally the case, there are not in this, as in other great towns, any number of persons of sufficient weight who could by their influence, or the number of their dependents, act with any effect in case of a disturbance, and as the wages given to journeymen are very high, it is . . . generally the practice for them to work for three days, in which they earn sufficient to enable them to drink and riot for the rest of the week, consequently no place can be more fit for seditious purposes.

The Sheffield society originated in meetings among "five or six mechanics" to discuss "the enormous high price of provisions," the "luxury and debauchery" of the court and "the mock representation of the people" in Parliament. By mid-1792 it had over two thousand members and its publications, including cheap editions of *The Rights of Man*, were widely circulated among "the lower classes of people" and were "read with avidity" in "the workshops of the manufacturers."[10]

By 1792, groups modeled on the Sheffield society had sprung up throughout the British Isles. Best known was the London Corresponding Society, organized early in 1792 by Thomas Hardy, a master shoemaker whose political education derived from the tracts published in the 1780s by the Society for Constitutional Information. Hardy seems to have been typical of late eighteenth-century artisan radicals. He described himself as "a plain, industrious citizen . . . of a contemplative and serious turn of mind," who avoided "all . . . scenes of dissipation." The first meeting, held in the Bell tavern, attracted only eight members, but by the end of 1792, the LCS claimed the adherence of several thousand "tradesmen, mechanicks, and shopkeepers," including both journeymen and masters in most of the myriad trades of London. One contemporary broadside observed that "the Poor have seldom time to attend to these public meetings, . . . they seldom understand the purpose of them, or foresee the effect of them upon their own interests." But by 1794, LCS meetings were attracting porters, dockside laborers and even gentlemen's servants.[11]

The emergence of independent political organization among artisans, shopkeepers and workingmen marked a decisive break with patterns of deference and paternalism. Even Hardy at first believed that once the LCS was founded, "men of talents would step forward, and we who were the first formers of it, who had neither time to spare from our daily employment, nor talents for conducting so important an undertaking, would withdraw into the background. . . . But it was soon found that an alarm was created among that class, by the uncommon appearance of the popular societies. . . ." As a result, men like Hardy were forced to take the lead in the work of political organization and the dissemination of radical literature. When the LCS drew up its first public address, many members were reluctant to sign, fearing a loss of middle- and upper-class patronage. As Hardy recalled, "I being the most independent in the society at that time," stepped forward, and the address, issued in April 1792, bore his name alone. But the very experience of participation in the LCS and kindred organizations helped many of Hardy's contemporaries free themselves from traditional patterns of dependence. "The moral effects of the Society," as one member later recalled, "were considerable. It induced men to read books, instead of wasting their time in public houses, it taught them to respect themselves. . . . The discussions in the divisions, in the Sunday evening readings, and in the small debating meetings, opened to them views which they had never before taken."[12]

Paine's writings provided for such men a political and social analysis which seemed to explain the inequities of British life.

An anti-radical print from 1798, depicting the members of the London Corresponding Society. Note the picture of Paine on the wall. *Gimbel Collection, American Philosophical Society*

More than any other individual, Paine became the hero of the radical societies. In Sheffield, the master cutlers sang new words to the tune of the national anthem:

> God save great Thomas Paine
> His "Rights of Man" to explain
> To every soul.
> He makes the blind to see
> What dupes and slaves they be
> And points out liberty
> From pole to pole.

And a London song echoed the sentiment:[13]

> There was a man whose name was Paine, a man of Common Sense,
> Who came from Philadelphia here, his knowledge to dispense;
> He prov'd that man had equal rights, as equal sons of nature,
> Deriv'd by universal grant, from Heaven's Legislature.
>
> He taught, that on the people's will all lawful pow'r depended,
> That governors were for the good of the governed intended;
> And many other wholesome truths, all form'd on reason's plan,
> He wrote within a little book, and call'd it Rights of Man.

The political ideology of the societies echoed that of Paine. As the artisan radical Francis Place later recalled, "All the leading members of the London Corresponding Society were republicans. . . . This they were taught by the writings of Thomas Paine." These societies shared Paine's utter contempt for existing institutions in England, his enthusiasm for the revolution in France, and his utopian image of America. One radical tract urged English workingmen to emigrate to America, where "no lordly peer tramples down the corn of the husbandman, and no proud prelate wrings from him the tithe of his industry." Many radicals of the 1790s still insisted that their demands embraced nothing more than a restoration of the ancient Anglo-Saxon constitution.

But such arguments were increasingly superceded by Paine's contempt for historical precedents and authorities and his orientation toward the future.[14]

The Rights of Man, as Paine declared, was "written in a style of thinking and expression different to what had been customary in England." It was typical of Paine that he linked "thinking and expression" in this way, and the pamphlets, broadsides, newspapers and public letters issued by the radical societies were modeled as much on Paine's literary style as on his political thought. Following Paine's literary example, radical publicists insisted on avoiding "the language of the schools," and on bringing their subject matter within the reach of "the meanest capacity." Aside from periodic bows to the ancient Anglo-Saxon constitution, they generally followed Paine in eschewing references to "worm-eaten volumes" or "a musty roll of parchment," appealing instead to "the gift of Him whom all nature obeys—Reason." Such writing was not easy for the radical artisans. In 1792, Paine himself had to assist the inexperienced members of the LCS in setting their ideas down on paper.[15]

In these political tracts, the LCS and kindred groups adopted and publicized Paine's language of radical change, even composing addresses containing dictionary-like redefinitions of old words:

REPUBLICAN—one who wishes to promote the general welfare of his country.
DEMOCRAT—a supporter of the rights and power of the people.
ARISTOCRAT—one who wishes to promote the interest of a few at the expense of the many.

The societies found the most difficulty in developing a meaning for the crucial term "equality." Again and again they were charged with being "levellers" whose demand for equality of rights embraced a desire to destroy all social distinctions and make

all property common. But the artisans, after all, were property-
owners themselves. "We have ever disclaimed the foolish idea of
levelling property," said a speaker at a Sheffield radical meeting,
"because our own property, the fruit of our labour, or of our
talents, might, by the example, be exposed to the invasion of the
first intruder." In 1795, in an attempt to end this political-linguis-
tic confusion, the LCS issued an address attempting to rescue the
word "equality" from the "base misrepresentations" which had
been imposed upon it:

> Social equality . . . appears to consist in the following things:
> 1. The Acknowledgement of equal rights.
> 2. The existence of equal laws for the security of those rights.
> 3. Equal and actual representation, by which, and which alone, the
> invasion of those laws can be prevented. . . . In their ideas of
> equality, they have never included (nor, till the associations of
> alarmists broached the frantic notion, could they ever have con-
> ceived that so wild and detestable a sentiment could have entered
> the brain of man) as the equalization of property, or the invasion of
> personal rights of possession.

Or, as a Leeds broadside put it, "'tis an Equality of Rights, not an
Equality of Property."[16]

Despite this solicitude for rights of property, the roots of the
radical movement of the 1790s lay in economic and social grievances far deeper than existed in contemporary America. Every
contemporary account of the societies' origins stressed that what
stimulated political inquiry among members was "the miserable
and wretched state the people were reduced to," the "numerous,
burthensome, and unnecessary taxes," the "oppressive game laws
and destructive monopolies," and all the other causes of "the
lower classes sinking into poverty, disgrace, and excesses." But in
typical Paineite fashion, these social ills were attributed primarily
to defects in the political system, and electoral reform was viewed
as "the groundwork" of all necessary social change. As the LCS

AN

EXPLANATION

OF THE

WORD EQUALITY.

THE perverse fenfe impofed on the word EQUALITY, by the folly or the fears of fome of our countrymen, is as dangerous as it is abfurd, and they may probably fee the day, when they may repent of having infufed into the minds of the people, a notion that the EQUALITY to be contended for, is an *equality of wealth and poffeffions*. If, by continually repeating this idea, the *uninformed*, or, (as they are arrogantly ftyled by the *penfioned* Mr. B****) the "SWINISH MULTITUDE," fhould take it into their heads, that they are juftified in *inforcing* fuch a fyftem, the confequences will reft upon thofe, who, by a perverfion of terms, have wickedly or foolifhly propagated fo dangerous a doctrine.

The Equality infifted on by the Friends of Reform, is an EQUALITY OF RIGHTS; or, in other words that *every perfon* may be equally entitled to the protection and benefits of fociety: may *equally* have a voice in the election of thofe who make the laws, by which he is affected in his *liberty*, his *life* or his *property*; and may have a fair opportunity of exerting to advantage any talents he may poffefs. The rule is not " *Let all mankind be perpetually equal*; " God and Nature have forbidden it—but " *Let all mankind ftart fair in the race of life*." The *inequality* derived from labor and fuccefsful enterprize, the refult of fuperior induftry and good fortune, is an *equality effential to the very exiftence of fociety*: and it naturally follows, that the property fo acquired fhould pafs *from a father to his children*. To render property infecure would deftroy all motives to exertion, and tear up public happinefs by the roots.

A   Such

Printed in 1792 by the Manchester Constitutional Society and distributed by radical groups throughout England, this broadside records the emergence of a new language of politics. *Public Record Office, London* explained in 1792, "reform one abuse and the others will all disappear":[17]

> soon then should we see our liberties restored, the press free, the laws simplified, . . . taxes diminished, and the necessaries of life and more within the reach of the poor, . . . old age better provided for, and sumptuous feasts at the expense of the starving poor less frequent.

It was this linking of political and social reform that explains why, in the countless resolutions honoring Paine, the "social chapter" of *The Rights of Man* was often singled out. Paine himself believed that it was his plan for a reduction of taxes and social legislation, not his assault on the English constitution, which led the government to prosecute him for sedition in 1792.[18]

The point is that beneath the political reform movement of the 1790s lay deep-seated social grievances and resentments which increasingly found articulate expression as the decade advanced. In contrast to the situation in America, Paineite radicalism was quickly transformed into a pervasive critique of the entire organization of English society. Paine, of course, helped to stimulate this transformation in *The Rights of Man,* but by the mid-1790s, as war with France led to an increase in taxation and poor harvests raised the price of food to unprecedented levels, even Paine's social proposals seemed inadequate to some radical leaders. From Thomas Spence's bookshop on London's Chancery Lane flowed a series of pamphlets and broadsides arguing that mere Parliamentary reform could never solve the social problems of eighteenth-century England. "Landlords and landlords only," Spence insisted, were "the oppressors of the people," and he developed an elaborate plan for land to be owned communally by democratically-elected parish governments and rented to the inhabitants in small parcels. In contrast to the abolition of private property in land, Paine's social proposals seemed tame indeed.

A rare portrayal of Paine in his original trade of staymaking, this 1793 cartoon shows him attempting to lace Brittania into an ill-fitting French corset. *Gimbel Collection, American Philosophical Society*

"I hear there is another Rights of Man by Spence, that goes farther than Paine's," said a character in one of the political dialogues Spence printed to propagate his ideas. "Yet," was the reply, "it goes no farther than it ought."[19]

Aside from a few devoted followers, Spence's ideas had little immediate impact on the radical movement of the 1790s, although his influence can be recognized in a wide variety of land reform plans in the nineteenth century. More influential in expanding the movement's social program was John Thelwall, the son of a silk mercer and the leading radical lecturer of the mid-1790s. Like Spence, Thelwall built upon the foundation laid by Paine, whom he described as "that great apostle of the Rights of Man." But Thelwall added to *The Rights of Man* his own version of *The Rights of Nature*—the right of every citizen to a fair share of the accumulated wealth of society. Thelwall not only publicly flaunted his radicalism—"I tell you in plain terms I am a republican, a downright *sansculotte*"— but was the only radical figure of these years to question Paine's uncritical picture of America. "I hear you are somewhat short of the true sansculotte liberty," he wrote to an American, "that you have too much veneration for property, too much religion, and too much law." Americans, he believed, were too fond of "respecting mankind in proportion to their property."[20]

The radical movement of the 1790s was suppressed with remarkable speed by the Pitt government. By the end of 1792, Paine had been tried and convicted *in absentia* for seditious libel, and a series of state trials of leaders of the societies and publishers of Paine's writings soon followed. (The government was offended by Paine's literary style as well as by his political principles: at his trial the Attorney-General asked the jury to "take into your consideration the phrase and the manner as well as the matter.") At the same time the government encouraged the formation of loyalist clubs which distributed anti-Paine tracts, burned countless effigies of Paine and were held responsible by the radicals for

Another example of the anti-Paine propaganda sponsored by the British government in the 1790s. *Gimbel Collection, American Philosophical Society*

mob attacks on radical leaders in Birmingham and Manchester. (One loyalist pamphlet ended with a "worker" declaring to his employer: "Right, master! and I thank you for explaining all this to me; . . . for I should not like to see a Frenchman lie with my wife, or take the bread out of my childrens' mouths.") In 1794, the radicals won a great victory when Hardy, Tooke and others were acquitted by a London jury—Hardy was carried by a huge throng through the streets of London. But after a final upsurge of popular radicalism in 1795 the government enacted the Two Acts, banning large public meetings and making prosecutions for treason easier, and within the next two years the popular movement was crushed.[21]

The radicalism of the 1790s, as E. P. Thompson so eloquently shows, was driven underground, not destroyed. From the agitation of these years flowed the major currents of nineteenth-century English radicalism—the traditions of self-education, rational criticism of political institutions, republicanism, support for revolutions overseas, an uncritical glorification of the United States and the validity of lower-class political organization. The political demands of the LCS became the six points of the Chartists; the attack on the privileged aristocracy became the basis for a radical sociology that contrasted the "producing" and "nonproducing" classes even as industrialization made such a social analysis increasingly obsolete. And there was the tradition of secularism and hostility to the established Anglican Church, which was stimulated by Paine's The Age of Reason, but which stemmed from the radicals' belief that the clergy and Church were among the bulwarks of the established order. The LCS was very careful to "avoid all religious disputes," but as Francis Place later recalled, "nearly all the leading members were either deists or atheists."[22]

It is symptomatic of the differences between American and British society at the end of the eighteenth century that Paine's political ideas were commonplace in the former but outlawed in the latter. In America, the political demands of Paineite radicals had largely been achieved by the 1790s and the social inequalities that inspired the English radical movement simply did not exist on the same scale (at least within white society). The "social chapter" of *The Rights of Man* attracted virtually no comment in contemporary America; most Americans seemed to agree with Paine that it was not relevant to the New World.

In America, men like Jefferson could easily endorse *The Rights of Man*, but in England the "respectable" reformers Hardy hoped would step forward to lead the reform movement were, with a few notable exceptions, frightened away either by the French Revolution or by the very fact of independent lower-class political activity. As a result, English society was polarized, politically and socially, as America never was. To men like Thomas Hardy, "the whole political world was basically alien and repulsive." This polarization led to the inevitable defeat of the fledgling radical movement, but encouraged the survival underground of a radical tradition. It was the experience of the 1790s which made *The Rights of Man* a "foundation-text of the English working-class movement," made Paine a recurrent hero in nineteenth-century radical circles and led generations of English radicals to echo the words of John Thelwall: "So long as the tongue of man can articulate the names of those heroes who have benefitted mankind, so long, in defiance of persecution, will the name of Thomas Paine resound throughout the world."[23]

III

The early 1790s saw Paine at his best—bringing radical ideas to a new audience, submitting contemporary institutions to a withering critique, raising the demand for far-reaching change. As a tribute to Paine for his writings in support of the Revolution, he was elected in 1792 to the French National Convention. Thus began the most enigmatic and controversial period of his life.

Why did the apostle of international revolution end up in jail in revolutionary Paris? The answer lies both in Paine's character and in the immense differences between the social and political situation in France and what he had experienced in England and America.

To some extent, unavoidable contingencies shaped Paine's French career. A man with no direct experience in the process of government, he had gone in well beyond his depth in the National Convention. His position as a foreigner, his ignorance of French, his personal contacts and his acceptance into the upper echelons of revolutionary society all prevented his full integration into the French scene, limited his perception of events and cut him off from the Parisian sans-culottes who, as the rough equivalents of the artisans of London and Philadelphia, seemed to be his natural constituency. There is also the question of the relevance of Paine's radicalism to the French context. Nothing he had witnessed in England or America could compare with the demands of conducting a revolutionary government at a time of war abroad and social crisis at home. His interpretation of events in France was shaped by his experiences in America, and his prescription for the ills of France was simply to follow the model laid down in the New World. In a sense, Paine's problems in France were grounded in the tension, evident in his American career as well, between his political radicalism and his free-market economic orientation. On such political issues as republicanism and universal suffrage, Paine was more consistently radical even than many Jacobins. But in the crisis of 1793, with the rising demand in Paris for a new social dimension to the Revolution, Paine was unwilling to abandon the commitment to laissez-faire and the sanctity of private property which he had brought with him to France.

Although it was not until 1792 that Paine became intimately involved in French affairs, by then he had already visited Paris on a number of occasions during the early years of the Revolution.

Like Jefferson, the American ambassador at Paris until 1790, Paine believed that the National Assembly which in 1789 remade France into a constitutional monarchy, abolished the remnants of feudal privilege, endorsed the principles of natural rights and expanded the right to vote, had constructed a "superb edifice." In January 1790, Paine wrote to Edmund Burke from Paris, "With respect to the politics of France, . . . if we distinguish the Revolution from the Constitution, we may say, that the first is compleat, and the second is in a fair prospect of being so." And in a sentence which must have been truly alarming to Burke, Paine exulted, "The Revolution in France is certainly a forerunner to other Revolutions in Europe."[24]

Paine's view of the French Revolution in these early years derived primarily not from direct experience with events, but from the convictions of his French associates. Paine spoke no French, although he seems to have understood the spoken idiom. Thus, his friends were of necessity either Americans like Jefferson or English-speaking Frenchmen. His closest associates were J. P. Brissot de Warville, Etienne Clavière, the Marquis de Condorcet, and others who in the early 1790s would become leaders of the Girondin group in the Convention.

In a sense, it was only natural that Paine would gravitate to such men, and not simply because they spoke English. It has been written of Jefferson that "the common denominator of all his friendships in France was good will toward America," and the same may be said for Paine. Paine's French associates shared his uncritical vision of the United States. Brissot, the son of a Chartres restaurateur, had become "a fanatical Americanist" in the 1780s as well as a critic of French political and social institutions. He greatly admired the Pennsylvania Constitution of 1776 and regarded the American Revolution as "an epoch in the annals of humanity," whose example should inspire the French to reform their own society. To Brissot, Americans were a simple, uncorrupted people living in an agrarian arcadia, and in 1787 he helped to create the Gallo-American Society, devoted to promoting commerce between the two nations.[25] Condorcet, with whom Paine developed a close friendship in the early 1790s, shared the uncritical Americanism of Paine's other French associates, holding out the American experience as an example of the possibility of beginning government anew and organizing a society devoid of class distinctions.[26]

These French reformers were quick to welcome American visitors to Paris. They befriended Franklin and Jefferson in the 1780s and extended a warm welcome to Paine. Brissot never tired of praising *Common Sense* and hoped to arouse French public opinion as Paine had inspired Americans. But the affinities between Paine and his French associates went even deeper than a mutual admiration for America and Thomas Paine. All were cosmopolitans who had traveled widely (Brissot had visited America in 1788) and who shared the ideal of world revolution. All were critics of slavery—Brissot was a leading figure in the French Society des Amis des Noirs. All believed in free trade as a vehicle of international cooperation and prosperity, and all were critical of paper money. Like Paine, Brissot and Condorcet were deists who believed in the perfectibility of man. All had contempt for the past, little use for existing European institutions and hoped that reforms on the American model would create a new France grounded on the principles of equality of rights, freedom of trade and international good will.[27] The fact that Brissot spoke English was more an illustration than a cause of the intellectual affinities between himself and Paine.

Despite the fact that Paine and his friends would become Girondins, it would be wrong to read Paine's later "moderation" back to his early participation in the Revolution. He returned to Paris in April 1791 after an absence of over a year. Along with his friends Condorcet, Brissot and Clavière, Paine became a regular member of the salon of Madame Roland. On the issue of a republic, Paine was far in advance of most of the prominent figures of the Revolution. Despite the fact that abstract discussions of replacing the constitutional monarchy with a republic were held at the Roland home, republicanism at this time was little more than "an aspiration entertained by a handful of idealists." Even radicals like Jean Paul Marat believed that republican government was not suitable for large, populous nations; while Marat demanded the deposition of Louis XVI, he envisioned the establishment of a regency, not the abolition of monarchy. As in America, it was Paine who issued the first outright call for the establishment of a republic. The occasion was the flight and subsequent capture of Louis XVI in June 1791. Paine, Brissot, Clavière and the young nobleman Achille Duchatelet formed a society to promote republicanism and collaborated on a short-lived newspaper, *Le Republicain*. And Paine, at no small risk to himself, wrote a republican manifesto which was translated into French by the English wife of Duchatelet and placarded on the doors of the Legislative Assembly—an action much resented by the members of that body.[28]

Paine left Paris in August 1791 and did not return until September of the following year. By then the situation in France was radically transformed. His friends Brissot and the Rolands were now leading figures in the loosely defined political grouping known as the Girondins. For a time in the spring of 1792, Roland had served in a Girondin ministry under the king, despite his republican inclinations. Indeed it was an unnatural alliance of Girondins and the Court which engineered the French declaration of war against Austria in April 1792. Only a few political leaders, including Maximilien Robespierre, opposed what Brissot termed the "war of the human race against its oppressors," ridiculing the idea that the peoples of Europe would rise in welcome to "armed missionaries" from France. Robespierre insisted on the necessity of consolidating the gains of the Revolution at home before embarking on foreign ventures.[29]

The war which began in 1792 shook the political and social

foundations of France. It created economic chaos, exposed the duplicity of the king, led to the creation of a revolutionary government and provided the occasion for the emergence of the Parisian sans-culottes as an independent force in national politics. An amalgam of wage-earners, artisans, shopkeepers and petty entrepreneurs, the sans-culottes were fervently committed to direct democracy and popular sovereignty, intensely hostile to men of great wealth and convinced that private property should be regulated in the interests of the urban consumer. The political education of the sans-culottes had begun in 1790 and 1791 in the lectures and newspapers of radical intellectuals like Paine's friend Nicholas de Bonneville, a romantic revolutionary whose journal, *La Bouche de Fer,* preached a kind of communism modeled on the society of the early Christians. By 1792, their demands for price controls and public employment, and for the right of local assemblies to dismiss elected officials, set them apart from both the Girondins and the emerging opposition group, the Jacobins. But as France suffered military defeat and as the Girondins vacillated between attacking the monarchy and seeking further power at court, the breach between them and the sans-culottes became unbridgable. In August 1792, a sans-culotte uprising in Paris overthrew the monarchy and as Prussian troops crossed into France, thousands of sans-culottes stormed the prisons, killing hundreds of "royalist" inmates. These "September Massacres" horrified the Girondins, converting them into advocates of law and order who demanded the removal of the national government from Paris.[30]

With the sans-culotte uprisings and the imprisonment of the king, the French monarchy came to an end. And as a further sign of the radical thrust of the "second revolution," the Legislative Assembly in August 1792 conferred honorary citizenship upon an unlikely group of seventeen foreigners, including Paine, Washington and Hamilton, as well as the British abolitionist William Wilberforce and the Polish patriot Thaddeus Kosciusko.

Shortly thereafter, when elections were held for the National Convention, Paine was one of two foreigners elected. (The other was Anacharsis Cloots, a Prussian nobleman who called himself the Orator of the Human Race and believed that as a universal republic, France should offer representation in the Convention to New York, China and Arabia.) At the very time that he was under indictment in England for sedition, Paine traveled to Calais. *The Rights of Man* had already been widely distributed in France, and in every town on his journey to Paris, Paine was honored as an authentic hero of the French Revolution.[31]

In September 1792, Paine took his seat in the Convention, a body whose first official action was to declare France a republic. At fifty-five, Paine was one of the oldest men in the body, and hampered by his meager French and limited familiarity with domestic affairs, he would play only a minor role in the Convention's deliberations. He spent much of his time with his Girondin friends and with a small colony of emigré English and Irish radicals who met weekly at White's Hotel to discuss the possibility of revolution in the British Isles. In early 1793, Paine moved to the outskirts of Paris. In America and in England Paine had moved freely in the worlds of the upper and lower classes, had been at home in the tavern as well as the salon. Now he associated exclusively with foreigners and with Frenchmen denounced by the Left as aristocrats. In striking contrast to his experience in America and England, Paine had no ties with any segment of the French lower classes, a situation which goes a long way toward explaining the difficulties he would soon encounter.[32]

As in America, Paine in France considered himself a man above party. When "the violence of party" appeared in the Convention, he said in 1794, "it was impossible for me to see upon what principle they differed—unless it was a contention for power. I acted however as I did in America, I connected myself with no party, but considered myself altogether a National Man." Nevertheless, in the political strife of 1793 Paine's personal connections,

his interest in world revolution, his laissez-faire economic outlook and his distaste for crowd violence, all drew him closer to the
Girondins than to the Jacobins. On many issues, there was little
difference between the two political groups, especially when contrasted with the radicalism of the sans-culottes. But in 1793, with a
foreign army on French soil, Paris under the control of a sans-
culotte-dominated Commune and disaffection rife in the provinces, it was the Jacobins who recognized that the situation called
for revolutionary, even dictatorial government, and who were
willing to compromise their laissez-faire economic views to satisfy
sans-culotte demands. In addition, the Jacobin leadership, more
provincial than Brissot and his followers, spoke no English and
distrusted foreigners, especially the foreign revolutionaries like
Paine who hoped the French would devote their energies to
stimulating revolution in other countries. The Girondins, cosmopolitan Parisians and representatives of the commercial port cities
of the Atlantic coast, were more internationalist in outlook. They
tended to view the French Revolution through the lens of the
American, believing that a prompt end to the Revolution
required only a republican Constitution. This was a view in which
Paine concurred. As he later explained:[33]

> Had a Constitution been established, the nation would then have
> had a bond of union, and every individual would have known the
> line of conduct he was to follow. But, instead of this, a revolutionary
> government, a thing without either principle or authority, was
> substituted in its place. . . .

At the outset of the Convention, however, Paine was not viewed
as the adherent of any political faction. Late in 1792, he was
placed on the committee charged with drafting a new constitution for France. The document, primarily the work of Condorcet,
was republican and democratic, although it incorporated a complex system of indirect elections. Paine has been credited with
helping to draft the Declaration of Rights, which included the

usual guarantees of liberty, equality and the right to resist oppression, and also affirmed as natural rights the free-market economic
principles Paine had embraced in America:[34]

> The right of property consists in the liberty of every man to make
> such a disposition of his possessions, capital, income and industry as
> he chooses.
> No citizen can be prevented from engaging in any kind of labor,
> commerce, or agriculture; he can manufacture, sell and transport
> every species of production. . . .
> No one can be deprived of the smallest portion of his property
> without his consent, except when a public need, legally established,
> plainly requires it, and then only on condition of a just, preliminary
> indemnity.

Aside from serving on this committee, Paine's only real involvement in Convention affairs came during the trial of Louis XVI
early in 1793. Long an opponent of capital punishment—a position deriving from his Quaker upbringing—Paine urged that the
King be imprisoned and at the end of the war banished to
America. He believed the example of mercy would not only
impress the rest of Europe, but would win approval in the United
States. Paine's speeches to the Convention—read in French by a
translator—impressed many delegates; a number specifically
cited his example in casting their own votes against execution. But
in the end, by a slim majority, Louis XVI was sentenced to death,
and he was executed in February 1793. Paine probably did not
understand that the trial was part of a complex struggle for power
between Girondins and Jacobins and that the result had seriously
challenged Girondin control of the Convention. Indeed, he had
differed with his Girondin friends in opposing a popular referendum on the King's fate, a remarkable vote which revealed that he
either did not realize how crucial the referendum proposal was to
Girondin political plans or, alternatively, that he was, as he
claimed, a man above party.
Nonetheless, in the eyes of the Jacobins, Paine's opposition to

the execution of Louis XVI linked him with the group around Brissot, an identification further strengthened in April 1793 when Paine testified at the trial of Jean Paul Marat. The trial was a final attempt by the Girondins to enhance their dwindling power in the Convention. A man of vast popularity among the sans-culottes, Marat was blamed by the Girondins for the September Massacres—as early as 1791 he had called for vengeance against the royal family and all counter-revolutionaries, as well as demanding that the property of the rich be confiscated to assist the poor. Paine's testimony concerned a question peripheral to the charges against Marat; it involved William Johnson, a young Englishman who had attempted suicide in Paris after exclaiming that Marat had assassinated liberty. But the confrontation between Paine and Marat was indeed a revealing one. Each prided himself on speaking the language of the people, but Marat's language was very different from Paine's. Marat's perpetual calls for violence and for the use of terror as a political weapon contrasted sharply with Paine's insistence that the Revolution adhere strictly to constitutional forms; Marat's assaults on the rich and open appeals to class hostility were the antithesis of Paine's belief in a republican society characterized above all by social harmony.[35]

After the execution of the King and the acquittal of Marat, Paine took little part in Convention debates. As the political struggle ran its course in 1793, he became increasingly disillusioned with events in France. If only the French adopted a constitution like the Americans, if only the Jacobins did not give in to sans-culotte demands for price controls, and if only the Convention could be removed from Paris, away from the increasingly frequent crowd demonstrations which intimidated the delegates, then political debate could be carried on in a spirit of reconciliation. In April, Paine wrote of his disillusionment to Jefferson: "Had this Revolution been conducted consistently with its principles, there was once a good prospect of extending liberty throughout the greatest part of Europe; but I now relinquish that hope."

In May, after several thousand sans-culottes surrounded the Convention demanding price controls and voices were raised for the arrest of prominent Girondin deputies as traitors (the close friend of the leading Girondins, General Dumouriez, had defected to the Austrians), Paine poured out his unhappiness to Danton. He asked that the government be removed from Paris, away from "the tumultuous misconduct with which the internal affairs of the present revolution" were conducted. He abandoned hope for international revolution, agreeing with Danton's belief that "all that now can be hoped for is limited to France only." He condemned the "spirit of denunciation" aimed at his Girondin friends. And, revealing again his belief that the French should be guided by the American experience, and by free-market economics instead of the "moral economy" of the sans-culottes, he firmly opposed legislative price controls:[36]

> I see also another embarrassing circumstance arising in Paris of which we have had full experience in America. I mean that of fixing the price of provisions. . . . In Philadelphia we undertook, among other regulations of this kind, to regulate the price of salt; the consequence was that no salt was brought to market. . . . [In addition], the assignats are not of the same value they were a year ago, and as the quantity increases the value of them will diminish.. . . Paper money in America fell so much in value from this excessive quantity of it, that in the year 1781 I gave three hundred paper dollars for one pair of worsted stockings.

On June 2, 1793, a huge crowd of Parisians surrounded the Convention, demanding the arrest of twenty-two Girondin members. Paine's name was not among them, but Danton, meeting him at the door, urged him to avoid danger and return home. During the summer, with his friends in jail and bound for the guillotine, Paine stayed in his suburban home, resorting increasingly to drink to ease his anxiety and despair. "I went little to the Convention," he later wrote, "and then only to make my appearance; because I found it impossible to join in their tremendous decrees, and useless and dangerous to oppose them."[37]

Only in October was Paine's name added to the list of deputies publicly accused of treason. It was almost inevitable that he would come under suspicion, for the Jacobin revolutionary government, faced with enormous dangers abroad and at home, had become increasingly distrustful of foreigners. Paine's friendship with the Girondins, his foreign birth, his commitment to world revolution, his obvious disapproval of the course of events in 1793, his opposition to the execution of Louis XVI, all made him vulnerable. In December Paine and Cloots—the two foreign deputies—were expelled from the Convention. Cloots was executed, and Paine was placed under arrest and lodged in the Luxembourg Palace, now a prison.[38]

Paine remained in the Luxembourg for ten months. The American ambassador in Paris, his erstwhile conservative critic Gouverneur Morris, did nothing to obtain his release. When a group of Americans petitioned in his behalf, the Convention's president replied that not only was Paine a citizen of England—a nation now at war with France—but that while his services as "the apostle of liberty" in America were still appreciated, "his genius has not understood that [Revolution] which has regenerated France." Paine remained in the Luxembourg while the Hebertists, then Danton and his followers, and finally Robespierre, were led to the guillotine. Even after the fall of the Jacobins in 1794, Paine was not freed, and it was not until the arrival of the new American ambassador, James Monroe, who claimed Paine as a citizen of the United States, that he was released—the "citizen of the world" saved by the principle of national citizenship.[39]

Soon after his release, Paine was reinstated as a member of the Convention. Meanwhile the conservative reaction against the Jacobin rule of the previous year continued unabated, and after

the suppression of the great sans-culotte insurrections of March
and May 1795, the popular masses of Paris disappeared almost
entirely from the political scene. One symbol of the swing to the
right was the Constitution of the Year III, adopted by the Convention in 1795, which abandoned the principle of universal
suffrage in favor of a complex system of indirect elections coupled with property qualifications for voting and office-holding.
The dissipirited remnants of the Jacobin party offered only mini-
mal resistance to these provisions; it was Paine who returned to
the Convention to denounce the betrayal of his cherished principle of political equality.[40] It is ironic that Paine, a so-called "moderate" within the French context, stood virtually alone in criticizing the new Constitution and in reaffirming the principle of
universal suffrage. But as always, when the first principles of
government were concerned, Paine's voice was clear, consistent,
and inflexible. Despite his lonely criticisms, the Constitution of
1795 was approved by the Convention, a new legislative body was
elected and Paine's unhappy career as a law-maker came to an
end.

IV

Despite his meager influence on French events, Paine's experience in the mid-1790s was not entirely one of failure. For he was
able to compose the last great pamphlets of his career—*The Age of
Reason* and *Agrarian Justice*. The manuscript of the first was
begun in 1793 and was completed during Paine's confinement in
Luxembourg prison. It was the rise of the dechristianization
movement in the fall and winter of 1793 which convinced Paine to
seek a mass audience for his religious views. He claimed that "the
people of France were running headlong into atheism" and that
he wrote *The Age of Reason* "lest in the general wreck of superstition, of false systems of government and false theology, we lose

sight of morality, of humanity, and of the theology that is true."
Yet it was this work which created Paine's reputation as an infidel
and an enemy of all religion.[41]

As in so many of his works, Paine said little that was strikingly
new in *The Age of Reason*. His expression of the deist's faith was
eloquent, but hardly original: "I believe in one God, and no more;
and I hope for happiness beyond this life. I believe in the equality
of man; and I believe that religious duties consist in doing justice,
loving mercy, and endeavouring to make our fellow-creatures
happy." He condemned existing religious institutions for attempting to "terrify and enslave mankind, and monopolize power and
profit," and he insisted that basic tenets of Christianity—revelation, miracles, the divine inspiration of the Bible—were incompatible with reason. For the Bible and revelation he substituted
Nature and natural laws as the source of religious knowledge.
"The word of God is the creation we behold," Paine declared,
"and it is in *this word*, which no human invention can counterfeit
or alter, that God speaketh universally to man." The power of
God was evident in "the immensity of the creation"; divine wisdom in "the unchangeable order" of the universe; God's benevolence in "the abundance with which He fills the earth." In place of
"the Christian system of faith," Paine proposed the study of
science as the only source of "true theology."

So far, little of what Paine had said would not have been
agreed to by men like Jefferson and Franklin, not to mention far
more aggressive European deists like Voltaire and Hume. But
even in Europe, most eighteenth-century deists had been content
to confine their religious opinions to upper-class salons, or to
pamphlets addressed to an educated audience. But in 1795, Paine
published a second part of *The Age of Reason*. If part one was
generalized and reasonable in disputing the tenets of Christianity,
part two was a book-by-book refutation of the Scriptures, in a
tone of outrage and ridicule. And, as always, Paine wrote in a
manner designed to reach a mass audience. "Were any girl that is

now with child," he asked, "to say, and even to swear to it, that she was gotten with child by a ghost, and that an angel told her so, would she be believed?" The story of Jonah and the whale was "a fit story for ridicule, if it was written to be believed; or of laughter, if it was intended to try what credulity could swallow; for if it could swallow Jonah and the whale, it could swallow anything." Previously, Paine had condemned all established churches; now he singled out Christianity for his bitterest assaults:

> Of all the systems of religion that ever were invented, there is none more derogatory to the Almighty, more unedifying to man, more repugnant to reason, and more contradictory in itself, than this thing called Christianity. Too absurd for belief, too impossible to convince, and too inconsistent for practice, it renders the heart torpid, or produces only atheists and fanatics.

It was to the "Bible of Creation," not the "stupid Bible of the Church," that men should turn for knowledge.[42]

Reprinted in countless editions and languages, *The Age of Reason* became the most popular deist work ever written. It brought ideas long common among the elites of the eighteenth century to a new popular audience and also gave deism a new, agressive, explicitly anti-Christian tone. Before Paine it had been possible to be both a Christian and a deist; now such a religious outlook became virtually untenable. *The Age of Reason* helped shake men free from deference to religious institutions, just as Paine's other writings led his readers to rethink their assumptions about politics and society. As a result, it aroused tremendous hostility from the clergy and the devout in Europe and America.

Throughout the nineteenth century, wherever freethinkers and deists gathered, Paine was certain to be revered as a hero. And yet, Paine's picture of religion and the Church was strangely limited. His view of the Bible was starkly literal and ignored its metaphoric and mythic qualities. He saw churches as "engines of

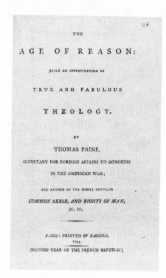

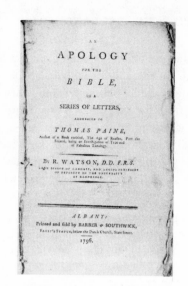

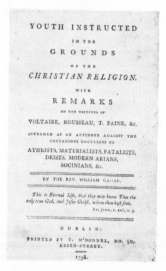

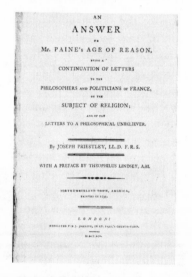

Paine's *The Age of Reason* stimulated countless replies defending revealed religion. The *Answer* by Joseph Priestley illustrates that many political radicals would not go along with Paine's attack on Christianity.

power" and allies of aristocracy and despotism—a view understandable enough in France and in much of Europe, where established churches enjoying legal privileges were bulwarks of the political status quo, but one which could not encompass independent, voluntary congregations of believers, or the reforming impulse unleashed by religious revivals. As a result, *The Age of Reason* outraged Dissenters as well as Anglicans, Quakers as well as Catholics, men who shared Paine's distaste for religious establishments and their pomp, power and conservatism, but would not follow him in rejecting the Bible and Christianity. Paine appealed to and greatly strengthened a popular tradition of secular anti-clerical radicalism, but at the same time isolated himself from the radical tradition inspired by evangelical Christianity.[43]

Like *The Age of Reason*, Paine's last great pamphlet, *Agrarian Justice*, helped to shape a tradition which flowed into nineteenth-century radicalism. The occasion for his writing was the French government's suppression in 1796 of the Conspiracy of the Equals of "Gracchus" Babeuf, "the first communist movement of modern times." Paine condemned Babeuf wholeheartedly, but the conspiracy led him for the first time to move beyond the view that poverty and economic inequalities were the result of differences in talent, defects in the political system and unfair taxation.

In all his previous writings, Paine had insisted that private property, as the fruit of individual labor, was a much an inviolate natural right as liberty. Now, he distinguished between two kinds of property: the bounty of nature, especially land, which he described as "the common property of the human race," and property created by the labor of men. To be sure, such a distinction was hardly original—it was implicit in the work of John Locke, from which so much of eighteenth-century property theory derived. Locke, however, had defined land as common property only in the state of nature; in civil society, it could legitimately be appropriated as the private property of individuals. But there was a potential radicalism in Locke's view, which was picked up and expanded by such eighteenth-century writers as William Ogilvie and Thomas Spence in England, and Babeuf in France, each of whom insisted that men retained a natural right to land and that a good part of existing property derived not from the labor of men, but from social institutions, and could therefore be regulated for the common good. In *Agrarian Justice,* Paine identified himself with this tradition. Since "all accumulation . . . of personal property, beyond what a man's own hands produce, is derived from living in society," he wrote, "he owes . . . a part of that accumulation back to society from which the whole came."

More than in any other essay, Paine seemed torn in *Agrarian Justice* between his customary desire to unite all classes in pursuit of what he perceived as the common good, and his sympathy for the plight of the European poor. On the one hand, he went out of his way to deny that equality of property was either possible or desirable, and to appeal directly to men of wealth, arguing that the only certain "security" for private property was a lessening of the distance between rich and poor. On the other hand, Paine had never been more vehement in his condemnation of existing economic inequalities:

> The present state of civilization is as odious as it is unjust. It is absolutely the opposite of what it should be, and it is necessary that a revolution should be made in it. The contrast of affluence and wretchedness continually meeting and offending the eye, is like dead and living bodies chained together. . . . The great mass of the poor are become an hereditary race, and it is next to impossible for them to get out of that state of themselves. . . . The condition of millions, in every country in Europe, is far worse than if they had been born before civilization began.

Paine even suggested that in too many cases, personal wealth was "the effect of paying too little for the labor that produced it; the consequence of which is that the working hand perishes in old age, and the employer abounds in affluence."

But, having reached the limits of his economic radicalism in such observations, Paine drew back. While Spence would forge this kind of thinking into a weapon against all private property in land, and Babeuf would use it to attack private property in general, Paine insisted he had no intention of interfering with existing property. As the full title of the pamphlet suggests, Paine sought a middle ground between a full-scale assault on private property and an uncritical acceptance of the existing order: "Agrarian Justice, Opposed to Agrarian Law, and to Agrarian Monopoly." ("Agrarian Law"—the equal division of existing property—had been a nightmare of both Girondins and Jacobins; its advocacy had been made a capital offense in 1792.) Paine's actual proposals seemed tame, indeed, when placed beside his expressions of indignation. Each proprietor of land, he argued, owed the state a "ground-rent" from which a fund would be created to pay everyone reaching the age of twenty-one a sum of fifteen pounds, "as a compensation, in part, for the loss of his or her natural inheritance, by the introduction of the system of landed property." And funds would also be provided for social security payments to all persons above the age of fifty. As in *The Rights of Man*, Paine's main emphasis was on eliminating poverty, rather than altering the system of private property.

Printed in French in 1796 and in an English edition the following year, *Agrarian Justice* did mark a departure in Paine's thinking, but it was a limited one. More radical land reformers like Thomas Spence considered the pamphlet a "dire disappointment" and condemned Paine's "poor beggerly stipends" as "contemptible and insulting" substitutes for "our lordly and just pretensions to the soil of our birth." But because of its argument that poverty was a product of civilization, not nature, and that among its causes was the alienation of land to private individuals, *Agrarian Justice* established Paine as one of the pioneers of the nineteenth-century land reform movement in Europe and America.[44]

The fact that *Agrarian Justice* was, in part, a comment on the Conspiracy of the Equals, illustrated the fact that Paine continued to be involved in French political affairs in the mid-1790s. Indeed, he developed close ties to two powerful members of the Directory which ruled France from November 1795 to the end of 1799: the devoted anti-Christian La Revellière-Lépeaux and the fanatical regicide and republican Barras. On several occasions, Paine employed his pen to defend the policies of the Directory and advised the government on ways of improving relations with the United States. He wrote an essay for circulation in America, condemning Jay's Treaty of 1794 establishing close commercial ties between Britain and the United States, and another lengthy pamphlet, printed by the French government, on the weaknesses of the British system of finance. He also composed a vitriolic attack on his former friend George Washington, whom Paine blamed for allowing him to languish in prison during the Terror. And Paine rushed into print to defend the anti-royalist coup of Fructidor (September 1797), which purged from the legislature its right-wing majority and temporarily "solidified the republican cause in France."[45]

Paine's major interests as the eighteenth century drew to a close were familiar ones for him—deism and European revolution. In January 1797 he joined the Society of Theophilanthropists, proponents of a form of deism sponsored by the Directory, particularly La Revellière-Lépeaux, as an alternative to Catholicism. Given permission by the government to hold services in religious buildings in Paris and the provinces, the Theophilanthropists attracted many republicans to their simple ceremonies in which humanitarian hymns were sung and the existence of God, the immortality of the soul and the golden rule were the sum of religious dogma. The movement reached a peak of influence in 1798 and then declined, to be finally suppressed after the accession of Napoleon. Although it challenged Catholicism for a time among officials and intellectuals, it never developed popular roots. (When La Revellière-Lépeaux told Talleyrand that he hoped Theophilanthropy would replace Catholicism as the religion of France, the cynical politician replied, "All you have to do is get yourself hanged, and revive the third day."[46])

Paine's other concern in these years was promoting republican revolutions outside France, especially in the British Isles. He had long been associated with emigré Irish radicals like Lord Edward Fitzgerald, and *The Rights of Man* had been widely circulated in Ireland. Paine used his influence with the Directory to urge French military assistance for a projected Irish uprising and his pleas won a sympathetic hearing from Barras and La Revellière-Lépeaux, both of whom, in the Girondin tradition, were expansionists and proponents of international revolution. But the French "invasion" of Ireland in 1798 was a failure, and when the coup of Napoleon overthrew the Directory in 1799, Paine's contacts with the government ceased. When Jefferson became president in America in 1801, Paine revived his long-suspended plan to return to the United States. Still disillusioned with the course of events in France, he retained the uncritical image of America he had done so much to popularize in Europe. When the English reformer Henry Redhead Yorke visited Paris, Paine told him:

> This is not a country for an honest man to live in; they do not understand any thing at all of the principles of free government, and the best way is to leave them to themselves. . . . I know of no Republic in the world except America, which is the only country for such men as you and I.

In 1802, at the age of sixty-five, Paine finally got his wish, and returned to the United States.[47]

V

Although fifteen years had passed since Paine had been in America, he had hardly been forgotten. All his writings of the

1790s had been reprinted in the United States. At the outset of the decade, Americans of every political persuasion had shown enthusiasm for Paine's writings. Both parts of *The Rights of Man* were widely circulated in the United States and excerpted in many newspapers, Federalist as well as Jeffersonian. *The Rights of Man,* declared one newspaper in 1791, was "not less popular in America at this day, than his *Common Sense* was in 1776." At the Independence Day celebration of the Tammany Society of New York in 1791, the toasts included: "Louis XVI and the patriots of France" and "The scourge of aristocracy—author of *Common Sense,* and *The Rights of Man."* And the poet Philip Freneau composed these adulatory lines "occasioned by reading Mr. Paine's Rights of Man:"[48]

> Rous'd by the Reason of his manly page,
> Once more shall Paine a listening world engage;
> From Reason's source, a bold reform he brings,
> By raising up mankind, he pulls down kings. . . .

It was not until 1793, with the execution of the King, the outbreak of war in Europe and President Washington's Proclamation of Neutrality, that the French Revolution became a partisan issue in American politics. Both Federalists and Republicans saw mirrored in European events their own fears for America—to Federalists the French Revolution was an example of the dangers of excessive democracy and social leveling; to Republicans the French were the defenders of the ideals of republicanism, and anyone who opposed the Revolution was a monarchist.[49] The year 1793 witnessed countless popular demonstrations of support for the French. In Philadelphia, French songs were sung in the streets, the *bonnet rouge* was everywhere and the French Revolution was toasted in the taverns. This was the year too of the emergence of the Democratic-Republican Societies, whose resolutions linked support for the French Revolution with the defense of republicanism at home. Composed of "every class of citizens,"

the societies in New York and Philadelphia attracted a wide
following among artisans, who were particularly enthusiastic in
their support for the Revolution, and who retained from the
1770s a special sense of identification with Paine. In 1793, the
General Society of Mechanics and Tradesmen of New York
toasted the success of the French armies, and "the mechanic,
Thomas Paine. . . ."[50]

The Democratic societies' enthusiasm for France, indeed,
seemed to outweigh Paine's own. At the very time that Paine was
in Luxembourg prison, thoroughly disillusioned with the course
of events in France, the Democratic Society of Pennsylvania
toasted "The Mountain [Jacobins]: May tyranny be chained at its
foot and may the light of liberty from its summit cheer and
illuminate the whole world." Nonetheless, Paine remained a hero
to the societies; indeed he has been given "the credit for father-
ing" them. This is an exaggeration, but it is true that *The Rights of
Man* was distributed by the societies more frequently than any
other work, and that the members shared Paine's internationalism, his intense commitment to republicanism and his hostility to
aristocracy and monarchy. And, as Paine had done in *The Rights
of Man,* the societies redefined the meaning of the word "democracy," using it simply as a synonym for republicanism, a government based on the will of the people. The ideological conflict over
the French Revolution made Paine's name anathema to many
Federalists, but the Democratic and mechanic organizations still
revered him:[51]

> Here's success to honest Tom Paine:
> May he live to enjoy what he well does explain,
> The just rights of Man may we never forget
> For they'll save Britain's friends from the bottomless Pitt.

The Democratic societies all but disappeared by 1795, but
much of their organization and ideology was absorbed into the
growing Jeffersonian Republican party. And Paine remained "a

near saint" to Republicans in the mid-1790s. The Republican press defended him against Federalist attacks and reprinted his criticisms of Jay's Treaty. Paine's writings resonated strongly with the "frenzy" of Anglophobia among Republicans and with the Jeffersonians' image of Federalists as pro-British "aristocrats" who desired to undermine republican government and had contempt for the common people. Even Paine's attack on George Washington did not affect his standing among Republicans; after all, strong denunciations of the President were standard fare in the opposition press by 1796. The Philadelphia *Aurora,* for example, hailed Washington's exit from office by observing that "the name of Washington" had become synomymous with "political iniquity" and "legalized corruption."[52]

What finally made Republicans pull back from too close an identification with Paine was *The Age of Reason.* In the mid-1790s, Paine's deist pamphlet went through seventeen editions in America and sold tens of thousands of copies. As a result, deism, which had previously been confined primarily to the educated classes and to a small number of rationalist mechanics, seemed to be becoming a popular movement. And while previous deists had been content to discuss their beliefs in private, the new deist organizations which arose in the 1790s were militant and proselytizing. Through pamphlets and lectures they launched a direct assault upon organized Christianity. *The Age of Reason* became the "Bible" of American deists, and Paine their hero. To the blind former Methodist preacher Elihu Palmer, the most prominent deist organizer of these years, Paine was "the undaunted champion of reason, and the resolute enemy of tyranny, bigotry and prejudice . . . probably the most useful man that ever existed on the face of the earth."[53]

From throughout the country in the mid-1790s came reports of a wave of "infidelity" and indifference to religion. Rev. Joseph Priestley, who emigrated to Pennsylvania in 1794, found on his arrival that the state was filled with "unbelievers." Priestley himself was considered dangerous by more orthodox Protestants since, as a Unitarian, he defended the doctrine of free will and rejected such "unreasonable" tenets of Christianity as the Trinity and the divinity of Christ. But Priestley could not follow Paine in denying the Bible as the revealed truth of Divine Providence, and he was alarmed that *The Age of Reason* was "much read," and had "made great impression here." Palmer's lectures attracted large audiences in New York and Philadelphia, and the irreligion among settlers in Kentucky, Ohio and Tennessee was notorious.[54] It was the apparent spread of infidelity, more than the French Revolution, which turned much of the Protestant clergy toward conservatism. And this was true not simply of Federalist New England Calvinists, but of such ardent Republicans as Methodists, Baptists and Presbyterians. Throughout the country, the Protestant clergy geared themselves for a battle in defense of the faith.[55]

When Jefferson's own religious beliefs became a political issue in the campaign of 1800, his supporters hastened to separate their candidate from too close an association with Paine. As one Republican observed in a Virginia newspaper, while *Common Sense* had been "the Bible of the American Revolution," and *The Rights of Man* was equally praiseworthy, "Mr. Paine's attack upon our most sacred religion . . . is not the question before the public" since "no such attack has ever been made by" Jefferson. Deism was not the only, or even the most important "republican religion" at the turn of the century. Jefferson rode to power on the votes of Methodists, Baptists and Presbyterians, their enthusiasm heightened by the religious revival which began in 1800. Paine had become more of an embarrassment than an asset to the Republican party. As one Jeffersonian society in New York resolved, "May his Rights of Man be handed down to our latest posterity, but may his Age of Reason never live to see the rising generation."[56]

The story of the remaining seven years of Paine's life is quickly told. He arrived in America in the fall of 1802, to a torrent of abuse from the Federalist press. A Boston journalist described Paine as "a lying, drunken, brutal infidel, who rejoices in the opportunity of basking and wallowing in the confusion, devastation, bloodshed, rapine and murder, in which his soul delights." To the Federalists, Paine was a convenient weapon with which to attack and embarrass Jefferson and raise anew the question of the President's religion. But there were also many Republicans who refused to welcome him. His old friend Samuel Adams, an enthusiastic supporter of the French Revolution during the 1790s, issued a public letter denouncing Paine for his "defense of infidelity." Benjamin Rush refused to see him, and innkeepers refused him service during his trip to Washington.

At first, Paine did receive a warm reception from Republican organizations in Philadelphia, New York and Washington, and visited Jefferson several times in the White House. Jefferson still had affection for Paine. In 1801, he had offered Paine transportation to the United States on a public vessel, adding that he would find that Americans had returned to the principles of 1776, in whose cause Paine had "steadily laboured and with as much effect as any man living." But soon after his return to America, Paine composed a series of letters for publication in the Republican press, reviving his hostility to John Adams and George Washington. Paine seemed locked into the issues of the past; his strong personal denunciation of Federalist leaders was out of keeping with the spirit of political reconciliation Jefferson was attempting to foster. Paine's friend William Duane, editor of the *Aurora* and himself a British radical forced to flee the country for his political views, warned Paine not to publish the letters. "I have fairly told him," Duane explained to Jefferson, "that he will be deserted by the only party that respects him or does not hate him—that all his political writings will be rendered useless—and even his fame destroyed." But Paine refused to listen, and Jefferson gently severed their relationship.[57]

In the last years of his life, Paine devoted most of his energies to religious writings. He contributed some seventeen essays to *The Prospect*, the deist journal edited by Elihu Palmer. As usual, he minced no words in his assaults on Christianity. "The hinting and intimating manner of writing that was formerly used on subjects of this kind," he explained, "produced skepticism, but not conviction. It is necessary to be bold." In general, his writings simply repeated the arguments of *The Age of Reason*, but on occasion flashes of the old style and incisiveness came through. One essay sparkled in its condemnation of the Blue Laws of Connecticut:[58]

> The word Sabbath means rest; that is cessation from labor, but the stupid Blue Laws of Connecticut make a labor of rest, for they oblige a person to sit still from sunrise to sunset on a Sabbath-day, which is hard work. . . . The gloomy Calvinist of Connecticut . . . shuts from his view the Temple of Creation. The sun shines no joy to him. The gladdening voice of nature calls on him in vain. He is deaf, dumb and blind to everything around that God has made. Such is the Sabbath-day of Connecticut.

Paine did, in his final years, contribute occasional essays to the Republican press on the political issues of the day. He strongly supported the Louisiana Purchase—indeed Paine was one of the first to suggest that America purchase not only the port of New Orleans, but the entire Louisiana Territory, an indication of his continued interest in the development of a continental American empire. Here, Paine was firmly within the mainstream of Republican party thought, but on some occasions he associated with the "left wing" of the Jeffersonian party—those who desired to see the democratic impulse of the Revolution extended and strengthened. In a number of states, the conflict between radical and conservative Jeffersonians centered on demands for reform of the legal system. Appealing to popular hostility to lawyers, reformers demanded that the power of the legal profession be weakened, that the ability of judges to interpret the law be reduced, that new codes of laws be adopted free from Latin phraseology and that British precedents be excluded from American courts.

In 1805, Paine published a number of essays in support of the movement for legal reform in Pennsylvania. His friend William Duane and backcountry Republicans led by John Binns, another radical British emigré, demanded that a convention be called to restore the Pennsylvania Constitution of 1776 (which had been radically revised in 1790), and to institute far-reaching changes in the legal system. Paine stated their case more effectively than any other writer and his essays were reprinted in the *Aurora* and distributed in pamphlet form by the Duane-Binns faction. Paine reiterated his admiration for the constitution of 1776, which "copied nothing from the English government" and was "comfortable to the Declaration of Independence" because, in contrast to the revised constitution of 1790, it contained no property qualifications for voting. And in support of the movement for simplification of the legal system, Paine proposed doing away with lawyers entirely in many cases, by allowing arbitration boards composed of merchants, farmers or mechanics to settle disputes within each occupation without the necessity of going to court.[59] Paine's writings on Louisiana and Pennsylvania politics in a sense were a culmination, or a reiteration, of the themes which had characterized his thought thirty years earlier during the American Revolution—a commitment to commercial expansion coupled with an intense democratic egalitarianism.

As in most other states, the movement for legal reform failed in Pennsylvania and, after this brief moment when he was once again a spokesman for radical Jeffersonians in the state, Paine slipped into obscurity. His final years were ones of "lonely, private misery." He was isolated from almost all his old associates and friends, and again began to drink heavily. Paine retired to his New Rochelle farm and then lived with a succession of friends in and near New York City. At the close of his life, Paine's visitors were said to be chiefly from among "the laboring class of emi-

grants." He died in 1809. Six mourners attended his funeral—
Madame Bonneville and her two sons, who had come to America
a few years after Paine's return, a Quaker and two Negroes.
And with the exception of a hostile, humorous poem in a Federalist
newspaper, his death passed virtually unnoticed in the American
press.[60]

Why had America rejected and then forgotten Paine? Certainly, as an aggressively anti-Christian deist who had done more
than any individual to popularize a critique of the Bible, Paine
could not have chosen a worse moment to return to America—in
the midst of a religious revival and at the outset of a century
which would be marked, especially in America, by an intense
pietism. "It is a basic difference between European and American
civilizations," writes the historian William McLoughlin, "that dis-
establishment was not engineered by atheistic *philosophes* shouting
'Écrasez l'infâme,' but by evangelical pietists shouting 'Freedom of
religion.' " The aggressive anti-clericalism and secularism so common in nineteenth-century Europe never found a congenial soil
in America, partly because, after the Revolution, there was no
established church with vast property holdings and institutionalized privilege to attack and partly because the Protestant
churches, far from being a bastion of the existing order, were the
source of much of the reforming fervor in American society. In
England, anti-clerical rationalism was a major component of
labor-radical thought throughout the nineteenth century; in
America, far more critics of society spoke the language of revivalist Protestantism and Christian perfectionism than of deist rationalism.[61]

In a sense, the real mystery about Paine's reception is not why
he was so bitterly attacked, but why virtually no one came to his
defense. Was Paine, as a symbol of the radical edge of the
American Revolution, unacceptable at a time when that radical
impulse seemed to have been largely exhausted? Did Paine's
America—the radical constituency among urban artisans—no

longer exist? Unfortunately, we know far too little about radical thought in early nineteenth-century America to answer such questions with any degree of certainty. It is significant, however, that support for the legal reform movement came largely from the rural areas of Pennsylvania and other states. The legal reformers quoted Paine's democratic writings more often than the works of any other author, but they either ignored or were ignorant of his economic views.

As for the artisans, they did not seem particularly alienated from the American social order in the generation between 1800 and 1830. American society and politics in these years seemed infinitely more open to mechanic and lower-class participation than was contemporary England. In France and England, the artisans and sans-culottes had entered politics in 1792, only to be forced to withdraw by the end of the decade. But in America, the artisans who entered politics during the American Revolution were there to stay. They continued to find opportunities for self-expression in politics, and they found political leaders, usually in the Jeffersonian party, whose ideology seemed consonant with their own. In England, by contrast, men like Thomas Hardy viewed the entire political system as alien and hostile, and the mass of British workers, deprived of the right to vote, lived in a virtual "political and social apartheid" in the early nineteenth century. This isolation was critical to the formation of English working-class consciousness, a consciousness in which Paine's critique of the aristocracy, monarchy and the political and social inequalities of English society, became essential parts.[62]

But what did this critique have to do with America? Not only had Americans already achieved the political goals demanded by English radicals—a wide suffrage, republican government, the absence of institutionalized legal privilege—but the burning social grievances which fueled English radicalism were not nearly as prevalent here. This is not to suggest that American society was without social problems. The famous 1806 strike of journeyman shoemakers against their master employers, which resulted in the trial and conviction of the leaders for conspiracy, symbolized the issues which had not been solved by political democracy and republicanism. But Paine said nothing about the trial; indeed, his republicanism, with its vision of a democratic order free from class conflict, was not well suited to deal with the economic questions raised by the strike.

The American political system did, however, even at this early date, seem remarkably able to absorb the energies and talents of disaffected European radicals. The contrast is indeed striking between America's rejection of Paine and the opportunities it offered to Paineite radicals who fled England in the 1790s. William Duane, John Binns and many others who fled England one step ahead of the law found positions as prominent Republican editors and party officials. Joseph Gales, to take one further example, had been one of the leading spirits of the Sheffield Constitutional Society until his flight to America in 1794; here, he became editor of the Raleigh *Register,* mayor of Raleigh and a leading figure in early nineteenth-century Jeffersonian politics. Men like Gales retained their Paineite republican ideals but viewed them as having been essentially fulfilled in America. And America seemed quite able to accept Paineites like Duane and Gales, who were not tainted by the sin of aggressive infidelity, while it rejected Paine himself.[63]

VI

In August 1809, shortly after Paine's death, the English-born New York City editor James Cheetham wrote to Paine's long-time friend Joel Barlow, asking for information for use in a prospective biography of Paine. Barlow wished him luck, but concluded that perhaps the time was not right to celebrate Paine's memory. "His own writings are his best life, and these are not read at present. The greater part of readers in the United States will not be persuaded, as long as their present feelings last, to consider him in any other light than as a drunkard and deist." Thirteen years later Thomas Jefferson was asked to allow one of his letters to Paine to appear in print. "No, my dear sir, not for this world," Jefferson replied. "Into what a hornet's nest would it thrust my head!"[64]

As the remarks of Barlow and Jefferson make clear, few Americans were prepared to speak kindly of Paine in the years immediately following his death. But, beginning in the mid-1820s, a veritable Paine revival took place. In 1825, a dinner was held in New York City to celebrate the anniversary of Paine's birth (January 29), and the occasion became an annual event. By the 1830s Paine birthday dinners were being held in cities such as Boston, Philadelphia, Cincinnati and Albany. At the height of the Paine enthusiasm, in 1834, some seven hundred men and women attended a ball following the New York birthday dinner at the City Saloon. Paine seemed to have become a popular figure once again.[65]

Who were the men and women who celebrated Paine's birthday and what did the memory of Paine mean to them? The dinners were closely associated with the emergence of the first class-conscious labor movement in American history. The ideology of the labor spokesmen echoed the premises of Paineite republicanism—a belief in natural rights and human perfectibility and a conviction that, in the absence of artificial privilege, republican government would ensure an economic abundance in which all classes could share. Combined with these beliefs was an early version of the labor theory of value, coupled with an assertion of the right of the worker to the "whole product of his labor." Such ideas stemmed from the influence of the "Ricardian Socialists" of the preceding thirty years—Englishmen like Patrick Colquhoun, William Thompson and John Gray and their American disciples Cornelius Blatchely and Thomas Skidmore. But the essential social outlook harked back to the Paineite distinction between the "producing" and "non-producing" classes and its corollary that through unfair taxation and economic privilege, the latter deprived the former of a part of the fruit of its labor.

A few of the early labor leaders did move beyond Paine's ideas to an attack on the existing system of private property. Skidmore, a Connecticut-born teacher, scientist and machinist and a great admirer of Paine's writings, developed an elaborate plan by which the state, by an on-going redistribution of property, would ensure an approximate economic equality. The title of Skidmore's pamphlet, *The Rights of Man to Property*, was meant to pay homage to Paine at the same time that it indicated the need to transcend Paineite republicanism in the quest for equality.[66]

Paine, according to one student, "captured the imagination" of the early labor movement. To "A Mechanic," Paine was "that noble patriot, who did more than any other writer of his day to disenthral the human mind from the fetters of prejudice and superstition." It was "a shame . . . to Americans, that they have never done justice to his memory." As this last sentence implies, the "Mechanic" was not a native-born American; in fact, he was a Scottish immigrant. And a closer look at the Paine birthday celebrations reveals that the leading organizers were almost entirely British-born. Paine's memory lived most strongly among men like William Carver, a native of Lewes who came to America in 1794 and befriended Paine in his final years; George Houston, who had been jailed in England for his anti-clerical writings; and George Henry Evans, a printer's apprentice who emigrated to the United States in 1820 and was a "radical in civil government, and in religion." The birthday dinner of 1825 was organized by Carver and Benjamin Offen, a self-educated shoemaker who had just arrived from England and was following the pattern set a few years earlier when the first Paine dinner was held in "an obscure tavern in London." And the subscription drive which resulted in the erection of a statue of Paine in New Rochelle in 1839 was organized by Gilbert Vale, an immigrant teacher and surveyor who also published a biography of Paine in 1841.[67]

Almost all the leading Paineites of the 1830s were enthusiastic deists; in most cases, an acceptance of the anti-religious outlook of *The Age of Reason* was still required to associate one's self with Paine. Although many of the dinners were sponsored by labor organizations, the toasts and speeches dealt far more extensively with religious questions than with larger social concerns. At one dinner, a toast described *The Age of Reason* as "a work containing more truth than any volume under the sun." And while toasts were generally offered to the memory of American heroes like George Washington and Benjamin Franklin, foreign rebels ranging from Simon Bolivar to William Tell, and to such republican subjects as free education and the memory of the French Revolution, crusading secularists were usually singled out for special praise—Richard Carlile, who had been jailed in England for publishing deist works in the 1820s, Abner Kneeland, prosecuted for "blasphemy" in Massachusetts, and such anti-clerical figures of the eighteenth century as Voltaire and Hume. When, in the mid-1830s, Tammany Hall sponsored the Paine dinner in an attempt to woo the votes of workingmen, the official toasts became rather more general—"Equal Rights, Free Discussion, The Press, The People"—but toasts from the floor continued in the deist vein.[68]

The issue which most disturbed the Paineites was what they perceived as a growing "priestly domination" in American society. The clergy were held responsible for the fact that "at one period, no man could approbate [Paine's] writings, or even lisp his name with praise, without being made to feel the rancor of a bewildered multitude." The Paineites were particularly alarmed by the Sabbatarian campaign for a halt to Sunday mail deliveries, which they viewed as the first step in a "union of Church and State." The toasts at the Paine dinners ridiculed religious revivalism and evangelical preaching. "Their best stock in trade," one Philadelphia diner proposed, "consists of hell and the devil. With these they frighten people out of their senses and then out of their money." And in typical deist terms they exalted the "empire of reason" and looked forward to the day when "Churches and Chapels may . . . be converted into Temples of the Sciences, and the Philosopher be cherished instead of the Priest."[69] Unlike their hero, speakers at the Paine dinners seemed both defensive and backward-looking, more concerned with the religious debates of the eighteenth century than with the pressing social and economic questions of their own day.

To the men and women who celebrated his birthday, Paine was above all a symbol of the evil effects of clerical persecution and the virtues of the free intellect, unfettered by "superstition." But while the leaders of the labor movement, at least in Philadelphia and New York, seem to have been deists (many of them influenced by the secularism of Robert Owen), it is difficult to believe that a majority of urban workingmen shared these religious views. On the issue of the "union of Church and State," to be sure, the Paineites could receive support from the official Democratic party, which took a strict Jeffersonian position on the separation of church and state, opposed Sabbatarianism and condemned their Whig opponents as the "religious party." But most labor organizations were conspicuously silent on questions of religion. Evangelical Protestantism was far more typical of the religious climate of the 1830s than Paineite deism, even, it seems likely, within the labor movement.[70]

Unfortunately, our knowledge of the early labor movement is still too sketchy to say with certainty what happened to the tradition of Paineite rationalism in the years which followed. It has recently been suggested that the depression of 1837–42 not only severely weakened labor organizations, but made native-born Protestant workingmen receptive to evangelical revivalism, nativism, temperance and the Sabbatarian movement, undermining the class consciousness which had been so widespread in the 1830s and pitting workers against one another along religious and ethnic lines. The nativist and evangelical upsurge submerged the secularist tradition and with it, the memory of Paine. True, the Paine birthday celebrations continued into the 1840s and beyond, but Paine's memory was now even more exclusively associated with free thinkers and secularists than in previous years. The only exception was the land reform movement, whose leaders, including George Henry Evans, still cited Paine's *Agrarian Justice* in support of their demands for free homesteads and "The People's Right to the Soil." *Agrarian Justice,* Evans declared at a Paine dinner in 1850, was "excellent material for building up democratic and social republics."[71]

Even among free thinkers, the old Paineite constituency was disappearing. The native-born deist movement seemed to have virtually died out by 1850, but it was succeeded by a new generation of anti-clerical immigrants. In 1859, the *Atlantic Monthly* described Paine as "only an indistinct shadow" to most Americans, noting that only a "small and threadbare sect of 'liberals,' as they call themselves," still revered Paine's memory. English immigrants and German refugees from the Revolution of 1848 dominated these "liberal" gatherings. It was at a meeting of English-born "infidels" in Cincinnati that Moncure D. Conway, the author of what is still in some ways the finest biography of Paine, was introduced to Paine's writings. "Paine had become to them," Conway later recalled, "more than the founder of a theistic church; he was the standard-bearer and apostle of religious freedom; to these freethinkers he was what George Fox was to the Quakers and John Wesley to the Methodists." The German '48ers, too, frequently quoted Paine in their attacks on "king-craft and priest-craft" and in opposing nativism, temperance, Sabbath laws and other attempts to use state power to promote the cultural ends of evangelical Protestantism. Paine birthday celebrations continued among German-Americans into the 1880s and 1890s, finally dying out around the turn of the century. Speakers frequently lamented that in a land he served so well, it seemed to be left to immigrants to promote the memory of Paine.[72]

What, then, was Paine's legacy? In England, he provided "working-class radicalism with its vocabulary, its standard of right and wrong, its interpretation of the past and its hopes for the future," as well as with a utopian image of America which was not seriously challenged among English radicals until the 1880s. Virtually every working-class radical in nineteenth-century England was strongly influenced by Paine.[73] In America, too, the republican heritage of the American Revolution became a major inspiration of nineteenth-century labor and radical ideology. Radicals would not only appeal to the Revolution to legitimate their own demands for change, but would seize on republican egalitarianism to attack large concentrations of power and property and to demand a reconstruction of American society. The irony is that Paine's republican language suffused the culture of nineteenth-century America, but that Paine himself was generally forgotten. Even the labor radicals who celebrated the Fourth of July and claimed descent from the heroes of the Revolution generally omitted Paine from the list of revolutionary forebears. Republican and democratic ideas could be obtained from Jefferson, without the added burden of Paine's aggressive anti-clericalism. It was only among those willing to accept him in full—his religious writings as well as political—that Paine remained a hero.

And yet Paine had contributed too much to the image Americans had of themselves and to the language in which they expressed their political and social aspirations, to be completely forgotten. It is significant that the two presidents we associate most closely with the democratic tradition in the nineteenth century—Andrew Jackson and Abraham Lincoln—were both admirers of Paine. Jackson's democratic beliefs and his commitment to the separation of church and state may explain the fact that he believed Paine deserved a place "in the hearts of all lovers of liberty." Lincoln remained an admirer of Paine and something of a religious skeptic after reading *The Age of Reason* in the 1830s. Neither Jackson nor Lincoln was the sort of man to be intimidated by the hostility to Paine in polite society. Nor was Walt Whitman, himself a former artisan, who delivered a Paine birthday speech in Philadelphia in 1877, or Eugene V. Debs, who insisted that the American socialist tradition was indebted to Paine. When, at the close of the nineteenth century, Theodore Roosevelt referred to Paine as a "filthy little atheist," there were still admirers of Paine who protested vehemently.

Today, Paine still seems "relevant," not only in his revolutionary internationalism and defiance of existing institutions, but because of his modern cast of mind, his rationalism and faith in human nature, his belief in the possibility of casting off the burden of the past and remaking institutions so as to "bring forward, by a quiet and regular operation, all that extent of capacity which never fails to appear in revolutions." There have always been and, we may hope, there will always be, men and women who echo Paine's conviction: "A share in two revolutions is living to some purpose."[74]

☆ ☆

NOTES

☆ ☆

ABBREVIATIONS USED IN NOTES

HSPa   Historical Society of Pennsylvania, Philadelphia
JAH   *Journal of American History*
PaH   *Pennsylvania History*
PaMHB   *Pennsylvania Magazine of History and Biography*
PRO   Public Record Office, London
WMQ   *William and Mary Quarterly*

INTRODUCTION

1. Charles Francis Adams, ed., *Familiar Letters of John Adams and His Wife Abigail Adams* (New York, 1876), 167; David Freeman Hawke, *Paine* (New York, 1974), 7.
2. Among useful works which isolate one aspect of Paine's thought are Joseph Dorfman, "The Economic Philosophy of Thomas Paine," *Political Science Quarterly*, LIII (September, 1938), 372–86; Howard Penniman, "Thomas Paine—Democrat," *American Political Science Review*, XXXVII (April, 1943),

244–62; Harry Hayden Clark, "Toward a Reinterpretation of Thomas Paine," *American Literature*, V (May, 1933), 133–45.

3. Hawke, *Paine*, is now the best one-volume biography, although Audrey Williamson, *Thomas Paine: His Life, Work, and Times* (New York, 1974) contains some information not in the Hawke work. Neither entirely supersedes Moncure Conway, *The Life of Thomas Paine* (2 vols.: New York, 1892).

4. See Bernard Friedman, "The Shaping of Radical Consciousness in Provincial New York," *JAH*, LVI (March, 1970), 781–801, esp. 795–96. However, while Friedman rightly warns against associating eighteenth-century radicalism with "the exclusive interests of a propertyless proletariat," he himself lumps together a variety of social aspirations and values under the anachronistic phrase "middle-class objectives" (796).

5. Bernard Bailyn, *The Ideological Origins of the American Revolution* (Cambridge, 1967); Gordon S. Wood, *The Creation of the American Republic, 1776–1787* (Chapel Hill, 1969); Pauline Maier, *From Resistance to Revolution* (New York, 1972).

6. This point is made in the important article by J. G. A. Pocock, "Virtue and Commerce in the Eighteenth Century," *Journal of Interdisciplinary History*, III (Summer, 1972), 119–34.

7. J. G. A. Pocock, *Politics, Language, and Time* (New York, 1971), 12, 38, 105, and *passim.* Cf. Walter J. Ong, *Rhetoric, Romance, and Technology* (Ithaca, 1971).

8. E. J. Hobsbawm, *Primitive Rebels* (New York, 1965), 126.

9. See below, Chapter 3, and R. R. Palmer, *The Age of the Democratic Revolution* (2 vols.: Princeton, 1959–64), I, 19–20. On the crucial importance of the changing meanings of words in the late eighteenth and early nineteenth centuries, see also Raymond Williams, *Culture and Society, 1780–1950* (Penguin ed., London, 1951), 13.

10. *Mémoirs de Madame Roland* (2 vols.: Paris, 1834 ed.), II, 295.

11. E. P. Thompson, *The Making of the English Working Class* (London, 1963), and the works by George Rudé, E. J. Hobsbawm, and Albert Soboul cited in Chapter 2 below.

12. Adams, ed., *Familiar Letters*, 149–50, 155; Page Smith, *John Adams* (2 vols.: Garden City, N. Y., 1962), II, 845.

13. Warren I. Susman, "History and the American Intellectual: Uses of a Usable Past," *American Quarterly*, XVI (1964), 257.

14. William Appleman Williams, *The Contours of American History* (London ed., 1961), 111; Cecelia M. Kenyon, "Republicanism and Radicalism in the American Revolution: An Old-Fashioned Interpretation," *WMQ*, 3 ser., XIX (April, 1962), 153–82.

15. There had been a few "professional pamphleteers" in the colonial period, but most were school teachers paid by political leaders to write occasional pamphlets for election campaigns, not men for whom pamphleteering was their major vocation. Gary B. Nash, "The Transformation of Urban Politics, 1700–1765," *JAH*, LX (December, 1973), 618–19.

CHAPTER ONE

1. *A Description of the Diocese of Norwich: or, the Present State of Norfolk and Suffolk* (London, 1735), 56–57; A. Leigh Hunt, *The Capital of the Ancient Kingdom of East Anglia* (London, 1870), 49; Daniel Defoe, *A Tour Thro' the Whole Island of Great Britain* (2 vols: London, 1968—orig. pub., 1724–26), I , 61–63.

2. The best treatment of Paine's early life in England is contained in Williamson, *Paine,* 11–59. See also Hawke, *Paine,* 7–21. All treatments of these years rely heavily on Francis Oldys [pseud. G. Chalmers], *The Life of Thomas Pain* (London, 1793 ed.).

3. R. Campbell, *The London Tradesman* (London, 1747), 224–26; *A General Description of All Trades Digested in Alphabetical Order* (London, 1747), 200; Oldys, *Pain,* 9–12.

4. Philip S. Foner, ed., *The Complete Writings of Thomas Paine* (2 vols.: New York, 1945), II, 1189.

5. Williamson, *Paine,* 19–20.

6. Foner, *Complete Writings,* II, 464.

7. Defoe, *A Tour,* I, 61–63, 120–22; William Page, ed., *The Victoria History of the County of Sussex* (London, 1905—), II, 199.

8. *Calendar of Home Office Papers of the Reign of George III, 1773–1775* (London, 1899), 39–42; John Bigelow, *The Complete Works of Benjamin Franklin* (10 vols.: New York, 1887), IV, 163; George Rudé, *The Crowd in History* (New York, 1964); T. S. Ashton, *An Economic History of England: The Eighteenth Century* (London, 1955), 225–27, 239.

9. M. Dorothy George, *London Life in the Eighteenth Century* (New York, 1965 ed.), 41–42, 83; Oldys, *Pain,* 9–12; George Rudé, *Hanoverian London, 1714–1808* (London, 1971), 82–84. Cf. Richard Hofstader, *America at 1750* (New York, 1971), 134: "Open the work of an English historian writing a general history of the eighteenth century, and you will soon be in the midst of a strong and necessary preoccupation with the grinding, unremitting poverty of the small farmer or the pestiferous, deadly squalor of the urban poor."

10. Foner, *Complete Writings,* I, 496; J. H. Plumb, *In the Light of History* (London, 1972), 9, 15–21; Rush quoted in Whitfield J. Bell, "Science and Humanity in Philadelphia, 1775–1790" (unpublished doctoral dissertation, University of Pennsylvania, 1947), 302. Cf. Daniel Boorstin, *The Lost World of Thomas Jefferson* (New York, 1948), 206, 209; Harry Hayden Clark, "Toward a Reinterpretation of Thomas Paine," 133–45.

11. Foner, *Complete Writings,* I, 164, 387; F. W. Gibbs, "Itinerant Lecturers in Natural Philosophy," *Ambix,* VIII (1960), 111–17; Nicholas Hans, *New Trends in Education in the Eighteenth Century* (London, 1951), 145–46, 152–53, 160–61; Plumb, *In the Light of History* 13–16.

12. Foner, *Complete Writings,* II, 1131, 1162, 1384; "George Lewis Scott," *Dictionary of National Biography,* XVII, 961.

13. Verner W. Crane, "The Club of Honest Whigs: Friends of Science and

Liberty," *WMQ*, 3 ser., XXIII (October, 1966), 210–33. Paine quotes Price in one of the *Crisis* essays: Foner, *Complete Writings*, I, 133. For the influence of Burgh and Priestley, see below, note 17.

14. Caroline Robbins, *The Eighteenth-Century Commonwealthman* (Cambridge, 1959); Bailyn, *Ideological Origins*, chs. 2–3; Lance G. Banning, "The Quarrel With Federalism: A Study in the Origins of Republican Thought" (unpublished doctoral dissertation, Washington University, 1972), 63–90, 103–08, 124; Pocock, "Virtue and Commerce in the Eighteenth Century," 119–34; Isaac Kramnick, *Bolingbroke and His Circle* (Cambridge, 1968). On the financial revolution, see also Sidney Homer, *A History of Interest Rates* (New Brunswick, 1963), 147–53.

15. John Cannon, *Parliamentary Reform, 1640–1832* (Cambridge, 1973), 45.

16. Anthony Lincoln, *Some Political and Social Ideas of English Dissent, 1763–1800* (Cambridge, 1938); Russell E. Richey, "The Origins of British Radicalism: The Changing Rationale for Dissent," *Eighteenth-Century Studies*, VII (Winter, 1973–74), 179–92; Staughton Lynd, *Intellectual Origins of American Radicalism* (New York, 1968), 19–25; Harold Perkin, *The Origins of Modern English Society, 1780–1900* (London, 1969), 34.

17. It is not entirely clear—and perhaps not very important—whether Paine read Burgh and Priestley in England or shortly after his arrival in America. He refers to Burgh in *Common Sense* (Foner, *Complete Writings*, I, 38). For the influence of Priestley on that work, see Felix Gilbert, "The English Background of American Isolationism in the Eighteenth Century," *WMQ*, 3 ser., I (April, 1944), 156–58. Paine later wrote that Franklin had given him some materials in 1775 to assist in the writing of *Common Sense*. But, according to Paine, "I had then formed the outlines of Common Sense, and finished nearly the first part"—the portion most indebted to Priestley's *Essay on the First Principles of Government*. (Foner, I, 88–89). If this is the case, it seems likely Paine read Priestley's pamphlet in England since it was never published in America after its initial printing in England in 1771, according to Charles Evans, *American Bibliography* (14 vols.: Worcester, 1941–59 ed.). Paine refers to knowing Tooke before his departure for America in New York *Public Advertiser*, August 22, 1807.

18. Robbins, *Eighteenth Century Commonwealthman*, 8; Ian R. Christie, *Wilkes, Wyvill, and Reform* (London, 1962), 2; James Burgh, *Political Disquisitions* (3 vols.: London, 1774–75), I, 9; II, 18.

19. Christopher Hill, *The World Turned Upside Down* (New York, 1972), 308; Christopher Hill, "Republicanism After the Restoration," *New Left Review*, III (May–June, 1960), 48; Thompson, *Making of the English Working Class*, 28–31; J. H. Plumb, "The Fascination of Republican Virtue Among the Known and the Unknown," in *The Development of a Revolutionary Mentality* (Washington, 1972), 57–61; J. H. Plumb, "Political Man," in James L. Clifford, ed., *Man Versus Society in Eighteenth Century Britain* (Cambridge, 1968), 15–16.

20. J. G. A. Pocock, *Politics, Language, and Time*, 145, 230; Charles Inglis, *The True Interest of America* (Philadelphia, 1776), 22; John Hall, *The Grounds and Reasons of Monarchy Considered* . . . , in *The Oceana and Other Works of James Harrington* (London, 1771), 3–30.

21. Lucy Sutherland, "The City of London in Eighteenth-Century Politics," in Richard Pares and A. J. P. Taylor, eds., *Essays Presented to Sir Lewis Namier* (London, 1956), 49–74; Rudé, *Hanoverian London*, x–xi, 98–99; Plumb, *In the Light of History*, 74.

22. Robbins, *Eighteenth-Century Commonwealthman*, 18; Plumb, "Political Man," 17; Christie, *Wilkes, Wyvill, and Reform*, 6–10; George Rudé, *Wilkes and Liberty* (Oxford, 1962); *Making of the English Working Class*, 69–70, 80; S. Maccoby, *English Radicalism, 1762–1785* (London, 1955), 110.

23. Foner, *Complete Works*, I, 172.

24. J. M. Connell, *Lewes, Its Religious History* (Lewes and London, 1931), 101–03, 110; Jacqueline Simpson, *The Folklore of Lewes* (London, 1973), 134–36. On millennialism, see Ernest Lee Tuveson, *Redeemer Nation: The Idea of America's Millennial Role* (Chicago, 1968), and the discussion and works cited in Chapter 4 below.

25. Simpson, *Folklore*, 134–35; *Sussex Weekly Advertiser, or Lewes Journal*, August 27, 1770.

26. *Sussex Weekly Advertiser, or Lewes Journal*, January 16, 30, March 20, August 7, 1769; Walter H. Godfrey, *At the Sign of the Bull, Lewes, with an Account of Thomas Paine's Residence* . . . (London, 1924), 28; Oldys, *Pain*, 29. The issues of June 5, October 23, 1769, June 4, 1770, and April 29, 1771, contain the letters of Junius. See also J. Steven Watson, *The Reign of George III, 1760–1815* (Oxford, 1960), 145; Williamson, *Paine*, 36.

27. William D. Cooper, *The Parliamentary History of the County of Sussex* (Lewes, 1834), 24; Basil Williams, *Carteret and Newcastle* (Cambridge, 1943), 32–34, 223; Page, ed., *Victoria History of Sussex*, I, 530–31; *A Poll, Taken by Samuel Ollive, and Thomas Scarce, Constables of the Borough of Lewes* . . . (Lewes, 1768). This unusual election contest can be followed in the Newcastle Papers, British Museum Add. Mss 32,988–89.

28. *Ancient and Modern History of Lewes and Brighthelmston* . . . (Lewes, 1795), 211–13, 270–73.

29. William D. Cooper, "Smuggling in Sussex," *Sussex Archaeological Collections*, X (1868), 69–94; Charles Fleet, *Glimpses of Our Ancestors in Sussex* (Brighton, 1878), 73–75; Edward Carson, *The Ancient and Rightful Customs* (London, 1972), 60; *Sussex Weekly Advertiser, or Lewes Journal*, March 20, 1770, May 31, 1773; Customs 48/18/278–79, Customs House Library, London; Malachy Prostlethwayt, *The Universal Dictionary of Trade and Commerce* (4th ed., 2 vols: London, 1764), I, Excise (no pagination).

30. Foner, *Complete Writings*, II, 464, 466; New York *Public Advertiser*, August 22, 1807.

31. Godfrey, *At the Sign of the Bull;* Plumb, *In the Light of History,* 19; Richard Burn and John Burn, *The Justice of the Peace, and Parish Officer* (4 vols.: London, 1797), II, 42; Verena Smith, ed., "The Town Book of Lewes 1702–1837," *Sussex Record Society,* LXIX (1972), 57–62; St. Michael's Parish, Vestry Minute Book, 1770–1773 entries, East Sussex Record Office, Lewes.
32. Foner, *Complete Writings,* I, 441; II, 4–11, 1129; Customs 48/18/415–16, Customs House Library. Cf. Henry Collins, "Paine's Economic Ideas," *Bulletin of the Thomas Paine Society* [England], IV (Autumn, 1967), 5–6.
33. Ian Watt, *The Rise of the Novel* (London, 1957), 36–48; Leslie Stephen, *English Literature and Society in the Eighteenth Century* (London, 1963 ed.), 60–61, 116; H. A. Innis, *Empire and Communication* (Oxford, 1950), 192–95; Levin L. Schücking, *The Sociology of Literary Taste* (London, 1944), 18; Joseph A. Schumpeter, *Capitalism, Socialism, and Democracy* (3rd ed.; London, 1950), 146–49.
34. Foner, *Complete Writings,* I, 441; Hawke, *Paine,* 17; *Sussex Weekly Advertiser, or Lewes Journal,* April 11, 1774.
35. Foner, *Complete Writings,* II, 11–12.
36. Wood, *Creation of the American Republic,* 98–99; Michael Kraus, *The Atlantic Civilization: Eighteenth Century Origins* (Ithaca, 1949), ch. 9.
37. Hawke, *Paine,* 25.

CHAPTER TWO

1. L. H. Butterfield, *Letters of Benjamin Rush* (2 vols.: Philadelphia, 1951), I, 450.
2. David F. Hawke, *In the Midst of A Revolution* (Philadelphia, 1961), 40–45; John K. Alexander, "The Philadelphia Numbers Game: An Analysis of Philadelphia's Eighteenth-Century Population," *PaMHB,* XCVIII (July, 1974), 314–24; Abbott Smith, *Colonists in Bondage* (Chapel Hill, 1947), 335–36; *Return of the Whole Number of Persons Within the Several Districts of the United States* (Philadelphia, 1791), 45. Alexander's is the most recent analysis of the perplexing subject of Philadelphia's population in the colonial period. A slightly lower estimate is given in Gary B. Nash, "Slaves and Slaveholders in Colonial Philadelphia," *WMQ,* 3 ser., XXX (April, 1973), 233.
3. Grant Miles Simon, "Houses and Early Life in Philadelphia," *Transactions, American Philosophical Society,* n. s., XLIII (March, 1953), 282; Whitfield J. Bell, "Some Aspects of the Social History of Pennsylvania, 1760–1790," *PaMHB,* LXII (July, 1938), 282–84; Bell, "Science and Humanity," *passim.*
4. Isaac Weld, *Travels Through the States of North America* (2 vols.: London, 1800), I, 53; Jackson Turner Main, *The Social Structure of Revolutionary America* (Princeton, 1965), 18, 25, 34; John F. Walzer, "Transportation in the Philadelphia Trading Area, 1740–1775" (unpublished doctoral dissertation, University of Wisconsin, 1968); James T. Lemon, *The Best Poor Man's Country: A Geographical Study of Early Southeastern Pennsylvania* (Baltimore, 1972); James

T. Lemon, "Urbanization and the Development of Eighteenth-Century South-eastern Pennsylvania and Adjacent Delaware," *WMQ*, 3 ser, XXIV (October, 1967), 505–06.

5. Carl Bridenbaugh, ed., "Patrick McRoberts' Tour Through the Northern Provinces of America, 1774–1775," *PaMHB*, LIX (1935), 167n.; Arthur L. Jensen, *The Maritime Commerce of Colonial Philadelphia* (Madison, 1963); James L. Henretta, *The Evolution of American Society, 1700–1815* (Lexington, 1973), 45–48.

6. Jensen, *Commerce*, 3–5; Henretta, *Evolution of American Society*, 78–79; Carl Bridenbaugh, *The Colonial Craftsman* (New York, 1950), 89–94; John J. Mc-Cusker, "Sources of Investment Capital in the Colonial Philadelphia Shipping Industry," *Journal of Economic History*, XXXII (March, 1972), 151–54; Jacob E. Cooke, ed., *The Federalist* (Middletown, 1961), 219.

7. Robert F. Oaks, "Philadelphia's Merchants and the American Revolution, 1765–1776" (unpublished doctoral dissertation, University of Southern California, 1970), 11–13. The most recent analysis of the distribution of wealth in Philadelphia is contained in Henretta, *Evolution of American Society*, 105–06 (based on figures gathered from probate and other records by Alice Hanson Jones.) In 1774, the top 10 per cent of the population owned 54.7 per cent of net wealth, and the next 10 per cent 14.6 per cent. An analysis of the even more unequal distribution of wealth in the city in the 1790s is Richard G. Miller, "Gentry and Entrepreneurs: A Socioeconomic Analysis of Philadelphia in the 1790's," *Rocky Mountain Social Science Journal*, XII (January, 1975), 71–84.

8. Carl Bridenbaugh, *Cities in Revolt* (New York, 1955), 139, 145; Frederick B. Tolles, "Town House and Country House: Inventories from the Estate of William Logan, 1776," *PaMHB*, LXXXII (October, 1958), 397–410; Carl Bridenbaugh and Jessica Bridenbaugh, *Rebels and Gentlemen: Philadelphia in the Age of Franklin* (New York, 1942), 182; Judith M. Diamondstone, "Philadelphia's Municipal Corporation, 1701–1776," *PaMHB*, LC (April, 1966), 183–201; Robert A. East, *Business Enterprise in the American Revolutionary Era* (New York, 1938), 13–14.

9. Frederick B. Tolles, *Meeting House and Counting House* (Chapel Hill, 1948), 112–14; Leonard Labaree *et al.*, eds., *The Papers of Benjamin Franklin* (New Haven, 1959—), XI, 324n.; Weld, *Travels*, I, 13.

10. Carl N. Degler, *Out of Our Past* (New York, 1959), 1; George Rogers Taylor, "American Economic Growth Before 1840: An Exploratory Essay," *Journal of Economic History*, XXIV (December, 1964), 432–33; Rowland Berthoff, *An Unsettled People* (New York, 1971), 48–52. Perhaps a word is in order concerning my understanding of the word "capitalism." I am using it here to describe not simply an economy dominated by the profit motive, monetary exchange, commodity production and market relations, but also as a specific social system and set of social relations in which labor itself has become a commodity. As we shall see, the era of the Revolution witnessed the full emergence of a free labor

market in Philadelphia, although the pre-capitalist system of petty commodity production, in which many laborers owned their own means of production, persisted well into the nineteenth century. See Karl Marx, *Capital* (3 vols.: Moscow, 1961), I, 714, 767, 774; Maurice Dobb, *Studies in the Development of Capitalism* (New York, 1963 ed.), 7–8.

11. Curtis B. Nettels, *The Emergence of a National Economy* (New York, 1962), 39; E. James Ferguson, *The American Revolution* (Homewood, Ill., 1974), 15; Bridenbaugh, *Cities in Revolt,* 71; Thomas C. Cochran, *Business in American Life* (New York, 1972), 19–24; Elisha P. Douglass, *The Coming of Age of American Business* (Chapel Hill, 1971), 24–26.

12. W. T. Baxter, *The House of Hancock: Business in Boston,* 1724–1775 (Cambridge, 1945), 294–95; East, *Business Enterprise,* 23–26; Jensen, *Commerce,* 10; William S. Sachs, "The Business Outlook in the Northern Colonies, 1750–1775" (unpublished doctoral dissertation, Columbia University, 1957), 22; Tolles, *Meeting House and Counting House,* 89–91; Robert A. East, "The Business Entrepreneur in a Changing Colonial Economy, 1763–1795," *Journal of Economic History,* VI (1946), Supplement, 20; Jacob M. Price, "Economic Function and the Growth of American Port Towns in the Eighteenth Century," *Perspectives in American History,* VIII (1974), 139.

13. Marc Engal and Joseph A. Ernst, "An Economic Interpretation of the American Revolution," *WMQ,* 3 ser., XXIX (January, 1972), 15–20; Douglass, *Coming of Age,* 20, 43; Marc Engal, "The Economic Development of the Thirteen Continental Colonies, 1720 to 1775," *WMQ,* 3 ser., XXXII (April, 1975), 215; Price, "Economic Function," 160; Charles H. Lincoln, *The Revolutionary Movement in Pennsylvania,* 1760–1776 (Philadelphia, 1901), 81–85.

14. Joseph A. Ernst, *Money and Politics in America,* 1755–1775 (Chapel Hill, 1973); Baxter, *House of Hancock,* 193, 204; East, *Business Enterprise,* 18–22; Wilbur C. Plummer, "Consumer Credit in Colonial Philadelphia," *PaMHB,* LXVI (October, 1942), 389–400; Henretta, *Evolution of American Society,* 182; Homer, *History of Interest Rates,* 155, 161, 274–75; Richard B. Morris, "The Organization of Production During the Colonial Period," in Harold F. Williamson, ed., *The Growth of the American Economy* (New York, 1951), 72–73; Bridenbaugh and Bridenbaugh, *Rebels and Gentlemen,* 206; Cochran, *Business,* 21–22.

15. Anne C. Bezanson *et al., Prices in Colonial Pennsylvania* (Philadelphia, 1935); Morton J. Horowitz, "The Historical Foundations of Modern Contract Law," *Harvard Law Review,* LXXXVII (March, 1974), 935–36. Bezanson, pp. 18–19, 46–47, shows that between 1749 and 1775 the price of bread in Philadelphia was essentially stable, although there was sharp temporary inflation in 1763 and 1772.

16. Donard R. Adams, Jr., "Wage Rates in the Early National Period: Philadelphia, 1785–1830," *Journal of Economic History,* XXVIII (September, 1968), 406, indicates that the traditional English pre-industrial wage hierarchy in which skilled workers received twice the pay of common laborers, characterized Philadelphia wage rates in the 1780s. See also Eric Hobsbawm, *Labouring*

Men (London, 1964), 346–47. Cf. Karl Marx's comment concerning levels of economic development: "The independent development of merchant's capital . . . stands in inverse proportion to the general economic development of society." Marx, *Capital* III, 322. The chapter from which this quotation is taken, "Historical Facts About Merchant's Capital" (III, ch. 20) is of great relevance to the colonial American economy.

17. Henretta, *Evolution of American Society*, 159; Nettels, *Emergence of a National Economy*, 22; Douglass, *Coming of Age*, 32; East, *Business Enterprise*, 43–46, 127, 285, 322–23; East, "Business Entrepreneur," 26.

18. Price, "Economic Function," 152–54.

19. The most extensive occupational analysis of Philadelphia's population is contained in Price, "Economic Function." Utilizing data from 1774 tax lists, he provides the occupations of 4407 male heads of household and single men, of whom I classify 48.1 per cent as artisans. (Price arranges his figures somewhat differently.) Figures from the 1772 tax lists generously supplied to me by Gary B. Nash of the University of California at Los Angeles paint a similar picture: of 3251 males listed, 50 per cent were artisans. I define an artisan as a property-owning producer of commodities (but artisanal "property" includes skill and tools) or a skilled craftsman owning his own tools but working for a contractor, as in the building trades. I include masters and journeymen, but not apprentices or laborers. For other definitions, see Charles S. Olton, "Philadelphia Artisans and the American Revolution" (unpublished doctoral dissertation, University of California, Berkeley, 1967), 4–13; Staughton Lynd, *Class Conflict, Slavery, and the United States Constitution* (Indianapolis, 1967), 82–84; Alfred F. Young, "Some Thoughts on Mechanic Participation in the American Revolution" (paper delivered at Third Annual Conference on Early American History, Newberry Library, November, 1974). My understanding of the eighteenth-century artisan has been greatly aided by Thompson, *Making of the English Working Class;* Albert Soboul, *The Sans Culottes*, trans. Rémy Inglis Hall (New York, 1972); and Arno S. Mayer's unpublished essay, "The Lower Middle Class as Historical Problem."

20. Main, *Social Structure*, 74–83, 133, 274–75; Bridenbaugh, *Colonial Craftsman, passim;* Jackson Turner Main, *The Sovereign States*, 1775–1783 (New York, 1973), 71–80; Blanche E. Hazard, *The Organization of the Boot and Shoe Industry in Massachusetts Before* 1875 (Cambridge, 1921), 32; Charles E. Peterson, "Carpenter's Hall," *Transactions*, American Philosophical Society, n. s., XLIII (March, 1953), 97; Bridenbaugh, *Cities in Revolt*, 268–69.

21. Henretta, *Evolution of American Society*, 105–06. Ten per cent of the artisans on the tax lists compiled by Gary Nash for 1772 were among the city's "official" poor—excused from taxes for having no property, or receiving assistance from the city or church charities. The crafts with the largest number of poor were weaver (26 per cent), breechmaker (20 per cent), bricklayer (20 per cent), cordwainer [shoemaker] (16 per cent). These figures do not include those taxed at only a pound or two or personal property, receiving help from craft

societies, etc. See also Alice Hanson Jones, "Wealth Estimates for the American Middle Colonies, 1774," *Economic Development and Cultural Change,* XVIII (July, 1970), 97–103.

22. Bridenbaugh, *Colonial Craftsman,* 141–42. The statistics utilized by Jacob Price, and those supplied by Gary Nash (see note 19 above), are quite consistent as to the relative size of the various Philadelphia trades:

	Price (1774)		Nash (1772)	
total male occupations listed	4407		3251	
total artisans	2121		1618	
building trades	433	20.4%	343	21.2%
clothing crafts	407	19.2	278	17.1
leather crafts	313	14.8	208	12.9
food processors	304	14.3	194	12.0
shipbuilding crafts	257	12.1	227	14.0
metal workers	190	9.0	124	8.6
furniture trades	74	3.5	67	4.1
others	143	6.7	177	10.8

23. Sam Bass Warner, Jr., *The Private City* (Philadelphia, 1968), 5–6, 16n.; Richard B. Morris, *Government and Labor in Early America* (New York, 1946), 42; Morris, "The Organization of Production," 74–75; Charles S. Olton, "Philadelphia's Mechanics in the First Decade of Revolution, 1765–1775," *JAH,* LIX (September, 1972), 315n.; Hazard, *Boot and Shoe Industry,* 29n.; Sachs, "Business Outlook," 12–13; John F. Watson, *Annals of Philadelphia* (3 vols.: Philadelphia, 1887), I, 174–76.

24. Watson, *Annals,* I, 241. Unfortunately, it is impossible to tell how many of the artisans were masters and how many were journeymen. One clue is that in the Federal Procession of July 4, 1788, celebrating the ratification of the Constitution, the official account listed two trades with masters counted separately from other workers: 16 master cabinet and chair-makers marched with 100 "apprentices and journeymen," and 10 master bricklayers marched with 100 "workmen." "Account of the Grand Federal Procession in Philadelphia," *American Museum,* IV (July, 1788), 57–75.

25. J. Thomas Scharf and Thompson Westcott, *History of Philadelphia, 1609–1884* (3 vols.: Philadelphia, 1884), I, 263–64; Johann David Schoepf, *Travels in the Confederation,* trans. Alfred J. Morrison (2 vols.: Philadelphia, 1911), I, 117–18; Lemon, *Best Poor Man's Country,* 30; Bridenbaugh, *Colonial Craftsman,* 172; Harry D. Berg, "The Organization of Business in Colonial Philadelphia," *PaH,* X (July, 1943), 159; Martha G. Fales, *Joseph Richardson and Family, Philadelphia Silversmiths* (Middletown, 1974), 62–68. This last work is an excellent portrait of the business life of a Philadelphia artisan family.

26. Watson, *Annals,* I, 175–76; Plummer, "Consumer Credit," 404–09; Berg, "Organization of Business," 157; Olton, "Philadelphia Artisans," 37–49, 104; Nettels, *Emergence of a National Economy,* 40–41; Douglass, *Coming of Age,* 27;

Victor S. Clark, *History of Manufactures in the United States* (3 vols.: New York, 1929), I, 111; Bridenbaugh, *Colonial Craftsman*, 111; David Montgomery, "The Working Classes of the Pre-Industrial City," *Labor History*, IX (Winter, 1968), 13–15.

27. Bridenbaugh and Bridenbaugh, *Rebels and Gentlemen*, 204; Plummer, "Consumer Credit," 388–89; Sachs, "Business Outlook," 269–70; Olton, "Philadelphia Artisans," 51–53, 293; Jensen, *Commerce*, 88–90, 297.

28. James H. Hutson, *Pennsylvania Politics, 1746–1770: The Movement for Royal Government* (Princeton, 1972), 131; Bridenbaugh, *Cities in Revolt*, 146–47; Paul W. Conner, *Poor Richard's Politicks* (New York, 1965), 12–15; Bridenbaugh, *Colonial Craftsman*, 129; New York *American Daily Advertiser*, July 10, 1794; Labaree, ed., *Franklin Papers*, XII, 180n.; Max Savelle, *Seeds of Liberty* (New York, 1948), 220–21.

29. "A Philadelphia Mechanic," *Pa. Independent Gazetteer*, October 8, 1785; *To the Tradesmen, Mechanics, Etc. of the Province of Pennsylvania*, Broadside, December 4, 1773.

30. Labaree, ed., *Franklin Papers*, III, 306; Albert H. Smyth, ed., *The Writings of Benjamin Franklin* (10 vols.: New York, 1905–07), V, 127. The statement about the shoemakers is from the Philadelphia *Public Ledger*, April 17, 1839, in Richard McLeod. "The Philadelphia Artisan, 1828–1850" (unpublished doctoral dissertation, University of Missouri, 1971), 26–27. Cf. Herbert G. Gutman, "Work, Culture and Society in Industrializing America, 1815–1919," *American Historical Review*, LXXVIII (June, 1973), 531–88; E. P. Thompson, "Time, Work Discipline and Industrial Capitalism," *Past and Present*, XXXVIII (1967), 58–97.

31. Olton, "Philadelphia's Mechanics," 313; James H. Hutson, "An Investigation of the Inarticulate: Philadelphia's White Oaks," *WMQ*, 3 ser., XXVIII (January, 1971), 9–10; Bridenbaugh and Bridenbaugh, *Rebels and Gentlemen*, 87–88, 240; Lincoln, *Revolutionary Movement*, 86; Watson, *Annals*, I, 176, 187; Main, *Sovereign States*, 80.

32. Bridenbaugh, *Colonial Craftsman*, 92; Bridenbaugh, *Cities in Revolt*, 272; Olton, "Philadelphia Artisans," 20–29; Warner, *Private City*, 7–15.

33. Main, *Social Structure*, 256; Plummer, "Consumer Credit," 391–94; Bridenbaugh and Bridenbaugh, *Rebels and Gentlemen*, 90, 355–57; Bridenbaugh, *Colonial Craftsman*, 169. Cf. Harry Braverman, *Labor and Monopoly Capital: The Degradation of Work in the Twentieth Century* (New York, 1974), 109, 133. A pioneering study of literacy in colonial New England finds that artisans there were generally literate, although less completely so than merchants and professionals. Kenneth A. Lockridge, *Literacy in Colonial New England* (New York, 1974).

34. J. E. Crowley, *This Sheba, Self: The Conceptualization of Economic Life in Eighteenth Century America* (Baltimore, 1974), 87; Warner, *Private City*, 8; Olton, "Philadelphia Artisans," 6–14, 74–80; "Account of the Grand Federal Procession";

John R. Commons *et al.*, eds., *A Documentary History of American Industrial Society* (10 vols.: New York, 1909–11), III, 26–30, 128–29; Roger W. Moss, Jr., "The Carpenter's Company of Philadelphia," *Historic Preservation*, III (July–September, 1974), 37–41.

35. John R. Commons *et al.*, *History of Labour in the United States* (4 vols.: New York, 1921–35), I, 45, 79; James A. Henretta, "Economic Development and Social Structure in Colonial Boston," *WMQ*, 3 ser., XXII (January, 1965), 75–92; *To the Tradesmen, Mechanics, Etc. of the Province of Pennsylvania*, Broadside, December 4, 1773. Cf. the comment of Karl Marx in *The German Ideology*, referring to medieval towns but perhaps applicable in this context as well: "Capital in these towns was a natural capital, consisting of a house, the tools of the craft and the natural, hereditary customers; and not being realizable, on account of the backwardness of commerce and the lack of circulation, it descended from father to son. Unlike modern capital, which can be assessed in money and which may be indifferently invested in this thing or that, this capital was directly connected with the particular work of the owner, inseparable from it and to this extent 'estate' capital." Marx, *Pre-Capitalist Economic Formations*, ed., E. J. Hobsbawm (New York, 1965), 130.

36. On the Lockean theory of property and its ambiguities, see Richard Schlatter, *Private Property: The History of an Idea* (New Brunswick, 1951), 151–59, 184; C. B. Macpherson, *The Political Theory of Possessive Individualism* (Oxford, 1962), 199–221; Paschal Larkin, *Property in the Eighteenth Century* (Dublin, 1930), 59–78.

37. Plummer, "Consumer Credit," 390–95; Olton, "Philadelphia Artisans," 67–89, 100–12, 134, 210–12; Morris, *Government and Labor*, 200; Cochran, *Business*, 19–20; Commons, ed., *Documentary History*, III, 34–39. Again, the comments of Marx are useful in understanding the nature of artisan production: "Though urban crafts are based substantially on exchange and the creation of exchange-values, the main object of production is not enrichment or exchange-value as exchange-value, but the subsistence of man as an artisan, as a master-craftsman, and consequently use-value. Production is therefore everywhere subordinate to a presupposed consumption, supply to demand, and its expansion is slow." Marx, *Pre-Capitalist Economic Formations*, 118.

38. Article 9, Taylor's Company Minutes, 1771–76, HSPa; Morris, *Government and Labor*, 188–202; Commons, *History of Labor*, I, 25, 75; Montgomery, "Working Classes," 6; Ian M. G. Quimby, "The Cordwainers' Protest," *Winterthur Portfolio*, III (1967), 83–101.

39. The approximate size of the involuntary labor force is estimated as follows: Warner, *Private City*, 6, estimates a total of 900 indentured servants and 600 slaves in Philadelphia in 1775—about the same as Gary Nash's estimate of 869 servants and 675 slaves. (Nash, "Slaves and Slaveowners," 246.) The best source on apprenticeship is "Records of Indentures of Individuals Bound out as Apprentices, Servants, Etc.," *Pennsylvania German Society Proceedings*, XVI

(1907). Between October 3, 1771, and October 2, 1772, 403 males were apprenticed to Philadelphians, almost all to artisans, for an average of 6.5 years service. Making allowances for runaways and those transferred out of the city, these figures suggest an estimate of between 1500 and 2000 male apprentices in the city in 1775.

40. "Records of Indentures," 1–135; Nash, "Slaves and Slaveowners," 249–50; Cheesman A. Herrick, *White Servitude in Pennsylvania* (Philadelphia, 1926), 74–75; Cordwainers' Fire Company Minutes, November 9, 1767, HSPa.

41. Karl Polanyi, *The Great Transformation* (Boston, 1957 ed.), 70; Macpherson, *Possessive Individualism*, 48–49.

42. Nash, "Slaves and Slaveowners," 236–41, 246; Lemon, *Best Poor Man's Country*, 10; Main, *Sovereign States*, 70–71; Smith, *Colonists in Bondage*, 240; Herrick, *White Servitude*, 207; Ian M. G. Quimby, "Apprenticeship in Colonial Philadelphia" (unpublished master's essay, University of Delaware, 1963), xiv, 52–53, 60, 71; Clark, *History of Manufactures*, I, 68.

43. Nash, "Slaves and Slaveowners," 247; Olton, "Philadelphia Artisans," 339; Samuel McKee, Jr., *Labor in Colonial New York* (New York, 1935), 88; Nettels, *Emergence*, 266–68. For a different view, see William Miller, "The Effects of the American Revolution on Indentured Servitude," *PaH*, VII (July, 1940), 131–41.

44. Olton, "Philadelphia's Mechanics," 314–15; Nettels, *Emergence*, 314–15; John K. Alexander, "Philadelphia's 'Other Half': Attitudes Toward Poverty and the Meaning of Poverty in Philadelphia, 1760–1800" (unpublished doctoral dissertation, University of Chicago, 1973), 33–35; Stephen J. Rosswurm, "'That They Were Grown Unruly': The Crowd and Lower-Classes in Philadelphia, 1765–1780" (unpublished master's essay, Northern Illinois University, 1974), 7–12; Bridenbaugh, *Cities in Revolt*, 86–87; John Swift to Customs Commissioners, November 15, 1770 (draft), Customs House Papers, HSPa. Jacob Price's figures indicate a lower class of sailors, wage-earners, porters, fishermen, peddlers, etc., comprising 1076 (24.4 per cent) of males on the tax lists.

45. Ferguson, *American Revolution*, 39; Allan Kulikoff, "The Progress of Inequality in Revolutionary Boston," *WMQ*, 3 ser., XXVIII (October, 1971), 375–411; Rudé, *Hanoverian London*, 83; Jeffrey Kaplow, "The Culture of Poverty in Paris on the Eve of the Revolution," *International Review of Social History*, XII (1967), 278–81.

46. Alexander, "Philadelphia's 'Other Half;'" Gary B. Nash, "Social Change and the Origins of the Revolution in the Cities," in Alfred F. Young, ed., *Explorations in the History of American Radicalism: The American Revolution* (DeKalb, 1976); Gary B. Nash, "Poverty in Pre-Revolutionary Philadelphia" (unpublished essay in the possession of Professor Nash); Samuel Hazard, ed., *The Register of Pennsylvania* (16 vols.: Philadelphia, 1828–36), II, 23–26, 379–86; VIII, 384.

47. Nash, "Social Change;" Alexander, "Philadelphia's 'Other Half,'" 153–65;

David J. Rothman, *The Discovery of the Asylum* (Boston, 1971), 28, 40; Bridenbaugh, *Rebels and Gentlemen*, 234; Philip Padelford, ed., *Colonial Panorama 1775* (San Marino, 1939), 18.

48. Labaree, ed., *Franklin Papers*, XI, 314–16; *Pa. Journal*, September 27, 1775; *Pa. Packet*, October 16, 1775; *Pa. Evening Post*, November 16, 1775.

49. Watson, *Annals*, I, 176, 187; Alexander, "Philadelphia's 'Other Half,'" 15–21, 46–49; Montgomery, "Working Classes," 13–16; Smyth, ed., *Writings of Franklin*, V, 123, 538. Cf. Thompson, *Making of the English Working Class*, 240–44, 253, 262, 740–41, 757–59.

50. Bridenbaugh and Bridenbaugh, *Rebels and Gentlemen*, 16; Watson, *Annals*, II, 265; Warner, *Private City*, 11.

51. Bridenbaugh, *Cities in Revolt*, 160, 169, 271, 316; Scharf and Westcott, *Philadelphia*, II, 866, 940–41, 981–82; Bridenbaugh and Bridenbaugh, *Rebels and Gentlemen*, 21; Warner, *Private City*, 19–20; Robert E. Graham, "The Taverns of Colonical Philadelphia," *Transactions*, American Philosophical Society, n. s., XLIII (March, 1953), 318–20; Watson, *Annals*, I, 463–64.

52. Darold D. Wax, "The Demand for Slave Labor in Colonial Pennsylvania," *PaH*, XXXIV (October, 1967), 331–45; Edward R. Turner, *The Negro in Pennsylvania* (Washington, 1911), 30–33, 38–41; Watson, *Annals*, I, 62; Morris, *Government and Labor*, 424–25n.; Ellis P. Oberholzer, *Philadelphia: A History of the City and its People* (4 vols.: Philadelphia, n. d.), I, 167–68; Scharf and Westcott, *Philadelphia*, I, 244; II, 936. David Brion Davis points out that we know virtually nothing about contacts between lower-class whites and blacks in the eighteenth century—the "independent and irreverent fraternizers" considered dangerous both north and south. David Brion Davis, *The Problem of Slavery in the Age of Revolution* (Ithaca, 1975), 279n. One attempt to analyze the "alley society" of Boston is Robert C. Twombly, "Black Resistance to Slavery in Massachusetts," in William O'Neill, ed., *Insights and Parallels* (Minneapolis, 1973), 26–28.

53. Watson, *Annals*, I, 364; Labaree, ed., *Franklin Papers*, I, 211–12; Scharf and Westcott, *Philadelphia*, I, 294; III, 2300; *Pa. Archives*, 8 ser., VIII, 7184–85.

54. Rosswurm, "'That They Were Grown Unruly,'" 25–30; Scharf and Westcott, *Philadelphia*, I, 257; Brooke Hindle, *The Pursuit of Science in Revolutionary America* (Chapel Hill, 1956), 249–53; Watson, *Annals*, I, 267–73, 375; II, 32. Cf. Raymond P. Stearns, *Science in the British Colonies of North America* (Urbana, 1970), 512–13.

55. Alexander Graydon, *Memoirs of His Own Times* (Philadelphia, 1846), 93; Warner, *Private City*, 19–20.

56. "Wilbraham," *Pa. Packet*, March 24, 1781. Cf. the important article by Rhys Isaac, "Evangelical Revolt: The Nature of the Baptists' Challenge to the Traditional Order in Virginia, 1765 to 1775," *WMQ*, 3 ser., XXXI (July, 1974), esp. 351–52, 362.

57. *Pa. Evening Post*, July 30, 1776; "Whitlocke," *Pa. Evening Post*, May 27, 1777; Charles W. Peale to Dr. David Ramsey, 1779? Peale Papers, American Philo-

dophical Society, Philadelphia; "Philadelphia Society Before the Revolution," *PaMHB*, XI (1887), 492.

58. Richard M. Brown, "Violence and the American Revolution," in Stephen G. Kurtz and James H. Hutson, eds., *Essays on the American Revolution*, (Chapel Hill, 1973), 94–97, 117–20; Rosswurm, "'That They Were Grown Unruly,'" 18–21, 36–76; Labaree, ed., *Franklin Papers*, II, 363–64; Scharf and Westcott, *Philadelphia*, I, 207; Watson, *Annals*, II, 496. Cf. Gordon S. Wood, "A Note on Mobs in the American Revolution," *WMQ*, 3 ser., XXIII (October, 1966), 635–42; George Rudé, *The Crowd in History* (New York, 1964); Thompson, *Making of the English Working Class*, 21, 62. The most thorough study of crowds during the American Revolution is Dirk Hoerder, *People and Mobs: Crowd Action in Massachusetts During the American Revolution*, 1765–1780 (Berlin, 1971).

59. Maier, *From Resistance to Revolution*, 1–11, 24, 57–59; Philip G. Davidson, *Propaganda and the American Revolution*, 1763–1783 (Chapel Hill, 1941), 58; Norman S. Cohen, "The Philadelphia Election Riot of 1742," *PaMHB*, XCII (July, 1968), 313–18; Labaree, ed., *Franklin Papers*, XI, 377n.; John Swift to Customs Commissioners, May 5, October 13, 1769, November 15, 1770 (drafts), Customs House Papers, HSPa; Jensen, *Maritime Commerce*, 145–52, 273n.; Rosswurm, "'That They Were Grown Unruly,'" 57–63.

60. Jesse Lemisch, "The Radicalism of the Inarticulate: Merchant Seamen in the Politics of Revolutionary America," in Alfred F. Young, ed., *Dissent: Explorations in the History of American Radicalism* (DeKalb, 1968), 37–82; John Hughes to Lords Commissioners of His Majesty's Treasury, January 13, 1766, Treasury Papers, Class One, 452:218, PRO (Library of Congress Transcripts); Jensen, *Commerce*, 151; Whitfield J. Bell, Jr., "Addenda to Watson's Annals of Philadelphia: Notes by Jacob Mordecai, 1836," *PaMHB*, XCVIII (April, 1974), 134; Horace M. Lippincott, *Early Philadelphia* (Philadelphia, 1917), 86–87; Summary of letter from John Hughes, October 12, 1765, Treasury Papers, Class One, PRO (Library of Congress Transcripts).

61. Hobsbawm, *Primitive Rebels*, 6–7, 116; Thompson, *Making of English Working Class*, 70–80; Gwyn A. Williams, *Artisans and Sans-Culottes* (New York, 1969), 57–60, 68.

62. Labaree, ed., *Franklin Papers*, III, 106; Conner, *Poor Richard*, 136–38; *Pa. Gazette*, June 15, 1774; Maier, *From Resistance to Revolution, passim;* Arthur M. Schlesinger, "Political Mobs and the American Revolution, 1765–1776," *Proceedings*, American Philosophical Society, XCIX (August, 1955), 249.

63. Edward Countryman, "The Problem of the Early American Crowd," *Journal of American Studies*, VII (April, 1973), 79–80; William Barton, *Memoirs of the Life of David Rittenhouse* (Philadelphia, 1813), 599; Peter Force, ed., *American Archives*, 4 ser., I, 342.

64. William S. Hanna, *Benjamin Franklin and Pennsylvania Politics* (Stanford, 1964), 2–3; Benjamin H. Newcomb, *Franklin and Galloway: A Political Partnership* (New Haven, 1972), 18–26, 84; G. B. Warden, "The Proprietary Group in Pennsylvania, 1754–1764," *WMQ*, 3 ser., XXI (July, 1964), 367–89; Rowland

Berthoff and John M. Murrin, "Feudalism, Communalism, and the Yeoman
Freeholder: The American Revolution Considered as a Social Accident," in
Kurtz and Hutson, eds., *Essays on the American Revolution,* 267; J. R. Pole,
Political Representation in England and the Origins of the American Republic (New
York, 1966), 112–21, 264; Hutson, *Pennsylvania Politics,* 130–32, 172. For the
most recent estimates of voting eligibility, see Hawke, *In the Midst of a Revolution,* 34n.; Richard A. Ryerson, "Leadership in Crisis, The Radical Committees
of Philadelphia and the Coming of the Revolution in Pennsylvania, 1765–
1776: A Study in the Revolutionary Process" (unpublished doctoral dissertation, Johns Hopkins University, 1972), 441n.

65. Warden, "Proprietary Group," 367–69; Dietmar Rothermund, *The Layman's
    Progress: Religious and Political Experience in Colonial Pennsylvania, 1740–1770*
    (Philadelphia, 1961), 124–28; Benjamin H. Newcomb, "Effects of the Stamp
    Act on Colonial Pennsylvania Politics," *WMQ,* 3 ser., XXIII (April, 1966),
    257–72; Hutson, *Pennsylvania Politics,* 195–215; Nash, "Transformation of
    Urban Politics," 626–31; Labaree, ed., *Franklin Papers,* XI, 290, XII, 315–16;
    Maier, *Resistance to Revolution,* 80.

66. Nash, "Transformation of Urban Politics," 627–32; Labaree, ed., *Franklin
    Papers,* XII, 218.

67. R. A. Ryerson, "Political Mobilization and the American Revolution: The
    Resistance Movement in Philadelphia, 1765 to 1776," *WMQ,* 3 ser., XXXI
    (October, 1974), 565–68; Olton, "Philadelphia Artisans," 141–56, 364; John J.
    Zimmerman, "Charles Thomson, 'The Sam Adams of Philadelphia.'" *Missis-
    sippi Valley Historical Review,* XLV (December, 1958), 464–80; Hutson, *Pennsyl-
    vania Politics,* 234–40; Jensen, *Commerce,* 186–91; Newcomb, *Franklin and
    Galloway,* 177, 203, 210–13; Labaree, ed., *Franklin Papers,* XVII, 228–29; John
    A. Schutz and Douglass Adair, eds., *The Spur of Fame: Dialogues of John Adams
    and Benjamin Rush, 1805–1813* (San Marino, Cal., 1966), 273; Engal and Ernst,
    "Economic Interpretation," 23.

68. Graydon, *Memoirs,* 134–35; Olton, "Philadelphia Artisans," 141–48, 161–64;
    Ryerson, "Political Mobilization," 568–77, 585–87.

69. *Pa. Archives,* 4 ser., III, 729.

70. Williams, *Artisans and Sans-Culottes, passim;* "A Lover of Liberty and a Mechan-
    ics' Friend," *To the Free and Patriotic Inhabitants of the City of Philadelphia,*
    Broadside, May 31, 1770; "A Brother Chip," *Pa. Gazette,* September 27, 1770;
    "A Mechanic," *Pa. Chronicle,* September 27, 1773; Labaree, ed., *Franklin
    Papers,* XVII, 249. Cf. The comment of Karl Polanyi: "purely economic
    matters are . . . incomparably less relevant to class behavior than questions of
    social recognition." Polanyi, *The Great Transformation,* 153.

71. Olton, "Philadelphia's Mechanics," 316; Ryerson, "Political Mobilization,"
    582–88.

72. Hanna, *Franklin and Pennsylvania Politics,* 32; Ryerson, "Leadership in Crisis,"
    428–33; Arthur J. Alexander, "Pennsylvania's Revolutionary Militia,"
    PaMHB, LXIX (January, 1945), 15–16.

73. *Pa. Gazette*, May 1, 1776; *Pa. Archives*, 8 ser., VIII, 7407–08; Ryerson, "Leadership in Crisis," 441; "The Lee Papers," New-York Historical Society *Collections* (4 vols.: 1871–74), I, 212; *Pa. Gazette*, February 14, August 28, 1776.
74. Broadside, June, 1776, Clymer Family Papers, HSPa; *Pa. Archives*, 2 ser., XIII, 579–80; 3 ser., XIV–XVI; 8 ser., VIII, 7406; account of meeting, July 25, 1775, of High Street Ward Militia Company, Peters Papers, VIII, 54, HSPa.
75. Hill, *World Turned Upside Down*, 51–53, 58, 103; H. N. Brailsford, *The Levellers and the English Revolution* (Stanford, 1961), 148–51; Arthur D. Graeff, "The Relations Between the Pennsylvania Germans and the British Authorities (1750–1776)," *Pennsylvania German Society Proceedings*, XLVII (1939), 212–43; Ryerson, "Political Mobilization," 578.
76. *Pa. Archives*, 8 ser., VIII, 7397–7405, 7409, 7422, 7438–39, 7449; *Pa. Gazette*, October 11, 1775, March 6, 1776; Elisha P. Douglass, *Rebels and Democrats* (Chapel Hill, 1955), 252. For a similar view of the politics of the revolutionary militia in Maryland, see David C. Skaggs, *Roots of Maryland Democracy, 1753–1776* (Westport, 1973), 156, 167–71.
77. *Pa. Archives*, 1 ser., V, 186–88; *Pa. Gazette*, September 13, 1775, Supplement, March 6, 1776; Ryerson, "Leadership in Crisis," 374–75; Ryerson, "Political Mobilization," 371–75; *To the Associators of the City of Philadelphia*, Broadside, May 18, 1775; Butterfield, ed., *Rush Letters*, I, 462; *Instructions for Inlisting Rifle-Men*, Broadside, March 14, 1776.
78. On this last point, see E. J. Hobsbawm, "Class Consciousness in History," in István Mezaros, ed., *Aspects of History and Class Consciousness* (London, 1971), 5–21; and Asa Briggs, "The Language of 'Class' in Early Nineteenth-Century England," in Asa Briggs and John Saville, eds., *Essays in Labour History* (London, 1960), 43–73.

CHAPTER THREE

1. John C. Miller, *Origins of the American Revolution* (Boston, 1943), 379; Foner, *Complete Writings*, II, 1161; Hawke, *Paine*, chapter 2; Lyon N. Richardson, *A History of Early American Magazines, 1741–1789* (New York, 1931), 177–79.
2. Foner, *Complete Writings*, II, 18, 33, 49, 54–55, 1109–10.
3. Foner, *Complete Writings*, I, 43; Miller, *Origins*, 416–17, 422, 446, 459.
4. Worthington C. Ford, ed., "Letters of William Duane," *Proceedings*, Massachusetts Historical Society, 2 ser., XX (1906–07), 279; Butterfield, ed., *Rush Letters*, II, 1007; Schutz and Adair, eds., *The Spur of Fame*, 151; *Pa. Evening Post*, February 22, 1776; Daniel J. Boorstin, *The Americans: The Colonial Experience* (New York, 1959), 309; Bernard Bailyn, "Common Sense," *American Heritage*, XXV (December, 1973), 36.
5. Foner, *Complete Writings*, II, 1480; Wood, *Creation of the American Republic*, 199–200, 223; W. Paul Adams, "Republicanism in Political Rhetoric Before 1776,"

Political Science Quarterly, LXXXV (September, 1970), 398–404; Maier, *Resistance to Revolution,* 288–95; Pauline Maier, "The Beginnings of American Republicanism," in *Development of a Revolutionary Mentality,* 99–104. On evangelicism and republicanism, see also below, Chapter 4.

6. Foner, *Complete Writings,* I, 4–16, 29.

7. Bailyn, *Ideological Origins,* 285; Thompson, *Making of the English Working Class,* 86–88; Foner, *Complete Writings,* I, 6, 28; Hawke, *Paine,* 43–44; Christopher Hill, "The Norman Yoke," in Hill, *Puritanism and Revolution* (London, 1958), 50–122.

8. J. M. Bumsted, "'Things in the Womb of Time:' Ideas of American Independence, 1633 to 1763," *WMQ,* 3 ser., XXXI (October, 1974), 533–64; Maier, *Resistance to Revolution,* 266–68; Foner, *Complete Writings,* 16–21, 25–26, 32, 41, 44, 400.

9. Foner, *Complete Writings,* I, 17–18, 24, 27–30, 45.

10. Foner, *Complete Writings,* I, 18, 20, 32–34, 41. Cf. Williams, *Contours of American History,* 116–19.

11. Foner, *Complete Writings,* I, 31, 45. Cf. Wood, *Creation,* 43–48, 91–118.

12. Thomas R. Adams, *American Independence: The Growth of an Idea* (Providence, 1965), xi–xii; Foner, *Complete Writings,* II, 1162–63; Hawke, *Paine,* 47.

13. *Pa. Evening Post,* February 13, March 26, 1776; Winthrop D. Jordan, "Familial Politics: Thomas Paine and the Killing of the King," *JAH,* LX (September, 1973), 295; *Pa. Packet,* Feburary 12, 1776.

14. L. H. Butterfield, ed., *Diary and Autobiography of John Adams* (4 vols.: Cambridge, 1961), III, 333.

15. On the concept of an American empire, see William Appleman Williams, "The Age of Mercantilism: An Interpretation of the American Political Economy, 1763 to 1828," *WMQ,* 3 ser., (October, 1958), 419–21; R. W. Van Alstyne, *The Rising American Empire* (New York, 1960), 1–6. Paine's comment is in Foner, *Complete Writings,* I, 119; he referred again to "the probability of empire" in 1779 (II, 202).

16. Foner, *Complete Writings,* I, 10–12; Butterfield, ed., *Adams Diary,* III, 333.

17. Tuveson, *Redeemer Nation,* 11–12, 20–24, 34–37; Yehoshura Arieli, *Individualism and Nationalism in American Ideology* (Cambridge, 1964), 71–73, 269–70.

18. John R. Howe, *From the Revolution Through the Age of Jackson* (Englewood Cliffs, 1973), 28–31; Margaret M. Willard, ed., *Letters on the American Revolution, 1774–1776* (Boston and New York, 1925), 274.

19. Foner, *Complete Writings,* I, 25; Bailyn, "Common Sense," 36–39; Bailyn, *Ideological Origins,* 12–19; Inglis, *The True Interest of America,* 34.

20. Douglass, *Rebels and Democrats,* 21; Foner, *Complete Writings,* II, 111; I, 260, 9, 18. Cf. Paine's footnote after using the word "soliloquy" in an April 1776 newspaper article: "As this piece may possibly fall into the hands of some who are not acquainted with the word soliloquy, for their information the sense of it is given, viz. 'talking to one's self.'" Foner, II, 74.

21. Watt, *Rise of the Novel,* 29–30, 54–59, 101–04, 194–96; James T. Boulton, *The*

Language of Politics in the Age of Wilkes and Burke (London, 1963), 19–23, 52, 252; James T. Boulton, ed., *Daniel Defoe* (New York, 1965), 2–9, 15; Hawke, *Paine,* 44; Nash, "Transformation of Urban Politics," 619–20.

22. Foner, *Complete Writings,* II, 78; I, 17, 376, 571.
23. Foner, *Complete Writings,* I, xviii; Franklin quoted in Benjamin Vaughan to Lord Shelburne, December 26, 1782 (copy), Gimbel Collection, American Philosophical Society; "Edmund Randolph's Essay," *Virginia Magazine of History and Biography* XLIII (1935), 306, Bailyn, *Ideological Origins,* 13–17. My analysis of Paine's literary style has been influenced by the excellent discussions in Thompson, *Making of the English Working Class,* 90–92; Harry Hayden Clark, "Thomas Paine's Theories of Rhetoric," *Transactions,* Wisconsin Academy of Sciences, Arts and Letters, XXVIII (1933), 307–09; J. H. Plumb, "The Public, Literature and the Arts in the Eighteenth Century," in Paul Fritz and David Williams, eds., *The Triumph of Culture: Eighteenth Century Perspectives* (Toronto, 1972), 27–48; and especially, Boulton, *Language of Politics.*
24. James T. Austin, *The Life of Elbridge Gerry* (Boston, 1859), 163; Hawke, *Paine,* 47; Miller, *Origins,* 467.
25. Foner, *Complete Writings,* II, 910. Cf. II, 1491.
26. Foner, *Complete Writings,* I, 369, 343; II, 191; Daniel J. Sisson, *The American Revolution of 1800* (New York, 1974), 42.
27. Wood, *Creation,* 57–59, 607–12; Richard J. Buel, Jr., "Democracy and the American Revolution: A Frame of Reference," *WMQ,* 3 ser., XXI (April, 1964), 169–70; Richard Hofstadter, *The Idea of a Party System* (Berkeley, 1969), 9–12, 29–30; Sisson, *American Revolution,* 26–40; Saul K. Padover, ed., *The Forging of American Federalism* (New York, 1965), 40–43; Arieli, *Individualism and Nationalism,* 193.
28. Macpherson, *Possessive Individualism,* 263–66; Foner, *Complete Writings,* II, 17, 286, 372, 578; Cooke, ed., *The Federalist,* 58–65, 351–52; T. H. Breen, "A Changing Labor Force and Race Relations in Virginia 1660–1710," *Journal of Social History,* VII (Fall, 1973), 3–25.
29. Foner, *Complete Writings,* I, 203. Cf. Paine's comment in *Pa. Packet,* April 4, 1782, that during the Revolutionary War, "something like poverty *began to appear*" (italics added).
30. Regina M. Morantz, "'Democracy' and 'Republic' in American Ideology, 1787–1840" (unpublished doctoral dissertation, Columbia University, 1971), 14–30; Giovanni Sartori, *Democratic Theory* (Detroit, 1962), 262; Bailyn, *Ideological Origins,* 57–61; Cooke, ed., *The Federalist,* 31, 58–59, 97, 349, 378; Wood, *Creation,* 205; Richard Hofstadter, *The American Political Tradition* (New York, 1948), 3–8; Arthur O. Lovejoy, *Reflections on Human Nature* (Baltimore, 1961), 37–65.
31. Foner, *Complete Writings,* I, 4–6; Stow Persons, "The Cyclical Theory of History in Eighteenth-Century America," *American Quarterly,* VI (Summer, 1954), 147–63; John Passmore, *The Perfectibility of Man* (London, 1970), 158–59, 195–96, 200–01; Tuveson, *Redeemer Nation,* 66–67.

32. Foner, *Complete Writings*, I, 371–72, 397.
33. Foner, *Complete Writings*, I, 4–5, 357, 406; George Woodcock, *Anarchism* (New York, 1962), 50.
34. Sheldon Wolin, *Politics and Vision* (Boston, 1960), 130–31, 291–92, 308–12; Elie Halévy, *The Growth of Philosophic Radicalism* (London, 1934), 189–91; Foner, *Complete Writings*, I, 357–61, 400.
35. Foner, *Complete Writings*, I, 404–05, 341.
36. Foner, *Complete Writings*, I, 9, 618–20; II, 580.
37. Foner, *Complete Writings*, I, 326, 355, 412.
38. Foner, *Complete Writings*, II, 286, 1142.
39. Foner, *Complete Writings*, II, 11; I, 90; Charles Coleman Sellers, *Charles Willson Peale* (New York, 1969), 331–32: *Pennsylvania Magazine* (May, 1775), 231–32.
40. Foner, *Complete Writings*, I, 63; II, 289, 369.
41. George Rudé, "Popular Protest in 18th Century Europe," in Fritz and Williams, eds., *The Triumph of Culture*, 293–95; Rudé, *Crowd in History*, 138–40; Foner, *Complete Writings*, II, 1296; I, 359; Maier, *Resistance to Revolution*, 13.
42. Foner, *Complete Writings*, I, 265–66. The phrase "the riots and outrages of 1780" refers to London's Gordon riots of that year.
43. Foner, *Complete Writings*, II, 399; Joseph Priestley, *An Account of a Society for Encouraging the Industrious Poor* (Birmingham, 1787). This learned divine, political reformer, and scientist, believed that because the English poor felt they had a "legal claim to subsistence," they had "no sufficient motive to exert themselves. . . . It is well known in all manufacturing places, that if the greater part of workmen can earn enough in three or four days to maintain themselves and their families for the week, they will never work any more; or if they do make any extraordinary gain, it is spent in alehouses. . . ." Since the mental outlook of the "lower ranks" did not "go beyond a subsistence for themselves, and the gratification of their own passions," Priestley proposed that poor rates be levied only on the poor themselves, as a form of forced saving or social security. (pp. 4–14). Priestley's house in Birmingham was destroyed by a mob in a famous riot of 1791.
44. Foner, *Complete Writings*, I, 355, 360, 405, 424, 431, 466–67; E. G. West, "Tom Paine's Voucher Scheme for Public Education," *Southern Economic Journal*, XXXIII (January, 1967), 378–82. West observes that Paine's stress on taxation as a cause of poverty reflects the incredibly regressive nature of British taxation in the late eighteenth century. The largest share of government revenue came from taxes on food and tobacco and only a small amount from direct taxes on land and property.
45. Gwyn A. Williams, "Tom Paine," *New Society*, August 6, 1970, 236. Cf. Lynd, *Class Conflict*, 94.
46. Foner, *Complete Writings*, I, 413–14. On the sociology of intellectuals see the classic treatments in Karl Mannheim, *Ideology and Utopia* (New York, 1936), 137–42; and Schumpeter, *Capitalism, Socialism, and Democracy*, 146–47.

47. Foner, *Complete Writings*, I, 169; II, 362, 621, 1228; "Outline for Common Sense," Gimbel Collection; Hawke, *Paine*, 47; Williams, "Paine," 237.
48. Hawke, *Paine*, 160.
49. Lynd, *Class Conflict*, 267.
50. Kramnick, *Bolingbroke, passim;* Robert Kelley, *The Transatlantic Persuasion* (New York, 1969), 104–05, 128–37; Caroline Robbins, "European Republicanism in the Century and a Half Before 1776," in *Development of a Revolutionary Mentality*, 50; Edmund S. Morgan, "Slavery and Freedom: The American Paradox," *JAH*, LIX (June, 1972), 7–9; Thomas Jefferson, *Notes on the State of Virginia* (New York, 1964 ed.), 157–58; Jackson Turner Main, *Political Parties Before the Constitution* (Chapel Hill, 1973), 406.
51. Boorstin, *The Lost World of Thomas Jefferson*, 147; Albert E. Bergh, ed., *The Writings of Thomas Jefferson* (20 vols.: Washington, 1903), V, 93; Jefferson, *Notes*, 157–58; Edmund S. Morgan, "The Puritan Ethic and the American Revolution," *WMQ*, 3 ser., XXIV (January, 1967), 36–41; Drew R. McCoy, "Republicanism and American Foreign Policy: James Madison and the Political Economy of Commercial Discrimination, 1789 to 1794," *WMQ*, 3 ser., XXXI (October, 1974), 633–46; Lynd, *Class Conflict*, 265; Arieli, *Individualism and Nationalism*, 155–63; Williams, "Mercantilism," 432–34.
52. Richard E. Ellis, *The Jeffersonian Crisis* (New York, 1971), 259–60. See also the interesting comments of R. R. Palmer on the contrast between France and England, where democratic, egalitarian ideas were strong in the cities and weak in the countryside, and America, where the bulk of the urban commercial classes were Federalists in the 1790s and the strength of Jeffersonianism lay among the yeomen. Palmer, "The Great Inversion: America and Europe in the Eighteenth-Century Revolution," in *Ideas in History*, ed., Richard Herr and Harold T. Parker (Durham, 1965), 3–19.
53. Hawke, *Paine*, 71; Lynd, *Class Conflict*, 268; Douglass G. Adair, "Experience Must be Our Only Guide: History, Democratic Theory, and the United States Constitution," in Ray A. Billington, ed., *The Reinterpretation of Early American History* (San Marino, Cal., 1966), 129–48; Pocock, *Politics, Language, and Time*, 100.
54. Foner, *Complete Writings*, I, 355; II, 1292; *Pennsylvania Magazine* (April, 1775), 157–58; Leo Marx, *The Machine in the Garden* (New York, 1964), 126–29; Kramnick, *Bolingbroke*, 193–94; Wood, *Creation*, 418–19: "Like Puritanism, of which it was a more relaxed, secularized version, republicanism was essentially anti-capitalistic. . . ." Cf. Pocock, "Virtue and Commerce," *passim*.

CHAPTER FOUR

1. Ryerson, "Leadership in Crisis," 368–71, 467–73, 547–56; Theodore Thayer, *Pennsylvania Politics and the Growth of Democracy, 1740–1776* (Harrisburg,

1953), 173–77; Bernard Mason, *The Road to Independence: The Revolutionary Movement in New York*, 1773–1777 (Lexington, 1966), 252–53; Merrill Jensen, *The Founding of a Nation* (New York, 1968), 687. Cf. the comment of "A Watchman," *Pa. Packet*, June 10, 1776, addressed to the pre-independence ruling elite: "Had you concurred in the present virtuous and necessary measure of instituting a new government, you would have probably continued to occupy your posts and offices . . . but you have now forfeited the confidence of the people, by despising their authority."

2. William Duane, Jr., ed., *Passages from the Remembrancer of Christopher Marshall* (Albany, 1877), reveals constant meetings among many of these men in 1775 and 1776. Hawke, *In the Midst*, carefully traces the activities of the radical group, but his conspiratorial interpretation leaves little room for questions about the group's social roots or popular support. Ryerson, "Leadership in Crisis," 545, revises Hawke's list of radical leaders.

3. A. M. Stackhouse, *Col. Timothy Matlack* (n. p., 1910); Bridenbaugh, *Cities in Revolt*, 365–66; Jacob C. Parsons, ed., *Extracts from the Diary of Jacob Hiltzheimer* (Philadelphia, 1893), 13–20, 44; "The Cock-Fighter," *PaMHB*, XLIV (1920), 73–76; Edmund Burnett, ed., *Letters of Members of the Continental Congress* (8 vols.: Washington, 1921–36), V, 281; "Consideration," *Pa. Gazette*, October 30, 1776; *An Epistle from Titus to Timothy*, Broadside, 1781. The imagery of cock-fighting was on occasion explicitly used in politics. One toast at a dinner of the Portland, Maine Republican Society in 1797 went: "May the spurs of the Republican Cock, prick every tyrant to the heart." Philip S. Foner, ed., *To Light the Torch of Truth: Documents of the Democratic-Republican Societies* (forthcoming).

4. Davis, *Problem of Slavery in the Age of Revolution*, 288–89; Alan Heimert, *Religion and the American Mind, from the Great Awakening to the Revolution* (Cambridge, 1966), 12–14, 59–60, 460–63, and *passim*.

5. Scharf and Westcott, *Philadelphia*, I, 261; Bridenbaugh, *Colonial Craftsman*, 165; Bridenbaugh and Bridenbaugh, *Rebels and Gentlemen*, 19; "Philadelphia Society Before the Revolution," *PaMHB*, XI (1887), 494; Guy Klett, *Presbyterianism in Colonial Pennsylvania* (Philadelphia, 1937), 151–54.

6. "The Lee Papers," III, 431; Bridenbaugh, *Colonial Craftsman*, 164; Wayne L. Bockelman and Owen S. Ireland, "The Internal Revolution in Pennsylvania: An Ethnic-Religious Interpretation," *PaH*, XLI (April, 1974), 125–60. However, the data presented in this article does not prove the authors' contention that "ethnic-religious conflict transcended section and class and was the most salient characteristic of the contending forces in Pennsylvania."

7. "Philadelphia Society," 285; Heimert, *Religion and the American Mind*, 387; Thayer, *Pennsylvania Politics*, 134–35, 185; John Hughes to Lords Commissioners of His Majesty's Customs, January 13, February 20, 1766, Treasury Papers, Class One, 452: 5, 218, PRO (Library of Congress Transcripts); Labaree, ed., *Franklin Papers*, XIII, 37. Cf. Peter A. Butzin, "Politics, Presby-

terianism and the Paxton Riots, 1763-64," *Journal of Presbyterian History*, LI (Spring, 1973), 79-83.

8. Wayland F. Dunaway, *The Scotch-Irish of Colonial Pennsylvania* (Chapel Hill, 1944), 11; Klett, *Presbyterianism in Colonial Pennsylvania*, 265; Willard, ed., *Letters on the American Revolution*, 315; Beatrice Kevitt Hofstadter, "Loyalties in Conflict: The Anglican Church in Eighteenth Century America" (unpublished doctoral dissertation, Columbia University, 1973), 3-4, 8-13, 68.

9. Butterfield, ed., *Letters of Rush*, I, 265; Herbert James Henderson, "Political Factions in the Continental Congress: 1774-1783" (unpublished doctoral dissertation, Columbia University, 1962), 45; Donald D'Elia, "The Republican Theology of Benjamin Rush," *PaH*, XXXIII (April, 1966), 187-203; David Freeman Hawke, *Benjamin Rush: Revolutionary Gadfly* (Indianpolis, 1971), 12-14.

10. Hawke, *Rush*, 83-86, 126-28; George W. Corner, ed., *The Autobiography of Benjamin Rush* (Philadelphia, 1948), 79, 84; *American Museum*, V (1789), 581-84 (a reprint of Rush's speech of 1775).

11. Hawke, *Rush*, 73, 157-58; Butterfield, ed., *Letters of Rush*, I, 18; II, 825-26; John A. Woods, ed., "The Correspondence of Benjamin Rush and Granville Sharp 1773-1809," *Journal of American Studies*, I (1967), 9.

12. Christopher Marshall to "Friend John," January 30, 1776; Marshall to "Esteemed Friend," September 22, 1774; Marshall to "J. P.," April 13, 1775, Marshall Letterbook, HSPa.

13. William G. McLoughlin, "The American Revolution As a Religious Revival: The 'Millennium in one Country,'" *New England Quarterly*, XL (March, 1967), 108-09; William G. McLoughlin, ed., *Isaac Backus on Church, State, and Calvinism* (Cambridge, 1968), 1, 29-30; John Hughes to Lords Commissioners of His Majesty's Treasury, January 13, 1766, Treasury Papers, Class One, 452:218, PRO (Library of Congress Transcripts).

14. *Pa. Packet*, February 7, 1782; William H. Egle, "The Constitutional Convention of 1776: Biographical Sketches of Its Members," *PaMHB*, III (1879), 198-99; Hawke, *In the Midst*, 105; Ryerson, "Leadership in Crisis," 334-37; Minutes, March 20, 1761, Cordwainers' Fire Company, HSPa.

15. David Freeman Hawke, "Dr. Thomas Young—'Eternal Fisher in Troubled Waters': Notes for a Biography," *New-York Historical Society Quarterly*, LIV (January, 1970), 7-29; Henry H. Edes, "Memoir of Dr. Thomas Young, 1731-1777," *Publications*, Colonial Society of Massachusetts, XI (1906-07), 2-54; John C. Miller, *Sam Adams, Pioneer in Propaganda* (Boston, 1936), 84-87, 198; Isaac Q. Leake, *Memoir of the Life and Times of General John Lamb* (Albany, 1850), 89. On Adams, see also William Appleman Williams, "Samuel Adams: Calvinist, Mercantilist, Revolutionary," *Studies on the Left*, I (Winter, 1960), 47-57.

16. Brooke Hindle, *David Rittenhouse* (Princeton, 1964); Henry D. Biddle, "Owen Biddle," *PaMHB*, XVI (1892), 299-329; Sellers, *Peale*; Boorstin, *Lost World of*

Thomas Jefferson, 13–22; Charles Willson Peale Autobiography (typescript copy), 40, Peale Papers, American Philosophical Society.

17. Barton, *Memoirs of Rittenhouse,* 568; Thompson, *Making of English Working Class,* 743; Morgan, "Puritan Ethic," 5–7.

18. Conrad Wright, *The Beginnings of Unitarianism in America* (Boston, 1955); Joseph Haroutunian, *Piety Versus Morality: The Passing of the New England Theology* (New York, 1932); Passmore, *Perfectibility of Man,* 135–47.

19. Herbert Morais, *Deism in Eighteenth Century America* (New York, 1943), 14–19, 80, and *passim;* Bridenbaugh and Bridenbaugh, *Rebels and Gentlemen,* 20; Jonathan Dickinson, *Familiar Letters Upon a Variety of Religious Subjects* (4th ed., Glasgow, 1775), 2; Article 12, Minutes, Taylor's Company, HSPa; Foner, *Complete Works,* II, 1434–39.

20. Butterfield, ed., *Letters of Rush,* I, 335.

21. Hawke, *In the Midst,* 184; Smith, *John Adams,* I, 245. Cf. Alfred F. Young, *The Democratic Republicans of New York: The Origins, 1763–1797* (Chapel Hill, 1967), 12; Douglass, *Rebels and Democrats,* 13–14.

22. Gerald Stourzh, *Alexander Hamilton and the Idea of Republican Government* (Stanford, 1970), 44, 55; Howe, *From the Revolution,* 2; Adams, "Republicanism in Political Rhetoric," 397–98; New York *Constitutional Gazette,* February 24, 1776.

23. Davidson, *Propaganda,* 253–54, 285, 293; Inglis, *True Interest of America,* vii, 10, 49–53, 79; [William Smith], *Plain Truth* (Philadelphia, 1776), 2, 8–12, 34–36; *Pa. Gazette,* March 20, 1776; Adams, "Republicanism in Political Rhetoric," 411–12; Pole, *Political Representation,* 266; Charles Sydnor, *Gentlemen Freeholders: Political Practices in Washington's Virginia* (Chapel Hill, 1952).

24. Adams, ed., *Familiar Letters of John Adams and Abigail Adams,* 146; *The Warren-Adams Letters* (2 vols.: Boston, 1917–25), I, 234; Butterfield, ed., *Diary of Adams,* III, 331–33; Charles Francis Adams, ed., *The Works of John Adams* (10 vols.: Boston, 1856), IX, 616–18; Buel, "Democracy and the American Revolution"; W. Stark, *America: Ideal and Reality* (London, 1947), 102–08; Marius Bewley, *The Eccentric Design* (New York, 1963), 26–31.

25. *Warren-Adams Letters,* I, 234, 339; Adams, ed., *Adams Works,* IX, 376–78; Pocock, *Politics, Language, and Time,* 90–131; Douglass, *Rebels and Democrats,* 29.

26. Wood, *Creation,* 72–73, 482; "Salus Populi," *Pa. Journal,* March 13, 1776; "Eudoxus," *Pa. Packet,* April 22, 1776; *Four Letters on Interesting Subjects* (Philadelphia, 1776); Robbins, "European Republicanism in the Century and a Half Before 1776," 50; E. A. J. Johnson, *The Foundations of American Economic Freedom: Government and Enterprise in the Age of Washington* (Minneapolis, 1973), 184; Stourzh, *Hamilton,* 230n.

27. "Salus Populi," *Pa. Journal,* March 13, 1776.

28. Sartori, *Democratic Theory,* 327; Sanford A. Lakoff, *Equality in Political Philosophy* (Cambridge, 1964), 89–90, 100, 113.

29. Berthoff and Murrin, "Feudalism, Communalism, and the Yeoman Free-

holder"; "Candidus," *Pa. Gazette*, March 6, 1776; "Cassandra," *Pa. Ledger*, April 13, 1776; *The Alarm*, Broadside, May, 1776; "Eudoxus," *Pa. Packet*, April 22, 1776; Leake, *Lamb*, 85; "Elector," *Pa. Gazette*, May 15, 1776.

30. "Elector," *Pa. Packet*, April 29, 1776; "Elector," *Pa. Gazette*, May 15, 1776; "To the Worthy Inhabitants," *Pa. Packet*, May 20, 1776; "Eudoxus," *Pa. Packet*, April 22, 1776.

31. "Elector,". *Pa. Packet*, April 29, 1776; "Elector," *Pa. Gazette*, May 15, 1776; Morgan, "Slavery and Freedom: The American Paradox."

32. Hawke, *In the Midst*, 18–21; Thayer, *Pennsylvania Politics*, 173–77; Ryerson, "Leadership in Crisis," 368–71, 439–40, 467–73, 547–56. "For seven years past," said one writer, "the aristocrats have not descended to look upon the ordinary person except at election time. . . . Be freemen and you will be companions for gentlemen annually." *Pa. Evening Post*, April 27, 1776.

33. Foner, *Complete Writings*, II, 63–64, 79, 84–85.

34. *Four Letters on Interesting Subjects*, 12; *The Genuine Principles of the Ancient Saxon or English Constitution* (Philadelphia, 1776); "Salus Populi," *Pa. Journal*, March 13, 1776; "Eudoxus," *Pa. Packet*, April 22, 1776; "Elector," *Pa. Packet*, April 29, 1776; "Elector," *Pa. Gazette*, May 15, 1776.

35. Hawke, *In the Midst*, 30–33, 113–46; Foner, *Complete Writings*, II, 86; Allan Nevins, *The American States During and After the Revolution, 1775–1789* (New York, 1924), 105n.

36. Douglass, *Rebels and Democrats*, 258; Hawke, *In the Midst*, 172; Ryerson, "Leadership in Crisis," 603–04.

37. *The Proceedings Relative to Calling the Conventions of 1776 and 1790* (Harrisburg, 1825), 38–39; *Extracts from the Proceedings of the Provincial Convention of Committees*, Broadside, 1776; *Pa. Archives*, 2 ser., III, 639–42.

38. *The Proceedings*, 39–41; Christopher Marshall to "J. B.," June 30, 1776; Marshall to Cannon, July 1, 1776; Marshall to ?, September 12, 1776, Marshall Letterbook, HSPa; Hawke, *In the Midst*, 160–61; Duane, ed., *Marshall Diary*, 79–81, 120.

39. *To the Several Battalions of Military Associators in the Province of Pennsylvania*, Broadside, June 26, 1776.

40. Nevins, *American States*, 149; "Christophus Scotus," *Pa. Packet*, October 29, 1776; Charles Page Smith, *James Wilson, Founding Father, 1742–1798* (Williamsburg, 1956), 108; William H. Smith, ed., *The St. Clair Papers* (2 vols.: Cincinnati, 1882), I, 371–73.

41. "Audax," *Pa. Freeman's Journal*, September 29, 1784; Butterfield, ed., *Letters of Rush*, I, 336; Connor, *Poor Richard*, 147–48; *The Proceedings*, 48–49; Hawke, *In the Midst*, 183–86; Foner, *Complete Writings*, II, 269–72.

42. J. Paul Selsam, "Brissot de Warville on the Pennsylvania Constitution of 1776," *PaMHB*, LXXII (January, 1948), 25–43.

43. *The Proceedings*, 54–65; "A Friend to Fair Elections," *Pa. Gazette*, March 22, 1786.

44. Robert A. Rutland, ed., *Papers of George Mason* (Chapel Hill, 1970—), I, 287–

89; *An Essay of a Declaration of Rights,* Broadside, 1776; *The Proceedings,* 54–57.

45. E. P. Walton, ed., *Records of the Council of Safety and Governor and Council of the State of Vermont* (8 vols.: Montpelier, 1873–80), I, 394–95.

46. Pole, *Political Representation,* 273–74; *Pa. Colonial Records,* X, 723–24.

47. "Diary of James Allen," *PaMHB,* IX (1885), 177; *At a Meeting, Held at the Philosophical Society Hall, October* 17, 1776, Broadside; C. Marshall to ?, September 20, 1776, Marshall Letterbook, HSPa.

48. Roland M. Baumann, "The Democratic-Republicans of Philadelphia: The Origins, 1776–1797" (unpublished doctoral dissertation, Pennsylvania State University, 1970), 28–33; Olton, "Philadelphia Artisans," 205–14; Graydon, *Memoirs,* 284–85.

49. Baumann, "Democratic-Republicans," 18; *Pa. Packet,* October 29, 1776; "Agricola," *Pa. Packet,* February 6, 1779; "Farmer," *Pa. Packet,* November 5, 1779.

50. "John Trusshoop," *Pa. Gazette,* November 13, 1776; *To the Free and Independent Electors of the City of Philadelphia,* Broadside, November 5, 1776; "The Considerate Freeman," *Pa. Packet,* November 26, 1776; "Whitlocke," *Pa. Evening Post,* May 27, June 4, 1777.

51. Hawke, *Rush,* 196–201; Butterfield, ed., *Rush Letters,* I, 137, 148, 152, 240, 409, 498, 530; Dagobert D. Runes, ed., *The Selected Writings of Benjamin Rush* (New York, 1947), 72–80; Rush to John Dickinson, March 20, 1778, Dickinson Papers, Library Company of Pennsylvania.

52. McLoughlin, "The American Revolution," 107; Wood, *Creation,* 428–29; Butterfield, ed., *Rush Letters,* I, 142, 270–73, 371, 413, 462–67, 523; Bell, "Science and Humanity," 65–74, 281–93; Runes, ed., *Writings of Rush,* 72, 332–33; Boorstin, *Lost World,* 181–82.

53. Hawke, *Paine,* 57–60; Foner, *Complete Writings,* I, 49.

54. Hawke, *Paine,* 66–75; Foner, *Complete Writings,* I, 65–67, 70–71, 77, 132–153–55.

55. Foner, *Complete Writings,* I, 73; "Consideration," *Pa. Gazette,* October 30, 1776; Force, *American Archives,* 5 ser., II, 1154–55; Baumann, "Democratic-Republicans," 19–20; *Pa. Archives,* 2 ser., I, 725; Duane, ed., *Remembrancer of Marshall,* 139; Walton, ed., *Records of Vermont,* I, 394–95.

56. *Pa. Gazette,* April 9, 1777; Foner, *Complete Writings,* II, 282–83.

57. Macpherson, *Possessive Individualism, passim;* Foner, *Complete Writings,* II, 285–87. I should note that recent work on the Levellers views their proposals regarding the franchise as being closer to universal manhood suffrage than Macpherson allows. He claims the Levellers meant to exclude all wage-earners, but this is challenged in Roger Howell, Jr. and David E. Brewster, "Reconsidering the Levellers; The Evidence of *The Moderate,*" *Past and Present,* XLVI (February, 1970), 68–86; and in Keith Thomas, "The Levellers and the Franchise," in G. E. Aylmer, ed., *The Interregnum: The Quest for Settlement, 1646–1660* (London, 1972), 57–78.

58. Foner, *Complete Writings,* I, 330; II, 285–87, 399, 578–81.

CHAPTER FIVE

1. E. P. Thompson, "The Moral Economy of the English Crowd in the Eighteenth Century," *Past and Present*, L (Feburary, 1971), 76–136; Louise A. Tilly, "The Food Riot as a Form of Political Conflict in France," *Journal of Interdisciplinary History*, II (Summer, 1971), 23–57; R. B. Rose, "Eighteenth Century Price Riots and Public Policy in England," *International Review of Social History*, VI (1961), 277–92; Rudé, *Crowd in History*, 21–45, 108–21, 228; Thompson, *Making of the English Working Class*, 62–67; Soboul, *The Sans Culottes*, 14–18, 59–60, 252–57.

2. The most recent work on these disorders is Walter J. Shelton, *English Hunger and Industrial Disorders: A Study of Social Conflict during the First Decade of George III's Reign* (New York, 1973). Unfortunately, it is far from an adequate treatment of the subject. See the review essay by Peter Linebaugh in *Bulletin* of Society for the Study of Labour History, XXVIII (Spring, 1974), 57–61, which refers to the London crowd incident of 1768, quoted above, on p. 61.

3. Quotation from Crowley, *This Sheba, Self*, 6; Richard Morris, "Labor and Mercantilism in the Revolutionary Era," in Richard Morris, ed., *The Era of the American Revolution* (New York, 1939), 76–91; East, *Business Enterprise*, 26–28; Morris, *Government and Labor, passim;* Bridenbaugh, *Cities in Revolt*, 280; Jensen, *Maritime Commerce*, 26; Horowitz, "Historical Foundations of Contract Law," 917–18, 923–27; Arthur M. Schlesinger, *The Colonial Merchants and the American Revolution, 1763–1776* (New York, 1957 ed.), 211, 498–99, 554–55, 584–85.

4. David Klingaman, "Food Surpluses and Deficits in the American Colonies, 1768–1772," *Journal of Economic History*, XXXI (September, 1971), 562–65; Maier, *Resistance to Revolution*, 4–5; Henretta, *Evolution of American Society*, 20, 70–72; Jensen, *Maritime Commerce*, 7–8; East, *Business Enterprise*, 16, 199; Bezanson, *Prices in Colonial Pennsylvania*, 12–19, 46–47; Anne Bezanson, "Inflation and Controls, Pennsylvania, 1774–1779," *Journal of Economic History*, VIII (1948), Supplement, 1–3; Bridenbaugh, *Cities in Revolt*, 79–80, 280, 283.

5. E. James Ferguson, *The Power of the Purse: A History of American Public Finance, 1776–1790* (Chapel Hill, 1961), xv, 2–19, 26–27; Howard R. Marraro, "Philip Mazzei on American Political, Social, and Economic Problems," *Journal of Southern History*, XV (August, 1949), 364; Foner, *Complete Writings*, I, 33, 98–99.

6. S. Weir Mitchell, "Historical Notes of Dr. Benjamin Rush, 1777," *PaMHB*, XXVII (1903), 131–39; Butterfield, ed., *Rush Letters,* I, 132.

7. William Graham Sumner, *The Financier and the Finances of the American Revolution* (2 vols.: New York, 1892), I, 55–59; Adams, ed., *Familiar Letters,* 239–40; Ferguson, *Power of the Purse*, 29–34; Burnett, ed., *Letters*, II, 233, 257, 340, 568; III, 167; *Connecticut State Records*, I, 599, 609–14; Ford, ed., *Journals*, VII,

124; IX, 956; XI, 569; C. H. Gardiner, *A Study in Dissent* (Urbana, 1968), 102–03, 108.

8. Oscar and Mary Handlin," Revolutionary Economic Policy in Massachusetts," *WMQ*, 3 ser., IV (January, 1947), 3–26; East, *Business Enterprise*, 203; Morris, "Labor and Mercantilism," 93–96, 103–106; Adams, ed., *Familiar Letters*, 286–87; Andrew M. Davis, "The Limitation of Prices in Massachusetts, 1776–1779," *Publications*, Colonial Society of Massachusetts, X (1905), 121–25; Theophilus Parsons, Jr., "The Old Conviction Versus the New Realities: New York Anti-Federalist Leaders and the Radical Whig Tradition" (unpublished doctoral dissertation, Columbia University, 1974), 16; John C. Fitzpatrick, ed., *The Writings of George Washington* (39 vols.: Washington, 1931–44), XIV, 313; Burnett, ed., *Letters*, III, 167–68, 202.

9. Schlesinger, *Colonial Merchants*, 211, 498–99, 554–55, 584–85; "A True Patriot," *Pa. Gazette*, April 14, 1779; *Pa. Evening Post*, April 18, 1776; *Pa. Archives*, 2 ser., III, 625–31; Ryerson, "Leadership in Crisis," 480–81; Corner, ed., *Rush Autobiography*, 116–17; Duane, ed., *Remembrancer of Marshall*, 58, 62, 74.

10. *Pa. Evening Post*, March 7, April 30, 1776; "A. B.," *Pa. Gazette*, September 3, 1777; Worthington Ford *et al.*, eds., *Journals of the Continental Congress* (34 vols.: Washington, 1904–37), IV, 320; Force, ed., *American Archives*, 4 ser., V, 85–86; "Luke," *Pa. Gazette*, March 13, 1776.

11. *Pa. Gazette*, June 12, August 28, 1776; *Journals of the House of Representatives of the Commonwealth of Pennsylvania* (Philadelphia, 1782), 69; *Pa. Packet*, October 22, 1776; *In Council of Safety*, Broadside, November 7, 1777; Brunhouse, *Counter-Revolution*, 51; Minutes of the Committee of Safety, Northumberland County, March 1777, 28–29, HSPa.

12. Smyth, ed., *Franklin Writings*, IV, 469–70; V, 535; Merrill D. Peterson, *Thomas Jefferson and the New Nation* (New York, 1970), 189, 304; Johnson, *Foundations of American Economic Freedom*, 7–8; East, *Business Enterprise*, 31; Joseph Dorfman, *The Economic Mind in American Civilization, 1606–1865* (2 vols.: New York, 1946), I, 215; "Rationalis," *New Jersey Gazette*, March 11, 1778; "Revolutionary Correspondence," Rhode Island Historical Society *Collections*, VI (1867), 193–94.

13. Thompson, "Moral Economy," 89–90; Adam Smith, *The Wealth of Nations* (Penguin ed., London, 1970), 119, 160–64, 246, 495; Wolin, *Politics and Vision*, 301.

14. Wood, *Creation*, 606–12; Williams, *Contours*, 32–41; Wolin, *Politics and Vision*, 323, 333; Max Horkheimer, *The Eclipse of Reason* (New York, 1947), 9–10, 19.

15. In fact, Smith's view of human nature was rather complex. In his earlier great work, *The Theory of Moral Sentiments*, Smith had taken a more positive view of humanity, positing conscience (the "man within his breast") and sympathy or fellow feeling, as qualities which not only animated much of human behavior, but fitted men to live in society. The apparent contradiction between Smith's

moral theory based on sympathy and his economic system, founded in self-interest, is what German historians used to call "Das Adam Smith Problem." It has never been resolved by historians. See Ralph Anspach, "The Implications of the *Theory of Moral Sentiments* for Adam Smith's Economic Thought," *History of Political Economy*, IV (Spring, 1972), 176–206; Halévy, *Philosophic Radicalism*, 90–91; Glenn A. Morrow, *The Ethical and Economic Theories of Adam Smith* (New York, 1923), 3–4.

16. Thompson, "Moral Economy," 89; Halévy, *Philosophic Radicalism*, 89, 107, 129; Morrow, *Ethical and Economic Theories*, 42, 72, 83; Robbins, *Eighteenth Century Commonwealthman*, 196; Duncan Forbes, "Scientific Whiggism: Adam Smith and John Millar," *Cambridge Journal*, VII (August, 1954), 646; Joseph Cropsey, *Polity and Economy: An Interpretation of the Principles of Adam Smith* (The Hague, 1957), ix, 62–65; George J. Sligter, "Smith's Travels on the Ship of State," *History of Political Economy*, III (Fall, 1971), 265. Paine could not have read *The Wealth of Nations* before writing *Common Sense*, but in the 1790's he several times referred favorably to Smith: Foner, *Complete Writings*, I, 282; II, 654, 664, 672.

17. Polanyi, *Great Transformation*, 3, 227; Smith, *Wealth of Nations*, 11, 77; Perkin, *Origins of Modern English Society*, 187, 224; Cropsey, *Polity and Economy*, xi, 65, 72, 80–81; Wolin, *Politics and Vision*, 301.

18. Cropsey, *Polity and Economy*, 2, 64; Wolin, *Politics and Vision*, 312–13.

19. Stark, *America: Ideal and Reality*, 9–10; Horkheimer, *Eclipse of Reason*, 138–40; Smith, *Wealth of Nations*, 169, 201, 391, 430–31; Perkin, *Origins of Modern English Society*, 27–28; Commons, ed., *Documentary History*, III, 151–52.

20. Polanyi, *Great Transformation*, 93, 111–24; Wolin, *Politics and Vision*, 317–21; Smith, *Wealth of Nations*, 115, 172–76, 181–84.

21. Robert W. Malcolmson, *Popular Recreations in English Society, 1700–1850* (Cambridge, 1973), 117.

22. Polanyi, *Great Transformation*, 68–69; Foner, *Complete Writings*, II, 483; Elizabeth Fox-Genovese, "The Many Faces of Moral Economy," *Past and Present*, LVIII (February, 1973), 161–68; "Artemon," *Pa. Gazette*, March 16, 1785.

23. Henderson, "Continental Congress," 114–21, 238–51; Hawke, *Paine*, chapter 6; Howe, *From the Revolution*, 9–15; Burnett, ed., *Letters*, II, 401; III, 437, 490–92; Jacob M. Price, *France and the Chesepeake* (2 vols.: Ann Arbor, 1973), II, 203–05; E. James Ferguson, *The Power of the Purse* (Chapel Hill, 1961), 71–81, 92–102; Clarence L. Ver Steeg, *Robert Morris: Revolutionary Financier* (Philadelphia, 1954), 13, 25; Douglass, *Coming of Age*, 30; Merrill Jensen, *The New Nation* (New York, 1950), 35.

24. Wood, *Creation*, 52–53, 68–69, 476–79; Richard Bushman, "Corruption and Power in Provincial America," in *Development of a Revolutionary Mentality*, 63–64; Heimert, *Religion and the American Mind*, 55–56, 261, 267, 434–35, 487, 495; Dorfman, *Economic Mind*, I, 117.

25. Wood, *Creation*, 416–21; Williams, "Samuel Adams," 47–57; Henderson,

"Continental Congress," 121–23, 252; East, *Business Enterprise*, 196–97; Harry
A. Cushing, ed., *The Writings of Samuel Adams* (4 vols.: New York, 1904–08),
IV, 7, 67; James C. Ballagh, ed., *The Letters of Richard Henry Lee* (2 vols.: New
York, 1911–14), II, 30, 33, 65; Burnett, ed., *Letters*, III, 438; Morgan, "Puritan
Ethic," 25–32; East, "Business Entrepreneur," 22. See also Curtis B. Nettels,
George Washington and American Independence (Boston, 1951), 3–4.

26. Foner, *Complete Writings*, I, 400, 20, 36, 80, 153; II, 5.

27. Foner, *Complete Writings*, II, 136, 141, 1176; Hawke, *Paine*, 89–94; "Plain
    Truth," *Pa. Packet*, December 21, 1778; "Candid," *Pa. Packet*, January 12,
    1779; "Common Sense [not Paine]," *Pa. Journal*, February 3, 1779.

28. Biddle, "Biddle," 315; Burnett, ed., *Letters*, III, 545; IV, 110; "The Lee
    Papers," III, 331; Paine to Henry Laurens, January 9, 1779, Gimbel Collec-
    tion, American Philosophical Society.

29. Anne Bezanson, *Prices and Inflation During the American Revolution: Pennsylva-
    nia, 1770–1790* (Philadelphia, 1951).

30. East, *Business Enterprise*, 34–35, 152; Ver Steeg, *Morris*, 53; Butterfield, ed.,
    Rush Letters, I, 120; Handlins, "Revolutionary Economic Policy," 16–17; War-
    ner, *Private City*, 29–30; Bernard Mason, "Entrepreneurial Activity in New
    York During the American Revolution," *Business History Review*, XL (Summer,
    1966), 196, 204–05.

31. Burnett, ed., *Letters*, IV, 92; "A. B.," *Pa. Gazette*, September 3, 1777; "Wilbra-
    ham," *Pa. Packet*, March 24, 1781; "A Citizen," *Pa. Packet*, August 20, 1778; "A
    Fair Trader," *Pa. Packet*, December 3, 1778.

32. Brunhouse, *Counter-Revolution*, 50; Hawke, *Rush*, 227; Scharf and Westcott,
    Philadelphia, I, 371–80, 389; Frederick D. Stone, "Pennsylvania Society One
    Hundred Years Ago, or the Reign of Continental Money," *PaMHB*, III
    (1879), 362–65; "Philanthropos," *Pa. Packet*, January 21, 1779. Cf. "A Coun-
    tryman," *Pa. Packet*, December 29, 1778; "A True Patriot," *Pa. Gazette*, April 7,
    1779.

33. Ford, ed., *Journals*, I, 78; Bridenbaugh and Bridenbaugh, *Rebels and Gentle-
    men*, 139–46; *Pa. Archives*, 1 ser., X, 141–43; *Pa. Packet*, September 3, 1778;
    Watson, *Annals*, I, 473; J. Thomas Jable, "The Pennsylvania Blue Laws of
    1779: A View of Pennsylvania Society and Politics During the American
    Revolution," *PaH*, XL (October, 1973), 420–25; *Pa. Freeman's Journal*, August
    8, 1781; Elizabeth Cometti, "Morals and the American Revolution, *South
    Atlantic Quarterly*, XLVI (January, 1947), 62–71.

34. Owen S. Ireland, "The Ethnic-Religious Dimensions of Pennsylvania Politics,
    1778–1779," *WMQ*, 3 ser., XXX (July, 1973), 441–42; *Pa. Packet*, March 25,
    30, April 1, 1779; *Pa. Gazette*, April 28, 1779; H. James Henderson, "Constitu-
    tionalists and Republicans in the Continental Congress, 1778–1786," *PaH*,
    XXXVI (April, 1969), 120, 130–32; *An Act for the Regulation of the Markets*,
    Broadside, April 1, 1779.

35. "A Hint," *Pa. Packet*, December 10, 1778.

36. Brunhouse, *Counter-Revolution*, 68–69; Scharf and Westcott, *Philadelphia*, I, 403; "A True Patriot," *Pa. Gazette*, May 5, 1779; Moses Hazen to Thomas McKean, September 28, 1778, McKean Papers, HSPs; *Pa. Archives*, 1 ser, VII, 392–94.

37. Duane, ed., *Marshall Remembrancer*, 217; *At a General Meeting of the Citizens of Philadelphia*, Broadside, May 25, 1779; Henry D. Biddle, ed., *Extracts from the Journal of Elizabeth Drinker* (Philadelphia, 1889), 116. On Roberdeau, see Labaree, ed., *Franklin Papers*, XVII, 81n.; *PaMHB*, IX (1885), 278–79n. A native of St. Christopher's in the West Indies, Roberdeau sold his estate there in 1779 to remove "a temptation that at some future day might fall in the way of my children to slave keeping, a practice I never can be reconciled to." Labaree, ed., *Franklin Papers*, XVII, 86.

38. Watson, *Annals*, II, 303–05; John W. Wallace, *An Old Philadelphian: Colonel William Bradford, The Patriot Printer of 1776* (Philadelphia, 1884), 304–05; Rosswurm, "'That They Were Grown Unruly,'" 126–27; *Pa. Archives*, 1 ser., VII, 461; Broadside, June 26, 1779; Charles W. Peale Diary, July 13, 1779, Peale Papers, American Philosophical Society; *Pa. Journal*, July 7, 1779.

39. W. B. Reed, *Life and Correspondence of Joseph Reed* (2 vols.: Philadelphia, 1847), II, 144; "Letters of Christopher Marshall to Peter Miller," *PaMHB*, XXVIII (1904), 76–77; Duane, ed., *Marshall Remembrancer*, 218–20; *Pa. Evening Post*, June 15, 1779; *Pa. Journal*, July 7, 1779; *Pa. Gazette*, July 7, 1779.

40. *Boston Gazette*, April 26, 1779; *Pa. Journal*, June 23, 30, 1779; *Pa. Packet*, July 13, August 12, 1779; *Massachusetts Spy*, July 1, 1779; *Continental Journal*, July 15, 1779; *Pa. Evening Post*, July 26, 1779.

41. Wood, *Creation*, 324; "A Farmer of Virginia," *Pa. Packet*, July 15, 31, 1779; Butterfield, ed., *Rush Letters*, I, 224, 229–35, 239; *Pa. Packet*, September 10, 1779.

42. Ver Steeg, *Morris*, 38; Johnson, *Foundations of American Economic Freedom*, 28–29, 168–71; Pelatiah Webster, *Political Essays* (Philadelphia, 1791), 9–20, 30–46 (quotation from page 20); *Pa. Packet*, September 10, 1779.

43. *Pa. Packet*, July 15, 1779; Bezanson, *Prices*, 336.

44. Jensen, *Commerce*, 31, 35; Olton, "Philadelphia Artisans," 42–48; "A Whig Shoemaker," *Pa. Packet*, July 15, 1779; "A Mechanic," *Pa. Evening Post*, July 22, 1779; "Committee," *Pa. Packet*, July 20, 1779.

45. Olton, "Philadelphia Artisans," 229–30, 319–20.

46. *Pa. Packet*, July 24, 1779; Foner, *Complete Writings*, II, 171–72.

47. "Junius," *Pa. Packet*, August 3, 1779; "Cato," *Pa. Evening Post*, July 9, 1779.

48. "Letter of Silas Deane to His Brother Simeon Deane," *PaMHB*, XVII (1893), 350; J. L. Bishop, *A History of American Manufactures* (2 vols.: Philadelphia, 1861–64), I, 570; *Pa. Evening Post*, August 2, 1779; *Pa. Packet*, July 29, 1779.

49. *In Council*, Broadside, July 8, 1779; Charles W. Peale Autobiography (typescript copy), Peale Papers; *Pa. Packet*, July 10, 29, September 11, 1779; *Pa. Archives*, 1 ser., VII, 621–22. Pennsylvania's Supreme Executive Council

endorsed the plan, but added that contributions would be credited only to taxes raised for continental purposes, not those for poor relief or for state uses.

50. *Pa. Packet,* August 5, 14, 28, September 10, 1779; Olton, "Philadelphia Artisans," 230; Edward Burd to Jasper Yeates, August 24, 1779, Yeates Papers, HSPa; "C____. S____.," *Pa. Packet,* September 11, 1779; *Pa. Gazette,* September 22, 1779.

51. John F. Roche, *Joseph Reed: A Moderate in the American Revolution* (New York, 1957), 116–21, 149–51, 158–60; Reed, *Reed,* I, 302; II, 139.

52. The most recent and best published account of the "Fort Wilson Riot" is John Alexander, "The Fort Wilson Incident of 1779: A Case Study of the Revolutionary Crowd," *WMQ,* 3 ser., XXXI (October, 1974), 589–612. Rosswurm, "'That They Were Grown Unruly,'" 143–67, provides a somewhat different analysis. C. Page Smith, "The Attack on Fort Wilson," *PaMHB,* LXXVIII (April, 1954), 177–88, contains some useful information, but is marred by the view that the underlying issue in the "riot" was "the lurking animal violence and panic that move in the wake of revolution" (p. 181). Cf. Reed, *Reed,* II, 150–52, 423–28; James Bayard to William B. Reed, November 15, 1825, Joseph Reed Papers, New-York Historical Society; Brunhouse, *Counter-Revolution,* 24; Stackhouse, *Matlack,* 12.

53. Butterfield, ed., *Rush Letters,* I, 240; "Journal of Samuel Rowland Fisher," *PaMHB,* XLI (1917), 169–70; Burnett, ed., *Letters,* IV, 468; Charles W. Peale Autobiography (typescript copy), 71–75, Peale Papers; Reed, *Reed,* II, 15; "C __ __. S ____.," *Pa. Packet,* October 16, 1779.

54. *Pa. Packet,* October 9, 12, 1779; *To the Merchants and Traders of Philadelphia,* Broadside, October 26, 1779.

55. *Pa. Gazette,* February 16, 1780; Burnett, ed., *Letters,* V, 4, 16, 23, 27, 40; Butterfield, ed., *Rush Letters,* I, 246; "Proceedings of a Convention to Regulate Prices," *Collections,* Massachusetts Historical Society, 7 ser., III (1902), 15–17; Roche, *Reed,* 172.

56. Burnett, ed., *Letters,* V, 36; Edmund C. Burnett, *The Continental Congress* (New York, 1941), 426–27; E. James Ferguson *et al.,* eds., *The Papers of Robert Morris, 1781–1784* (Pittsburgh, 1973–), I, 180–81; Francis Wharton, ed., *The Revolutionary Diplomatic Correspondence of the United States* (6 vols.: Washington, 1889), V, 58–59; Ferguson, *Power of the Purse,* 115–16, 136–37; Main, *Sovereign States,* 253–62.

57. Brunhouse, *Counter-Revolution,* 83–84, 94–95; Roche, *Reed,* 172–74; Diary of George Nelson, March 18, 1780, HSPa; East, *Business Enterprise,* 208; Robert Morris to Stacey Hepburn, September 23, 1779, Society Collections, HSPa; Olton, "Philadelphia Artisans," 245–47; Raymond E. Hayes, "Business Regulation in Early Pennsylvania," *Temple Law Quarterly,* X (Feburary, 1936), 155–65.

58. Louis Hartz, *Economic Policy and Democratic Thought: Pennsylvania, 1776–1860* (Cambridge, 1948), 206, 291; *The Proceedings,* 87, 113; Reed, *Reed,* II, 140;

"To the Inhabitants of America," *Pa. Packet,* March 11, 1780 [identified as Gouverneur Morris in Jared Sparks, *The Life of Gouverneur Morris* (3 vols.: Boston, 1832), I, 218–19]; Richard C. Bull, "The Constitutional Significance of Early Pennsylvania Price-Fixing Legislation," *Temple Law Quarterly,* XI (April, 1937), 317–19.

59. Hartz, *Economic Policy, passim;* Horowitz, "The Historical Foundations of Contract Law," 932–35, 940–45; George Logan, *Letters Addressed to the Yeomanry* (Philadelphia, 1791), 18, 41–42.
60. Foner, *Complete Writings,* I, 185; II, 228–29, 1336.
61. Foner, *Complete Writings,* I, 439.

CHAPTER SIX

1. Burton A. Konkle, *George Bryan and the Constitution of Pennsylvania, 1731–1791* (Philadelphia, 1932), 189, 202–03; *Pa. Gazette,* December 1, 1779; Brunhouse, *Counter-Revolution,* 77–81; Ireland, "Ethnic-Religious Dimension," 424–27, 436–37; James Cannon to Joseph Reed, May 12, 1780, Gratz Manuscripts, HSPa; *Pa. Packet,* February 7, 1782; Duane, ed., *Marshall Remembrancer,* 171, 187, 197, 209, 233, 238, 247; Williamson, *Paine,* 94.
2. Edwin G. Burrows, "Albert Gallatin and the Political Economy of Republicanism" (unpublished doctoral dissertation, Columbia University, 1973), 176–79, 184; Brunhouse, *Counter-Revolution,* 157–58; "One of the Majority," *Pa. Journal,* March 20, 1784; *Pa. Packet,* March 12, 1785; Constitutionalist Broadside, August, 1783; Main, *Sovereign States,* 395.
3. Brunhouse, *Counter-Revolution,* 63, 82, 149; Olton, "Philadelphia Artisans," 245–47, 284–97; "A Hint," *Pa. Packet,* June 28, 1783; "A Friend to Mechanics," *Pa. Gazette,* June 25, 1783; "A Constitutionalist," *Pa. Independent Gazetteer,* January 15, 1785; "A Tradesman," *Pa. Independent Gazetteer,* January 22, 1785.
4. "Irish Cooper," *Pa. Journal,* March 20, 1782; "A Brother Mechanic," *Pa. Independent Gazetteer,* October 11, 1783; "A Philadelphia Mechanic," *Pa. Independent Gazetteer,* October 8, 1785; "A Mechanic," *Pa. Independent Gazetteer,* January 8, 1785; "To the Mechanics," *Pa. Gazette,* September 13, 1786.
5. *Colonial Records of Pennsylvania,* XII, 319; Watson, *Annals.* I, 327; Schoepf, *Travels in the Confederation,* I, 99; Brunhouse, *Counter-Revolution,* 107, 140–42.
6. Foner, *Complete Writings,* I, 169–70; II, 383–84, 1183–87.
7. Hawke, *Paine,* 108–09, 115–20; Rutland, ed., *Papers of George Mason,* II, 699.
8. Wharton, ed., *Revolutionary Diplomatic Correspondence,* V, 134–35n.; Memorandum; February 10, 1782 (photostat of original in Library of Congress); Gimbel Collection, American Philosophical Society; Paine to Robert Morris, April 7, 1782 (photostat), Gimbel Collection; Foner, *Complete Writings,* II, 283; Hawke, *Paine,* 121–30.
9. Ferguson, *Power of the Purse,* 120–21; E. James Ferguson, "The Nationalists of

1781–1783 and the Economic Interpretation of the Constitution," *JAH*, LVI (September, 1969), 241–61; Wood, *Creation*, 403–05.

10. Foner, *Complete Writings*, I, 232–34; II, 333–47, 364, 1213–14.
11. Hawke, *Paine*, 135–47; Arnold K. King, "Thomas Paine in America, 1774–1787" (unpublished doctoral dissertation, University of Chicago, 1951), 325–45.
12. Janet Wilson, "The Bank of North America and Pennsylvania Politics, 1781–1787," *PaMHB*, LXVI (January, 1942), 3–28; Bray Hammond, *Banks and Politics in America* (Princeton, 1957), 42–52; Herman E. Kroos, "Financial Institutions," in David T. Gilchrist, ed., *The Growth of the Seaport Cities, 1790–1825* (Charlottesville, 1967), 115–23; M. L. Bradbury, "Legal Privilege and the Bank of North America," *PaMHB*, XCVI (April, 1972), 139–66; Baumann, "Democratic-Republicans," 38–49; Brunhouse, *Counter-Revolution*, 111, 150; George D. Rappaport, "The Sources and Early Development of Hostility to Banks in Early American Thought" (unpublished doctoral dissertation, New York University, 1970), 12–14, 32–33, 89.
13. Baumann, "Democratic-Republicans," 50–51; Henderson, "Constitutionalists and Republicans," 138–41; Main, *Political Parties*, 193.
14. Matthew Carey, ed., *Debates and Proceedings of the General Assembly of Pennsylvania* . . . (Philadelphia, 1786), 52–57, 62–69, 79, 130; Bradbury, "Legal Privilege," 148–49.
15. Carey, ed., *Debates*, 57, 66; "Atticus," *Pa. Packet*, June 28, 1786.
16. Forrest McDonald, *E Pluribus Unum* (Boston, 1965), 48–51; Main, *Political Parties*, 186; Carey, ed., *Debates*, 113.
17. *Remarks on a Pamphlet Entitled 'Considerations on the Bank of North America'* (Philadelphia, 1785), 11–14; "Colbert," *Pa. Packet*, March 31, 1785; Olton, "Philadelphia Artisans," 273–80, 302–05, 318–23; *Pa. Packet*, March 29, 1786.
18. "Candid," *Pa. Gazette*, April 6, 1785; "An Old Banker," *Pa. Gazette*, March 30, 1785; "Nestor," *Pa. Gazette*, July 19, 1786; Robert G. McCloskey, ed., *The Works of James Wilson* (2 vols.: Cambridge, 1967), II, 833–39.
19. *Pa. Gazette*, December 21, 1785, February 15, 1786; Paine to Thomas Mifflin, December 19, 1785, Gimbel Collection; Foner, *Complete Writings*, II, 382.
20. "Common Sense," *Pa. Packet*, November 7, 1786; "Common Sense," *Pa. Packet*, August 21, 1786; Hammond, *Banks and Politics*, 60–61; Foner, *Complete Writings*, II, 404–06; Homer, *History of Interest Rates*, 153–54.
21. Foner, *Complete Writings*, II, 415; McCloskey, ed., *Works of Wilson*, II, 835–36; Smith, *Wealth of Nations*, 393–98, 419–26.
22. Foner, *Complete Writings*, II, 376, 395, 413, 991; Hawke, *Paine*, 154; Hartz, *Economic Policy*, 250, 304; "Atticus," *Pa. Packet*, May 8, 1786.
23. Foner, *Complete Writings*, II, 391, 416, 424, 428; *Pa. Gazette*, December 21, 1785, September 20, 1786.
24. Foner, *Complete Writings*, II, 1247, 1255, 390.
25. Foner, *Complete Writings*, II, 409; I, 390; "Common Sense," *Pa. Gazette*, September 20, 1786.

26. Foner, *Complete Writings*, II, 426, 1256. Cf. Klett, *Presbyterians*, 262; "A Friend to Prosperity," *Pa. Gazette*, November 29, 1786; Walzer, "Transportation in Philadelphia Trading Area," 48–49, 313.

27. "Atticus," *Pa. Packet*, April 25, 1786; Hawke, *Paine*, 156–57; *Pa. Gazette*, January 25, 1786.

28. Hawke, *Paine*, 164–69; Paine to George Clymer, December 13, 1786, Gimbel Collection; Foner, *Complete Writings*, II, 909; Minutes, Society for Political Enquiries, HSPa; Paine to Edmund Burke, August 7, 1788, Gimbel Collection.

29. Louis Gottschalk, *Lafayette Between the American and French Revolutions* (Chicago, 1950), 374–75; Foner, *Complete Writings*, I, 44; II, 332, 691–93, 1390–91; Sisson, *Revolution of 1800*, 108.

30. Wood, *Creation*, 497–547. This view, of course, goes back at least as far as Charles A. Beard's *An Economic Interpretation of the Constitution* (New York, 1913).

31. Lynd, *Class Conflict*, 123–26; Konkle, *Bryan*, 301–05; Adams, "Wage Rates," 405; Charles L. Chandler, *Early Shipbuilding in Pennsylvania, 1683–1812* (Philadelphia, 1932), 29; "A Citizen," *Pa. Gazette*, April 2, 1788.

32. Olton, "Philadelphia Artisans," 309–11, 342–57; "A Federalist," *Pa. Independent Gazetteer*, October 15, 1787; "A Bricklayer," February 15, 1788; "Sidney," *Pa. Gazette*, April 2, 1788; John B. McMaster and Frederick D. Stone, eds., *Pennsylvania and the Federal Constitution* (Philadelphia, 1888), 605, 615; "One of the People," *Pa. Gazette*, October 17, 1787.

33. "Account of the Grand Federal Procession," 57–75; Quimby, "The Cordwainers' Protest," 87; Watson, *Annals*, II, 345–46.

34. Butterfield, ed., *Rush Letters*, I, 470–75; *Pa. Gazette*, March 19, 1788; Marx, *Machine in the Garden*, 166.

CHAPTER SEVEN

1. Ian R. Christie, *Wilkes, Wyvill, and Reform;* Pole, *Political Representation*, 436–68; John W. Osborne, *John Cartwright* (Cambridge, 1972), 17–26, 38, 52; SCI Minute Book, TS 11/1133/1, 7, 43, PRO; Hawke, *Paine*, 179, 195, 202–06.

2. Edmund Burke, *Reflections on the Revolution in France* (Penguin ed., London, 1968), R. R. Fennessy, *Burke, Paine, and the Rights of Man* (The Hague, 1963).

3. Fennessy, *Burke and Paine*, 85; Paine to Thomas Jefferson, January 15, 1789, Jefferson Papers, Library of Congress; TS 11/961/166–68, PRO.

4. Boulton, *Language of Politics*, 139–43; Foner, *Complete Writings*, I, 318–19; Hawke, *Paine*, 221–22.

5. Foner, *Complete Writings*, I, 251–54, 260, 278–80, 289, 326–27, 344.

6. Foner, *Complete Writings*, II, 471; I, 355–58, 360–61, 370–72, 376–78, 410, 414–17, 424–41; R. R. Palmer, *The Age of the Democratic Revolution* (2 vols.: Princeton, 1959–65), I, 19.

7. Thompson, *Making of the English Working Class*, 93–94; Henry Collins, "The London Corresponding Society," in *Democracy and the Labour Movement*, ed., John Saville (London, 1954), 108; Cannon, *Parliamentary Reform*, 120.

8. Thompson, *Making of the English Working Class*, 107–08; *Annual Register*, 1792, 172; Hawke, *Paine*, 240–46; Christopher Wyvill, *Political Papers* (6 vols.: York, 1794–1804), V, iii–vi, xiv–xvi, 51.

9. Thompson, *Making of the English Working Class*, 17–21; W. A. L. Seaman, "British Democratic Societies in the Period of the French Revolution" (unpublished doctoral dissertation, University of London, 1954); Eugene C. Black, *The Association* (Cambridge, 1963), 225–27.

10. John Horne Tooke to Sheffield Constitutional Society, TS 11/951/3495, PRO; Col. DeLancey to Secretary Henry Dundas, June 13, 1792, HO 42/20/176, PRO: Thompson, *Making of the English Working Class*, 150–51; ? to Rev. H. Zouch, December 28, 1791, Fitzwilliam Papers, F. P. 44/2, Sheffield Central Library.

11. Place Collection, Add. MSS 27,808, f. 13; 27, 811, f. 5; 27, 815, f. 180; 27, 817, f. 67, British Museum; *Memoir of Thomas Hardy* (London, 1832), 4–8, 12–13, 59–60; *War*, Broadside, Manchester, December 10, 1792: TS 11/959/3505, PRO; Thompson, *Making of the English Working Class*, 133, 155–57; Seaman, "Democratic Societies," 29–34.

12. Place Collection, Add. MSS, 27,812, f. 64; 27,814, ff. 29–30; 27,808, f. 59. Cf. TS 11/960/3506(1), PRO: the comment of William Hatton, the keeper of a London butter warehouse who in 1791 wished to publish his thoughts on the French Revolution: "Aware that it would be deemed by many (and probably by some of my customers) the high [sic] of presumption, for a man in my line of life, to give publicly in print, his opinion, so freely as I had done, on so important a subject, I therefore thought it most prudent to adopt the signature of 'A Citizen of the World.'"

13. John Wilson, *The Songs of Joseph Mather* (Sheffield, 1862), 56–57; *Politics for the People*, pt. II, no. 1 (1794), 3–4.

14. Place Collection, Add. MSS 27,808, f. 113; Seaman, "Democratic Societies," 209–16, 234–35; TS 11/965/3510A, PRO; Arthur Sheps, "Ideological Immigrants in Revolutionary America," in *City and Society in the 18th Century*, eds., Paul Fritz and David Williams (Toronto, 1973), 232–34. *To the Parliament and People of Great Britain*, LCS Broadside, November 23, 1795; Hill, "The Norman Yoke;" "List of Toasts": TS 11/959/3505, PRO; Seaman, "Democratic Societies," 93–94; *Address of the British Convention Assembled at Edinburgh* (London, 1793), 4–7.

15. Foner, *Complete Writings*, II, 348; Editor, *The Patriot*, to Thomas Hardy, June 14, November 22, 1792: TS 11/958/3503, PRO; *The Patriot*, I, 450; II, 110–11; Place Collection, Add. MSS 27,811, f. 6.

16. TS 11/951/3495; TS 11/764/29, PRO; *Proceedings of the Public Meeting Held in Sheffield*, (Sheffield, 1794), 15; *To the Parliament and People of Great Britain*, LCS Broadside, November 23, 1795; *Address of Leeds Constitutional Society*, Broadside, April 11, 1793: TS 24/3/30A, PRO.

17. Place Collection, Add. MSS 27,814, f. 29; *Proceedings of the Public Meeting Held in Sheffield*, 29–30; LCS Address, August 6, 1792: TS 11/958/3503, PRO; Pole, *Political Representation*, 477–78.

18. Draft resolution, Sheffield Society for Constitutional Information, March 14, 1794, MSS M. D. 251, Sheffield Central Library; Resolution of Manchester Society: TS 11/951/3495, PRO; Foner, *Complete Writings*, II, 479; *Appendix to the Second Report from the Committee of Secrecy*, 9: TS 11/964/3510, PRO.

19. *Revolutions Without Bloodshed* (London, 1794), 2–3; Allen Davenport, *The Life, Writings, and Principles of Thomas Spence* (London, 1836); P. M. Kemp-Ashraf, ed., "Selected Writings of Thomas Spence 1750–1814," in *Life and Literature of the Working Class: Essays in Honour of William Gallacher* (Berlin, 1966), 267–354; Thomas Spence, *The Restorer of Society, to Its Natural State* (London, 1801); [Thomas Spence], *The End of Oppression* (London, nd), 3: TS 24/3/16, PRO.

20. Place Collection, Add. MSS, 27,808, f. 151; [John Thelwall], *Peaceful Discussion, and not Tumultuary Violence* . . . (London, 1795), 9–10, 15; Thompson, *Making of the English Working Class*, 157–60; Charles Cestre, *John Thelwall* (London, 1906); John Thelwall, *The Rights of Nature* (2nd ed., London, 1796); Thelwall to "Dear Allum," February 13, 1794: TS 11/960/3497, PRO; [John Thelwall], *The Natural and Constitutional Rights of Britons* (London, 1795), 83.

21. Boulton, *Language of Politics*, 250; Thompson, *Making of the English Working Class*, 106, 114–16, 132–35, 145–47, 174–76; Black, *The Association*, 234–74; Sheffield *Register*, August 22, 1793; Carl B. Cone, *The English Jacobins* (New York. 1968), 149. 210–11; *Annual Register*, 1795, 37, 43, 47.

22. Thompson, *Making of the English Working Class*, 99, 179–85; Williams, *Artisans and Sans-Culottes*, 112; Thelwall lectures: TS 11/951/3495, PRO; Sheffield Constitutional Society to LCS, June 14, 1792: TS 24/9/6, PRO; Place Collection, Add. MSS 27,808, ff. 115–16; 27,814, f. 30.

23. Williams, *Artisans and Sans-Culottes*, 72; Thompson, *Making of the English Working Class*, 90, 177–82; [John Thelwall], *The Tribune*, II (1795), 181.

24. Hawke, *Paine*, 178–79, 183, 200–03, 226–29; Sisson, *The Revolution of 1800*, 106, 168–70; Paine to Edmund Burke, January 17, 1790 (copy), Gimbel Collection, American Philosophical Society.

25. Hawke, *Paine*, 228, 266; Lawrence S. Kaplan, *Jefferson and France* (New Haven, 1967), 21; Eloise Ellery, *Brissot de Warville* (Boston and New York, 1915), 4, 49, 126–27, 133; Selsam, "Brissot de Warville," 25–43; Robert C. Darnton, "The Gallo-American Society" (unpublished B. Phil. thesis, Oxford University. 1962); J. P. Brissot, *New Travels in the United States of America*. ed.. Durand Echeverria (Cambridge, 1964). ix–xix; Durand Echeverria. *Mirage in the West* (Princeton, 1957), 152–58: Leonore B. Loft. "Brissot: Revolutionary and Disciple of the *Philosophes*" (unpublished doctoral dissertation, Columbia University, 1971), 36–42; Joyce Appleby, "America as a Model for the Radical French Reformers of 1789," *WMQ*, 3 ser., XXVIII (April, 1971), 274–85.

26. J. Salwyn Schapiro, *Condorcet and the Rise of Liberalism* (New York, 1934), 76–79, 219–30; Lakoff, *Equality in Political Philsophy*, 102–04.

27. Echeverria, *Mirage in the West*, 119–20, 144–45; Loft. "Brissot," 34–35, 169–

74, 201; Palmer, *Age of Democratic Revolution*, II, 55–56; Davis, *Problem of Slavery in the Age of Revolution*, 138–44; Ellery, *Brissot*, 24–27, 42–45, 82, 144, 416; Schapiro, *Condorcet*, 87, 148, 161–62, 182, 266; Durand Echeverria, ed., "Condorcet's *The Influence of the American Revolution on Europe*," *WMQ*, 3 ser., XXV (January, 1968), 85–108.

28. Gita May, *Madame Roland and the Age of Revolution* (New York, 1970), 177–88, 194; Ellery, *Brissot*, 113, 121; Albert Mathiez, *The French Revolution*, trans. Catherine A. Phillips (New York, 1964), 121–22, 129, 205, 210; Robert Darnton, *Mesmerism and the End of the Enlightenment in France* (Cambridge, 1968), 132–35; Louis R. Gottschalk, *Jean Paul Marat: A Study in Radicalism* (New York, 1927), 75–77, 98–99, 106; Georges Lefebvre, *The French Revolution*, trans. Elizabeth M. Evanson (2 vols.: New York, 1962), I, 174–75, 208; Moncure D. Conway, "Adventures of Paine in London and Paris," *The Open Court*, VIII (July 12, 1894), 4144; Foner, *Complete Writings*, II, 517–20.

29. M. J. Sydenham, *The Girondins* (London, 1961), 101–07; Norman Hampson, *A Social History of the French Revolution* (Toronto, 1963), 132–38; Ellery, *Brissot*, 231–32; Lefebvre, *French Revolution*, I, 217–25; May, *Madame Roland*, 201–12; George Rudé, *Revolutionary Europe, 1783–1815* (London, 1964), 211.

30. Rudé, *Revolutionary Europe*, 124; Soboul, *The Sans Culottes*; R. Cobb, "The People in the French Revolution," *Past and Present*, XV (April, 1959), 60–72; Palmer, *Age of Democratic Revolution*, II, 46–48, 105; Hampson, *Social History*, 147–53; Ellery, *Brissot*, 340. On Bonneville, see Georges Duval, *Histoire de la Littérature Révolutionnaire* (Paris, 1879), 254–304.

31. Palmer, *Age of Democratic Revolution*, II, 54; Alfred O. Aldridge, *Man of Reason: The Life of Thomas Paine* (Philadelphia, 1959), 176; Alison Patrick, *The Men of the First French Republic* (Baltimore, 1972), 176–78; Michael Walzer, ed., *Regicide and Revolution* (Cambridge, 1974), 127; Hawke, *Paine*, 256–57.

32. Hawke, *Paine*, 259–62, 279–80; John G. Alger, *Englishmen in the French Revolution* (London, 1889), 98; Foner, *Complete Writings*, II, 538. An indication of Paine's minor role in French affairs is the fact that the standard biographical directory of Convention members erroneously states that Paine was assassinated in 1806. A. Kuscinski, *Dictionnaire des Conventionnels* (Paris, 1917), 414–15.

33. Foner, *Complete Writings*, II, 587, 1342–43; Lefebvre, *French Revolution*, I, 214; II, 160; Sydenham, *Girondins*, 208; Hampson, *Social History*, 157; Rudé, *Revolutionary Europe*, 133–38.

34. Sydenham, *Girondins*, 149; Foner, *Complete Writings*, II, 558–59; Schapiro, *Condorcet*, 93–100.

35. Walzer, ed., *Regicide and Revolution*, 59–66, 127–28, 208; Sydenham, *Girondins*, 139–42; Mathiez, *French Revolution*, 263; Hawke, *Paine*, 282; Gottschalk, *Marat*, 96–99, 121, 157–59.

36. Foner, *Complete Writings*, II, 1331, 1335–36. On the issue of price controls, see Hampson, *Social History*, 161–67, 192–96; Sydenham, *Girondins*, 151–69; Williams, *Artisans and Sans-Culottes*, 41–44, 53–55; Soboul, *Sans Culottes, passim*.

37. Palmer, *Age of Democratic Revolution*, II, 110; Williamson, *Paine*, 205–08; Hawke, *Paine*, 281–89.

38. Hawke, *Paine*, 289–90; Palmer, *Age of Democratic Revolution*, II, 116–21; Isser Woloch, *Jacobin Legacy* (Princeton, 1970), 8–10.

39. Conway, *Paine*, II, 109; Tighe Hopkins, *The Dungeons of Old Paris* (New York, 1897), 175–89; Hawke, *Paine*, 296–306.

40. Hampson, *Social History*, 237–42; Woloch, *Jacobin Legacy*, 20; Foner, *Complete Writings*, II, 583–94.

41. Palmer, *Age of Democratic Revolution*, II, 115; Hampson, *Social History*, 200; Foner, *Complete Writings*, II, 1435–37.

42. Foner, *Complete Writings*, I, 464, 482, 487, 574, 600, 603; Hawke, *Paine*, 294.

43. John Derry, *The Radical Tradition, Tom Paine to Lloyd George* (London, 1967), 34–37.

44. Lefebvre, *French Revolution*, II, 175–76; Mathiez, *French Revolution*, 211, 306; K. D. Tönnesson, "The Babouvists: From Utopia to Practical Socialism," *Past and Present*, XXII (July, 1962), 60–76; Foner, *Complete Writings*, I, 605–21; Schlatter, *Private Property*, 174–77; Larkin, *Property in the Eighteenth Century*, 128–30, 196–97; T. Spence, *The Rights of Infants . . . To Which are Added . . . Strictures on Paine's Agrarian Justice* (London, 1797), 3, 11, 14–16.

45. Georgia Robison, *Revelliere-Lepeaux, Citizen Director*, 1753–1824 (New York, 1938), 117; Foner, *Complete Writings*, II, 568, 594–606; 690, 719; Woloch, *Jacobin Legacy*, 65–66, 76–83, 274.

46. Albert Mathiez, *La Théophilanthropie et le Cult Décadaire* (Paris, 1904); Robison, *Revelliere-Lepeaux*, 161–81; Conway, *Paine*, II, 294.

47. Rudé, *Revolutionary Europe*, 212; Moncure D. Conway, "The Paine Club in Paris," *The Open Court*, VIII (August 30, 1894), 4199–4202; Conway, *Paine*, II, 301–02, 443–44. Cf. A. W. Smith, "Irish Rebels and English Radicals," *Past and Present*, VII (April, 1955), 78–85; W. E. H. Lecky, *A History of Ireland in the Eighteenth Century* (5 vols.: London, 1902–03), III, IV, *passim*.

48. Philadelphia *Federal Gazette*, cited in New York *Packet*, May 26, 1791; New York *Journal*, July 13, 1791; New York *Daily Advertiser*, May 27, 1791.

49. Banning, "The Quarrel With Federalism," 330–32; Richard J. Buel, *Securing the Revolution* (Ithaca, 1972), 36–42; Young, *Democratic-Republicans of New York*, 207, 349–50.

50. Charles D. Hazen, *Contemporary American Opinion of the French Revolution* (Baltimore, 1897), 164–72; Watson, *Annals of Philadelphia*, I, 180; Eugene P. Link, *Democratic-Republican Societies*, 1790–1800 (New York, 1942); Baumann, "Democratic-Republicans," 441–49; Young, *Democratic-Republicans of New York*, 395; New York *Journal*, January 5, 1793.

51. Democratic Society of Pennsylvania, Minutes, May 1, 1794, HSPa; Link, *Democratic-Republican Societies*, 104; Foner, ed., *To Light the Torch of Truth* (manuscript copy), 242, 247, 737; New York *Journal*, July 8, 1795.

52. Young, *Democratic-Republicans of New York*, 366, 579; Donald Stewart, *The Opposition Press of the Federalist Period* (Albany, 1969), chs. 6–7, 528, 544;

Norman V. Blantz, "Editors and Issues: The Party Press in Philadelphia, 1789–1801" (unpublished doctoral dissertation, Penn State University, 1974), 160–68, 181; Banning, "Quarrel with Federalism," 368–70; Margaret Woodbury, "Public Opinion in Philadelphia, 1789–1801," *Smith College Studies in History*, V (October, 1919), 25.

53. Morais, *Deism*, 65, 120–32; Samuel Bernstein, "The Subject of Revolution in Post-Revolutionary America," *Stüdien uber die Revolution* (Berlin, 1969), 191–92; G. Adolf Koch, *Republican Religion* (New York, 1933), 71–87.

54. "Correspondence of John Adams and Mercy Warren," *Collections*, Massachusetts Historical Society, 5 ser., IV (1878), 376; John T. Rutt, ed., *The Theological and Miscellaneous Works of Joseph Priestley* (2 vols.: London, 1832), I, pt. 2, 272–76; Morais, *Deism*, 156, 174; Albert Post, *Popular Freethought in America*, 1825–1850 (New York, 1943), 19–27.

55. Gary B. Nash, "The American Clergy and the French Revolution," *WMQ*, 3 ser., XXII (July, 1965), 392–412; James H. Smylie, "Clerical Perspectives on Deism: Paine's *The Age of Reason* in Virginia," *Eighteenth-Century Studies*, VI (Winter, 1972–73), 203–20; Young, *Democratic-Republicans of New York*, 404, 568–70.

56. "A Scots Correspondent," Richmond *Examiner*, November 21, 1800; William Gribbin, "Republican Religion and the American Churches in the Early National Period," *The Historian*, XXXV (November, 1972), 61–74; Heimert, *Religion and the American Mind from the Great Awakening to the Revolution*, 538–41; Paul Goodman, *The Democratic-Republicans of Massachusetts* (Cambridge, 1964), 86–96; Stewart, *Opposition Press*, 396–400, 407; Russell B. Nye, *The Cultural Life of the New Nation* (New York, 1960), 213–15; Young, *Democratic-Republicans of New York*, 404.

57. Dumas Malone, *Jefferson the President: First Term, 1801–1805* (Boston, 1970), 192–200; Jerry W. Knudson, "The Rage Around Tom Paine: Newspaper Reaction to his Homecoming in 1802," *New-York Historical Society Quarterly*, LIII (January, 1969), 34–63; Miller, *Sam Adams*, 393–96; Foner, *Complete Writings*, II, 908, 915–17, 1433; Koch, *Republican Religion*, 131–33; Worthington C. Ford, ed., "Letters of William Duane," *Proceedings*, Massachusetts Historical Society, 2 ser., XX (1906–07), 279.

58. Foner, *Complete Writings*, II, 788–89, 804, 1426.

59. Foner, *Complete Writings*, II, 963, 992–1004; Hawke, *Paine*, 362; Stewart, *Opposition Press*, 391–92; Kim T. Phillips, "William Duane, Revolutionary Editor" (unpublished doctoral dissertation, University of California, Berkeley, 1968), 180–84; Ellis, *The Jeffersonian Crisis*, 161–75.

60. Hawke, *Paine*, 384–97; Koch, *Republican Religion*, 137–38; Philadelphia *United States Gazette*, November 16, 1809.

61. William G. McLoughlin, "Pietism and the American Character," *American Quarterly*, XVII (Summer, 1965), 166–69; Palmer, *Age of Democratic Revolution*, I, 193; Herbert G. Gutman, "Protestantism and the American Labor Move-

ment: The Christian Spirit in the Gilded Age," *American Historical Review,*
LXXII (October, 1966), 74–101.

62. Ellis, *Jeffersonian Crisis,* 252–59; Montgomery, "The Working Classes of the
Pre-Industrial City," 13; Williams, *Artisans and Sans-Culottes,* vi; Thompson,
Making of the English Working Class 157, 175–81.

63. Richard J. Twomey, "Jacobins and Jeffersonians: Anglo-American Radicalism
in the United States, 1790–1820" (unpublished doctoral dissertation, Northern Illinois University, 1974); Ray Boston, "The Impact of 'Foreign Liars' on
the American Press (1790–1800)" *Journalism Quarterly,* L (Winter, 1973), 722–
30; Robert N. Elliott, Jr., *The Raleigh Register,* 1799–1863 (Chapel Hill, 1955),
v–vi, 5–41; William E. Ames, *A History of the National Intelligencer* (Chapel Hill,
1972), 73–86.

64. Charles B. Todd, *The Life and Letters of Joel Barlow* (New York, 1886), 236–39;
Conway, *Paine,* II, 310–11n.

65. I am indebted to an unpublished essay by Mr. John Jentz, a graduate student
at the City University of New York, "The Celebration of Tom Paine's Birthday, 1825–1844"; *Workingman's Advocate,* February 7, 1835; Post, *Popular
Freethought,* 155–59.

66. Edward Pessen, *Most Uncommon Jacksonians* (Albany, 1967), 103–10; Maurice
F. Neufield, "Realms of Thought and Organized Labor in the Age of Jack-
son," *Labor History,* X (Winter, 1969), 5–43; Louis H. Arky, "The Mechanics'
Union of Trade Associations and the Formation of the Philadelphia Working-
men's Movement," *PaMHB,* LXXVI (April, 1952), 143–48; Ronald L. Meek,
Studies in the Labor Theory of Value (London, 1958), 125–28; David A. Harris,
Socialist Origins in the United States (Assen, The Netherlands, 1966), 10–11, 91–
99.

67. Bruce G. Laurie, "The Working People of Philadelphia 1827–1853" (unpublished doctoral dissertation, University of Pittsburgh, 1971), 41; "A Mechanic,"
Workingman's Advocate, February 6, 1830; Jentz, "Celebration," 16–18; Frank
Thistlethwaite, *America and the Atlantic Community: Anglo-American Aspects,*
1790–1850 (New York, 1963 ed.), 59–60, 68–69; F. W. Evans, *Autobiography of
a Shaker* (Mt. Lebanon, New York, 1869), 10–11, 16, 26.

68. *Workingman's Advocate,* February 6, March 6, 1830; February 16, 1833; February 7, 1835; *The Correspondent,* February 2, 9, 1828.

69. *Workingman's Advocate,* February 11, 1832; February 9, 1833; February 15,
1834; *The Correspondent,* February 9, 1828; *An Oration Delivered by Joseph W.
Pomroy, on the Birthday of Thomas Paine* (Philadelphia, 1838), 10; Jentz, "Celebration," 21–26, 37–38.

70. Laurie, "Working People," 41–43; Lee Benson, *The Concept of Jacksonian
Democracy* (Princeton, 1961), 193–96; Pessen, *Most Uncommon Jacksonians,* 111;
Walter Hugins, *Jacksonian Democracy and the Working Class* (Stanford, 1960),
134–35; John F. C. Harrison, *Quest for the New Moral World* (New York, 1969),
42, 86–87.

71. David Montgomery, "The Shuttle and the Cross: Weavers and Artisans in the Kensington Riots of 1844," *Journal of Social History*, V (Summer, 1972), 411–46; Pessen, *Most Uncommon Jacksonians*, 149; *Workingman's Advocate*, February 1, 1845; Helene S. Zahler, *Eastern Workingmen and National Land Policy, 1829–1862* (New York, 1941), 52n.–53n.

72. "Thomas Paine's Second Appearance in the United States," *Atlantic Monthly*, IV (July, 1859), 15; Mark O. Kistler, "German-American Liberalism and Thomas Paine," *American Quarterly*, XIV (Spring, 1962), 81–91; *Celebration of the 119th Anniversary of the Birthday of Thomas Paine* (Cincinnati, 1856); Moncure D. Conway, *Autobiography, Memories and Experiences* (2 vols.: Boston and New York, 1904), I, 304–05.

73. Derry, *Radical Tradition*, 32; London *Daily Herald*, June 25, 1932; Norman J. Gossman, "Republicanism in Nineteenth Century England," *International Review of Social History*, VII (1962), 47–62; Henry Pelling, *America and the British Left* (London, 1956).

74. Dixon Wechter, "Hero in Reverse," *Virginia Quarterly Review*, XVIII (Spring, 1942), 253; Floyd Stovall, *Walt Whitman: Prose Works* (2 vols: New York, 1963), I, 140–41; Paul M. Angle, ed., *Herndon's Life of Lincoln* (New York, 1930), xiv, 102, 355–56; Foner, *Complete Writings*, I, 368; Hawke, *Paine*, 200.

Acknowledgments

In the course of researching and writing this book, I have incurred enormous obligations to many persons for their advice, criticism, and encouragement, and I welcome the opportunity to thank them. My greatest debt is owed to Professor Alfred Young of Northern Illinois University. During the past few years, Professor Young has shared with me his unrivaled knowledge of the era of the American Revolution, offered advice and encouragement on numerous occasions, given me access to his own important research on artisans in the Revolution, and read with meticulous care successive drafts of this manuscript. His criticisms made me sharpen and rethink many aspects of the book's argument, and his unselfishness in making his ideas and materials available to me have been striking examples of scholarly cooperation and generosity.

I am also grateful to Professor Warren Susman of Rutgers University, who several times discussed with me at length the problems of analyzing American radicalism and the career of Thomas Paine, and who gave a detailed critical reading to two drafts of this work. My good friends Leonard Liggio of City

☆ 313 ☆

ACKNOWLEDGMENTS

College and Fred Siegel of Empire State College took time out from their own projects to read drafts of this book and to share with me their extensive knowledge of eighteenth-century political and social history. Gary Nash of the University of California, Los Angeles, generously allowed me to read his unpublished work on poverty in revolutionary Philadelphia and supplied me with a print-out of data concerning occupations and income in Philadelphia which he had gathered in the course of his own work. And John K. Alexander of the University of Cincinnati sent me his dissertation on attitudes toward poverty in eighteenth-century Philadelphia and generously provided me with a list of newspaper references to Paine which he had gathered during his own research.

I am also indebted to David Hawke and Audrey Williamson, both of whom allowed me to read, in manuscript, biographies of Paine which have since appeared in print. Stephen J. Rosswurm sent me a copy of his important Master's essay on lower-class politics in revolutionary Philadelphia, and my friend Edwin Burrows of Brooklyn College made available a portion of his work in progress on Albert Gallatin and criticized an early draft of this book. Arno Mayer of Princeton University sent me his unpublished essay on the lower-middle class, and his colleague Robert Darnton allowed me to read his unpublished Oxford University B. Phil thesis on the Gallo-American society. And my uncle Philip S. Foner of Lincoln University, sent me the manuscript of his forthcoming collection of documents concerning the Democratic-Republican societies. I also wish to thank Robert Mutch and David Gordon, who discussed with me the problems of interpreting the eighteenth-century American economy, and Richard M. Andrews of John Jay College and Isser Woloch of Columbia University, both of whom made important suggestions about Paine's experiences in France.

During the time I spent engaged in research in England, I was fortunate to be able to discuss Paine and his career with George Rudé, E. J. Hobsbawm, and E. P. Thompson, and to benefit from their extensive knowledge of the history of the English lower classes in the eighteenth century. As should be clear from a reading of this book, my own understanding of Paine's career was strongly influenced by the writings of these three scholars.

A large number of friends read one or another version of this manuscript and I want to thank them for their time and advice: Angus Cameron, Leon Fink, Elizabeth Fox-Genovese, Eugene Genovese, Herbert Gutman, Hubert Hammond, Jr., Michael Merrill, David Montgomery, Richard Morris, Mark Naison, Eric Perkins, Jonah Raskin, Allan Schiffman, James P. Shenton, Michael Wallace, Arthur Wang, Michael Weisser, and Gordon Wood.

Much of the research for this book was conducted during a year when, thanks to a fellowship from the American Council of Learned Societies, I was able to take time off from teaching. And a summer grant from the Faculty Research Award Program of the City University of New York enabled me to complete the research. I also want to thank the staffs of the various libraries I visited, especially the librarians at the British Museum, Public Record Office, New-York Historical Society, Historical Society of Pennsylvania, Library Company of Philadelphia, and American Philosophical Society. I am especially grateful to Mrs. Steffans, custodian of the Gimbel Collection at the American Philosophical Society, and to Ms. Stephanie Munsing and Ms. Marie Korey of the Library Company, for their assistance.

Mark Hirsch, then a student at City College, did an excellent job as my research assistant in the summer of 1974, and Robert Achs photographed materials at the Library Company for use in the illustrations. I also want to thank Harriet Serenkin, an excellent assistant editor at Oxford University Press, and my editor Sheldon Meyer, who pretended to be unconcerned when I told him him I was suspending work on another book, already under contract to Oxford, to write this one instead. And I am grateful to Lynn Garafola for a suberb job of editing and for assisting and encouraging me in numerous ways to complete this book.

I have dedicated this book to my father, Jack D. Foner, who has exemplified in his own life much of what is best and most admirable in the life and ideals of Thomas Paine.

INDEX